Generic Goals and Generic Practices

GG 1 Achieve Specific Goals

- GP 1.1 Perform Specific Practices

GG 2 Institutionalize a Managed Process

- GP 2.1 Establish an Organizational Policy
- GP 2.2 Plan the Process
- GP 2.3 Provide Resources
- GP 2.4 Assign Responsibility
- GP 2.5 Train People
- GP 2.6 Manage Configurations
- GP 2.7 Identify and Involve Relevant Stakeholders
- GP 2.8 Monitor and Control the Process
- GP 2.9 Objectively Evaluate Adherence
- GP 2.10 Review Status with Higher Level Management

GG 3 Institutionalize a Defined Process

- GP 3.1 Establish a Defined Process
- GP 3.2 Collect Improvement Information

GG 4 Institutionalize a Quantitatively Managed Process

- GP 4.1 Establish Quantitative Objectives for the Process
- GP 4.2 Stabilize Subprocess Performance

GG 5 Institutionalize an Optimizing Process

- GP 5.1 Ensure Continuous Process Improvement
- GP 5.2 Correct Root Causes of Problems

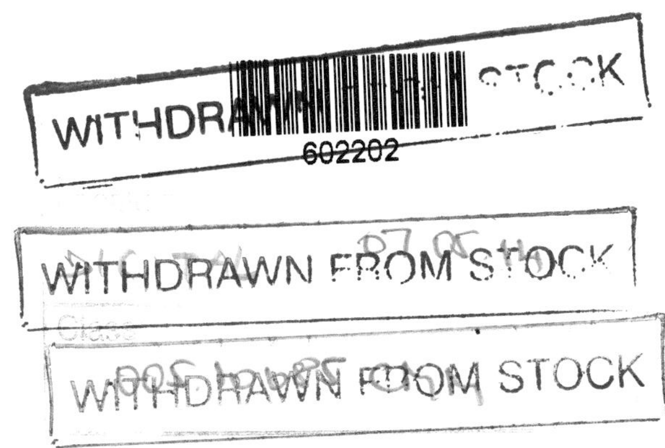

CMMI®-ACQ

CMMI®-ACQ

Guidelines for Improving the Acquisition of Products and Services

Brian P. Gallagher
Mike Phillips
Karen J. Richter
Sandy Shrum

Addison-Wesley

Upper Saddle River, NJ • Boston • Indianapolis • San Francisco
New York • Toronto • Montreal • London • Munich • Paris • Madrid
Capetown • Sydney • Tokyo • Singapore • Mexico City

The SEI Series in Software Engineering

The publisher offers excellent discounts on this book when ordered in quantity for bulk purchases or special sales, which may include electronic versions and/or custom covers and content particular to your business, training goals, marketing focus, and branding interests. For more information, please contact: U. S. Corporate and Government Sales (800) 382-3419, corpsales@pearsontechgroup.com.

For sales outside the United States, please contact: International Sales international@pearsoned.com.

Visit us on the Web: www.informit.com/aw

Library of Congress Cataloging-in-Publication Data

CMMI-ACQ : guidelines for improving the acquisition of products and services / Brian P. Gallagher ... [et al.].

p. cm.

Includes bibliographical references and index.

ISBN 978-0-321-58035-1 (hardcover : alk. paper) 1. Capability maturity model (Computer software) I. Gallagher, Brian P.

QA76.758.C556 2008

005.1068'5—dc22

2008042588

Pearson Education, Inc.
Rights and Contracts Department
501 Boylston Street, Suite 900
Boston, MA 02116
Fax: (617) 671-3447

ISBN-13: 978-0-321-58035-1
ISBN-10: 0-321-58035-4

Text printed in the United States on recycled paper at Courier in Westford, Massachusetts.
First printing, December 2008

CONTENTS

FOREWORD

A Commercial Perspective

Every day more companies are realizing that their market, competition, and economics have changed. Supported by advances in technology, companies previously operating within a single country or region now find themselves competing in a global marketplace. Within these enterprises, the information technology (IT) organization must partner with business leaders to transform the organization, develop global business processes, and introduce technology that supports these processes and drives collaboration and innovation on a global basis.

Similar to the way that businesses must adopt a new operating model and grow new skills, IT organizations themselves must adopt new practices and develop new skills to be successful. One of the key skills necessary for organizational growth is the successful management of technology sourcing and acquisition. Creating business solutions today involves obtaining, integrating, and managing skills and services from a variety of sources. These include networking, security, hosting, and disaster recovery, in addition to the more commonly thought of tasks such as design and coding. In many instances, solutions involve ERP, COTS, or BPO deployments, where there is little, if any, actual development activity. Clearly, the operating model of technology organizations has shifted from internal development to acquisition. In fact, recent studies have shown that nearly 75 percent of total global IT budgets are spent on purchases (Forrester 2006). In today's environment, it is difficult for IT organizations to be competitive unless they excel in acquisition. The SEI has recognized this and responded with the creation of the Capability Maturity Model for Acquisition (CMMI-ACQ).

In creating the CMMI-ACQ, the SEI realized that the process of acquiring technology is significantly different from running an internal development organization. Organizations that acquire technology must build strong relationships with the business, understand business strategy, develop enterprise-level technology architectures, protect intellectual property, and source technology that aligns with all of the above. Effective acquisition requires developing clear requirements, soliciting bids, negotiating scope and price, managing supplier commitment delivery, and ensuring that the business is prepared for the technology. The acquisition team must ensure that suppliers understand the business objective of the acquisition and are aligned to deliver the right value to the business.

At General Motors (GM), we sell and deliver the best transportation products and services to our customers in more than 200 countries around the globe. To accomplish this, our employees and partners collaborate globally on vehicle design, manufacturing, distribution, marketing, and sales of more than nine million vehicles annually. In addition, GM has an incredibly robust research organization that is pioneering the development of new technologies, including electric vehicles, hybrid drivetrains, and bio-fuel engines. To ensure that GM maintains a leadership position in the automotive industry, we continuously invest in system capabilities that drive collaboration and innovation throughout GM's global organization.

The Information Systems and Services (IS&S) organization is responsible for delivering and operating IT globally for GM. The IS&S organization is structured and operates in an acquisition model for the development, operation, and maintenance of all systems. GM has an internal staff responsible for business knowledge, technical strategy, and supplier management. Complementing the GM internal staff, we partner with the world's best IT suppliers for the actual design, construction, deployment, and operation of technology. This structure ensures that GM employees remain accountable for all aspects of IT performance while leveraging the talent, scalability, and global footprint of multiple suppliers.

When developing the organization structure and processes to support our acquisition model, we searched for frameworks and benchmarking tools to measure our performance against accepted best practices. We reviewed many models and concluded that the existing models focused on best practices and maturity levels for organizations that develop technology. No models or guides were truly appropriate for the customers of the technology. Rather than developing an internal model unique to GM, we leveraged our successful history with CMMI-DEV and partnered with the Software Engineering Institute (SEI) to create a model for the acquirers, or customers, of technology. The SEI offered a wealth of expertise to support this. It contributed internal expertise and access to other major technology acquirers in both the government and commercial areas. Looking forward, the SEI is able to provide training, implementation assistance, and appraisals to support industry adoption.

The result of our partnership with the SEI was the CMMI-ACQ, the model upon which this book is based. This new CMMI model provides GM with a road map to help focus our resources on continuously improving the management of our global environment. The model reinforces key competencies that we must maintain within GM; these include business knowledge, requirement skills, and technical architecture to drive strategy. They also include program management, project management, and contract management, to drive delivery and value for our business.

With IT essential to virtually all aspects of world commerce, this landmark new model can produce broad benefits for businesses in all industries. Businesses that take full advantage of the model can enhance their IT operations and better serve their customers, just as we have done here at GM. Such organizations will understand that although they work with partners to design, develop, and operate systems, they must remain accountable to the business for the entire solution. The CMMI-ACQ describes the necessary practices in requirements, sourcing, architecture management, and project management to support this.

I believe the CMMI-ACQ will be adopted by many organizations and will continue to evolve. Our environment is one in which suppliers must work collaboratively with other suppliers and in which new systems need to integrate into a complex network of other systems. The technologies will continue to evolve, as will supplier and acquirer business models. The CMMI-ACQ will have to keep pace, and we look forward to our continued relationship with the SEI to make sure that the CMMI-ACQ continues to be a valuable tool for GM and other technology acquirers.

I congratulate the various contributors that delivered the CMMI-ACQ maturity model. I also want to commend the authors of this book for taking the CMMI-ACQ and making it more relevant for commercial and government organizations. The authors' notes provide context and perspective for the reader to relate to these practical concepts. The case studies provide real-world examples that create a vision for organizations to pursue.

Effectively managing technology suppliers, while retaining business relationships and technology strategy, is a competence that virtually all organizations will need to develop. Until now, the resources to guide organization in this development were scarce. The CMMI-ACQ is a valuable guide in this area. It provides a framework based on proven best practices, a path for adopting the practices, and a standard method for assessing your progress and maturity. I commend the SEI for the creation of the model and encourage organizations to utilize it on their journey to acquisition maturity.

—Ralph Szygenda
Chief Information Officer and Group Vice President
General Motors Corporation
Detroit, Michigan

FOREWORD

A Government Perspective

I do not often have the pleasure of writing a foreword for an extraordinary piece of work as that presented in this text. What the CMMI-ACQ team has done is unique and offers a tremendous tool to greatly improve the acquisition process within the Department of Defense (DoD). The twenty-first century is challenging our old ways of managing projects and programs—particularly, *complex* projects and programs. This text provides a method for meeting that *challenge.*

In my more than 30 years in the DoD acquisition business, I have worked on, reviewed, and assessed countless programs. All successful programs (despite what you may have heard, the successes far outnumber the failures) have a set of common traits that I call the "3 Rs." The first "R" is the customer's "requirement." In the DoD, it is what the warfighter wants in order to accomplish his mission. The second "R" is for "resources." Here "resources" refers not only to funding but equally to the presence of "the right processes" to acquire the capability the warfighter requested. And finally, the third "R" is for "the right people." In other words, having the right people who are educated, trained, and experienced to understand the requirement and know how to use the right processes, and the funding to meet the cost, schedule, and performance demands of the program.

I have used the "3 Rs" approach for decades and I have encouraged others to use it. Although we strive to get requirement growth under control and the right people in place for long periods of time, the truth of the matter is that we do neither very well. And that reality most likely will not change in the foreseeable future.

However, I have observed that if you have strong and effective processes, this reality is effectively addressed by accommodating the enviable changes in requirements and people. That is the SEI's strong suit as evidenced by its CMMI approach to software, which has helped scores of companies and government program offices with software-intensive programs. Now that approach is being applied to acquisition. In short, the CMMI-ACQ model offers a powerful tool to put in place strong, adaptive, effective processes to manage the acquisition of products and services for warfighters.

The timing of CMMI-ACQ could not be better. The DoD is suffering losses in all of its acquisition areas: in terms of numbers of people as well as expertise. As older employees leave government work, their expertise goes with them. And even though the DoD is projected to maintain its current acquisition work force numbers, the experience of the incoming work force has created a knowledge/expertise shortfall. The CMMI-ACQ tool offers a way for program managers and others to mitigate the impact of this shortfall.

It has been a joy reading and understanding what this text presents. I trust you will gain the same appreciation as you read and use this text. My hat is off to the world-class talent of the CMMI-ACQ team who devoted so much time and effort to this project, and to the SEI for constantly pushing the art of the possible and the pursuit of excellence.

And now, I invite you to read, learn, and help yourself and others meet the *challenge* of the twenty-first century.

—Hon. Claude M. Bolton, Jr., DSc
DAU Executive in Residence
Defense Acquisition University
Fort Belvior, Virginia

PREFACE

A growing trend in business and government alike is one that has organizations purchasing, outsourcing, and acquiring products and services to deliver or assemble and deliver to their customers. Instead of focusing on the development of products and services, organizations are focusing on acquiring the best products and services developed by other organizations.

Because of this new emphasis in organizations, there is a lack of experience to draw on in the organization or even to hire that makes it difficult to be successful in this acquisition environment. The factors to consider are different.

The CMMI Product Team and its sponsors acknowledge this trend and have created the CMMI for Acquisition (CMMI-ACQ) model to help these organizations by codifying best practices. These best practices apply to processes critical to the successful acquisition of products and services and cover the important processes involved in an acquisition environment.

What Is CMMI?

CMMI (Capability Maturity Model Integration) is the name given to the collection of models that comprise best practices designed to help organizations improve the performance of their processes and the training and appraisals that support these models. A CMMI model documents activities important to different aspects of the processes needed to deliver products and services to a customer. The CMMI model contained in this book, CMMI-ACQ, is a model designed specifically for organizations that acquire products and services, including large, complex systems.

The first CMMI model was developed by a product team from industry, government, and the Software Engineering Institute (SEI) for the application of process improvement in the development of products and services.

What Is CMMI for Acquisition?

The CMMI-ACQ model was developed in a slightly different way. The first step was taken by General Motors, in collaboration with the SEI and with approval of the CMMI Sponsors and Steering Group. An author team in its Information Technology department developed the initial draft of the Acquisition model as the special report *Adapting CMMI for Acquisition Organizations: A Preliminary Report* [Dodson 2006]. The SEI released this report on its Web site. The CMMI Product Team sought input about this report from organizations that acquire products and services as a major part of the business processes. Organizations were also recruited to pilot this report to see how well it helped those who used it.

In the meantime, the CMMI Product Team formed a model development team that would use the report as a basis to form a CMMI model. Gathering input from those who piloted and reviewed the preliminary report, the CMMI-ACQ development team began work on just that. This team consisted of members from government, industry, and the SEI to ensure a wide variety of perspectives, just as other CMMI model development teams had in the past. This team subsequently created CMMI for Acquisition, Version 1.2 (CMMI-ACQ, V1.2). This model was released in November 2007 as a new member of the CMMI Product Suite and is included in this book with elements we've added.

We, as book authors, added tips and hints to all of the model's process areas to help you apply the practices in your organization. We've also added a case study from General Motors that describes how CMMI-ACQ has worked in that organization. Further, we've included important information about and for the government's use of CMMI-ACQ and the government's special needs.

Purpose

The purpose of this book is to present acquisition best practices by including the full CMMI-ACQ, V1.2 model as well as other information to help you apply these practices in your organization. This other information takes the form of tips, hints, and cross-references that supplement the model practices and additional chapters that focus on the needs of industry and government.

The CMMI-ACQ, V1.2 model is a collection of best practices generated from the CMMI V1.2 Architecture and Framework. This collection's best practices apply to professionals in both government and industry who acquire products and services for their customers and endusers.

The CMMI-ACQ model provides guidance for those who initiate and manage the acquisition of products and services that meet the needs of the customer and enduser. Although suppliers may provide artifacts useful to the processes addressed in CMMI-ACQ, the focus of the model is on the processes of the acquiring organization. CMMI-ACQ integrates bodies of knowledge that are essential to these processes.

The supplier-executed portion of the activities integral to the acquisition of products and services may use the CMMI for Development (CMMI-DEV) model [SEI 2006a]. In cases where the acquirer is also a product or service developer (e.g., taking responsibility for the first few layers of product development and integration), CMMI-DEV (in particular, the Requirements Development, Technical Solution, and Product Integration process areas) are useful for improving the acquirer's product or service development processes.

Contributors to CMMI for Acquisition

Many talented people were involved in the development of the CMMI v1.2 Product Suite, which includes both CMMI for Acquisition and CMMI for Development. Three primary groups involved in this development were the CMMI Steering Group, Product Team, and Configuration Control Board.

The Steering Group approved the architecture for adding additional areas of interest to the CMMI Product Suite by approving the concept of "constellations" built from the CMMI Model Framework (CMF) and CMMI Architecture. A *constellation* is a collection of components used to construct models, training materials, and appraisal materials in an area of interest (e.g., acquisition and development).

The Steering Group initiated the development of the Acquisition constellation, recognizing the importance of providing best practices to acquirers. The Steering Group provided guidance for the development of the CMMI-ACQ model and its accompanying training materials by guiding and approving plans of the Product Team, providing consultation on significant CMMI project issues, and ensuring involvement from a variety of interested communities.

The Product Team wrote, reviewed, revised, discussed, and agreed on the structure and technical content of the CMMI Product Suite, including the framework, models, training, and appraisal materials. Development activities were based on multiple inputs. These inputs included an A-Specification and guidance specific to each release provided by the Steering Group, source models, change requests received from the user community, and input received from pilots and other stakeholders.

The CMMI Configuration Control Board (CCB) is the official mechanism for controlling changes to CMMI models, the SCAMPI appraisal method, and *Introduction to CMMI* training. As such, this group ensures integrity over the life of the product suite by reviewing all proposed changes to the baseline and approving only those changes that satisfy identified issues and meet criteria for the upcoming release.

The Acquisition Advisory Board acted as the configuration control board for the Acquisition constellation, approving all changes to the initial draft of the CMMI-ACQ contained in the special report. Consisting of experts in the field of acquisition, this group ensured the integrity of the constellation using the same review process as the CMMI CCB.

Members of the groups involved in developing CMMI-ACQ, V1.2 are listed in Appendix C.

Audience

The audience for CMMI-ACQ is anyone interested in process improvement in an acquisition environment. Whether you are familiar with the concept of Capability Maturity Models or are seeking information to get started on your improvement efforts, CMMI-ACQ will be useful to you. This model is also intended for organizations that want to use a reference model for an appraisal of their acquisition-related processes.[1]

1. An *appraisal* is an examination of one or more processes by a trained team of professionals using a reference model (e.g., CMMI-ACQ) as the basis for determining strengths and weaknesses.

Organization of This Book

The organization of the book is similar to the CMMI-ACQ model available on the SEI Web site. However, we added a few features that are not found in that document.

- We added tips, hints, and cross-references in the margins throughout the process areas to help you better understand, apply, or find more information about the content of the process areas.
- We added two additional chapters in Part One. The first, Chapter 6, describes the special needs of government acquisition organizations and how CMMI-ACQ can support improving processes in that environment. The second, Chapter 7, demonstrates how CMMI-ACQ can successfully be applied in industry and the benefits that can result from its use.
- Process area sections have tabs that help you to quickly open the book to just the spot you need.
- An index is provided to help you find specific information quickly.

The book is organized into three main parts:

- Part One—About CMMI for Acquisition
- Part Two—Generic Goals and Generic Practices, and the Process Areas
- Part Three—The Appendices and Glossary

Part One, "About CMMI for Acquisition," consists of seven chapters.

- Chapter 1, "Introduction," offers a broad view of CMMI and the Acquisition constellation, concepts of process improvement, the history of models used for process improvement, and different process improvement approaches.
- Chapter 2, "Process Area Components," describes all of the components of the CMMI-ACQ process areas.
- Chapter 3, "Tying It All Together," assembles the model components and explains the concepts of maturity levels and capability levels.
- Chapter 4, "Relationships among Process Areas," provides insight into the meaning and interactions of the CMMI-ACQ process areas.
- Chapter 5, "Using CMMI Models," describes paths to adoption and the use of CMMI-ACQ for process improvement and benchmarking of practices in an acquisition organization.
- Chapter 6, "Using CMMI-ACQ in Government," describes the special needs of the government acquisition environment and how CMMI-ACQ provides a helpful tool for improvement.

- Chapter 7, "Using CMMI-ACQ in Industry: General Motors Case Study," describes the experiences of General Motors as it applied CMMI-ACQ best practices in the organization and the benefits that resulted.

Part Two, "Generic Goals and Generic Practices, and the Process Areas," contains all of the CMMI model's required and expected components. It also contains related informative components, including subpractices, notes, examples, and typical work products.

Part Two contains 23 sections. The first section contains the generic goals and practices. The remaining 22 sections each represent one of the CMMI-ACQ process areas.[2] To make these process areas easy to find, they are organized alphabetically by process area acronym and have tabs on the outside edge of the page. Each section contains descriptions of goals, best practices, and examples. Plus, we've added tips, hints, and cross-references in the outer margins to help explain concepts and relationships and to provide other useful information.

Part Three, "The Appendices and Glossary," consists of four sections.

- Appendix A, "References," contains references you can use to locate documented sources of information such as reports, process improvement models, industry standards, and books that are related to CMMI-ACQ.
- Appendix B, "Acronyms," defines the acronyms used in the model.
- Appendix C, "Project Participants," contains lists of team members and their organizations who participated in the development of CMMI-ACQ, Version 1.2.
- Appendix D, "Glossary," defines many of the terms used in CMMI-ACQ.

How to Use This Book

Whether you are new to process improvement, new to CMMI, or already familiar with CMMI, Part One can help you understand why CMMI-ACQ is the guide to use for improving your acquisition processes.

2. A *process area* is a cluster of related best practices in an area, which when implemented collectively, satisfies a set of goals considered important for making significant improvement in that area. This concept is covered in detail in Chapter 2.

Readers New to Process Improvement

If you are new to process improvement or new to the Capability Maturity Model (CMM) concept, we suggest that you read Chapter 1, "Introduction," first. Chapter 1 contains an overview of process improvement that explains what CMMI is all about.

Next, skim Part Two, including generic goals and practices and specific goals and practices, to get a feel for the scope of the best practices contained in the model. Pay close attention to the purpose and introductory notes at the beginning of each process area.

In Part Three, look through the references in Appendix A and select additional sources you think would be beneficial to read before moving forward with using CMMI-ACQ. Read through the acronyms and glossary to become familiar with the language of CMMI. Then, go back and read the details of Part Two, including the tips and hints.

Readers Experienced with Process Improvement

If you are new to CMMI but have experience with other process improvement models, such as the Software Acquisition CMM, you will immediately recognize many similarities in their structure and content.

We recommend that you read Part One to understand how CMMI is different from other process improvement models. If you have experience with other models, you may want to select which sections to read first. Read Part Two with an eye for best practices you recognize from the models that you have already used. By identifying familiar material, you will gain an understanding of what is new and what has been carried over or is familiar from the models you already know. Review the tips, hints, and cross-references to see details and relationships that will help you understand CMMI better.

Next, review the glossary to understand how some terminology may differ from that used in the process improvement models you know. Many concepts are repeated, but they may be called something different.

Readers Familiar with CMMI

If you have reviewed or used a CMMI model before, you will quickly recognize the CMMI concepts discussed and the best practices presented. Focus in on the tips, hints, and cross-references in the process areas to discover new ideas, relationships, or details you may have missed before.

Additional Information and Reader Feedback

Many sources of information about CMMI are available, such as the background and history of the CMMI models, as well as the benefits of using CMMI models. Many of these sources are listed in Appendix A and are also published on the CMMI Web site—www.sei.cmu.edu/cmmi/.

Your suggestions for improving CMMI are welcome. For information on how to provide feedback, see the CMMI Web site at www.sei.cmu.edu/cmmi/models/change-requests.html. If you have questions about CMMI, send e-mail to cmmi-comments@sei.cmu.edu.

ACKNOWLEDGMENTS

This book wouldn't be possible without the work of multiple people from multiple organizations dedicated to CMMI-based process improvement. The complete CMMI-ACQ model is contained in the book, which was created by the CMMI Product Team. The tips and hints we added were based on those created by the work of Mary Beth Chrissis, Mike Konrad, and Sandy Shrum in the book *CMMI®: Guidelines for Process Integration and Product Improvement.*

The CMMI-ACQ model development team included members from different organizations and backgrounds. Ultimately, without the work of those involved in the CMMI project since it began in 1998, this book would not exist.

The General Motors team created the report on which the CMMI-ACQ model was based. That team consisted of the following members: Kathryn Dodson, Matt Fisher, Hubert F. Hofmann, Keith Kost, Gowri S. Ramani, and Deborah K. Yedlin.

The CMMI-ACQ development team developed what is now CMMI-ACQ, V1.2, from that report and inputs from lots of users and reviewers. That team consisted of the following members: Lloyd Anderson, Larry Baker, Roger Bate, Rhonda Brown, Aaron Clouse, Brad Doohan, Tom Keuten, Mike Konrad, Keith Kost, Mahav S. Panwar, Mike Phillips, Margaret Porteus, George Prosnik, Karen Richter, John Scibilia, Sandy Shrum, and Deborah K. Yedlin.

We would also like to acknowledge those who directly contributed to this book.

We want to thank Bill Peterson for his support and for his leadership of the Software Engineering Process Management Program (which includes CMMI) at the SEI.

We have special thanks for the contributors to Chapters 6 and 7. All of these authors were willing to share their insights and experiences and met aggressive deadlines to do so. These contributors were Andrew D. Boyd, Richard Freeman, Richard Frost, Tom Keuten, and Craig Meyers. We are delighted that they agreed to contribute their experiences to our book.

We are grateful to the reviewers of this book, Lloyd Anderson and Richard Barbour. Their useful comments helped us to improve the book and to better convey our ideas.

Special thanks go to Addison-Wesley Publishing Partner, Peter Gordon, for his assistance, experience, and advice. We'd also like to thank Kim Boedigheimer, Julie Nahil, Audrey Doyle, and Dmitri Korzh for their help with the design, editing, and final production of this book.

From Brian P. Gallagher

I would like to thank my wife, Valerie, and my daughters, Ashley, Caitlin, and Rachel, for their patience, understanding, and support. I would like to dedicate my contribution to this book to the memory of our son, Brian. Only 24 years with us—not a day goes by without you in our thoughts, prayers, and hearts.

From Mike Phillips

I would like to thank my wife, Connie, for her understanding and acknowledging the time to help create this book with a great team. I owe my CMMI perspectives to Drs. Roger Bate and Mike Konrad—and my acquisition perspectives to leaders in the Air Force, such as Generals Ron Yates, Dick Scofield, Ralph Tourino, and Keith Glenn. I hope this book pays dividends on all of their investments in time and energy.

From Karen J. Richter

I would like to thank my sponsors from the Office of the Under Secretary of Defense for Acquisition, Technology and Logistics (OUSD [AT&L]), Mr. Mark Schaeffer and Ms. Kristen Baldwin, for their unwavering and continued support for my CMMI work over the past ten years. At the Institute for Defense Analyses (IDA), I would like to thank the Vice President for Finances, Ms. Ruth Greenstein, and my Division Director, Mr. Mike Leonard, for their support to coauthor this book.

From Sandy Shrum

I would like to thank my coauthors, Karen, Mike, and Brian. It has been a joy and a privilege to work with all three of them on this book and through the years. I'd also like to thank the colleagues I've worked with on CMMI development and support projects over the past ten years. I've learned a lot and have had lots of fun doing it. My work with them has given me opportunities I would not have otherwise experienced. Finally, I'd like to thank my boyfriend, Jimmy, for his loving support and for helping me keep my focus and sense of humor through all the hours of work required to coauthor this book.

PART ONE

About CMMI for Acquisition

CHAPTER 1

INTRODUCTION

Now more than ever, organizations are increasingly becoming acquirers[1] of needed capabilities by obtaining products and services from suppliers and developing fewer of these capabilities in-house. The intent of this widely adopted business strategy is to improve an organization's operational efficiencies by leveraging suppliers' capabilities to deliver quality solutions rapidly, at a lower cost, and with the most appropriate technology.

AUTHORS' NOTE

It has been challenging to name the CMMI for Acquisition (CMMI-ACQ) model and this book. The reason is that the activities covered in these documents are called different things in different industries, organizations, and even countries. Instructors who teach CMMI-ACQ ask their students to tell the class what these activities are called in their organizations. At last count, more than 20 different terms were used to refer to what we call "acquisition." Our choice to use "acquisition" is consistent with the term used to describe these activities in ISO 15288.

Acquisition of needed capabilities is challenging because acquirers must take overall accountability for satisfying the user of the needed capability while allowing the supplier to perform the tasks necessary to develop and provide the solution.

According to recent studies, 20 percent to 25 percent of large information technology (IT) acquisition projects fail within two years and 50 percent fail within five years. Mismanagement, an inability to articulate customer needs, poor requirements definition, inadequate supplier selection and contracting processes, insufficient technology selection procedures, and uncontrolled requirements changes are factors that

1. In CMMI-ACQ, the terms *project* and *acquirer* refer to the acquisition project; the term *organization* refers to the acquisition organization.

contribute to project failure. Responsibility is shared by both the supplier and the acquirer. The majority of project failures could be avoided if the acquirer learned how to properly prepare for, engage with, and manage suppliers.

AUTHORS' NOTE

A March 2008 report from the Government Accountability Office (GAO) found that 95 programs in the 2007 portfolio of major defense acquisition programs exceeded original estimates by $295 million, with deliveries almost two years late, on average. Total acquisition costs for these 95 programs had risen 26 percent, compared with 6 percent in 2000. Sixty-three percent had changed requirements after starting development, and about half of the programs experienced at least a 25 percent increase in expected lines of software code [GAO: Defense Acquisition, 2008].

In addition to these challenges, an overall key to a successful acquirer–supplier relationship is communication.

AUTHORS' NOTE

General Motors Information Technology is a leader in working with its suppliers. See the case study in Chapter 7 to learn more about how sophisticated the relationships and communication can be with suppliers.

Unfortunately, many organizations have not invested in the capabilities necessary to effectively manage projects in an acquisition environment. Too often acquirers disengage from the project once the supplier is hired. Too late they discover that the project is not on schedule, deadlines will not be met, the technology selected is not viable, and the project has failed.

The acquirer has a focused set of major objectives. These objectives include the requirement to maintain a relationship with the final users of the capability to fully comprehend their needs. The acquirer owns the project, executes overall project management, and is accountable for delivering the needed capabilities to the users. Thus, these acquirer responsibilities may extend beyond ensuring that the right capability is delivered by chosen suppliers to include such activities as integrating the overall product or service, transitioning it into operation, and obtaining insight into its appropriateness and adequacy to continue to meet customer needs.

CMMI for Acquisition (CMMI-ACQ) provides an opportunity to avoid or eliminate barriers in the acquisition process through practices and terminology that transcend the interests of individual departments or groups.

AUTHORS' NOTE

If the acquirer and its suppliers are both using CMMI, they have a common language they can use to enhance the relationship even further.

This document provides guidance to help the acquirer apply CMMI best practices.

CMMI-ACQ contains 22 process areas. Of those, 16 are CMMI Model Foundation (CMF) process areas that cover process management, project management, and support. We will discuss CMF in more detail later in this chapter.

AUTHORS' NOTE

The CMF concept is what enables CMMI to be integrated for both supplier and acquirer use. The shared content across models for different domains enables organizations in different domains (e.g., acquirers and suppliers) to work together more effectively. It also enables large organizations to use multiple CMMI models without a huge investment in learning new terminology, concepts, and procedures.

Six process areas focus on practices specific to acquisition addressing agreement management, acquisition requirements development, acquisition technical management, acquisition validation, acquisition verification, and solicitation and supplier agreement development.

All CMMI-ACQ model practices focus on the activities of the acquirer. Those activities include supplier sourcing, supplier agreement development and award, and management of the acquisition of capabilities, including the acquisition of both products and services. Supplier activities are not addressed in this document. Suppliers and acquirers who also develop products and services should consider using the CMMI for Development (CMMI-DEV) model.

About Capability Maturity Models

In its research to help organizations develop and maintain quality products and services, the Software Engineering Institute (SEI) has identified several dimensions that an organization can focus on to improve its business. Figure 1.1 illustrates the three critical dimensions on which organizations typically focus: people, procedures and methods, and tools and equipment.

But what holds everything together? It is the processes used in your organization. Processes allow you to align the way you do business.

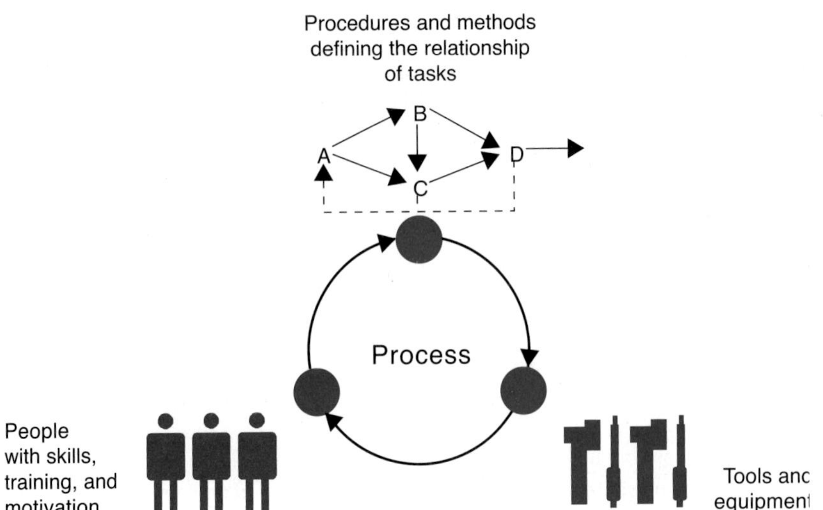

FIGURE 1.1
The Three Critical Dimensions

They allow you to address scalability and provide a way to incorporate knowledge of how to do things better. Processes allow you to leverage your resources and to examine business trends.

AUTHORS' NOTE

Another advantage of using CMMI models for improvement is that they are extremely flexible. CMMI doesn't dictate what processes to use, what tools to buy, or who should perform particular processes. CMMI provides a framework of flexible best practices that can be applied to meet the organization's business objectives, no matter what they are.

This is not to say that people and technology are not important. We are living in a world where technology is changing by an order of magnitude every ten years. Similarly, people typically work for many companies throughout their careers. We live in a dynamic world. A focus on process provides the infrastructure and stability necessary to deal with an ever-changing world and to maximize the productivity of people and the use of technology to be more competitive.

Manufacturing has long recognized the importance of process effectiveness and efficiency. Today, many organizations in manufacturing and service industries recognize the importance of quality processes. Process helps an organization's work force meet business objectives by helping them work smarter, not harder, and with improved consistency. Effective processes also provide a vehicle for introducing and using new technology in a way that best meets the organization's business objectives.

In the 1930s, Walter Shewhart began work in process improvement with his principles of statistical quality control [Shewhart 1931]. These principles were refined by W. Edwards Deming [Deming 1986], Phillip Crosby [Crosby 1979], and Joseph Juran [Juran 1988]. Watts Humphrey, Ron Radice, and others extended these principles even further and began to apply them to software in their work at IBM and the SEI [Humphrey 1989]. Humphrey's book, *Managing the Software Process*, provides a description of the basic principles and concepts on which many of the Capability Maturity Models (CMMs) are based.

The SEI has taken the process management premise, "the quality of a system or product is highly influenced by the quality of the process used to develop and maintain it," and defined CMMs that embody this premise. The belief in this premise is seen worldwide in quality movements, as evidenced by the International Organization for Standardization/International Electrotechnical Commission (ISO/IEC) body of standards.

CMMs focus on improving processes in an organization. They contain the essential elements of effective processes for one or more disciplines and describe an evolutionary improvement path from ad hoc, immature processes to disciplined, mature processes with improved quality and effectiveness.

The SEI created the first CMM designed for software organizations and published it in a book, *Capability Maturity Model: Guidelines for Improving the Software Process* [SEI 1995].

Today, CMMI is an application of the principles introduced almost a century ago to this never-ending cycle of process improvement. The value of this process improvement approach has been confirmed over time. Organizations have experienced increased productivity and quality, improved cycle time, and more accurate and predictable schedules and budgets [Gibson 2006].

Evolution of CMMI

Figure 1.2 illustrates the models that were integrated into CMMI-DEV and CMMI-ACQ. Developing a set of integrated models involved more than simply combining existing model materials. Using processes that promote consensus, the CMMI Product Team built a framework that accommodates multiple constellations.

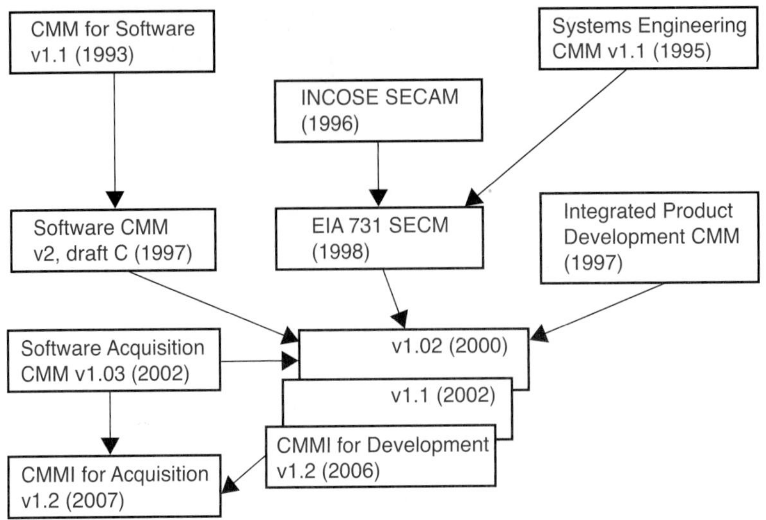

FIGURE 1.2
The History of CMMs[2]

> **AUTHORS' NOTE**
> Another CMMI model is currently "in the works" as this book is being written. In 2009 the CMMI for Services model will be released. It supports organizations that establish, manage, and delivery services.

CMMI Framework Architecture

The CMMI Framework Architecture provides the structure needed to produce CMMI models, training, and appraisal components. To allow the use of multiple models within the CMMI Framework, model components are classified as either common to all CMMI models or applicable to a specific model. The common material is called the *CMMI Model Foundation*, or *CMF*.

The components of the CMF are required to be a part of every model generated from the framework. Those components are combined with material applicable to an area of interest to produce a model. Some of this material is shared among areas of interest, and other portions are unique to only one area of interest.

A *constellation* is defined as a collection of components that are used to construct models, training materials, and appraisal materials in an

2. EIA 731 SECM is the Electronic Industries Alliance standard 731, or the Systems Engineering Capability Model. INCOSE SECAM is the International Council on Systems Engineering Capability Assessment Model [EIA 2002].

area of interest (e.g., acquisition and development). The Acquisition constellation's model is called *CMMI for Acquisition*, or *CMMI-ACQ*.

CMMI for Acquisition

The CMMI Steering Group initially approved an introductory collection of acquisition best practices called the *Acquisition Module (CMMI-AM)*, which was based on the CMMI Framework. Although it sought to capture best practices, it was not intended to become an appraisable model or a suitable model for process improvement purposes.

AUTHORS' NOTE

The Acquisition Module was updated after CMMI-ACQ was released. Now called the "CMMI for Acquisition Primer, Version 1.2," it continues to be an introduction to CMMI-based improvement for acquisition organizations. The primer is an SEI report (CMU/SEI-2008-TR-010) that you can find at www.sei.cmu.edu/publications/.

General Motors partnered with the SEI to create the initial draft Acquisition model that was the basis for this model. This model represents the work of many organizations and individuals.

Acquirers should use professional judgment and common sense to interpret this model for their organizations. That is, although the process areas described in this model depict behaviors that are considered best practice for most acquirers, all process areas and practices should be interpreted using an in-depth knowledge of CMMI-ACQ, organizational constraints, and the business environment.

AUTHORS' NOTE

Every CMMI model must be used within the framework of the organization's business objectives. An organization's processes should not be restructured to match a CMMI model's structure.

This document is a reference model that covers the acquisition of needed capabilities. Capabilities are acquired in many industries, including aerospace, banking, computer hardware, software, defense, automobile manufacturing, and telecommunications. All of these industries can use CMMI-ACQ.

CHAPTER 2

PROCESS AREA COMPONENTS

This chapter describes the components found in each process area, as well as in the generic goals and generic practices. Understanding the meaning of these components is critical to effectively using the information in Part Two of this book. If you are unfamiliar with the contents of Part Two, you may want to skim the Generic Goals and Generic Practices section of Part Two, along with a couple of process area sections, to get a general feel for the content and layout before reading this chapter.

Required, Expected, and Informative Components

Model components are grouped into three categories—required, expected, and informative—which reflect how to interpret them.

Required Components

Required components describe what an organization must achieve to satisfy a process area. This achievement must be visibly implemented in an organization's processes. The required components in CMMI are the specific and generic goals. Goal satisfaction is used in appraisals as the basis for deciding whether a process area has been satisfied.

Expected Components

Expected components describe what an organization may implement to achieve a required component. Expected components guide those who implement improvements or perform appraisals. The expected components in CMMI are the specific and generic practices.

Before goals can be considered satisfied, either the practices as described, or acceptable alternatives to them, must be present in the planned and implemented processes of the organization.

AUTHORS' NOTE
The required and expected components are also referred to as the normative material (versus the informative material).

Informative Components

Informative components provide details that help organizations understand the required and expected components. Subpractices, typical work products, goal and practice titles, goal and practice notes, examples, and references are examples of informative model components.

For CMMI for Acquisition (CMMI-ACQ), typical supplier deliverables are added informative components due to the interaction between supplier and acquirer processes.

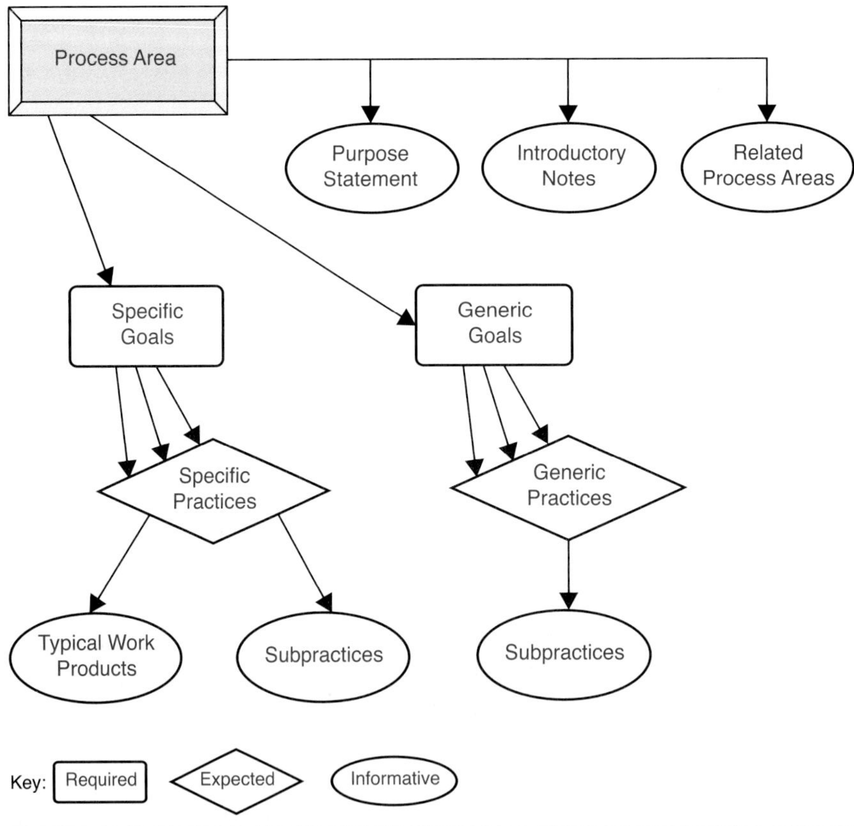

FIGURE 2.1
CMMI Model Components

The CMMI glossary of terms in Part Three of this book is not a required, expected, or informative component of CMMI models. You should interpret the terms in the glossary in the context of the model component in which they appear.

Components Associated with Part Two

The model components associated with Part Two can be summarized to illustrate their relationships, as shown in Figure 2.1.

AUTHORS' NOTE
All model components are important because the informative material helps you to understand the expected and required material. It is best to take these model components as a whole. If you understand all three types of material, you can then understand all the pieces and how they fit together to form a framework that can benefit your organization.

The following sections provide detailed descriptions of CMMI model components.

Process Areas

A process area is a cluster of related practices in an area that, when implemented collectively, satisfy a set of goals considered important for making improvement in that area.

There are 22 process areas, presented here in alphabetical order by acronym:

- Agreement Management (AM)
- Acquisition Requirements Development (ARD)
- Acquisition Technical Management (ATM)
- Acquisition Validation (AVAL)
- Acquisition Verification (AVER)
- Causal Analysis and Resolution (CAR)
- Configuration Management (CM)
- Decision Analysis and Resolution (DAR)
- Integrated Project Management (IPM)
- Measurement and Analysis (MA)
- Organizational Innovation and Deployment (OID)
- Organizational Process Definition (OPD)
- Organizational Process Focus (OPF)

- Organizational Process Performance (OPP)
- Organizational Training (OT)
- Project Monitoring and Control (PMC)
- Project Planning (PP)
- Process and Product Quality Assurance (PPQA)
- Quantitative Project Management (QPM)
- Requirements Management (REQM)
- Risk Management (RSKM)
- Solicitation and Supplier Agreement Development (SSAD)

AUTHORS' NOTE

Every time we release a model someone tells us that the process areas are not in alphabetical order. Since most users after a short time refer to the process areas by their acronym, it made sense to list them alphabetically by acronym instead of by full name.

Purpose Statements

A purpose statement describes the purpose of the process area and is an informative component.

For example, the purpose statement of the Organizational Process Definition process area is "The purpose of Organizational Process Definition (OPD) is to establish and maintain a usable set of organizational process assets and work environment standards."

AUTHORS' NOTE

All purpose statements follow the same sentence structure and always contain the process area acronym. An easy way to find a process area in an electronic file is to search for part or all of the purpose statement.

Introductory Notes

The introductory notes section of the process area describes the major concepts covered in the process area and is an informative component.

An example from the introductory notes of the Project Planning process area is "Planning begins with requirements that define the product and project."

Related Process Areas

The related process areas section lists references to related process areas and reflects the high-level relationships among the process areas. The related process areas section is an informative component.

An example of a reference found in the related process areas section of the Project Planning process area is "Refer to the Risk Management process area for more information about identifying and managing risks."

Specific Goals

A specific goal describes the unique characteristics that must be present to satisfy the process area. A specific goal is a required model component and is used in appraisals to help determine whether a process area is satisfied.

For example, a specific goal from the Configuration Management process area is "Integrity of baselines is established and maintained."

Only the statement of the specific goal is a required model component. The title of a specific goal (preceded by the goal number) and notes associated with the goal are considered informative model components.

Generic Goals

Generic goals are called *generic* because the same goal statement applies to multiple process areas. A generic goal describes the characteristics that must be present to institutionalize the processes that implement a process area. A generic goal is a required model component and is used in appraisals to determine whether a process area is satisfied. (See the Generic Goals and Generic Practices section in Part Two for a more detailed description of generic goals.)

An example of a generic goal is "The process is institutionalized as a defined process."

Only the statement of the generic goal is a required model component. The title of a generic goal (preceded by the goal number) and notes associated with the goal are considered informative model components.

Specific Goal and Practice Summaries

The specific goal and practice summary provides a high-level summary of the specific goals, which are required components, and the specific practices, which are expected components. The specific goal and practice summary is an informative component.

AUTHORS' NOTE

The specific goal and practice summary shows you at a glance a high-level summary of what is contained in a process area.

Specific Practices

A specific practice is the description of an activity that is considered important in achieving the associated specific goal. The specific practices describe the activities that are expected to result in achievement of the specific goals of a process area. A specific practice is an expected model component.

For example, a specific practice from the Project Monitoring and Control process area is "Monitor commitments against those identified in the project plan."

Only the statement of the specific practice is an expected model component. The title of a specific practice (preceded by the practice number) and notes associated with the specific practice are considered informative model components.

Typical Work Products

The typical work products section lists sample output from a specific practice. These examples are called *typical* work products because there are often other work products that are just as effective but are not listed. A typical work product is an informative model component.

For example, a typical work product for the specific practice "Monitor actual values of project planning parameters against the project plan" in the Project Monitoring and Control process area is "Records of significant deviations."

Typical Supplier Deliverables

To aid the acquirer, typical supplier deliverables are also provided. A typical supplier deliverable represents an artifact that is input into or supports the acquirer's implementation of the practice.

AUTHORS' NOTE

CMMI-ACQ includes a process area component called "typical supplier deliverables." After extended discussion, this new component was included because it presents lists of often very valuable inputs to the acquirers' processes that yield, in turn, the typical work products of the acquirers' activities. These were included to enable synergy across the acquirer–supplier team, particularly when both organizations are using the same book of CMMI best practices. Supplier deliverables do not become evidence for appraisals as typical work products often do, but providing these deliverables may aid projects during early planning and acquisition requirements development so that a more complete solicitation can be prepared.

For example, a typical supplier deliverable for the specific practice "Perform activities with the supplier as specified in the supplier agreement" in the Agreement Management process area is "Supplier project progress and performance reports."

Subpractices

A subpractice is a detailed description that provides guidance for interpreting and implementing a specific or generic practice. Subpractices may be worded as though they are prescriptive, but they are actually an informative component meant only to provide ideas that may be useful for process improvement.

For example, a subpractice for the specific practice "Take corrective action on identified issues" in the Project Monitoring and Control process area is "Determine and document the appropriate actions needed to address identified issues."

Generic Practices

Generic practices are called *generic* because the same practice applies to multiple process areas. A generic practice is the description of an activity that is considered important in achieving the associated generic goal. A generic practice is an expected model component.

For example, a generic practice for the generic goal "The process is institutionalized as a managed process" is "Provide adequate resources for performing the process, developing the work products, and providing the services of the process."

Only the statement of the generic practice is an expected model component. The title of a generic practice (preceded by the practice number) and notes associated with the practice are considered informative model components.

Supporting Informative Components

There are many places in the model where further information is needed to describe a concept. This informative material is provided in the form of the following components:

- Notes
- Examples
- References

Notes

A note is text that can accompany nearly any other model component. It may provide detail, background, or rationale. A note is an informative model component.

For example, a note that accompanies the specific practice "Implement selected action proposals developed in causal analysis" in the Causal Analysis and Resolution process area is "Only changes that prove to be of value should be considered for broad implementation."

Examples

An example is a component comprising text and often a list of items, usually in a box, that can accompany nearly any other component and provides one or more examples to clarify a concept or described activity. An example is an informative model component.

The following is an example that accompanies the subpractice "Document noncompliance issues when they cannot be resolved in the project" under the specific practice "Communicate quality issues and ensure the resolution of noncompliance issues with the staff and managers" in the Process and Product Quality Assurance process area.

Examples of ways to resolve noncompliance in the project include the following:

- Fixing the noncompliance
- Changing the process descriptions, standards, or procedures that were violated
- Obtaining a waiver to cover the noncompliance

References

A reference is a pointer to additional or more detailed information in related process areas and can accompany nearly any other model component. A reference is an informative model component.

For example, a reference that accompanies the specific practice "Select subprocesses that compose the project's defined process based on historical stability and capability data" in the Quantitative Project Management process area is "Refer to the Organizational Process Definition process area for more information about the organization's process asset library, which might include a process element of known and needed capability."

AUTHORS' NOTE

The difference between a reference that appears in the Related Process Areas section of a process area and one that appears elsewhere in the process area is that the references in the Related Process Area section represent more fundamental or important relationships and apply to the whole process area.

Numbering Scheme

Specific and generic goals are numbered sequentially. Each specific goal begins with the prefix *SG* (e.g., SG 1). Each generic goal begins with the prefix *GG* (e.g., GG 2).

Specific and generic practices also are numbered sequentially. Each specific practice begins with the prefix *SP*, followed by a number in the form *x.y* (e.g., SP 1.1). The *x* is the same number as the goal to which the specific practice maps. The *y* is the sequence number of the specific practice under the specific goal.

An example of specific practice numbering is in the Project Planning process area. The first specific practice is numbered SP 1.1 and the second is SP 1.2.

Each generic practice begins with the prefix *GP*, followed by a number in the form *x.y* (e.g., GP 1.1).

The *x* corresponds to the number of the generic goal. The *y* is the sequence number of the generic practice under the generic goal. For example, the first generic practice associated with GP 2 is numbered GP 2.1 and the second is GP 2.2.

Typographical Conventions

The typographical conventions used in this model were designed to enable you to select what you need and use it effectively. We present model components in formats that allow you to find them quickly on the page.

Figures 2.2 and 2.3 are sample pages from process areas in Part Two; they show the different process area components, labeled so that you can identify them. Notice that components differ typographically so that you can easily identify each one.

Process Area Name

Process Area Category

Maturity Level

Purpose

Introductory Notes

DECISION ANALYSIS AND RESOLUTION

A Support Process Area at Maturity Level 3

Purpose

The purpose of Decision Analysis and Resolution (DAR) is to analyze possible decisions using a formal evaluation process that evaluates identified alternatives against established criteria.

TIP

DAR provides organizations with a criteria-based approach to making important decisions objectively.

DAR

Introductory Notes

The Decision Analysis and Resolution process area involves establishing guidelines to determine which issues should be subject to a formal evaluation process and applying formal evaluation processes to these issues.

A formal evaluation process is a structured approach to evaluating alternative solutions against established criteria to determine a recommended solution.

A formal evaluation process involves the following actions:

- Establishing the criteria for evaluating alternatives
- Identifying alternative solutions
- Selecting methods for evaluating alternatives
- Evaluating alternative solutions using established criteria and methods
- Selecting recommended solutions from alternatives based on evaluation criteria

HINT

Many key acquisition decisions are made early in a project's lifecycle and have a major impact on project outcomes. Start by using formal evaluation methods on these key decisions before using them for selected day-to-day decisions. An effective source selection process or well-thought-out lifecycle milestone decisions are results of classic DAR activities.

Rather than using the phrase *alternative solutions to address issues* each time, in this process area, one of two shorter phrases are used: *alternative solutions* or *alternatives*.

A repeatable criteria-based decision-making process is especially important, both for making critical decisions that define and guide the acquisition process and later for critical decisions made with the selected supplier. The establishment of a formal process for decision

TIP

DAR takes the blame out of decision making. A bad decision is made when all the necessary information that might impact the decision was not considered and relevant stakeholders were not consulted.

239

FIGURE 2.2
Sample Page from Decision Analysis and Resolution

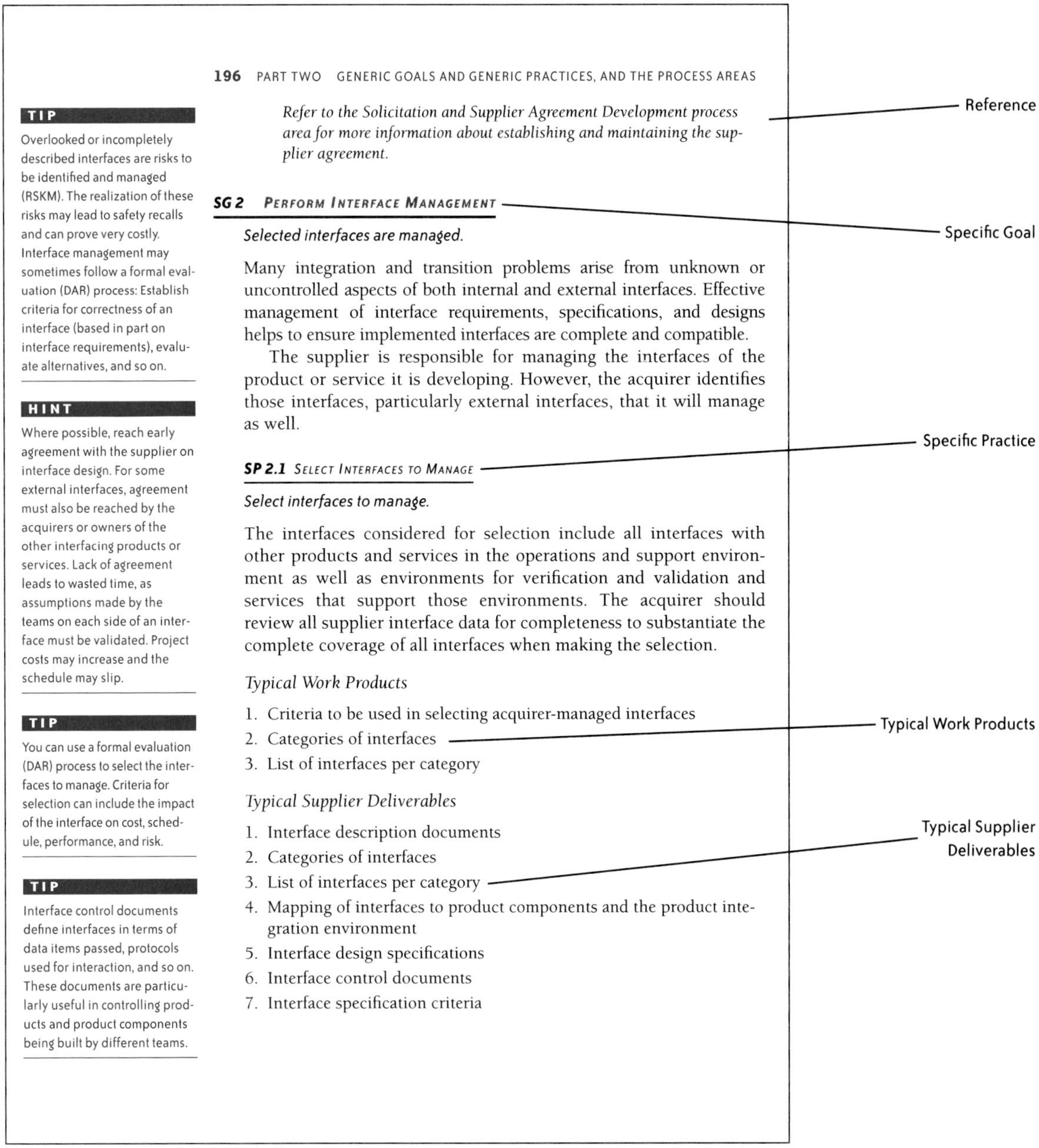

196 PART TWO GENERIC GOALS AND GENERIC PRACTICES, AND THE PROCESS AREAS

TIP

Overlooked or incompletely described interfaces are risks to be identified and managed (RSKM). The realization of these risks may lead to safety recalls and can prove very costly. Interface management may sometimes follow a formal evaluation (DAR) process: Establish criteria for correctness of an interface (based in part on interface requirements), evaluate alternatives, and so on.

HINT

Where possible, reach early agreement with the supplier on interface design. For some external interfaces, agreement must also be reached by the acquirers or owners of the other interfacing products or services. Lack of agreement leads to wasted time, as assumptions made by the teams on each side of an interface must be validated. Project costs may increase and the schedule may slip.

TIP

You can use a formal evaluation (DAR) process to select the interfaces to manage. Criteria for selection can include the impact of the interface on cost, schedule, performance, and risk.

TIP

Interface control documents define interfaces in terms of data items passed, protocols used for interaction, and so on. These documents are particularly useful in controlling products and product components being built by different teams.

Refer to the Solicitation and Supplier Agreement Development process area for more information about establishing and maintaining the supplier agreement. — Reference

SG 2 PERFORM INTERFACE MANAGEMENT — Specific Goal

Selected interfaces are managed.

Many integration and transition problems arise from unknown or uncontrolled aspects of both internal and external interfaces. Effective management of interface requirements, specifications, and designs helps to ensure implemented interfaces are complete and compatible.

The supplier is responsible for managing the interfaces of the product or service it is developing. However, the acquirer identifies those interfaces, particularly external interfaces, that it will manage as well.

SP 2.1 SELECT INTERFACES TO MANAGE — Specific Practice

Select interfaces to manage.

The interfaces considered for selection include all interfaces with other products and services in the operations and support environment as well as environments for verification and validation and services that support those environments. The acquirer should review all supplier interface data for completeness to substantiate the complete coverage of all interfaces when making the selection.

Typical Work Products — Typical Work Products

1. Criteria to be used in selecting acquirer-managed interfaces
2. Categories of interfaces
3. List of interfaces per category

Typical Supplier Deliverables — Typical Supplier Deliverables

1. Interface description documents
2. Categories of interfaces
3. List of interfaces per category
4. Mapping of interfaces to product components and the product integration environment
5. Interface design specifications
6. Interface control documents
7. Interface specification criteria

FIGURE 2.3
Sample Page from Acquisition Technical Management

CHAPTER 3

TYING IT ALL TOGETHER

Now that you have been introduced to the components of CMMI models, you need to understand how they fit together to meet your process improvement needs. This chapter introduces the concept of *levels* and shows how the process areas are organized and used.

CMMI-ACQ does not specify that a project or organization must follow a particular acquisition process flow or that a certain number of deliverables per day or specific performance targets be achieved—only that they have processes in place for adequately addressing acquisition-related practices. To determine whether this is so, a project or organization maps its processes to the process areas contained in this document.

The mapping of processes to process areas enables acquirers to track their progress against the CMMI-ACQ model as they implement processes. It is not intended that every process area of the CMMI-ACQ will map one to one with a given organization's or project's processes.

AUTHORS' NOTE
Think of CMMI-ACQ practices as characteristics that should be present in your processes to help reduce risk, not as checklist items to be blindly followed.

Understanding Levels

Levels are used in CMMI to describe an evolutionary path recommended for an organization that wants to improve the processes it uses to acquire capabilities, including products and services. Levels can also be the outcome of the rating activity in appraisals.[1]

1. For more information about appraisals, refer to *Appraisal Requirements for CMMI* and the *Standard CMMI Appraisal Method for Process Improvement Method Definition Document* [SEI 2006c, SEI 2006b].

Appraisals can apply to entire companies or to smaller groups such as a small group of projects or a division in a company.

AUTHORS' NOTE
Levels are useful for benchmarking your capabilities against a publicly reviewed set of practices and establishing improvement priorities. However, be sure to consider the entire team's capabilities (e.g., acquirer, supplier, and end user) when trying to maximize the outcomes and reduce risk on a particular project.

AUTHORS' NOTE
For guidance on how to use CMMI to help reduce project risk across the entire team, see the Software Engineering Institute (SEI) report, "Understanding and Leveraging a Supplier's CMMI Efforts: A Guidebook for Acquirers" (CMU/SEI-2007-TR-004).

CMMI supports two improvement paths using levels. One path enables organizations to incrementally improve processes corresponding to an individual process area (or process areas) selected by the organization. The other path enables organizations to improve a set of related processes by incrementally addressing successive sets of process areas.

These two improvement paths are associated with the two types of levels: capability levels and maturity levels. These levels correspond to two approaches to process improvement, called *representations*. The two representations are *continuous* and *staged*. The continuous representation has *capability levels*. The staged representation has *maturity levels*.

Regardless of which representation you select, the *level* concept is the same. Levels characterize improvement from an ill-defined state to a state that uses quantitative information to determine and manage improvements that are needed to meet an organization's business objectives.

To reach a particular level, an organization must satisfy all of the appropriate goals of the process area or set of process areas that are targeted for improvement, regardless of whether it is a capability or a maturity level.

Both representations provide ways to implement process improvement to achieve business objectives, and both provide the same essential content and use the same model components.

Structures of the Continuous and Staged Representations

Figure 3.1 illustrates the structures of the continuous and staged representations. The differences jump out at you immediately when you look at these structures. The staged representation utilizes maturity levels, whereas the continuous representation utilizes capability levels.

What may strike you as you compare these two representations is their similarity. Both have many of the same components (e.g., process areas, specific goals, and specific practices), and these components have the same hierarchy and configuration.

What is not readily apparent from the high-level view in Figure 3.1 is that the continuous representation focuses on process area capability as measured by capability levels and the staged representation focuses on organizational maturity as measured by maturity levels. The following dimensions (the capability/maturity dimensions) of CMMI are

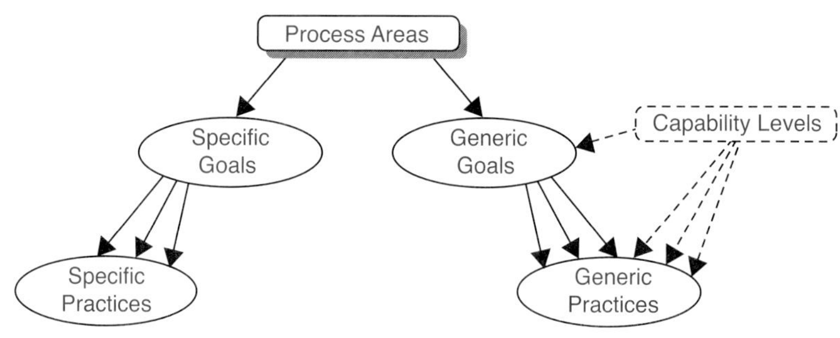

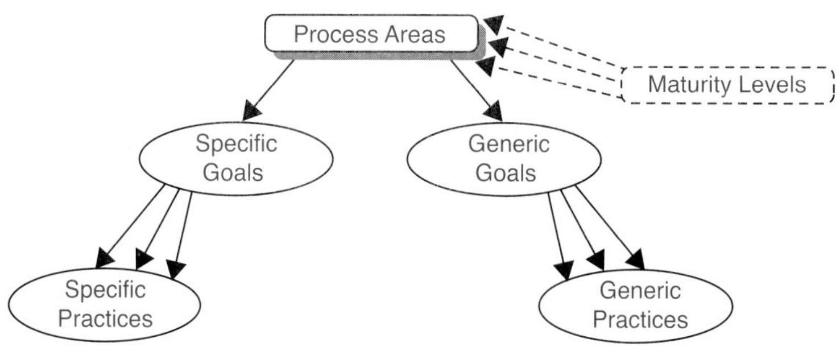

FIGURE 3.1
Structure of the Continuous and Staged Representations

used for benchmarking and appraisal activities, as well as for guiding an organization's improvement efforts.

- Capability levels apply to an organization's process improvement achievement in individual process areas. These levels are a means for incrementally improving the processes corresponding to a given process area. There are six capability levels, which are numbered 0 through 5.
- Maturity levels apply to an organization's process improvement achievement across multiple process areas. These levels are a means of predicting the general outcomes of the next project undertaken. There are five maturity levels, numbered 1 through 5.

Table 3.1 compares the six capability levels to the five maturity levels. Notice that the names of four of the levels are the same in both representations. The differences are that there is no maturity level 0, and at level 1 the capability level is *Performed*, whereas the maturity level is *Initial*. Therefore, the starting point is different.

The continuous representation is concerned with selecting both a particular process area to improve and the desired capability level for that process area. In this context, whether a process is performed or incomplete is important. Therefore, the name *incomplete* is given to the continuous representation starting point.

Because the staged representation is concerned with the overall maturity of the organization, whether individual processes are performed or incomplete is not the primary focus. Therefore, the name *initial* is given to the staged representation starting point.

Both capability levels and maturity levels provide a way to measure how well organizations can and do improve their processes. However, the associated approach to process improvement is different.

TABLE 3.1 Comparison of Capability and Maturity Levels

Level	*Continuous Representation Capability Levels*	*Staged Representation Maturity Levels*
Level 0	Incomplete	(not applicable)
Level 1	Performed	Initial
Level 2	Managed	Managed
Level 3	Defined	Defined
Level 4	Quantitatively Managed	Quantitatively Managed
Level 5	Optimizing	Optimizing

Understanding Capability Levels

To support those using the continuous representation, all CMMI models reflect capability levels in their design and content.

The six capability levels, designated by the numbers 0 through 5, are as follows:

0. Incomplete
1. Performed
2. Managed
3. Defined
4. Quantitatively Managed
5. Optimizing

A capability level for a process area is achieved when all of the generic goals are satisfied up to that level. The fact that capability levels 2 through 5 use the same terms as generic goals 2 through 5 is intentional because each of these generic goals and practices reflects the meaning of the capability levels of the goals and practices. (See the Generic Goals and Generic Practices section in Part Two for more information about generic goals and practices.) A short description of each capability level follows.

Capability Level 0: Incomplete

An *incomplete process* is a process that either is not performed or is partially performed. One or more of the specific goals of the process area are not satisfied, and no generic goals exist for this level since there is no reason to institutionalize a partially performed process.

Capability Level 1: Performed

A capability level 1 process is characterized as a *performed process*. A performed process is a process that satisfies the specific goals of the process area. It supports and enables the work needed to acquire capabilities.

Although capability level 1 results in important improvements, those improvements can be lost over time if they are not institutionalized. The application of institutionalization (the CMMI generic practices at capability levels 2 through 5) helps to ensure that improvements are maintained.

Capability Level 2: Managed

A capability level 2 process is characterized as a *managed process*. A managed process is a performed (capability level 1) process that has the basic infrastructure in place to support the process. It is planned and executed in accordance with policy; employs skilled people who have adequate resources to produce controlled outputs; involves relevant stakeholders; is monitored, controlled, and reviewed; and is evaluated for adherence to its process description. The process discipline reflected by capability level 2 helps to ensure that existing practices are retained during times of stress.

Capability Level 3: Defined

A capability level 3 process is characterized as a *defined process*. A defined process is a managed (capability level 2) process that is tailored from the organization's set of standard processes according to the organization's tailoring guidelines, and it contributes work products, measures, and other process improvement information to the organizational process assets.

A critical distinction between capability levels 2 and 3 is the scope of standards, process descriptions, and procedures. At capability level 2, the standards, process descriptions, and procedures may be quite different in each specific instance of the process (e.g., on a particular project). At capability level 3, the standards, process descriptions, and procedures for a project are tailored from the organization's set of standard processes to suit a particular project or organizational unit and therefore are more consistent, except for the differences allowed by the tailoring guidelines.

Another critical distinction is that at capability level 3, processes are typically described more rigorously than at capability level 2. A defined process clearly states the purpose, inputs, entry criteria, activities, roles, measures, verification steps, outputs, and exit criteria. At capability level 3, processes are managed more proactively using an understanding of the interrelationships of the process activities and detailed measures of the process, its work products, and its services.

Capability Level 4: Quantitatively Managed

A capability level 4 process is characterized as a *quantitatively managed process*. A quantitatively managed process is a defined (capability level 3) process that is controlled using statistical and other quantitative techniques. Quantitative objectives for quality and process performance are established and used as criteria in managing the process. Quality and process performance is understood in statistical terms and is managed throughout the life of the process.

Capability Level 5: Optimizing

A capability level 5 process is characterized as an *optimizing process*. An optimizing process is a quantitatively managed (capability level 4) process that is improved based on an understanding of the common causes of variation inherent in the process. The focus of an optimizing process is on continually improving the range of process performance through both incremental and innovative improvements.

Remember that capability levels 2 through 5 use the same terms as generic goals 2 through 5, and a detailed description of these terms appears in the Generic Goals and Generic Practices section in Part Two of this book.

Advancing through Capability Levels

The capability levels of a process area are achieved through the application of generic practices or suitable alternatives to the processes associated with that process area.

Reaching capability level 1 for a process area is equivalent to saying that the processes associated with that process area are *performed processes*.

Reaching capability level 2 for a process area is equivalent to saying that there is a policy that indicates you will perform the process. There is a plan for performing it, resources are provided, responsibilities are assigned, training to perform it is provided, selected work products related to performing the process are controlled, and so on. In other words, a capability level 2 process can be planned and monitored just like any project or support activity.

Reaching capability level 3 for a process area assumes that an organizational standard process exists that is associated with that process area and that can be tailored to the needs of the project. The processes in the organization are now more consistently defined and applied because they are based on organizational standard processes.

Reaching capability level 4 for a process area assumes that this process area is a key business driver that the organization wants to manage using quantitative and statistical techniques. This analysis gives the organization more visibility into the performance of selected subprocesses, which will make it more competitive in the marketplace.

Reaching capability level 5 for a process area assumes that you have stabilized the selected subprocesses and that you want to reduce the common causes of variation in that process. Remember that variation is a natural occurrence in any process, so although it is conceptually feasible to improve all processes, it is not economical to improve all processes to level 5. Again, you want to concentrate on those processes that help you to meet your business objectives.

Understanding Maturity Levels

To support those using the staged representation, all CMMI models reflect maturity levels in their design and content. A maturity level consists of related specific and generic practices for a predefined set of process areas that improve the organization's overall performance. The maturity level of an organization provides a way to predict an organization's performance in a given discipline or set of disciplines. Experience has shown that organizations do their best when they focus their process improvement efforts on a manageable number of process areas at a time and that those areas require increasing sophistication as the organization improves.

A maturity level is a defined evolutionary plateau for organizational process improvement. Each maturity level matures an important subset of the organization's processes, preparing it to move to the next maturity level. The maturity levels are measured by the achievement of the specific and generic goals associated with each predefined set of process areas.

There are five maturity levels, each a layer in the foundation for ongoing process improvement, designated by the numbers 1 through 5:

1. Initial
2. Managed
3. Defined
4. Quantitatively Managed
5. Optimizing

Remember that maturity levels 2 through 5 use the same terms as capability levels 2 through 5. This was intentional because the concepts of maturity levels and capability levels are complementary. Maturity levels are used to characterize organizational improvement relative to a set of process areas, and capability levels characterize organizational improvement relative to an individual process area.

Maturity Level 1: Initial

At maturity level 1, processes are usually ad hoc and chaotic. The organization usually does not provide a stable environment to support processes. Success in these organizations depends on the competence and heroics of the people in the organization and not on the use of proven processes. In spite of this chaos, maturity level 1 organizations acquire products and services that often work but frequently exceed the budget and schedule documented in their plans.

Maturity level 1 organizations are characterized by a tendency to overcommit, abandonment of processes in a time of crisis, and an inability to repeat their successes.

Maturity Level 2: Managed

At maturity level 2, projects establish the foundation for an organization to become an effective acquirer of needed capabilities by institutionalizing basic project management and supplier management practices. Projects define a supplier strategy, create project plans, and monitor and control the project to ensure that the product or service is delivered as planned. The acquirer establishes an agreement with suppliers supporting the projects and manages such agreements to ensure that each supplier delivers on its commitments. The acquirer develops and manages customer and contractual requirements. Configuration management and process and product quality assurance are institutionalized, and the acquirer also develops the capability to measure and analyze process performance.

At maturity level 2, projects, processes, work products, and services are managed. The acquirer ensures that processes are planned in accordance with policy. To execute the process, the acquirer provides adequate resources, assigns responsibility for performing the process, trains people on the process, and ensures that the designated work products of the process are under appropriate levels of configuration management. The acquirer identifies and involves appropriate stakeholders and periodically monitors and controls the process. Process adherence is periodically evaluated and process performance is shared with senior management. The process discipline reflected by maturity level 2 helps to ensure that existing practices are retained during times of stress.

Maturity Level 3: Defined

At maturity level 3, acquirers use defined processes for managing projects and suppliers. They embed tenets of project management and acquisition best practices, such as integrated project management and acquisition technical management, into the standard process set. The acquirer verifies that selected work products meet their requirements and validates products and services to ensure that they fulfill their intended use in the intended environment. These processes are well characterized and understood and are described in standards, procedures, tools, and methods.

The organization's set of standard processes, which is the basis for maturity level 3, is established and improved over time. These standard processes are used to establish consistency across the organization. Projects establish their defined processes by tailoring the organization's set of standard processes according to tailoring guidelines. (See the glossary for a definition of "organization's set of standard processes.")

A critical distinction between maturity levels 2 and 3 is the scope of standards, process descriptions, and procedures. At maturity level 2, the standards, process descriptions, and procedures may be quite different in each specific instance of the process (e.g., on a particular project). At maturity level 3, the standards, process descriptions, and procedures for a project are tailored from the organization's set of standard processes to suit a particular project or organizational unit and therefore are more consistent except for the differences allowed by the tailoring guidelines.

Another critical distinction is that at maturity level 3, processes are typically described more rigorously than at maturity level 2. A defined process clearly states the purpose, inputs, entry criteria, activities, roles, measures, verification steps, outputs, and exit criteria. At maturity level 3, processes are managed more proactively using an understanding of the interrelationships of process activities and detailed measures of the process, its work products, and its services.

At maturity level 3, the organization must further mature the maturity level 2 process areas. Generic practices associated with generic goal 3 that were not addressed at maturity level 2 are applied to achieve maturity level 3.

Due to the acquirer–supplier relationship, the need for early and aggressive detection of risk is compounded by the complexity of projects acquiring products and services. The purpose of risk management is to identify and assess project risks during project planning and to manage these risks throughout the project.

Maturity Level 4: Quantitatively Managed

At maturity level 4, acquirers establish quantitative objectives for quality and process performance and use them as criteria in managing processes. Quantitative objectives are based on the needs of the customer, end users, organization, and process implementers. Quality and process performance is understood in statistical terms and is managed throughout the life of the processes.

For selected subprocesses, specific measures of process performance are collected and statistically analyzed. When selecting processes or subprocesses for analysis, it is critical to understand the relationships among different processes and subprocesses and their impact on the acquirer's and supplier's performance relative to delivering the product specified by the customer. Such an approach helps to ensure that quantitative and statistical management is applied where it has the most overall value to the business. Supplier process performance is analyzed as it interfaces with acquirer processes, through data and measures submitted by the supplier. Performance models are used to set performance objectives for both acquirer and supplier performance and to help both parties achieve their objectives.

A critical distinction between maturity levels 3 and 4 is the predictability of process performance. At maturity level 4, the performance of processes is controlled using statistical and other quantitative techniques and is quantitatively predictable. At maturity level 3, processes are typically only qualitatively predictable.

Maturity Level 5: Optimizing

At maturity level 5, an organization continually improves its processes based on a quantitative understanding of the common causes of variation inherent in processes. (See the definition of "common cause of process variation" in the glossary.)

Maturity level 5 focuses on continually improving process performance through incremental and innovative process and technology improvements that enhance the acquirer's and its suppliers' ability to meet the acquirer's quality and process-performance objectives.

Quantitative process improvement objectives for the organization are established, continually revised to reflect changing business objectives, and used as criteria in managing process improvement. The effects of deployed process improvements are measured and compared to quantitative process improvement objectives. Both the defined processes and the organization's set of standard processes are targets of measurable improvement activities.

The acquirer typically achieves its quality and performance objectives through coordination with its suppliers. The acquirer typically focuses on capability differentiation and collaborative supplier management. Achievement of these objectives also depends on the acquirer's being able to effectively evaluate and deploy proposed improvements to processes and technologies. For best results, members of the acquirer–supplier network participate in the acquirer's process and technology improvement activities. Process improvement proposals are systematically gathered and addressed.

A critical distinction between maturity levels 4 and 5 is the type of process variation addressed. At maturity level 4, the organization is concerned with addressing special causes of process variation and providing statistical predictability of results. Although processes may produce predictable results, the results may be insufficient to achieve established objectives. At maturity level 5, the organization is concerned with addressing common causes of process variation and with changing the process (to shift the mean of the process performance or reduce the inherent process variation experienced) to improve process performance and to achieve established quantitative process improvement objectives.

Advancing through Maturity Levels

Organizations can achieve progressive improvements in their organizational maturity by achieving control first at the project level and continuing to the most advanced level—organization-wide continuous process improvement—using both quantitative and qualitative data to make decisions.

Since improved organizational maturity is associated with improvement in the range of expected results that can be achieved by an organization, it is one way of predicting the general outcomes of the organization's next project. For instance, at maturity level 2, the organization has been elevated from ad hoc to disciplined by establishing sound project management. As your organization achieves generic and specific goals for the set of process areas in a maturity level, you are increasing your organizational maturity and reaping the benefits of process improvement. Because each maturity level forms a necessary foundation for the next level, trying to skip maturity levels is usually counterproductive.

At the same time, you must recognize that process improvement efforts should focus on the needs of the organization in the context of its business environment and that process areas at higher maturity levels address the current needs of an organization or project. For example, organizations seeking to move from maturity level 1 to maturity level 2 are frequently encouraged to establish a process group, which is addressed by the Organizational Process Focus process area that resides at maturity level 3. Although a process group is not a necessary characteristic of a maturity level 2 organization, it can be a useful part of the organization's approach to achieving maturity level 2.

This situation is sometimes characterized as establishing a maturity level 1 process group to bootstrap the maturity level 1 organization to maturity level 2. Maturity level 1 process improvement activities may depend primarily on the insight and competence of the process group staff until an infrastructure to support more disciplined and widespread improvement is in place.

Organizations can institute process improvements anytime they choose, even before they are prepared to advance to the maturity level at which the specific practice is recommended. In such situations, however, organizations should understand that the success of these improvements is at risk because the foundation for their successful institutionalization has not been completed. Processes without the proper foundation may fail at the point they are needed most—when they are under stress.

A defined process that is characteristic of a maturity level 3 organization can be placed at great risk if maturity level 2 management practices are deficient. For example, management may commit to a poorly planned schedule or fail to control changes to baselined requirements. Similarly, many organizations prematurely collect the detailed data characteristic of maturity level 4 only to find the data uninterpretable because of inconsistencies in processes and measurement definitions.

Process Areas

Process areas are viewed differently in continuous and staged representations. Figure 3.2 compares views of how process areas are used in the continuous representation and in the staged representation.

The continuous representation enables an organization to choose the focus of its process improvement efforts by choosing those process areas, or sets of interrelated process areas, that best benefit the organization and its business objectives. Although there are some limits on what an organization can choose because of the dependencies among process areas, the organization has considerable freedom in its selection.

AUTHORS' NOTE

When selecting which process areas to use to improve your organization's processes, take a risk-based approach. For example, if most projects have difficulty selecting appropriate acquisition strategies or can't effectively perform trade studies, Decision Analysis and Resolution might be a good place to start.

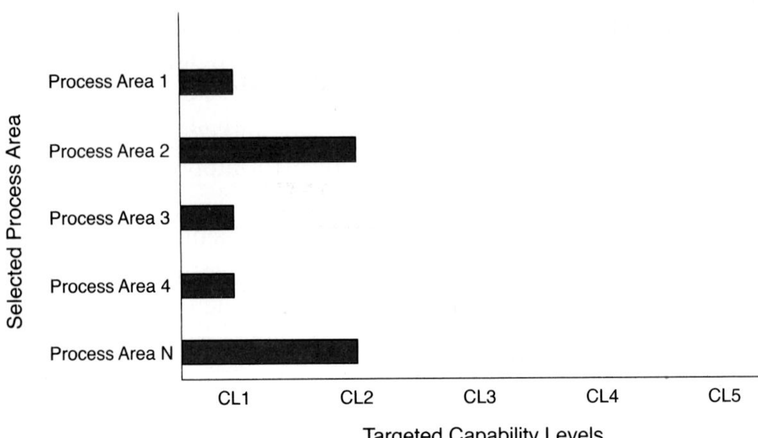

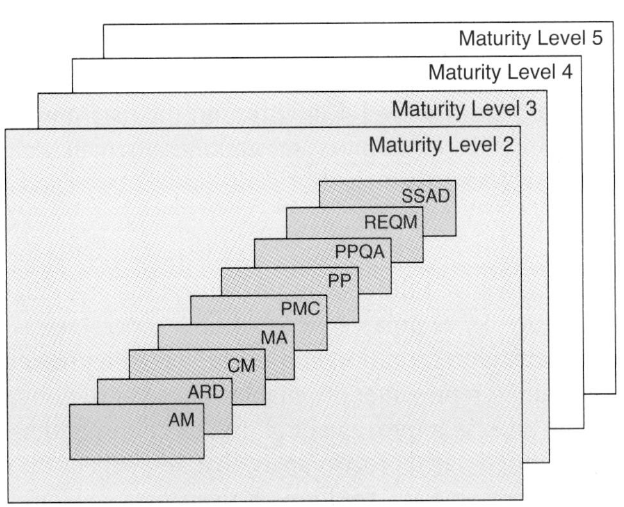

FIGURE 3.2
Process Areas in Continuous and Staged Representations

To support those using the continuous representation, process areas are organized into four categories: Process Management, Project Management, Acquisition, and Support. These categories emphasize some of the key relationships that exist among the process areas.

Once you select process areas, you must also select how much you would like to mature processes associated with those process areas (i.e., select the appropriate capability level). Capability levels and generic goals and practices support the improvement of processes associated with individual process areas. For example, an organization may wish to reach capability level 2 in one process area and capability level 4 in another. As the organization reaches a capability level, it sets its sights on the next capability level for one of these same process areas, or it decides to widen its view and address a larger number of process areas.

AUTHORS' NOTE

Consider improving processes that cross acquirer–supplier boundaries, such as the requirements process, and perform joint acquirer–supplier improvement activities.

This selection of a combination of process areas and capability levels is typically described in a target profile. A target profile defines all of the process areas to be addressed and the targeted capability level for each. This profile governs which goals and practices the organization will address in its process improvement efforts.

Most organizations, at minimum, target capability level 1, which requires that all specific goals of the process area be achieved. However, organizations that target capability levels higher than 1 concentrate on the institutionalization of selected processes in the organization by implementing the associated generic goals and practices.

The staged representation provides a predetermined path of improvement from maturity level 1 to maturity level 5 that involves achieving the goals of the process areas at each maturity level. To support those using the staged representation, process areas are grouped by maturity level, indicating which process areas to implement to achieve each maturity level. For example, at maturity level 2, there is a set of process areas that an organization would use to guide its process improvement until it can achieve all the goals of all these process areas. Once maturity level 2 is achieved, the organization focuses its efforts on maturity level 3 process areas, and so on. The generic goals that apply to each process area are also predetermined. Generic goal 2 applies to maturity level 2 and generic goal 3 applies to maturity levels 3 through 5.

Table 3.2 provides a list of CMMI-ACQ process areas and their associated categories and maturity levels.

TABLE 3.2 Process Areas and Their Associated Categories and Maturity Levels

Process Area	*Category*	*Maturity Level*
Agreement Management (AM)	Acquisition	2
Acquisition Requirements Development (ARD)	Acquisition	2
Acquisition Technical Management (ATM)	Acquisition	3
Acquisition Validation (AVAL)	Acquisition	3
Acquisition Verification (AVER)	Acquisition	3
Causal Analysis and Resolution (CAR)	Support	5
Configuration Management (CM)	Support	2
Decision Analysis and Resolution (DAR)	Support	3
Integrated Project Management (IPM)	Project Management	3
Measurement and Analysis (MA)	Support	2
Organizational Innovation and Deployment (OID)	Process Management	5
Organizational Process Definition (OPD)	Process Management	3
Organizational Process Focus (OPF)	Process Management	3
Organizational Process Performance (OPP)	Process Management	4
Organizational Training (OT)	Process Management	3
Project Monitoring and Control (PMC)	Project Management	2
Project Planning (PP)	Project Management	2
Process and Product Quality Assurance (PPQA)	Support	2
Quantitative Project Management (QPM)	Project Management	4
Requirements Management (REQM)	Project Management	2
Risk Management (RSKM)	Project Management	3
Solicitation and Supplier Agreement Development (SSAD)	Acquisition	2

Equivalent Staging

Equivalent staging is a way to compare results from using the continuous representation to those of the staged representation. In essence, if you measured improvement relative to selected process areas using capability levels in the continuous representation, how would you compare that to maturity levels? Is this possible?

Up to this point, we have not discussed process appraisals in much detail. The Standard CMMI Appraisal Method for Process Improvement (SCAMPI) method[2] is used to appraise organizations

2. The SCAMPI method is described in Chapter 5.

using CMMI, and one result of an appraisal is a rating [SEI 2006b, Ahern 2008]. If the continuous representation is used for an appraisal, the rating is a capability level profile. If the staged representation is used for an appraisal, the rating is a maturity level (e.g., maturity level 3) rating.

A capability level profile is a list of process areas and the corresponding capability level achieved for each. This profile enables an organization to track its capability level by process area. The profile is an *achievement profile* when it represents the organization's actual progress for each process area. Alternatively, the profile is a *target profile* when it represents the organization's planned process improvement objectives. Figure 3.3 illustrates a combined target and achievement profile. The gray portion of each bar represents what has been achieved. The unshaded portion represents what remains to be accomplished to meet the target profile.

An achievement profile, when compared with a target profile, enables an organization to plan and track its progress for each selected process area. Maintaining capability level profiles is advisable when using the continuous representation.

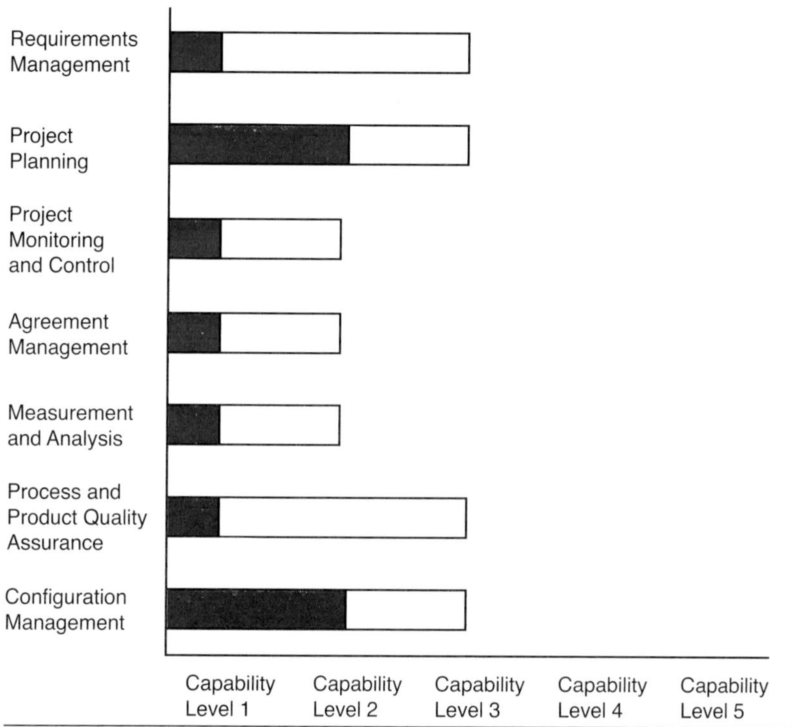

FIGURE 3.3
An Example of a Target and Achievement Profile

Target staging is a sequence of target profiles that describes the path of process improvement for the organization to follow. When building target profiles, the organization should pay attention to the dependencies between generic practices and process areas. If a generic practice depends on a process area, either to carry out the generic practice or to provide a prerequisite product, the generic practice may be much less effective when the process area is not implemented.[3]

Although there are many reasons to use the continuous representation, ratings consisting of capability level profiles are limited in their ability to provide organizations with a way to generally compare themselves with other organizations. Capability level profiles could be used if each organization selected the same process areas; however, maturity levels have been used to compare organizations for years and already provide predefined sets of process areas.

Because of this situation, equivalent staging was created. Equivalent staging enables an organization using the continuous representation for an appraisal to convert a capability level profile to the associated maturity level rating.

The most effective way to depict equivalent staging is to provide a sequence of target profiles, each of which is equivalent to a maturity level rating of the staged representation. The result is a target staging that is equivalent to the maturity levels of the staged representation.

Figure 3.4 shows a summary of the target profiles that must be achieved when using the continuous representation to be equivalent to maturity levels 2 through 5. Each shaded area in the capability level columns represents a target profile that is equivalent to a maturity level.

The following rules summarize equivalent staging.

- To achieve maturity level 2, all process areas assigned to maturity level 2 must achieve capability level 2 or higher.
- To achieve maturity level 3, all process areas assigned to maturity levels 2 and 3 must achieve capability level 3 or higher.
- To achieve maturity level 4, all process areas assigned to maturity levels 2, 3, and 4 must achieve capability level 3 or higher.
- To achieve maturity level 5, all process areas must achieve capability level 3 or higher.

These rules and the table for equivalent staging are complete; however, you may ask why target profiles 4 and 5 do not extend into the CL4 and CL5 columns. The reason is that maturity level 4 process

---

3. See Table 8.2 in the Generic Goals and Generic Practices section of Part Two for more information about the dependencies between generic practices and process areas.

Name	Abbr	ML	CL1	CL2	CL3	CL4	CL5
Agreement Management	AM	2					
Acquisition Requirements Development	ARD	2					
Configuration Management	CM	2					
Measurement and Analysis	MA	2					
Project Monitoring and Control	PMC	2	Target Profile 2				
Project Planning	PP	2					
Process and Product Quality Assurance	PPQA	2					
Requirements Management	REQM	2					
Solicitation and Supplier Agreement Development	SSAD	2					
Acquisition Technical Management	ATM	3					
Acquisition Validation	AVAL	3		Target Profile 3			
Acquisition Verification	AVER	3					
Decision Analysis and Resolution	DAR	3					
Integrated Project Management	IPM	3					
Organizational Process Definition	OPD	3					
Organizational Process Focus	OPF	3					
Organizational Training	OT	3					
Risk Management	RSKM	3					
Organizational Process Performance	OPP	4		Target Profile 4			
Quantitative Project Management	QPM	4					
Causal Analysis and Resolution	CAR	5		Target Profile 5			
Organizational Innovation and Deployment	OID	5					

FIGURE 3.4
Target Profiles and Equivalent Staging

areas describe a selection of the subprocesses to be stabilized based, in part, on the quality and process-performance objectives of the organization and projects. Not every process area will be addressed in the selection, and CMMI does not presume in advance which process areas might be addressed in the selection.

So, the achievement of capability level 4 for process areas cannot be predetermined, because the choices depend on the selections made by the organization in its implementation of the maturity level 4 process areas. Thus, Figure 3.4 does not show target profile 4 extending into the CL4 column, although some process areas will have achieved capability level 4. The situation for maturity level 5 and target profile 5 is similar.

The existence of equivalent staging should not discourage users of the continuous representation from establishing target profiles that extend above capability level 3. Such a target profile would be determined in part by the selections the organization makes to meet its business objectives.

CHAPTER 4

RELATIONSHIPS AMONG PROCESS AREAS

In this chapter we describe the key relationships among process areas to help you see the acquirer's view of process improvement and which process areas build on the implementation of other process areas.

The relationships among multiple process areas, including the information and artifacts that flow from one process area to another—illustrated by the figure and descriptions in this chapter—help you see a larger view of process implementation and improvement.

Successful process improvement initiatives must be driven by the organization's business objectives. For example, a common business objective is to reduce the time it takes to get a product to market. The process improvement objective derived from that might be to improve the project management processes to ensure on-time delivery. Those improvements rely on best practices in the Project Planning and Project Monitoring and Control process areas.

Although we group process areas in this chapter to simplify the discussion of their relationships, process areas often interact and have an effect on one another regardless of their group, category, or level. For example, the Decision Analysis and Resolution process area (a Support process area at maturity level 3) contains specific practices that address the formal evaluation process used in the Solicitation and Supplier Agreement Development process area (an Acquisition process area at maturity level 2) to select suppliers for acquirer management.

Being aware of the key relationships that exist among CMMI process areas will help you apply CMMI in a useful and productive way. Relationships among process areas are described in more detail in the references in each process area, and specifically in the Related Process Areas section of each process area in Part Two. Refer to Chapter 2 for more information about references.

Figure 4.1 illustrates key relationships among CMMI for Acquisition (CMMI-ACQ) process areas.

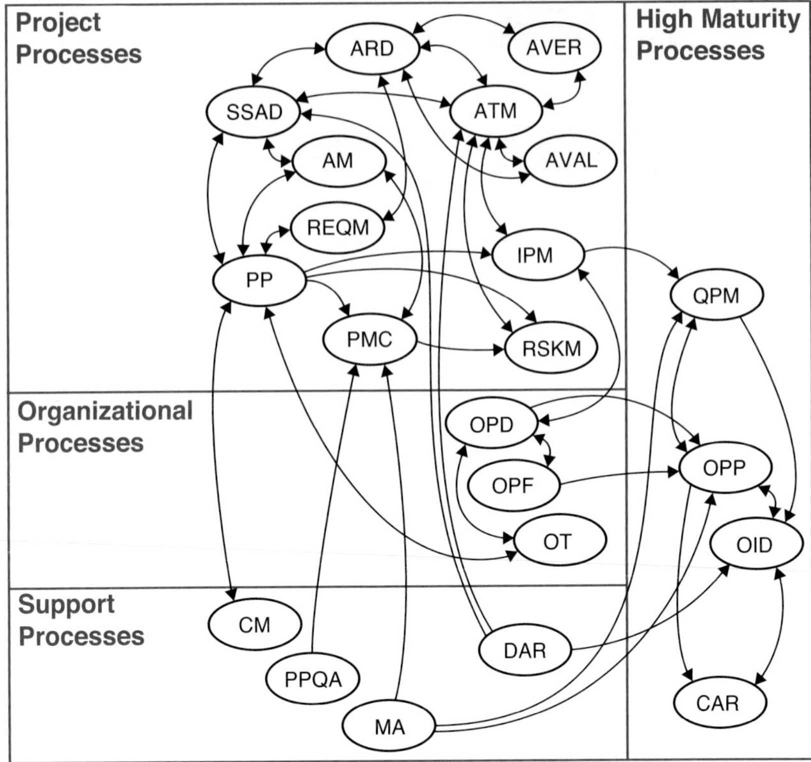

FIGURE 4.1
Key Relationships among CMMI-ACQ Process Areas

AUTHORS' NOTE

The model uses the process area categories of Project Management, Process Management, and Support for the CMMI Model Foundation (CMF) process areas and groups all of the additional process areas into the Acquisition category. This nomenclature is useful for building and sharing models; however, in this chapter the process areas are organized into groups that are more functional and descriptive to support process implementation. These groups—Project, Organizational, Support, and High Maturity—are depicted in Figure 4.1.

Project Processes

The project process areas contain practices that address acquirer activities related to establishing, executing, and transitioning an acquisition project.

The project process areas of CMMI-ACQ are as follows:

- Project Planning (PP)
- Acquisition Requirements Development (ARD)
- Requirements Management (REQM)
- Solicitation and Supplier Agreement Development (SSAD)
- Agreement Management (AM)
- Project Monitoring and Control (PMC)
- Integrated Project Management (IPM)
- Risk Management (RSKM)
- Acquisition Technical Management (ATM)
- Acquisition Verification (AVER)
- Acquisition Validation (AVAL)

The Project Planning process area includes practices for determining the acquisition strategy, developing the project plan, involving stakeholders appropriately, obtaining commitment to the plan, and maintaining the plan.

Planning begins with the acquisition strategy, which provides the framework for the acquisition project and its plans. The project plan covers the project management and acquisition activities performed by the project. Other plans (e.g., plans for transition to operations and support, configuration management, verification, and measurement and analysis) from relevant stakeholders that affect the project are reviewed, and commitments with those stakeholders for their contributions to the project are established.

Once the acquisition strategy is established using Project Planning practices, the strategy is used to focus on specifying customer and contractual requirements that express customer value in Acquisition Requirements Development practices. Customer needs are established and translated into customer requirements. The set of customer requirements is prioritized, and a set of contractual requirements, including design constraints, is developed.

Development of contractual requirements and operational scenarios also depends on the acquisition strategy developed using Project Planning practices. This set of contractual requirements is used in Solicitation and Supplier Agreement Development practices to select suppliers and establish a supplier agreement to acquire the product or service. The product or service is designed and implemented by the supplier consistent with the acquirer's contractual requirements and design constraints.

Requirements are maintained using Requirements Management practices. These practices describe activities for obtaining and controlling requirement changes and ensuring that other relevant plans and data are kept current. They also describe the traceability of requirements from customer to contractual requirements and supplier agreements. Requirements Management practices interact with Acquisition Requirements Development practices. All changes to contractual requirements must be reflected in the supplier agreements, which are established and maintained using Solicitation and Supplier Agreement Development practices.

The Solicitation and Supplier Agreement Development process area defines practices for preparing a solicitation package, selecting a capable supplier, and establishing and maintaining the supplier agreement. The acquisition strategy developed using Project Planning practices and the contractual requirements developed using Acquisition Requirements Development practices are required to prepare for Solicitation and Supplier Agreement Development practices. An agreement is developed to acquire the product or service by identifying potential suppliers, developing the solicitation package, and distributing it to potential suppliers. The acquirer evaluates the proposed solutions and negotiates with the supplier to finalize the agreement so that both the acquirer and the supplier have a mutual understanding of the agreement. This agreement is established and maintained using Solicitation and Supplier Agreement Development, but the execution of the agreement is performed using Agreement Management practices.

The acquirer uses Agreement Management practices to manage the supplier agreement by performing the acquirer activities defined in the supplier agreement, monitoring selected supplier processes, accepting the product or service, and managing supplier invoices.

After a supplier is selected and a supplier agreement is established, the acquirer continues to apply Requirements Management practices to manage customer and contractual requirements, while the selected supplier is managing the refined product and product component requirements. Using Requirements Management practices ensures that changes to requirements are reflected in project plans, activities, and work products. This cycle of changes may affect or be affected by other processes; thus, the requirements management process is a dynamic and often recursive sequence of events.

The Project Monitoring and Control process area contains practices for monitoring and controlling acquirer activities and overseeing the supplier's progress and performance according to project plans. The process area includes coverage of monitoring and controlling the transition to operations and support that was planned using Project Planning practices.

Project Monitoring and Control practices also cover the activities of taking corrective action. The project plan specifies the appropriate level of project monitoring, the frequency of progress reviews, and the measures used to monitor progress. Progress is determined primarily by comparing the project status to the plan. When the actual status deviates significantly from expected values, corrective actions are taken, as appropriate. These actions may include replanning, which requires using Project Planning practices.

As the acquirer's processes improve in capability, Integrated Project Management practices are used to manage the project using a defined process tailored from the organization's set of standard processes (Organizational Process Definition). The project uses and contributes to the organization's process assets, the project's work environment is established and maintained from the organization's work environment standards, and integrated teams are established using the organization's rules and guidelines. The project's relevant stakeholders coordinate their efforts in a timely manner through the identification, negotiation, and tracking of critical dependencies and the resolution of coordination issues.

In the acquirer–supplier relationship, the need for an early and aggressive detection of risk is compounded by the complexity of projects acquiring products or services. The purpose of Risk Management is to identify and assess project risks during the project planning process and to manage these risks throughout the project.

The acquirer has a dual role: First, assess and manage overall project risks for the duration of the project, and second, assess and manage risks associated with the performance of the supplier. As the acquisition progresses to the selection of a supplier, the risks specific to the supplier's technical and management approach become more important to the success of the acquisition.

Although risk identification and monitoring are covered in the Project Planning and Project Monitoring and Control process areas, using the Risk Management process area enables the acquirer to take a continuing, forward-looking approach to managing risks with activities that include identification of risk parameters, risk assessments, and risk mitigation.

Acquisition Technical Management practices are used to combine the project's defined process and risk management activities to perform technical and interface management. This management includes activities such as managing the technical evaluation of selected supplier products and services, conducting technical reviews with the supplier, and managing selected interfaces throughout the project's lifecycle. Acquisition Technical Management practices, Agreement Management practices, and Project Monitoring and Control practices are all used in concert, as they all contain reviews that are conducted throughout the project.

Using Acquisition Verification practices ensures that the acquirer's selected work products meet specified requirements. Using Acquisition Verification practices also enables the acquirer to select work products and verification methods to verify acquirer work products against specified requirements.

Acquisition Verification practices also are used to address peer reviews. Peer reviews are a proven method for removing defects early, and they provide valuable insight into the work products and product components being developed and maintained by the acquirer.

The acquirer uses Acquisition Validation processes to ensure that the products or services received from the supplier will fulfill the relevant stakeholders' needs. Products and services are incrementally validated against the customer's needs.

Validation may be performed in the actual operational environment or in a simulated operational environment. Coordination with the customer on the validation requirements is an important element of this process area.

The scope of the Acquisition Validation process area includes the validation of products, product components, selected intermediate work products, and processes. These validated elements may often require reverification and revalidation. Issues discovered during validation are usually resolved using Acquisition Requirements Development practices or by working with the supplier through the supplier agreement and technical reviews.

As mentioned earlier, Integrated Project Management processes establish a defined process and integrated plan for managing all the activities of the project. These activities include all of the project processes described earlier, from Project Planning through Acquisition Validation. The organization's set of standard processes and other process assets provide critical guidance to projects for establishing a defined process and plan. How the organization creates and deploys such process assets for use by the whole organization, along with other forms of critical project support, is the subject of the next section.

Organizational Processes

Organizational process areas contain the cross-project activities related to defining, planning, deploying, implementing, monitoring, controlling, appraising, measuring, and improving processes.

The organizational process areas contain practices that provide the acquiring organization with a capability to develop and deploy processes and supporting assets and to document and share best practices and learning across the organization.

The organizational process areas of CMMI-ACQ are as follows:

- Organizational Process Focus (OPF)
- Organizational Process Definition (OPD)
- Organizational Training (OT)

Organizational Process Focus practices help the acquiring organization to plan, implement, and deploy organizational process improvements based on an understanding of the current strengths and weaknesses of the organization's processes and process assets. Candidate improvements to the organization's processes are obtained through activities in the processes of related projects. These activities include generating process improvement proposals, measuring processes, collecting lessons learned in implementing the processes, and evaluating products and services.

Using Organizational Process Focus practices, the acquirer encourages participation of suppliers in process improvement activities. Suppliers may be involved in developing process action plans if processes that define interfaces between the acquirer and supplier are targeted for improvement.

Organizational Process Definition practices form the basis for establishing and maintaining the organization's set of standard processes, work environment standards, rules and guidelines for the operation of integrated teams, and other assets based on the organization's process needs and objectives.

These other assets include descriptions of lifecycle models, process-tailoring guidelines, and process-related documentation and data. Projects tailor the organization's set of standard processes to create their defined processes using Integrated Project Management practices. Experiences and work products from performing these defined processes, including measurement data, process descriptions, process artifacts, and lessons learned, are incorporated, as appropriate, into the organization's set of standard processes and other assets.

The acquirer's set of standard processes may also describe standard interactions with suppliers. Supplier interactions are typically characterized by the deliverables expected from suppliers, acceptance criteria applicable to those deliverables, standards (e.g., architecture and technology standards), and standard milestone and progress reviews. The acquirer defines in the supplier agreement how changes to organizational process assets that impact the supplier (e.g., standard supplier deliverables and acceptance criteria) are deployed.

The purpose of implementing Organizational Training practices is to develop people's skills and knowledge so that they can perform their roles effectively and efficiently. For example, an acquiring organization may want to develop its project managers' capability in managing supplier agreements.

Using Organizational Training practices helps the acquirer identify the strategic training needs of the organization as well as the tactical training needs that are common across projects and support groups. In particular, training is created or obtained to develop the skills required to perform the organization's set of standard processes. The main components of training include a managed training development program, documented plans, personnel with appropriate knowledge, and mechanisms for measuring the effectiveness of the training program.

Support Processes

Support process areas cover the activities that support acquisition and address processes that are used in the context of performing other processes. The support process areas address acquisition project processes and may address processes that apply more generally to the organization. For example, Process and Product Quality Assurance practices can be used to provide an objective evaluation of the processes and work products described in all of the process areas.

Although all support process areas rely on other process areas for input, some support process areas provide support functions that also help to implement several generic practices.

The support process areas of CMMI-ACQ are as follows:

- Measurement and Analysis (MA)
- Process and Product Quality Assurance (PPQA)
- Configuration Management (CM)
- Decision Analysis and Resolution (DAR)

The Measurement and Analysis process area is related to other process areas because its practices guide projects and organizations in aligning measurement needs and objectives with a measurement approach that provides objective results. These results can be used to make informed decisions and to take appropriate corrective actions.

An acquirer uses Measurement and Analysis practices to support the information needs of the organization and the project. Some of this information may be needed from the acquirer, some from the supplier, and some from all of the parts of a project. Solicitation and Supplier Agreement Development describes how these measures are specified in the solicitation process and supplier agreement. The measurement results from the acquirer and supplier support project, supplier, and technical reviews through Project Monitoring and Control, Agreement Management, and Acquisition Technical Management.

The Process and Product Quality Assurance process area is related to all process areas because it describes specific practices for objectively evaluating performed processes and work products against applicable process descriptions, standards, and procedures, and by ensuring that issues arising from these evaluations are addressed. Process and Product Quality Assurance practices support the acquisition of high-quality products and services by providing the acquirer with appropriate visibility into, and feedback on, the processes and associated work products throughout the life of the project.

The Configuration Management process area is related to all process areas because its practices describe establishing and maintaining the integrity of work products using configuration identification, configuration control, configuration status accounting, and configuration audits. The work products placed under configuration control include the products that are delivered to the customer, designated internal work products, acquired products, tools, and other items that are used in creating and describing these work products.

Examples of work products that may be placed under configuration control include plans, process descriptions, and requirements. Suppliers may play a part in any of these activities on behalf of the acquirer, so the supplier agreement should specify the configuration management roles and responsibilities of the acquirer and the supplier. Configuration management of acquired products (both final and interim products) created by the suppliers requires monitoring to ensure that project requirements are met.

The Decision Analysis and Resolution process area is related to all process areas because its practices describe the activities of determining which issues should be subjected to a formal evaluation process and then applying a formal evaluation process to them. A repeatable Decision Analysis and Resolution process is important for an acquirer when making the critical decisions that define and guide the acquisition process, and later when critical decisions are made with the selected supplier.

High Maturity Processes

High maturity process areas describe practices that further align organizational, project, and support processes with the organization's business objectives. These process areas describe practices at both the organizational and the project level for establishing objectives for quality and process performance, monitoring variation in the organization's and projects' processes, evaluating the impacts of proposed changes to those processes, and systematically deploying processes across the organization. To effectively implement these practices, mature measurement and analysis processes are needed.

The acquirer achieves an effective implementation of high maturity practices by ensuring that all members of the organization collect and analyze measurements and propose and evaluate changes to processes. In other words, high maturity practices should be integrated as much as possible into the practices in other process areas.

The high maturity process areas of CMMI-ACQ are as follows:

- Organizational Process Performance (OPP)
- Quantitative Project Management (QPM)
- Causal Analysis and Resolution (CAR)
- Organizational Innovation and Deployment (OID)

At the organizational level, Organizational Process Performance practices are used to derive quantitative objectives for quality and process performance from the organization's business objectives. The organization provides projects and support groups with common measures, process-performance baselines, and process-performance models. These organizational assets support quantitative project management and the statistical management of critical subprocesses for both projects and support groups.

The organization analyzes the process-performance data collected from these defined processes to develop a quantitative understanding of product quality, service quality, and the performance of the organization's set of standard processes.

At the project level, acquirers use Quantitative Project Management practices when applying quantitative and statistical techniques to manage process performance and product quality. Quality and process-performance objectives for the project are based on the objectives established by the organization. Through an evaluation of which subprocesses will help the project best achieve its objectives, the project's defined process is composed.

The project's defined process comprises, in part, process elements and subprocesses for which process performance can be predicted. At a minimum, the process variation of subprocesses critical to achieving the project's quality and process-performance objectives must be understood. Corrective action is taken when special causes of process variation are identified.

Acquirers use Causal Analysis and Resolution practices to guide identification of root causes of selected defects and other problems and taking action to prevent their reoccurrence. Although the project's defined processes are the principal targets for identifying the cause of the defect, the process improvement proposals they create target the organization's set of standard processes, which will prevent reoccurrence of the selected defects across the organization. These processes may be used to improve the performance of a subprocess, focusing on the central tendency of a product or process attribute, its spread, or both.

At the organizational level, Organizational Innovation and Deployment practices are used to select and deploy proposed incremental and innovative improvements that improve the organization's ability to meet its quality and process-performance objectives. Identifying promising incremental and innovative improvements should involve an empowered work force that is aligned with the organization's business values and objectives. The selection of improvements to deploy is based on a quantitative understanding of the benefits and costs of deploying candidate improvements, and the funding available.

Together, the high maturity processes provide the organization with an improved capability to achieve its quantitative objectives for quality and process performance.

CHAPTER 5

USING CMMI MODELS

The complexity of today's products demands an integrated view of how organizations do business. CMMI can reduce the cost of process improvement across enterprises that depend on multiple functions or groups to produce products and services.

To achieve this integrated view, the CMMI Framework includes common terminology, common model components, common appraisal methods, and common training materials. This chapter describes how organizations can use the CMMI Product Suite not only to improve their quality, reduce their costs, and optimize their schedules, but also to gauge how well their process improvement program is working.

Adopting CMMI

Research has shown that the most powerful initial step toward process improvement is to build organizational support through strong senior management sponsorship. To gain senior management sponsorship, it is often beneficial to expose senior management to the performance results experienced by others who have used CMMI to improve their processes [Gibson 2006].

For more information about CMMI performance results, see the Software Engineering Institute (SEI) Web site at www.sei.cmu.edu/cmmi/results.html.

The senior manager, once he or she is committed as the process improvement sponsor, must be actively involved in the CMMI-based process improvement effort. Activities performed by the senior management sponsor include, but are not limited to, the following.

- Influence the organization to adopt CMMI.
- Choose the best people to manage the process improvement effort.
- Monitor the process improvement effort personally.

- Be a visible advocate and spokesperson for the process improvement effort.
- Ensure that adequate resources are available to enable the process improvement effort to be successful.

Given sufficient senior management sponsorship, the next step is to establish a strong, technically competent process group that represents relevant stakeholders to guide process improvement efforts.

For an organization with a mission to develop software-intensive systems, the process group might include engineers representing the different technical disciplines across the organization and other selected members based on the business needs that are driving improvement. For example, a system administrator may focus on information technology (IT) support, whereas a marketing representative may focus on integrating customers' needs. Both members could make powerful contributions to the process group.

Once your organization decides to adopt CMMI, planning can begin with an improvement approach such as the Initiating, Diagnosing, Establishing, Acting, and Learning (IDEAL) model [McFeeley 1996]. For more information about the IDEAL model, see the SEI Web site at www.sei.cmu.edu/ideal/.

AUTHORS' NOTE

The SEI's Mastering Process Improvement course combines the use of CMMI models and the IDEAL model to establish a process improvement program that can result in real, positive change.

Your Process Improvement Program

Use the CMMI Product Suite to help establish your organization's process improvement program. Using the product suite for this purpose can be a relatively informal process that involves understanding and applying CMMI best practices to your organization. Or it can be a formal process that involves extensive training, creation of a process improvement infrastructure, appraisals, and more.

Selections That Influence Your Program

You must make three selections to apply CMMI to your organization for process improvement.

1. Select a part of the organization.

2. Select a model.
3. Select a representation.

Selecting the projects to be involved in your process improvement program is critical. If you select a group that is too large, it may be too much for the initial improvement effort. Your selection should also consider how homogeneous the group is (i.e., whether all members are software engineers, whether they all work on the same product or business line, etc.).

The process of selecting the representation to be used has some guidelines because of how CMMI models are built. If your organization likes the idea of maturity levels and the staged representation, your improvement road map is already defined. If your organization likes the continuous representation, you can select nearly any process area or group of process areas to guide improvement, although dependencies among process areas should be considered when making such a selection.

As the process improvement plans and activities progress, other important selections must be made, including which appraisal method should be used, which projects should be appraised, how training for personnel should be secured, and which personnel should be trained.

CMMI Models

CMMI models describe best practices that organizations have found to be productive and useful to achieving their business objectives. Regardless of your organization, you must use professional judgment when interpreting CMMI best practices for your situation, needs, and business objectives. Although process areas depict the characteristics of an organization committed to process improvement, you must interpret the process areas, using an in-depth knowledge of CMMI, your organization, the business environment, and the specific circumstances involved.

As you begin to use a CMMI model to improve your organization's processes, map your real-world processes to CMMI process areas. This mapping enables you to initially judge and later track your organization's level of conformance to the CMMI model you are using and to identify opportunities for improvement.

To interpret practices, it is important to consider the overall context in which these practices are used and to determine how well the practices satisfy the goals of a process area in that context. CMMI models do not prescribe or imply processes that are right for any organization or project. Instead, CMMI describes the minimum criteria necessary to plan and implement processes selected by the organization for improvement based on business objectives.

CMMI practices purposely use nonspecific phrases such as *relevant stakeholders, as appropriate,* and *as necessary* to accommodate the needs of different organizations and projects. The specific needs of a project may also differ at various points in the project's life.

Using CMMI Appraisals

Many organizations find value in measuring their progress by conducting an appraisal and earning a maturity level rating or a capability level achievement profile. These types of appraisals are typically conducted for one or more of the following reasons:

- To determine how well the organization's processes compare to CMMI best practices and to identify areas where improvement can be made
- To inform external customers and suppliers about how well the organization's processes compare to CMMI best practices
- To meet the contractual requirements of one or more customers

AUTHORS' NOTE

You can find guidance for an acquirer on interpreting the results of a supplier's appraisal in the SEI report, "Understanding and Leveraging a Supplier's CMMI Efforts: A Guidebook for Acquirers" (CMU/SEI-2007-TR-004), at www.sei.cmu.edu/publications/.

Appraisals of organizations using a CMMI model must conform to the requirements defined in the Appraisal Requirements for CMMI (ARC) document. Appraisals focus on identifying improvement opportunities and comparing the organization's processes to CMMI best practices. Appraisal teams use a CMMI model and ARC-conformant appraisal method to guide their evaluation of the organization and their reporting of conclusions. The appraisal results are used (e.g., by a process group) to plan improvements for the organization.

Appraisal Requirements for CMMI

The Appraisal Requirements for CMMI (ARC) document describes the requirements for several types of appraisals. A full benchmarking class of appraisal is defined as a Class A appraisal method. Less formal methods are defined as Class B or Class C methods. The ARC document was designed to help improve consistency across appraisal methods and to help appraisal method developers, sponsors, and users understand the tradeoffs associated with various methods [SEI 2006c].

Depending on the purpose of the appraisal and the nature of the circumstances, one class may be preferred over the others. Sometimes self-assessments, initial appraisals, quick-look or mini-appraisals, incremental appraisals, or external appraisals are appropriate; at other times a formal benchmarking appraisal is appropriate.

A particular appraisal method is declared an ARC Class A, B, or C appraisal method based on the sets of ARC requirements that the method developer addressed when designing the method.

More information about the ARC is available on the SEI Web site at www.sei.cmu.edu/cmmi/appraisals/index.html.

SCAMPI Appraisal Methods

The Standard CMMI Appraisal Method for Process Improvement (SCAMPI) A appraisal method is the generally accepted method used for conducting ARC Class A appraisals using CMMI models. The SCAMPI A Method Definition Document (MDD) defines rules for ensuring the consistency of SCAMPI A appraisal ratings [SEI 2006b]. For benchmarking against other organizations, appraisals must ensure consistent ratings. The achievement of a specific maturity level or the satisfaction of a process area must mean the same thing for different appraised organizations.

The SCAMPI family of appraisals includes Class A, B, and C appraisal methods. The SCAMPI A appraisal method is the officially recognized and most rigorous method. It is the only method that can result in benchmark quality ratings. SCAMPI B and C appraisal methods provide organizations with improvement information that is less formal than the results of a SCAMPI A appraisal, but nonetheless help the organization to identify improvement opportunities.

More information about SCAMPI methods is available on the SEI Web site at www.sei.cmu.edu/cmmi/appraisals/index.html.

Appraisal Considerations

Choices that affect a CMMI-based appraisal include the following:

- The CMMI model
- The appraisal scope, including the organizational unit to be appraised, the CMMI process areas to be investigated, and the maturity level or capability levels to be appraised
- The appraisal method
- The appraisal team members
- The appraisal participants selected from the appraisal entities to be interviewed
- The appraisal outputs (e.g., ratings or instantiation-specific findings)
- The appraisal constraints (e.g., time spent on-site)

The SCAMPI MDD allows the selection of predefined options for use in an appraisal. These appraisal options are designed to help organizations align CMMI with their business needs and objectives.

CMMI appraisal plans and results must always include a description of the appraisal options, model scope, and organizational scope selected. This documentation confirms whether an appraisal meets the requirements for benchmarking.

For organizations that wish to appraise multiple functions or groups, CMMI's integrated approach enables some economy of scale in model and appraisal training. One appraisal method can provide separate or combined results for multiple functions.

AUTHORS' NOTE

Appraisals that use multiple CMMI models in one organization or appraisals that span both acquirer and supplier organizations in a single event will need to be piloted as the use of CMMI for Acquisition (CMMI-ACQ) for appraisals grows. The CMMI Web site will have the most current information about acceptable approaches as the SEI gathers information regarding approaches that seem to be most effective.

The appraisal principles for CMMI are the same as those used in appraisals for other process improvement models. Those principles are as follows:

- Senior management sponsorship[1]
- A focus on the organization's business objectives
- Confidentiality for interviewees
- Use of a documented appraisal method
- Use of a process reference model (e.g., a CMMI model) as a base

1. Experience has shown that the most critical factor influencing successful process improvement and appraisals is senior management sponsorship.

- A collaborative team approach
- A focus on actions for process improvement

CMMI-Related Training

Whether your organization is new to process improvement or is already familiar with process improvement models, training is a key element in its ability to adopt CMMI. The SEI and its Partners provide an initial set of courses, but your organization may wish to supplement these courses with its own instruction. This approach allows your organization to focus on areas that provide the greatest business value.

The SEI and its Partners offer a course that provides a basic overview of CMMI-ACQ. The SEI also offers the Intermediate Concepts of CMMI course to those who plan to become more deeply involved in CMMI adoption or appraisal—for example, those who will guide improvement as part of a process group, those who will lead SCAMPI appraisals, and those who will teach the Introduction to CMMI course.

Current information about CMMI-related training is available on the SEI Web site at www.sei.cmu.edu/cmmi/training/.

CHAPTER 6

USING CMMI-ACQ IN GOVERNMENT

This chapter highlights some of the successes and challenges that government organizations (based in the United States or elsewhere) have experienced as they have sought to improve their acquisition processes. Links to elements of the CMMI for Acquisition (CMMI-ACQ) model are included in this discussion to demonstrate not only how these successes and challenges influenced the existing model, but also how they offer opportunities for future model development.

Critical Issues in Government Acquisition

by Mike Phillips and Brian Gallagher

"Big A" versus "Little a" Acquisition

As the CMMI Product Team began to consider how to construct a CMMI model to address the acquisition area of interest, the U.S. Department of Defense (DoD) was considering a critical report, the "Defense Acquisition Performance Assessment Report" (a.k.a. the DAPA report) [Kadish 2006]. In his letter delivering the report to Deputy Secretary of Defense Gordon England, the panel chair, Gen. Kadish, noted:

"Although our Acquisition System has produced the most effective weapon systems in the world, leadership periodically loses confidence in its efficiency. Multiple studies and improvements to the Acquisition System have been proposed—all with varying degrees of success. Our approach was broader than most of these studies. We addressed the 'big A' Acquisition System because it includes all the management systems that DoD uses not only the narrow processes traditionally thought of as acquisition. The problems DoD faces are deeply imbedded in the 'big A' management systems not just the 'little a' processes. We concluded that these processes must be stable for incremental change to be effective—they are not."

As the CMMI Product Team began to develop the CMMI-ACQ model—a model we wanted to apply to both commercial and government organizations—we considered tackling the issues raised in the DAPA report. However, successful model adoption requires an organization to embrace the ideas (i.e., best practices) of the model for effective improvement of the processes involved. As the preceding quote illustrates, in addition to organizations traditionally thought of as the "acquisition system" ("little a") in the DoD, there are also organizations that are associated with the "big A," including the Joint Capabilities Integration and Development System (JCIDS) and the Planning, Programming, Budgeting, and Execution (PPBE) system. These systems are governed by different stakeholders, directives, and instructions. To be effective, the model would need to be adopted at an extremely high level—by the DoD itself. Because of this situation, we resolved with our sponsor in the Office of the Secretary of Defense to focus on the kinds of "little a" organizations that are able to address CMMI best practices once the decision for a materiel solution has been reached.

However, we often find that models can have an impact beyond what might be perceived to be the "limits" of process control. The remainder of this section highlights some of the clear leverage points at which the model supports DAPA recommendations for improvement.

Figure 6.1 illustrates the issues and the relative importance of each issue as observed by the DAPA project team in reviewing previous recommendations and speaking to experts. The most important issues are labeled [Kadish 2006].

We would never claim that the CMMI-ACQ model offers a complete solution to all of the significant key issues in Figure 6.1; however, building capabilities addressed in the CMMI-ACQ model does offer opportunities to address many of the risks captured in these issue areas. In the text that follows, we limit the discussion of each issue to one paragraph.

Acquisition Strategy

This is one of the more significant additions to the CMMI Model Foundation (CMF) to support the acquisition area of interest. Multiple process area locations (including Acquisition Requirements Development and Solicitation and Supplier Agreement Development) were considered before placing the acquisition strategy practice into Project Planning. Feedback from various acquisition organizations noted that many different organizational elements are stakeholders in strategy development, but its criticality to the overall plan suggested an effective fit as part of this process area. We also found that some projects might

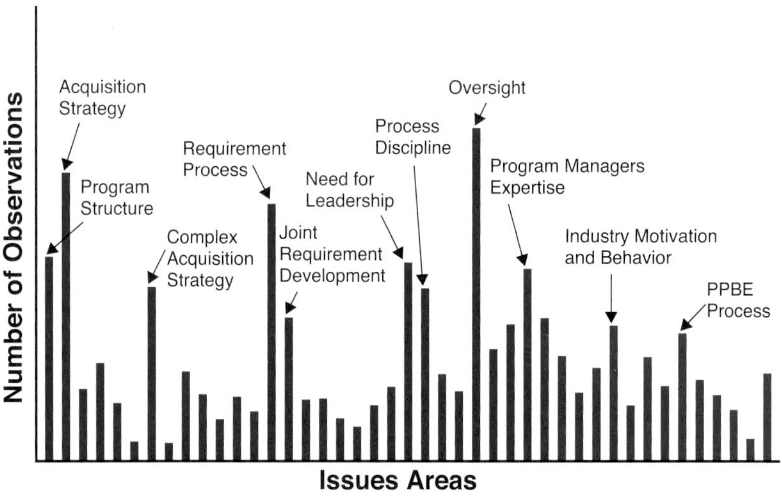

FIGURE 6.1
Observations by Issue Area

develop the initial strategy before the formal establishment of full acquisition offices, which would then accept the long-term management responsibility of the strategy. Note that the practice does not demand a specific strategy, but does expect the strategy to be a planning artifact. The full practice, "Establish and maintain the acquisition strategy," in Project Planning specific practice 1.1, recognizes that maintenance may require strategy updates if the changing environment reflects that need. The DAPA report (p. 14) calls out some recommended strategies in the DoD environment [Kadish 2006].

Additional discussion is contained in the section Acquisition Strategy: Planning for Success, later in this chapter.

Program Structure

Although a model such as CMMI-ACQ should not direct specific organizational structures, the CMMI Product Team looked for ways to encourage improved operations on programs. Most significant might be practices for creating and managing integrated teams with effective rules and guidelines. The DAPA report (p. 76) noted deficiencies in operation. Organizations following model guidance may be better able to address these shortfalls.

Requirement Process

The CMMI-ACQ Product Team recognized the vital role played by effective requirements development. The team assigned Acquisition

Requirements Development to maturity level 2 (Requirements Development is at maturity level 3 in the CMMI for Development or CMMI-DEV model). Key to this effectiveness is one of the significant differences between the CMMI-ACQ and CMMI-DEV versions of "Requirements Development," played out in specific goal 2, "Customer requirements are refined and elaborated into contractual requirements." The importance of this activity cannot be underemphasized, as poor requirements are likely to be the most troubling type of "defect" that the acquisition organization can inject into the system. The DAPA report notes that often, requirement errors are injected late into the acquisition system. Examples in the report included operational test requirements unspecified by the user. Although the model cannot address such issues directly, it does provide a framework that aids in the traceability of requirements to the source, which in turn allows the more successful resolution of issues. (The Requirements Management process area also aids in this traceability.)

Oversight

Several features in CMMI-ACQ should help users address the oversight issue. Probably the most significant help is in the Acquisition Technical Management process area, which recognizes the need for the effective technical oversight of development activities. Acquisition Technical Management couples with the companion process area of Agreement Management, which addresses business issues with the supplier via contractual mechanisms. For those familiar with CMMI model construction, the generic practice associated with reviewing all model activities with senior management gives yet another opportunity to resolve issues.

Need for Leadership, Program Managers Expertise, and Process Discipline

We have grouped leadership, program managers expertise, and process discipline issues together because they reflect the specific purpose of creating CMMI-ACQ—to provide best practices that enable leadership; to develop capabilities within acquisition organizations; and to instill process discipline where clarity might previously have been lacking. Here the linkage between DAPA report issues and CMMI-ACQ is not specific, but very general.

Complex Acquisition System and PPBE Process

Alas, for complex acquisition system and PPBE process issues, the model does not have any specific assistance to offer. However, the effective development of the high maturity elements of process-performance modeling, particularly if shared by both the acquirer and the system development team, may help address the challenges of "big A" budgetary exercises with more accurate analyses than otherwise would be produced.

System of Systems Acquisition Challenges

Although CMMI-ACQ is aimed primarily at the acquisition of products and services, it also has some practices that would be especially important in addressing system of systems issues. Because of the importance of this topic in government acquisition, we decided to add this discussion and the Interoperable Acquisition section later in this chapter to assist readers who are facing the challenges associated with systems of systems.

A source document for this segment is *Interoperable Acquisition for Systems of Systems: The Challenges* [Smith 2006], which describes the ever-increasing interdependence of systems necessary to provide needed capabilities to the user. As an example cited in the document, on one key satellite communications program, at least five separate and independent acquisition programs needed to achieve successful completion before the actual capability could be delivered to the various military services. The increasing emphasis on net-centric operations and service-oriented architectures added to the challenge. Figure 6.2 provides a visual depiction of some of the complexity.

Figure 6.2 shows the many ways that complexity grows quickly as the number of critical programmatic interfaces grows. Each dependency creates a risk for at least one of the organizations. The figure suggests that for two of the programs, a shared reporting directorate can aid in mitigating risks. This kind of challenge can be described as one in which applying recursion is sufficient. The system is composed of subsystems, and a single overarching management structure controls the subordinate elements. In many large program offices, the system might be an aircraft with its supporting maintenance systems and required training systems. All elements may be separate programs, but coordination occurs within a single management structure. The figure, however, shows the additional challenges evident when there is not a single management structure. Critical parts of the capability are delivered by separate management structures, often with widely different motivators and priorities.

Although the model was not constructed to specifically solve these challenges, especially the existence of separate management

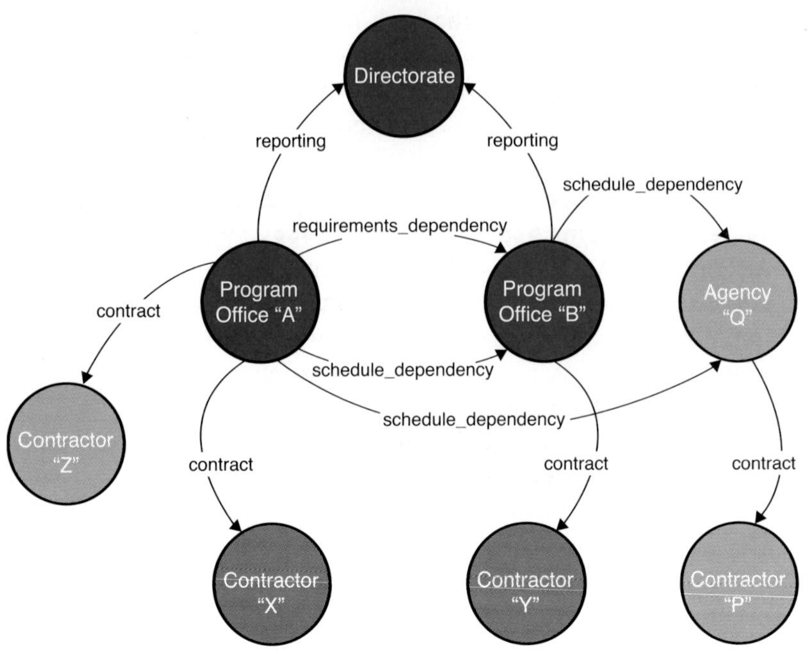

FIGURE 6.2
System of Systems Acquisition Challenges

structures, the complexity was familiar to CMMI-ACQ authors. Those of you who have used the Capability Maturity Model (CMM) or CMMI model in the past will recognize the Risk Management process area in this model. In addition to noting that there are significant risks in managing the delivery of a system through any outside agent, such as a supplier, the model also includes the value of recognizing both internal and external sources of risk. The following note is part of Risk Management specific practice 1.1:

"Identifying risk sources provides a basis for systematically examining changing situations over time to uncover circumstances that impact the ability of the project to meet its objectives. Risk sources are both internal and external to the project. As the project progresses, additional sources of risk may be identified. Establishing categories for risks provides a mechanism for collecting and organizing risks as well as ensuring appropriate scrutiny and management attention to risks that can have serious consequences on meeting project objectives."

Varying approaches to addressing risks across multiple programs and organizations have been taken. One of these, Team Risk Management, has been documented by the Software Engineering Institute

(SEI) [Higuera 1994]. CMMI-ACQ anticipated the need for flexible organizational structures to address these kinds of issues and chose to expect that organizations establish and maintain integrated teams crossing organizational boundaries rather than making it an option, as it is in CMMI-DEV. The following is part of Organizational Process Definition specific practice 1.7:

"In an acquisition organization, integrated teams are useful not just in the acquirer's organization but between the acquirer and supplier and among the acquirer, supplier, and other relevant stakeholders, as appropriate. Integrated teaming may be especially important in a system of systems environment."

Perhaps the most flexible and powerful model feature used to address the complexities of systems of systems is the effective employment of the specific practices in the second specific goal of Acquisition Technical Management. These practices require successfully managing needed interfaces among the system being focused on and other systems not under the project's direct control. It is set up first in Acquisition Requirements Development:

"Develop interface requirements of the acquired product to other products in the intended environment." (ARD SP 2.1.2)

The installation of the specific goal in Acquisition Technical Management as part of overseeing effective system development from the acquirer's perspective is powerful for addressing system of systems problems. The following note is part of Acquisition Technical Management specific goal 2:

"Many integration and transition problems arise from unknown or uncontrolled aspects of both internal and external interfaces. Effective management of interface requirements, specifications, and designs helps to ensure implemented interfaces are complete and compatible."

The supplier is responsible for managing the interfaces of the product or service it is developing. However, the acquirer identifies those interfaces, particularly external interfaces, that it will manage as well.

Although these model features provide a basis for addressing some of the challenges of delivering the capabilities desired in a system of systems environment, the methods best suited for various acquisition environments await further development in future documents. CMMI-ACQ is positioned to aid that development and mitigate the risks inherent in these acquisitions.

Acquisition Strategy: Planning for Success

by Brian Gallagher

Adapted from "Techniques for Developing an Acquisition Strategy by Profiling Software Risks," CMU/SEI-2006-TR-002

As previously discussed, CMMI-ACQ's Project Planning process area asks the program to establish and maintain an acquisition strategy. You will also see references to the acquisition strategy called out in many other CMMI-ACQ process areas.

What is an acquisition strategy, and how does it relate to other planning documents discussed in CMMI-ACQ?

The Defense Acquisition University (DAU) uses the following definition of acquisition planning:

"The process by which the efforts of all personnel responsible for an acquisition are coordinated and integrated through a comprehensive plan for fulfilling the agency need in a timely manner and at a reasonable cost. It is performed throughout the lifecycle and includes developing an overall acquisition strategy for managing the acquisition and a written acquisition plan (AP)."

Acquisition planning is the act of defining and maintaining an overall approach for a program. Acquisition planning guides all elements of program execution to transform the mission need into a fielded system that is fully supported and delivers the desired capability. The goal of acquisition planning is to provide a road map that is followed to maximize the chances of successfully fielding a system that meets users' needs within cost and schedule constraints. Acquisition planning is an iterative process; feedback loops impact future acquisition planning activities.

An *acquisition strategy*, when formulated carefully, is a means of addressing program risks via program structure. The DAU uses the following definition of acquisition strategy:

"A business and technical management approach designed to achieve program objectives within the resource constraints imposed. It is the framework for planning, directing, contracting for, and managing a program. It provides a master schedule for research, development, test, production, fielding, modification, postproduction management, and other activities essential for program success. The acquisition strategy is the basis for formulating functional plans and strategies (e.g., test and evaluation

master plan [TEMP], acquisition plan [AP], competition, systems engineering, etc.)."

The best acquisition strategy for a given program directly addresses that program's highest-priority risks. High-priority risks can be technical if no one has yet built a component that meets some critical aspect of the system or has never combined mature components in the way that is required. Risks can be programmatic if the system must be designed to accommodate predefined cost or schedule constraints. Or risks can be mission-related when the characteristics of a system that meets the need cannot be fully articulated and agreed on by stakeholders. Each program faces a unique set of risks, so the corresponding acquisition strategy must be unique to address them.

The risks a program faces also evolve through the life of the program. The acquisition strategy and the plans developed based on that strategy must also evolve. Figure 6.3 shows the iterative nature of acquisition strategy development and planning.

The process usually starts with an articulation of user needs requiring a material solution and identification of alternatives to satisfy those needs (e.g., an analysis of alternatives [AoA]). A technology development strategy is then developed to mature the technologies required for the selected alternative. Next, the acquisition strategy is developed to guide the program through its life. As the strategy is executed, refinements are made. In the DoD, the acquisition strategy is required and formally reviewed at major program milestones (e.g., Milestone B [MS B]).

The terms *acquisition planning, acquisition strategy,* and *acquisition plan* are frequently used interchangeably, which causes much confusion. A program's acquisition strategy is different from its acquisition plan, but both are artifacts of acquisition planning. All strategies can be plans, but not all plans can be strategies. In the context of acquisition, strategies are high-level decisions that direct the development of more detailed plans, which guide the execution of a program. Careful planning of what is to be done, who will do it, and when it will be done is required.

Developing an all-encompassing acquisition strategy for a program is a daunting activity. As with many complex endeavors, often the best way to begin is to break the complex activity down into simpler, more manageable tasks. When developing an acquisition strategy, a program manager's first task is to define the elements of that strategy. When defining strategy elements, it is useful to ask the question, "What acquisition choices must I make in structuring this

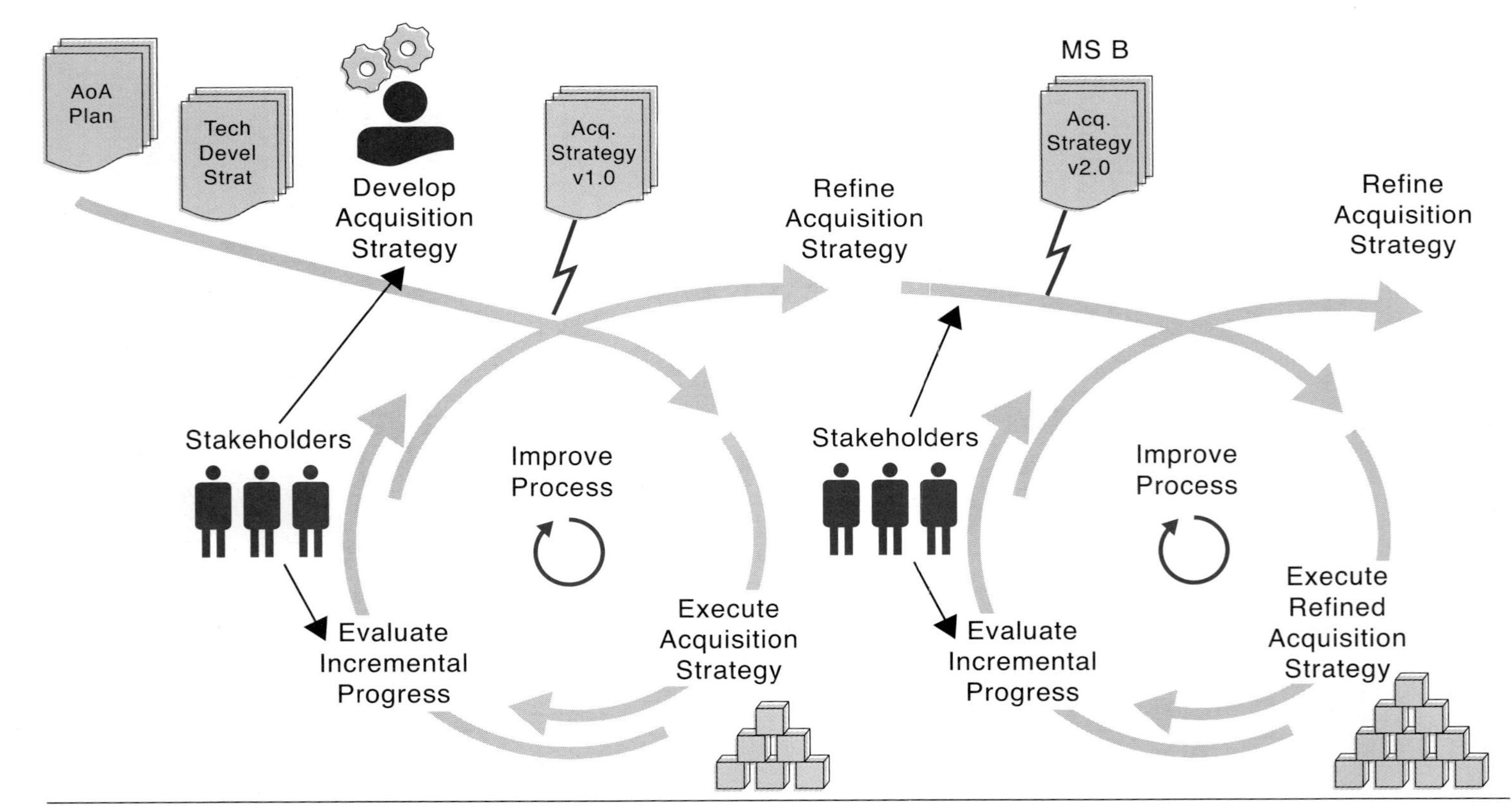

FIGURE 6.3
The Iterative Nature of Acquisition Strategy Development

program?" Inevitably, asking this question leads to more detailed questions, such as the following.

- What acquisition approach should I use?
- What type of solicitation will work best?
- How will I monitor my contractor's activities?

The result of these choices defines the acquisition strategy. Identifying strategy elements is the first step in this process.

The DAU's *Defense Acquisition Guidebook* defines 18 strategy considerations that should be addressed when formulating an acquisition strategy [DoD 2006]. These considerations include the following:

Acquisition Approach	Interoperability
Best Practices	Modular Open Systems Approach
Business Considerations	Product Support
Capability Needs Summary	Program Structure
Environment, Safety, Occupational Health	Relief, Exemption, and Waiver
Human Systems Integration	Research and Technology Protection
Information Assurance	Resource Management
Information Technology	Risk Management
Integrated Test and Evaluation	Systems Engineering

One of the most important strategy considerations is defining the acquisition approach. The acquisition approach strategy element defines the approach the program will use to achieve full capability. Typically, this approach is either single-step, incremental, or evolutionary, as illustrated in Figure 6.4.

For readers who are experienced with development approaches, the decision to use single-step, incremental, or evolutionary approaches seems natural and is driven by program risk. When acquiring a capability that has been developed many times before and there are known solutions, a single-step approach may be warranted. However, most systems are more complex and require either an incremental or an evolutionary approach. The most important aspect to understand is the difference between the acquisition approach and the development approach used by your supplier. You can use a single-step approach as an acquisition strategy while the developer is using an incremental development approach. At times, a different approach may be selected for different parts of the program. Figure 6.5 depicts the acquirer using a single-step approach while the developer is using an incremental approach. Figure 6.6 shows the acquirer using an evolutionary

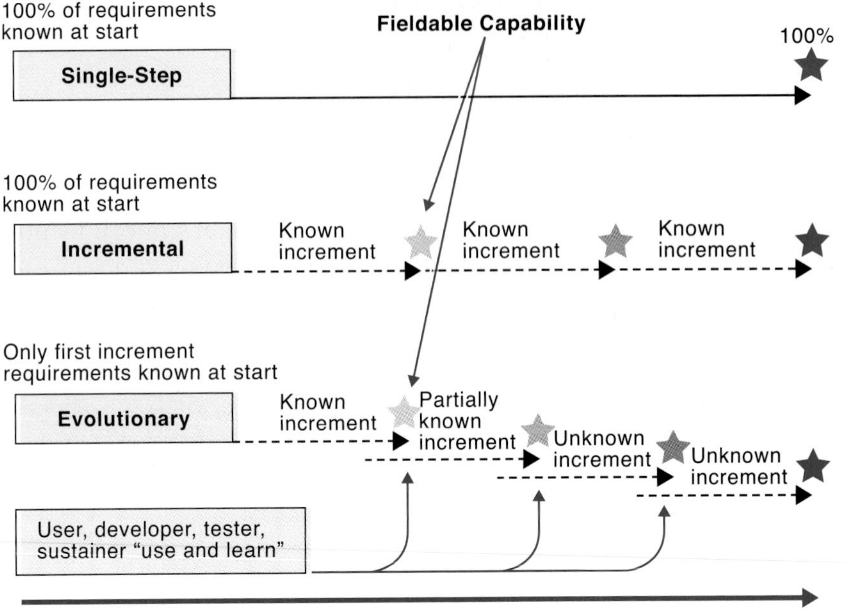

FIGURE 6.4
Defining an Acquisition Approach

approach and the developer using a mix of single-step, incremental, and evolutionary (spiral) approaches.

The acquisition approach is just one of many decisions an acquirer makes when developing the acquisition strategy. Most choices are made based on a careful examination of risk. Each project is unique, and the acquisition strategy is unique and becomes one of the most important guiding artifacts for all stakeholders. The decisions made and documented in the acquisition strategy help to mitigate the highest risks to the program and provide a road map that all stakeholders can understand, share, and analyze to help the project succeed.

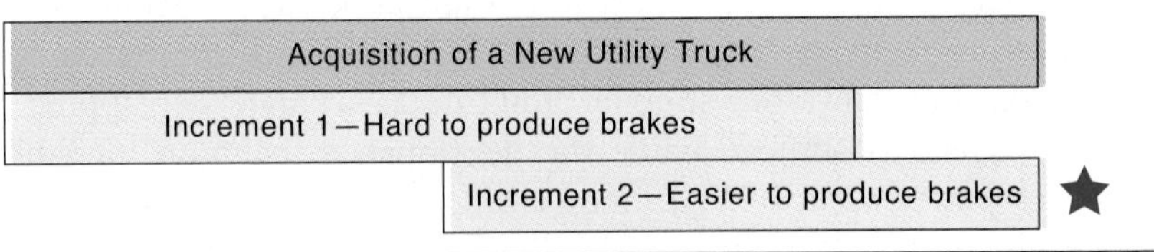

FIGURE 6.5
Single-Step Acquisition with an Incremental Development Approach

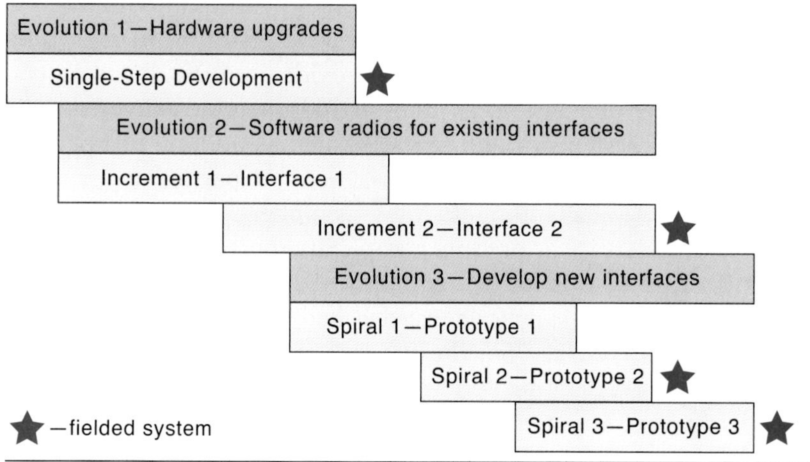

FIGURE 6.6
Evolutionary Acquisition with Mixed Development Approaches

Agreements: They Are Not Just with Suppliers

by Mike Phillips

When creating the CMMI-ACQ model, we wrestled with finding ways to properly discuss the myriad agreements that are needed for an acquisition program to be successful. In this section, I offer some thoughts related to the multiple types of agreements possible in acquisitions based on my experiences in government acquisition over the past 30 years.

Central to a successful acquisition process is the key contractual agreement between the acquirer and the supplier. To describe the agreements for this relationship, we built on the excellent foundation provided by the Supplier Agreement Management (SAM) process area from CMMI-DEV and legacy documents, such as the Software Acquisition CMM published in the 1990s [SEI 2002, SEI 2006a]. However, the product team knew that other agreements must be carefully developed and managed over the life of many acquisitions, and that the model had to cover these types of agreements as well. Figure 6.2 is a reminder of the need for multiple agreements given the complexity of many of today's acquisitions.

In many government organizations, the acquisition discipline is established and maintained in specific organizations that are chartered to handle acquisition tasks for a variety of using organizations. Often the acquirers do not simply provide products to customers that the supplier delivers "as is," but instead integrate delivered products with other systems or add services, such as training or upgrades, all of which may come from other agencies, departments, or organizations not typically thought of as suppliers. These other acquirer activities increase as product complexity increases.

Because of this known complexity, the product team knew that the definition of *supplier agreement* had to be broad and cover more than just a contract. So, the product team settled on the following definition: "A documented agreement between the acquirer and supplier (e.g., contract, license, or memorandum of agreement)."

The focus of the Acquisition Requirements Development process area is to ensure that customer needs are translated into customer requirements and that those requirements are used to develop contractual requirements. Although the product team agreed to call these "contractual" requirements, they knew the application of these requirements had to be broader.

Thus, contractual requirements are defined as follows: "The result of the analysis and refinement of customer requirements into a set of requirements suitable to be included in one or more solicitation packages, formal contracts, or supplier agreements between the acquirer and other appropriate organizations."

Practices in the Solicitation and Supplier Agreement Development and Agreement Management process areas are particularly helpful, as the need for other types of documented agreements increases with system complexity. An example of these kinds of agreements is the program-manager-to-program-manager agreement type that the U.S. Navy uses to help integrate combat systems and C4I in surface ships during new construction and modernization.

Another helpful process area to use when integrating a large product is Acquisition Technical Management. Specific goal 2 is particularly useful because it focuses on the critical interfaces that likely have become the responsibility of the acquisition organization. Notes in this goal state: "The supplier is responsible for managing the interfaces of the product or service it is developing. However, the acquirer identifies those interfaces, particularly external interfaces, that it will manage as well."

This statement recognizes that the acquirer's role often extends beyond simply ensuring a good product from a supplier. In the introductory notes of this process area, the acquirer is encouraged to use more of CMMI-DEV's Engineering process areas if "the acquirer assumes the role of overall systems engineer, architect, or integrator for the product."

Clearly many acquisitions are relatively simple and direct, ensuring delivery of a new capability to the customer by establishing contracts with selected suppliers. However, the model provides an excellent starting point for the types of complex arrangements that often are seen in government today.

Acquisition Verification: The Challenges

by Mike Phillips

Having been a military test pilot and director of tests for the B-2 Spirit Stealth Bomber acquisition program for the U.S. Air Force (USAF), I am particularly interested in the interactions between the testing aspects contained in the two companion models of CMMI-DEV and CMMI-ACQ. This section provides some perspectives I hope are helpful for those of you who need to work on verification issues across the acquirer–supplier boundary, particularly in government.

When we created the process areas for the Acquisition category, the product team knew we needed to expand the limited supplier agreement coverage in SAM (in the CMMI-DEV model) to address the business aspects critical to acquisition. However, we knew we also needed to cover the technical aspects that were "close cousins" to the process areas in the Engineering process area category in CMMI-DEV. We tried to maximize the commonality between the two models so that both collections of process areas would be tightly related in the project lifecycle. For a significant part of the lifecycle, the two models represent two "lenses" observing the same total effort. Certainly testing seemed to be a strongly correlated element in both models.

As you read through the CMMI-ACQ process areas of Acquisition Verification and Acquisition Validation, notice that the wording is either identical or quite similar to the wording in the CMMI-DEV process areas of Verification and Validation. This commonality was intentional to maintain bridges between the acquirer and supplier teams, which often must work together effectively.

Throughout my military career, I often worked on teams that crossed the boundaries of government and industry to conserve resources and employ the expertise needed for complex test events, such as flight testing. Combined test teams were commonly used. Often these teams conducted flight test missions in which both verification and validation tasks were conducted. The government, in these cases, helped the contractor test the specification and provided critical insight into the usability of the system.

Each model, however, must maintain a distinct purpose from its perspective (whether supplier or acquirer) while maximizing desirable synergies. Consider Validation and Acquisition Validation first. There is little real distinction between these two process areas, since the purpose of both is the same: to satisfy the ultimate customer with products and services that provide the needed utility in the end-use environment. The value proposition is not different—dissatisfied customers are often as upset with the acquisition organization as with the supplier of the product that has not satisfied the users. So, the difference between Validation and Acquisition Validation is quite small.

With Verification and Acquisition Verification, however, the commonality is strong in one sense—both emphasize assurance that work products are properly verified by a variety of techniques, but each process area focuses on the work products produced and controlled in its own domain. So, whereas Verification focuses on the verification of *supplier* work products, Acquisition Verification focuses on the verification of *acquirer* work products.

The CMMI-ACQ product team saw the value of focusing on acquirer work products, such as solicitation packages, supplier agreements and plans, requirements documents, and design constraints developed by the acquirer. These work products require thoughtful verification using powerful tools, such as peer reviews to remove defects. Since defective requirements are among the most expensive to find and address because they often are discovered late in development, improvements in verifying requirements have great value.

Verifying the work products developed by the supplier is covered in Verification and is the responsibility of the supplier, who is presumably using CMMI-DEV. The acquirer may *assist* in verification activities, since such assistance may be mutually beneficial to both the acquirer and the supplier. However, conducting the verification of the product or service developed by the supplier is ultimately performed by the supplier.

The acquirer's interests during supplier verification activities are captured in two other process areas. During much of development, supplier deliverables are used as a way to gauge development progress. Monitoring that progress and reviewing the supplier's technical solutions and verification results are covered by Acquisition Technical Management.

All of the process areas discussed thus far (Verification, Validation, Acquisition Verification, Acquisition Validation, Acquisition Technical Management, and Agreement Management) have elements of the stuff we call "testing." Testing is, in fact, a subset of the wider concept often known as "verification." I'll use my B-2 experience as an example.

Early in B-2 development, the B-2 System Program Office (SPO) prepared a test and evaluation master plan, or TEMP. This plan is required in DoD acquisition and demands careful attention to the various methods that the government requires for the contractor's verification environment. The B-2 TEMP outlined the major testing activities necessary to deliver a B-2 to the using command in the USAF. This plan delineated a collection of classic developmental test activities called "developmental test and evaluation." From a model perspective, these activities would be part of the supplier's Verification activities during development. Fortunately, we had the supplier's system test plan, an initial deliverable document to the government, to help us create the developmental test and evaluation portions of the TEMP. Receiving the right supplier deliverables to review and use is part of what the Solicitation and Supplier Agreement Development process area is about.

The TEMP also addressed operational test and evaluation activities, which included operational pilots and maintenance personnel to ensure operational utility. These activities map to both Validation and Acquisition Validation. From a model perspective, many of the operational elements included in the TEMP were the result of mission and basing scenarios codeveloped with the customer. These activities map to practices in Acquisition Requirements Development.

The TEMP also described a large number of ancillary test-related activities such as wind tunnel testing and radar reflectivity testing. These earlier activities are best mapped to the practices of Acquisition Technical Management. They are the technical activities the acquisition, organization uses to analyze the suppliers' candidate solution and review the suppliers' technical progress. As noted in Acquisition Technical Management, when all of the technical aspects have been analyzed and reviewed to the satisfaction of the acquirer, the system is ready for acceptance testing. In the B-2 example, that was a rigorous physical configuration audit and functional configuration audit to account for all of the essential elements of the system.

The testing and audits ensured that a fully capable aircraft was delivered to the using command. The physical configuration audit activities are part of the "Conduct Technical Reviews" specific practice in Acquisition Technical Management.

Much of the emphasis in CMMI-ACQ reminds acquirers of their responsibilities for the key work products and processes under their control. Many of us have observed the value of conducting peer reviews on critical requirements documents, from the initial delivery that becomes part of a Request for Proposal (RFP) to the oft-needed engineering change proposals. But my history with planning the testing efforts for the B-2 led me to point out a significant use of Acquisition Verification associated with the effective preparation of the TEMP. The test facilities typically were provided by the government, often a mix between the DoD and other government agencies, such as NASA and what is now the Department of Energy.

Many people have stated that "an untestable requirement is problematic." Therefore, to complete a viable TEMP, the acquisition team must determine the criteria for requirements satisfaction and the verification environment that is needed to enable requirements satisfaction to be judged accurately. Here are a few of the questions that I believe complement Acquisition Verification best practices to help improve the quality of the government work product called the TEMP.

What confidence do we have that a specific verification environment, whether it is a government site or a contractor site, can accurately measure the performance we are demanding?

Are results obtained in a constrained test environment scalable to represent specified performance requirements?

Can limited experience be extrapolated to represent long-term needs for reliability and maintainability?

When might it be more cost-effective to accept data gathered at the suppliers' facilities?

When might it be essential to use a government facility to ensure confidence in test results?

These and similar questions demonstrate the need for early attention to Acquisition Verification practices, particularly those under the first Acquisition Verification–specific goal, "Prepare for Verification." These practices, of course, then support specific goal 3 activities that verify acquisition work products. These work products, in turn, often provide or augment the verification environment in which the system being acquired demonstrates its performance.

These questions also help to differentiate the need to ensure a viable verification environment for the acquiring organization from the more familiar need to support the suppliers' verification of work products.

Interoperable Acquisition

by Craig Meyers

The term *interoperability* has long been used in an operational context. For example, it relates to the ability of machines to "plug and play." However, there is no reason to limit interoperability to an operational context.

Recent work at the SEI has broadened the concept of interoperability to apply in other contexts. A main result of this work is the System of Systems Interoperability (SOSI) model [Morris 2004], a diagram of which appears in Figure 6.7. This model is designed for application to a system of systems context in which there are more and broader interactions than one typically finds in a program- and system-centric context.

Taking a vertical perspective of Figure 6.7, we introduce activities related to program management, system construction, and system operation. However, what is important to recognize is the need for interaction among different acquisition functions. It is this recognition that warrants a broader perspective of the concept of interoperability. Figure 6.7 shows three different aspects of interoperability. Although

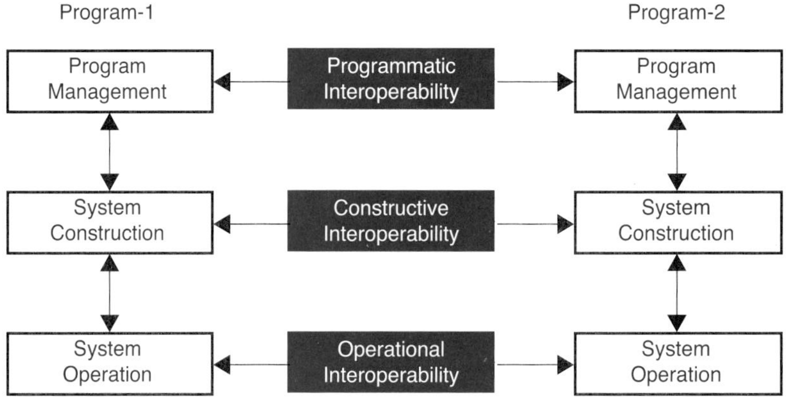

FIGURE 6.7
System of Systems Interoperability Model

we recognize that operational interoperability is the traditional use of the term, we also introduce programmatic interoperability, constructive interoperability, and interoperable acquisition [Meyers 2008].

Programmatic Interoperability

Programmatic interoperability is interoperability with regard to the functions of program management, regardless of the organization that performs those functions.

It may be natural to interpret programmatic interoperability as occurring only between program offices, but such an interpretation is insufficient. Multiple professionals collaborate with respect to program management. In addition to the program manager, relevant participants may include staff members from a program executive office, a service acquisition executive, independent cost analysts, and so on. Each of these professionals performs a necessary function related to the management of a program. In fact, contractor representation may also be included. The report "Exploring Programmatic Interoperability: Army Future Force Workshop" [Smith 2005] provides an example of the application of the principles of programmatic interoperability.

Constructive Interoperability

The concept of constructive interoperability may be defined in a similar manner as programmatic interoperability. Constructive interoperability is interoperability with regard to the functions of system construction, regardless of the organization that performs those functions.

Again, it may be natural to think of constructive interoperability as something that occurs between contractors, but that would limit its scope. For example, other organizations that may participate in the construction of a system might include a subcontractor, a supplier of commercial-of-the-shelf (COTS) products, independent consultants, an independent verification and validation organization, or a testing organization. And yes, a program management representative may also participate in the function of system construction. Each of these organizations performs a valuable function in the construction of a system.

An example of programmatic interoperability is the case in which a program is developing a software component that will be used by another program. For this transaction to occur, the program offices must interact with regard to such tasks as schedule synchronization, for example. Other interactions may be required, such as joint risk management. However, as we noted earlier, other organizations will play a role. For example, the development of an acquisition strategy may require interaction with the organizations responsible for its approval.

You can apply this example to the context of constructive interoperability as well. For one program office to provide a product to another, a corresponding agreement must exist among the relevant contractors. Such an agreement is often expressed in an *associate contractor agreement* (such an agreement would be called a *supplier agreement* in CMMI-ACQ). It is also possible that the separate contractors would seek out suppliers in a collective manner to maximize the chance of achieving an interoperable product.

Interoperable Acquisition

The preceding example, although focusing on the aspects of interoperability, does not address the integration of those aspects. This topic enlarges the scope of discussion and leads us to define interoperable acquisition.

Interoperable acquisition is the collection of interactions that take place among the functions necessary to acquire, develop, and maintain systems to provide interoperable capabilities.

In essence, interoperable acquisition is the integration of the various aspects of interoperability. For example, in regard to the previous example, although two program offices may agree on the need for the construction of a system, such construction will require interactions among the program offices and their respective contractors, as well as among the contractors themselves.

There are clearly implications for acquisition in the context of a system of systems[1] and CMMI-ACQ. For example, CMMI-ACQ includes the Solicitation and Supplier Agreement Development and Agreement Management process areas, which relate to agreement management. As the previous discussion illustrates, the nature of agreements—their formation and execution—is important in the context of a system of systems and interoperable acquisition. These agreements may be developed to serve acquisition management or to aid in the construction of systems that must participate in a larger context.

Other areas of relevance deal with requirements management and schedule management, as discussed in the reports "Requirements

1. We do not use the expression "acquisition of a system of systems," as this implies acquisition of a monolithic nature that is counter to the concept of a system of systems in which autonomy of the constituents is a prime consideration. As a colleague once said, "Systems of systems are accreted, not designed." This may be a bit strong, but it conveys a relevant and meaningful notion.

Management in a System of Systems Context: A Workshop" [Meyers 2006a] and "Schedule Considerations for Interoperable Acquisition" [Meyers 2006c], respectively. Another related topic is that of risk management considerations for interoperable acquisition. This topic is covered in the report "Risk Management Considerations for Interoperable Acquisition" [Meyers 2006b]. Some common threads exist among these topics, including the following:

- Developing and adhering to agreements that manage the necessary interactions
- Defining information, including its syntax, but also (and more importantly) its semantics
- Providing mechanisms for sharing information
- Engaging in collaborative behavior necessary to meet the needs of the operational community

Each of these topics must be considered in the application of CMMI-ACQ and CMMI-DEV to a system of systems context, perhaps with necessary extensions, to meet the goals of interoperable acquisition. Therefore, the application of maturity models to acquisition in a system of systems context is quite relevant!

Transition to Operations: Delivering Value

by Brian Gallagher

CMMI-ACQ includes two practices, one each in Project Planning and Project Monitoring and Control, related to transitioning products and services into operational use. As shown in Figure 6.8, one of the primary responsibilities of the acquirer, in addition to the acceptance of products and services from suppliers, is to ensure a successful transition of capability into operational use, including logistical considerations initially as well as throughout the life of the product or service.

Planning and monitoring transition to operations and support activities involves the processes used to transition new or evolved products and services into operational use, as well as their transition to maintenance or support organizations. Many projects fail during later lifecycle phases because the operational user is ill-prepared to accept the capability into day-to-day operations. Failure also stems from the inability to support the capability delivered, due to inadequate initial sparing or the inability to evolve the capability as the operational mission changes.

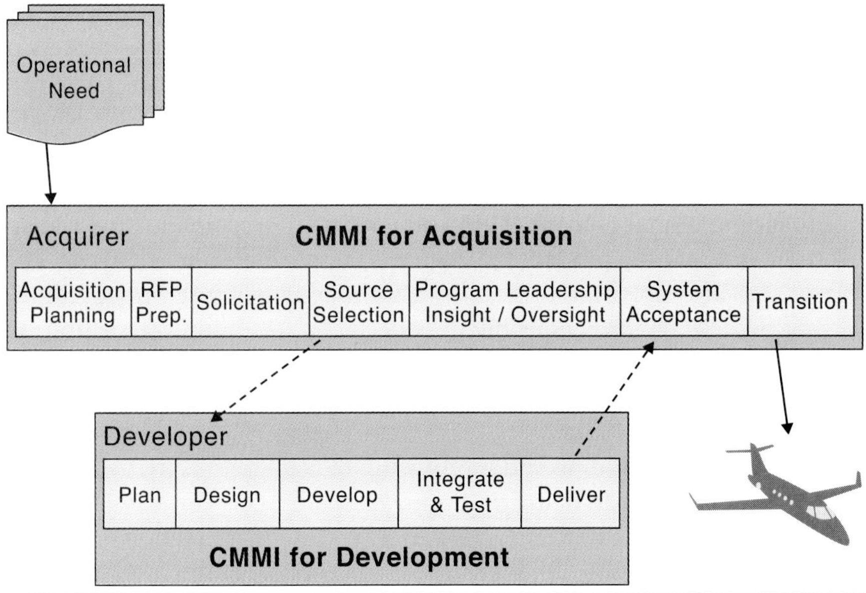

FIGURE 6.8
The Role of the Acquirer

Maintenance and support responsibilities may not be the responsibility of the original supplier. Sometimes an acquisition organization decides to maintain the new capability in-house. There may be other reasons, economic or otherwise, when it makes sense to recompete support activities. In these cases, the acquisition project must ensure that it has access to everything that is required to sustain the capability. This required access would include all design documentation as well as development environments, test equipment, simulators, and models.

The acquisition project is responsible for ensuring that acquired products not only meet their specified requirements (see the Acquisition Technical Management process area) and can be used in the intended environment (see the Acquisition Validation process area), but also that they can be transitioned into operational use to achieve the users' desired operational capabilities and can be maintained and sustained over their intended lifecycles.

The acquisition project is responsible for ensuring that reasonable planning for transition into operations is conducted (see Project Planning specific practice 2.7, "Plan for Transition to Operations and Support"), clear transition criteria exist and are agreed to by relevant stakeholders, and planning is completed for product maintenance and support of products after they become operational. These plans should include reasonable accommodation for known and potential evolution of products and their eventual removal from operational use.

This transition planning should be conducted early in the acquisition lifecycle to ensure that the acquisition strategy and other planning documents reflect transition and support decisions. In addition, contractual documentation must reflect these decisions to ensure that operational personnel are equipped and prepared for the transition and that the product or service is supportable after delivery. The project also must monitor its transition activities (see Project Monitoring and Control specific practice 1.8, "Monitor Transition to Operations and Support") to ensure that operational users are prepared for the transition and that the capability is sustainable once it is delivered.

Adequate planning and monitoring of transition activities is critical to success when delivering value to customers. The acquirer plays an important role in these activities by setting the direction, planning for implementation, and ensuring that the acquirer and supplier implement transition activities.

CMMI: The Heart of the U.S. Air Force's Systems Engineering Assessment Model

by Andrew D. Boyd and Richard Freeman

When the USAF consolidated various systems engineering assessment models into a single model for use across the entire USAF, the effort was made significantly easier due in large part to the fact that every model used to build the expanded USAF model was based on CMMI content and concepts.

In the late 1990s, pressure was mounting for the DoD to dramatically change the way it acquired, fielded, and sustained weapons systems. Faced with increasingly critical Government Accountability Office (GAO) reports and a barrage of media headlines reporting on multimillion-dollar program cost overruns, late deliveries, and systems that failed to perform at desired levels, the DoD began to implement what was called "acquisition reform." Most believed that the root of the problem rested with the government's hands-on approach to be intimately involved in requirements generation, design, and production processes. The DoD exerted control primarily through government-published specifications, standards, methods, and rules, which were codified into contractual documents.

These documents directed, often in excruciating detail, how contractors were required to design and build systems. Many thought that the government unnecessarily was bridling commercial contractors, who were strongly advocating that if they were free of these inhibitors, they could deliver better products at lower costs. This dual onslaught from the media and contractors resulted in sweeping changes that included rescinding a large number of military specifications and standards, slashing program documentation requirements, and greatly reducing the size of government acquisition program offices. The language of contracts was changed to specify the desired capability and allowed contractors the freedom to determine how to best deliver this capability. This action effectively transferred systems engineering to the sole purview of the contractors. Responsibility for the delivery of viable solutions ultimately remained squarely with the government, which was now relying heavily on contractors to deliver.

What resulted was a vacuum in which neither the government nor the contractors accomplished the necessary systems engineering. And over the following decade, the government's organic systems engineering capabilities virtually disappeared. This absence of systems engineering capability became increasingly apparent on multiple-system (i.e., systems-of-systems) programs in which more than one contractor was involved. Overall acquisition performance did not improve, and in many instances it worsened. Although many acquisition reform initiatives were beneficial, it became increasingly clear that the loss of integrated systems engineering was a principal driver behind continued cost overruns, schedule slips, and performance failures.

One service's response was in the USAF, when on February 14, 2003, it announced the establishment of the Air Force Center for Systems Engineering (AF CSE). The AF CSE was chartered to "revitalize" systems engineering across the USAF. Simultaneously, three of the four major USAF acquisition centers initiated efforts to swing the systems engineering pendulum back the other way. To regain some level of capability, each center used a process-based approach to address the challenge. Independently, each of these three centers turned to the CMMI construct and began to tailor it to create a model to be used within their various program offices, thereby molding it to meet the specific needs of these separate acquisition organizations.

Recognizing the potential of this approach, and with an eye toward standardizing systems engineering processes across all of the USAF centers (i.e., acquisition, test, and sustainment), in 2006 the AF CSE was tasked to do the following.

- Develop and field a single Air Force Systems Engineering Assessment Model (AF SEAM).
- Involve all major USAF centers (acquisition, test, and sustainment).
- Leverage current systems engineering CMMI-based assessment models in various stages of development or use at USAF centers.

In summer 2007, following initial research and data gathering, the AF CSE established a working group composed of members from the eight major centers across the USAF (four acquisition centers, one test center, and three sustainment centers). Assembled members included those who had either built their individual center models or would be responsible for the AF SEAM going forward. The team's first objective was to develop a consistent understanding of systems engineering through mutual agreement of process categories and associated definitions. Once this understanding was established, the team members would use these process areas and, building on the best practices of existing models, together develop a single AF SEAM which would have the following characteristics.

- It would be viewed as adding value by program managers and therefore would be "pulled" for use to aid in the following:
  - Ensuring that standardized core systems engineering processes are in place and being followed
  - Reducing technical risk
  - Improving program performance
- It would be scalable for use by all programs and projects across the entire USAF:
  - Based on self-assessment
  - Capable of independent verification
- It would be a vehicle for sharing systems engineering lessons learned as well as best practices.
- It would be easy to maintain.

To ensure a consistent understanding of systems engineering across the USAF and to provide the foundation on which to build AF SEAM, the working group clearly defined the ten systems engineering process areas (presented in the following list in alphabetical order):

CM	Configuration Management
DA	Decision Analysis
D	Design
M	Manufacturing

PP	Project Planning
R	Requirements
RM	Risk Management
S	Sustainment
TMC	Technical Management & Control
V	Verification & Validation

The model's structure is based on the CMMI construct of process areas, specific goals, specific practices, and generic practices. AF SEAM has the ten process areas in the preceding list amplified by 33 specific goals, 119 specific practices, and 7 generic practices. Each practice includes a title, a description, typical work products, references to source requirements and/or guidance, and additional considerations to provide context. Although some process areas are largely an extract from CMMI, others are combinations of specific practices from multiple CMMI process areas and other sources. Additionally, two process areas not explicitly covered in CMMI were added, namely Manufacturing and Sustainment.

To aid in the establishment of a systems engineering process baseline and in turn achieve the various goals stated earlier, programs and projects will undergo one or more assessments followed by continuous process improvement. An assessment focuses on process existence and use and therefore serves as a leading indicator of potential future performance. The assessment is not a determination of product quality or a report card on the people or the organization (i.e., lagging indicators). To allow for full USAF-wide scalability, the assessment method is intentionally designed to support either a one- or two-step process. In the first step, each program or project performs a self-assessment using the model to verify process existence, identify local references, and identify work products for each specific practice and generic practice—in other words, "grading" itself. If leadership determines that verification is beneficial, a second independent assessment is performed. This verification is conducted by an external team that verifies the results of the self-assessment and rates each specific practice and generic practice as either "satisfied" or "not satisfied." Results are provided back to the program or project as output of the independent assessment. The information is presented in a manner that promotes the sharing of best practices and facilitates reallocation of resources to underperforming processes. The AF SEAM development working group also developed training for leaders, self-assessors, and independent assessors, who are provided this training on a "just-in-time" basis.

The future of the AF SEAM looks bright. With a long history of using multiple CMMI-based models across the USAF, significant cultural inroads have been made to secure the acceptance of a process-based approach. The creation and use of a single USAF-wide Systems Engineering Assessment Model will aid significantly in the revitalization of sound systems engineering practices and in turn will facilitate the provision of mission-capable systems and systems of systems on time and within budget.

(The views expressed herein do not represent an official position of the DoD or the USAF.)

Acquisition Improvement: Identifying and Removing Process Constraints

by Brian Gallagher

Most process improvement approaches are based on a similar pedigree that traces back to the same foundation established by process improvement gurus, such as Shewhart, Deming, Juran, Ishikawa, Taguchi, Humphrey, and others. The improvement approaches embodied in CMMI, Lean, Six Sigma, the Theory of Constraints, Total Quality Management, and other methods all embrace an improvement paradigm that can be boiled down to these simple steps.

1. Define the system you want to improve.
2. Understand the scope of the system.
3. Define the goals and objectives for the system.
4. Determine constraints to achieving objectives.
5. Make a plan to remove the constraints.
6. Learn lessons and do it again.

These simple steps comprise an improvement pattern that is evident in the Plan-Do-Check-Act (PDCA) improvement loop, Six Sigma's Define, Measure, Analyze, Improve, Control (DMAIC) improvement methodology, the military's Observe-Orient-Decide-Act (OODA) loop, and the SEI's Initiating, Diagnosing, Establishing, Acting, and Learning (IDEAL) method shown in Figure 6.9.

All of these improvement paradigms share a common goal: to improve the effectiveness and efficiency of a system. That *system* can be a manufacturing assembly line, the decision process used by military pilots, a development organization, an acquisition project, or any other entity or process that can be defined, observed, and improved.

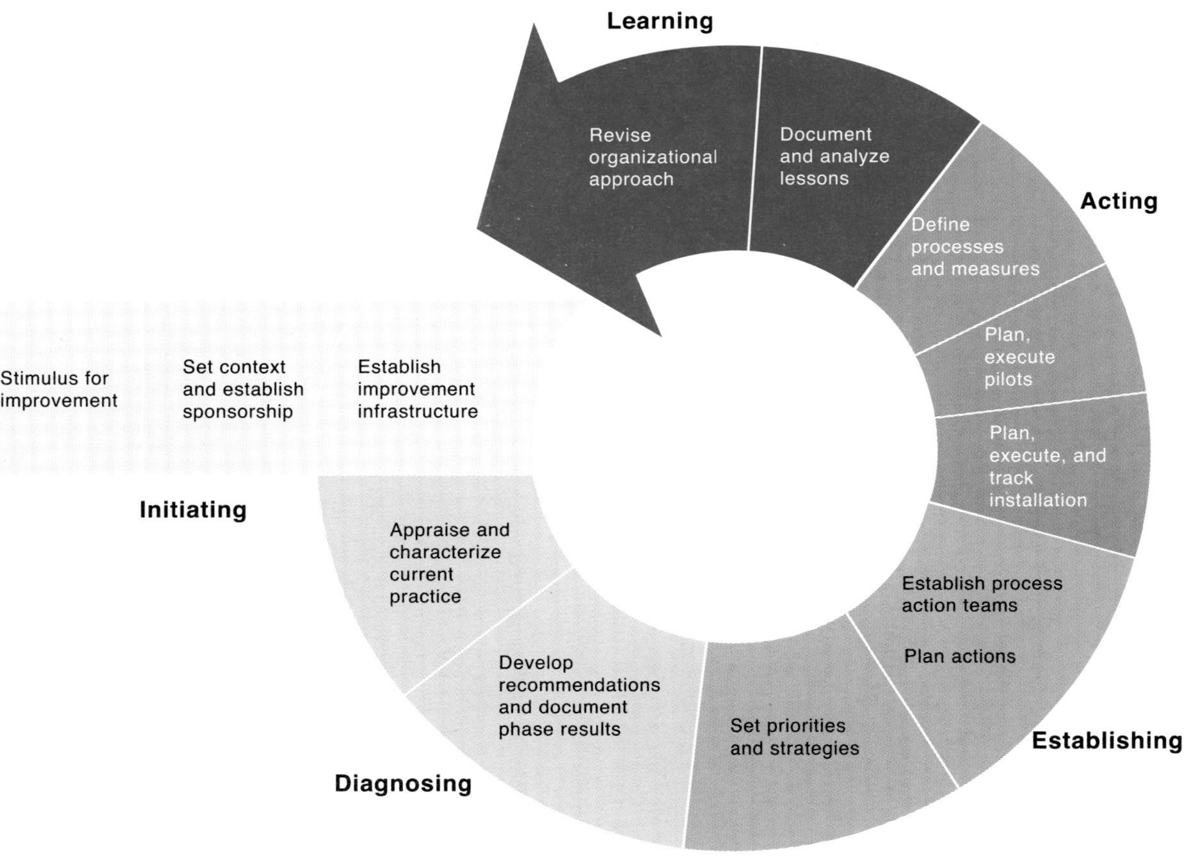

FIGURE 6.9
The SEI's IDEAL Model

One mistake individuals and organizations make when embarking on an improvement path is to force a decision to choose one improvement methodology over another as though each approach is mutually exclusive. An example is committing an organization to using CMMI or Lean Six Sigma or the Theory of Constraints before understanding how to take advantage of the tool kits provided by each approach and selecting the tools that make the most sense for the culture of the organization and the problem at hand. The following case study illustrates how one organization took advantage of using the Theory of Constraints with CMMI.

Case Study: Combining CMMI and the Theory of Constraints

One government agency had just completed a Standard CMMI Appraisal Method for Process Improvement (SCAMPI) appraisal with a CMMI model on its 12 most important customer projects—all managed within a Project Management Organization (PMO) under the direction of a senior executive. The PMO was a virtual organization consisting of a class of projects that the agency decided needed additional focus due to their criticality from a customer perspective. Although the entire acquisition and engineering staff numbered close to 5,000 employees, the senior executive committed to delivering these 12 projects on time, even at the expense of less important projects. Each project had a well-defined set of process requirements to include start-up and planning activities and was subject to monthly Program Management Reviews (PMRs) to track progress, resolve work issues, and manage risk. With its clear focus on project success, the PMO easily achieved CMMI maturity level 2.

On the heels of the SCAMPI appraisal, the agency was directed to move much of its customer-facing functionality to the Web, enabling customers to take advantage of a wide variety of self-service applications. This Web-based system was a new technology for the agency, and many of its employees and contractors had experience only with mainframe or client/server systems. To learn how to successfully deliver capability using this new technology, the senior executive visited several Internet-based commercial organizations and found that one key factor of their success was the ability to deliver customer value within very short time frames—usually between 30 and 90 days. Armed with this information, the executive decried that all Internet-based projects were to immediately establish a 90-day delivery schedule. Confident with this new direction and eager to see results, he asked the Internet projects to be part of the scope of projects in the next SCAMPI appraisal to validate the approach.

The agency's process improvement consultant realized that trying to do a formal SCAMPI appraisal on an organization struggling to adopt a new, more agile methodology while learning a new Web-based technology and under pressure to deliver in 90 days wasn't the best option given the timing of all the recent changes. She explored the idea of conducting a risk assessment or other technical intervention, but found that the word *risk* was overloaded in the agency context and so she needed a different approach. She finally suggested using the Theory of Constraints to help identify and mitigate some of the process-related constraints facing the agency.

The Theory of Constraints is a system-level management philosophy that suggests all systems may be compared to chains. Each chain is composed of various links with unique strengths and weaknesses. The weakest link (i.e., the constraint) in the chain is not generally eliminated; rather it is strengthened by following an organized process, thus allowing for improvement in the system. By systematically identifying the weakest link, and strengthening it, the system as a whole sees improvement. The first step in improving the system is to identify all of the system's constraints.

A constraint is an obstacle to the successful completion of an endeavor. Think about how constraints would differ depending on the following endeavors:

- Driving from Miami to Las Vegas
- Walking across a busy street
- Digging a ditch
- Building a shed
- Acquiring a new space launch vehicle
- Fighting a battle

Constraints are not context-free; you can't know your constraints until you know your endeavor. For the Internet project endeavor, the senior executive selected a rather wordy "picture of success":

"The Internet acquisition projects are scheduled and defined based upon agency priorities and the availability of resources from all involved components, and the application releases that support those initiatives are planned, developed, and implemented within established time frames using established procedures to produce quality systems."

The problem the consultant faced was how to systematically identify the constraints. Where should she look and how would she make sure she covered all the important processes employed by the agency?

Since the agency was familiar with CMMI, she decided to use the practices in CMMI as a taxonomy to help identify constraints. Instead of looking for evidence of compliance to the practice statements as you would in a SCAMPI appraisal, she asked interviewees to judge how well the practices were implemented and the impact of implementation on successful achievement of the "picture of success." Consider the difference in an interview session between the two:

SCAMPI Appraisal

Question: "How do you establish estimates?"

Answer: "We follow a documented procedure...involve stakeholders...obtain proper sign-off and commitment...."

CMMI-Based Constraint Identification

Question: "Given your 'picture of success,' do you have any concerns about the way you establish estimates?"

Answer: "Our estimates are based on productivity rates that are twice what our contractors have ever been able to accomplish. There's no way we'll meet our current schedule."

After six intense interview sessions involving 40 agency personnel and contractors, 103 individual constraint statements were gathered and affinity-grouped into the following constraint areas:

- Establishing, Communicating, and Measuring Agency Goals
- Legacy versus Internet
- Lack of Trained and Experienced Resources
- Lack of Coordination and Integration
- Internet-Driven Change
- Product Quality and Integrity
- Team Performance
- Imposed Standards and Mandates
- Requirements Definition and Management
- Unprecedented Delivery Paradigm
- Fixed 90-day Schedule

Further analysis using cause and effect tools helped to identify how each constraint affected the other. This further analysis also allowed the consultant to produce the hierarchical interrelationship digraph depicted in Figure 6.10.

The results of this analysis helped the senior executive decide which constraints needed to be resolved to help improve the quality

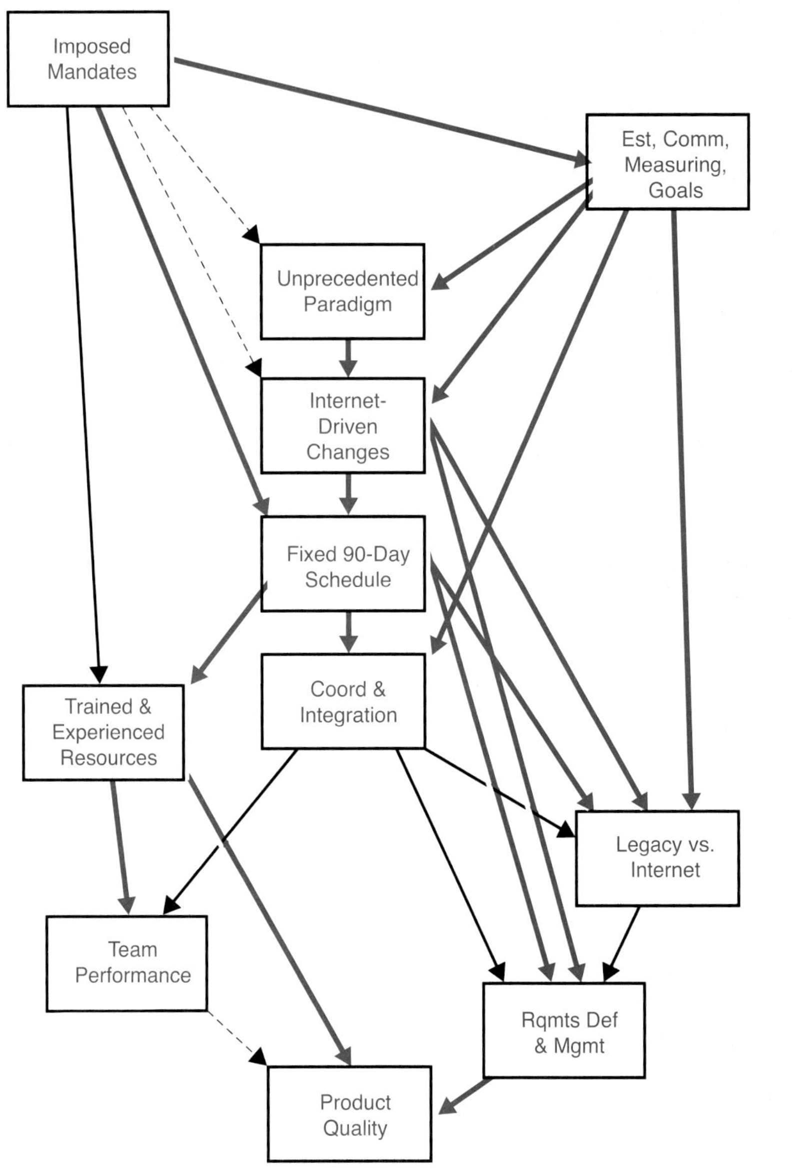

FIGURE 6.10
Hierarchical Interrelationship Digraph

of the delivered systems. The higher up in the diagram you can affect, the more impact you can achieve.

The senior executive decided that the "Imposed Mandates" constraint was outside his span of control. However, many of the other constraints were either directly within his control or at least within his sphere of influence. He decided to charter improvement teams to tackle the following constraints:

- Establishing, Communicating, and Measuring Goals
- Internet versus Legacy (combined with Lack of Coordination and Integration)
- Internet-Driven Changes

The improvement teams used a well-defined improvement approach that helped them explore each constraint in detail, establish an improvement goal, perform root cause analysis, identify barriers and enablers to success, and establish strategies and milestones to accomplish the goal.

The process improvement consultant recognized that using CMMI alone wasn't appropriate for the challenges facing the agency, and brought concepts and tools from another improvement approach—the Theory of Constraints—to help the agency recognize and remove critical process-related constraints. She helped establish improvement strategies and helped the agency avert a pending crisis, setting them on an improvement course that served them well. Today, the agency's PMO manages both legacy and Internet-based projects, is an exemplar for other agencies, and demonstrated its process prowess by successfully achieving CMMI maturity level 3.

This case study also illustrates how using CMMI for process improvement fits into the DoD-wide Continuous Process Improvement (CPI)/Lean Six Sigma (LSS) Program, which includes the Lean, Six Sigma, and Theory of Constraints tools and methods for process improvement [DoD 2008].

CHAPTER 7

USING CMMI-ACQ IN INDUSTRY: GENERAL MOTORS CASE STUDY

by Richard Frost and Tom Keuten

Executive Summary

Information Systems & Services (IS&S) is the global information technology (IT) organization for General Motors (GM). IS&S is focused on partnering with GM's business units to drive innovation and efficiency throughout the global GM enterprise. To accomplish this, IS&S determined the need to develop a new global sourcing structure and drive simplification, standardization, and collaboration among and with its supplier network. When designing its new global sourcing structure, GM approached the Software Engineering Institute (SEI) for guidance and best practices applicable to companies that manage suppliers. The two organizations jointly realized that the current maturity models were focused on development—not acquisition—and the IT industry was looking for a model to help acquirers. Together, they partnered with industry and government leaders from around the globe to create the CMMI for Acquisition (CMMI-ACQ) model. GM became an early adopter of the CMMI-ACQ model and used it as a framework to help benchmark its organization and processes as it moved a new global model of IT sourcing with suppliers.

GM used the CMMI-ACQ model to identify the key competencies that IS&S must retain in this environment in which all IT development and support is sourced. Within GM, the IS&S department is recognized as the strategic hub of IT (see Figure 7.1). The IS&S staff does not create or operate systems; instead, it develops deep knowledge of GM's business processes and develops enterprise and systems

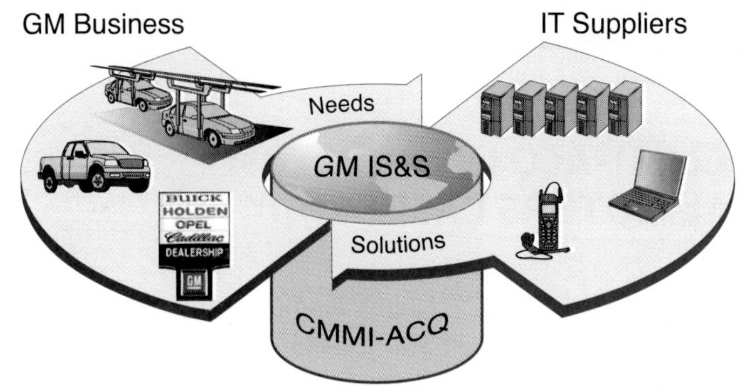

FIGURE 7.1
GM's IS&S and the CMMI-ACQ

engineering architectures for those processes. IS&S then brokers relationships with suppliers to build, operate, and secure systems.

In this role, the IS&S organization strategically builds competencies in business requirements (to maintain knowledge of the business), systems engineering (to drive technology standards and target architectures), and project management (to ensure successful system delivery). These core competencies correspond directly to process areas in the CMMI-ACQ model. GM also uses all of the other practices in the CMMI-ACQ model to help IS&S further define the system delivery processes and drive acquisition maturity across the organization.

Prior to the creation of the CMMI-ACQ model, IS&S successfully used the CMMI for Development (CMMI-DEV) model to standardize processes globally. As the organization matured in its acquisition capabilities, it realized that the practices for a customer, or acquirer, of technology are substantially different from the practices of development organizations. With this insight, GM now uses CMMI-ACQ as a model for its processes as a customer of technology systems. IS&S continues to understand the value of the CMMI-DEV model and requires its development suppliers to leverage the CMMI-DEV model to benchmark and continuously improve their processes. GM suppliers conduct regular appraisals and share their appraisal results and improvement plans with GM. GM also partners with its suppliers during its CMMI-ACQ appraisals. This practice helps to ensure that suppliers understand GM acquisition processes and reveals opportunities to improve GM and supplier interaction.

One of the fundamental principles implemented by GM's new sourcing model is that suppliers truly collaborate with each other and with GM. A set of suppliers is targeted for each functional or business area within GM. The suppliers then work to understand the business environment and bring business and technological innovation to GM. When projects are identified, GM partners with integration suppliers to develop the requirements, design, and target architecture. The final design, construction, and deployment are delivered by development suppliers on a firm fixed-price basis. These processes are standardized globally and are a key aspect of GM's implementation of the CMMI-ACQ. Development suppliers are compensated only for functionality delivered to the business. They are not compensated on a time and materials or cost-plus basis. This approach to compensation ensures that development suppliers understand the business problem, properly identify project risks, and work jointly with IS&S to ensure that business value is delivered to GM customers.

A second fundamental principle implemented by GM is that IS&S does not mandate how suppliers develop systems. GM recognizes that its IT suppliers are software development organizations that have mature processes for developing systems. GM and its suppliers agree on the deliverables for each project, and the suppliers are allowed to determine and use the appropriate development methodology.

GM has developed global standard processes based on CMMI-ACQ that describe the overall delivery processes and the processes executed internally by GM. These processes specify the activities and deliverables required at each phase of the project. They are supported by contracts that define the touch points and deliverables. The contracts also specify that suppliers have to develop their own processes which enable quick responses to new development requests and effective and efficient system delivery. Utilizing these global processes, both GM and supplier teams spend less time working on sales activities and proposals, and devote more time to innovation and development of new solutions to move the business.

Reducing the costs of these activities, as well as simplifying the IT landscape, allows greater investment in new and innovative technologies. This development work is more effective because of improvements in requirements. By jointly collaborating on and defining technology standards, GM is also able to leverage the innovation of its top suppliers without sacrificing the ownership and direction of its technical environment. The new GM-Supplier business model, CMMI-ACQ processes, and continuous improvement have allowed GM IS&S to deliver more capabilities to its business customers while lowering its costs to one of the lowest per vehicle in the automotive industry.

The entire GM organization is focused on building great cars and trucks, developing the next generation of fuel-efficient drivetrains, and ensuring that GM continues to excel in vehicle styling and quality. IS&S has realized significant benefits from using CMMI-ACQ such that GM's IT is well positioned to fully support and mobilize these corporate goals.

Overview of General Motors

General Motors Corp. (NYSE: GM) is a large automotive vehicle manufacturer and focuses on building great cars and trucks for the global market. The corporation is headquartered in the United States; however, GM operates as a truly global company and has a network of design, manufacturing, service, and marketing facilities supported by about two hundred sixty-six thousand employees located around the globe.

In 2007, GM sold 9.3 million units globally. GM has a sophisticated branding strategy that consists of global brands such as Cadillac, Chevrolet, and Saab; and regional brands including Buick, GMC, GM Daewoo, Holden, Opel, Pontiac, Saturn, and Vauxhall. GM manufactures vehicles in more than 35 countries using 375 million square feet of manufacturing space. These products are distributed globally and are sold in more than 200 countries through an extensive dealer network. GM also participates in several joint ventures that produce vehicles for local and emerging markets.

The vehicles designed by GM are some of the most sophisticated and complex products in the marketplace. Each vehicle is a custom-configured product that contains approximately five thousand unique parts and assemblies. The manufacturing process requires a complex supply chain that obtains materials from more than 3,200 sources globally. These materials are delivered every day to GM manufacturing facilities "just-in-time" for production.

GM is also a leader in the automotive telematics industry. GM's OnStar division provides real-time communication with vehicles to provide safety, security, and information services to vehicle owners and passengers. OnStar services include crash notification, medical emergency support, stolen-vehicle recovery assistance, vehicle maintenance monitoring, concierge services, and turn-by-turn navigation services.

Considering the breadth of its enterprise, the complexity of its products, and the volume of its business, GM is one of the most complex organizations in the world. The management team and employee base within GM are focused on building great cars and trucks and on bringing innovative vehicle products and services to the global market. The IS&S organization is focused on enabling this innovation, reducing technology complexity, and ensuring that GM's IT systems are secure and can rapidly respond to new market directions.

Overview of GM Information Systems & Services (IS&S)

GM Information Systems & Services (IS&S) provides IT products and services to the GM business globally. The continuing objective of IS&S is to provide world-class IT that propels GM to global leadership in transportation products and related services. IS&S is led by Group Vice President and CIO Ralph Szygenda, who is also a member of GM's most senior management committee, the GM Automotive Strategy Board. Mr. Szygenda has led the IS&S organization through several transformations as it has evolved to support and foster innovation within GM.

First-Generation Sourcing

Historically, GM has been an early adopter and pioneer in IT. This distinction was often necessitated by the complexity and scale of the GM operations. However, before 1984 there was no central IT organization within GM, and the regional structures sourced the majority of IT products and services. Only a few core systems were used globally.

In 1984, GM entered its first generation of IT sourcing by purchasing a global IT services company that was a leader in large-scale IT systems. GM utilized this firm as the sole supplier of IT services to the enterprise. Supplier personnel interacted directly with the GM business and were tasked with building a common global infrastructure, simplifying diverse systems, and providing common service globally. Within GM, this is referred to as the first-generation sourcing model (see Figure 7.2). It provided GM with the benefit of a single IT provider to optimize infrastructure and operations.

Second-Generation Sourcing

In the mid-1990s, GM senior management realized that IT was a strategic part of business operations and that IT strategy and accountability must be internal to the organization and must not reside with a supplier. With this insight, GM designed and entered its second-generation sourcing model in 1996. This model included creating IS&S and recruiting GM's first global CIO. The global CIO

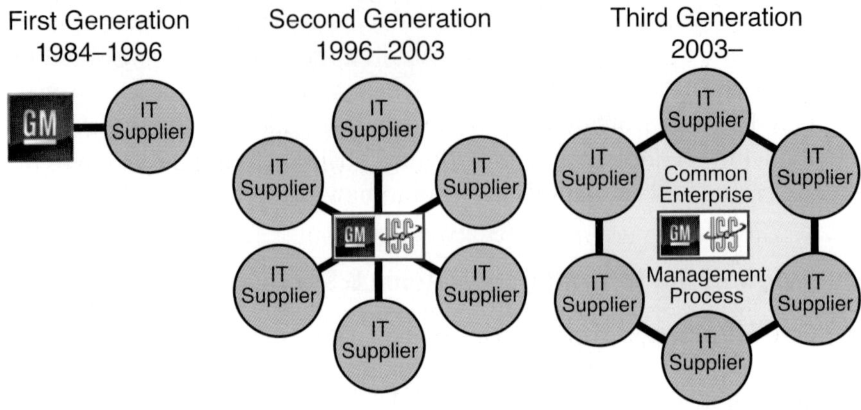

FIGURE 7.2
The Evolution of GM's IT Sourcing Model

developed the mission for IS&S and built the IS&S organization to drive the strategy and deliver innovation to the organization. This creation of IS&S and partnership with multiple suppliers is known as the second-generation sourcing model. In this model, the IS&S department became the primary interface to the business, understood the business strategy, and selected the systems and technology. IS&S then selected IT partners to develop, implement, and operate the business information systems.

The key benefit of the second-generation model was that GM developed internal IT capabilities. As an internal organization, IS&S was able to develop strategies and standards that drove the strategic interests of GM. In this model, GM also began to manage key technical development and support teams to obtain business and systems knowledge that had migrated to the supplier base. With this knowledge, IS&S was able to engage alternative suppliers for IT projects and sustain its activities. The new supplier base helped to drive new innovation with GM but introduced the complexity of GM having to manage a significant number of suppliers. It often required IS&S personnel to oversee integration activities, perform low-level problem solving, and resolve supplier-to-supplier technical and communication issues. During this time, GM also began to adopt CMMI-DEV as a model of best practices to standardize processes globally.

Third-Generation Sourcing

By 2003, IS&S had developed sufficient business and system knowledge to begin to structure GM's third-generation IT sourcing model. The primary goals of the new model were to drive standardization, simplification, and collaboration throughout GM's global IT structure. The third-generation model completed the transition of IS&S from a regionally aligned structure to a global structure.

When developing the third-generation model, GM leadership analyzed the benefits and realizations of the first- and second-generation sourcing models. They also analyzed the results that GM obtained from a multiyear initiative using CMMI-DEV to drive improvement and standardization across IS&S. With this data, GM approached the SEI for guidance and best practices for sourcing or acquisition organizations. After further review, the two organizations concluded that CMMI-DEV is an excellent model for organizations that develop systems but does not provide the right guidance for organizations that source or acquire systems. This interaction started what was eventually to become CMMI-ACQ, a new CMMI model focused on the capabilities of the acquirer. The analysis, along with the joint work on CMMI-ACQ with suppliers and other high-performing acquisition organizations, helped GM to establish some guiding principles for structuring the third-generation sourcing model. These principles include the following.

- GM IS&S will maintain the relationship with the business, understand the business strategy and process, and be accountable for delivering the solution to the business.
- With knowledge of the business strategy, GM IS&S will determine the business process impact, develop system requirements, and define the technical architecture for all systems.
- GM will standardize on a set of suppliers to provide system development and sustain activities aligned with GM business processes (e.g., manufacturing, supply chain, marketing, OnStar, and engineering).
- Suppliers are expected to bring business process domain expertise and technological innovation.
- Suppliers are expected to understand the GM environment, collaborate, and resolve integration issues without GM involvement.
- The pricing of all projects will be firm fixed price and payment will be based on tangible business deliverables.

In addition to the guiding principles for supplier sourcing, GM understood that it must align its internal IS&S organization to the global lines of business within GM. Prior to this adjustment, the IT strategy was driven by regional needs and each region was responsible for developing and managing global solutions. Regional business leaders would engage the regional IS&S units to help them with IT needs. GM realized that this model made it difficult to drive simplification because of the different priorities and business cycles of the regions. IS&S leaders now understood that simplification and standardization could be achieved only if the strategy was aligned with line-of-business goals, global solutions were developed to satisfy the strategy, and regional deployments of solutions were coordinated with regional business cycles.

IS&S Factory Structure

To support the objectives of simplification and standardization, the IS&S organizational structure was aligned into three global virtual "factories" (see Figure 7.3). The System Delivery Factory (SDF) consists of line-of-business or business process area organizations and is responsible for development, enhancement, deployment, and standardization of all systems globally. The Services Factory (SF) has global responsibility for all operations, infrastructure, network, and IT security for GM. Supporting both of these is the Business Management Factory (BMF). The BMF organization provides essential services such as central contracting support, compliance, finance management, and business strategy development to the other factories. The leadership, strategy, and management of each factory are provided by GM executives. Each virtual factory also partners with a supplier to provide integration, project support, quality, and coordination services.

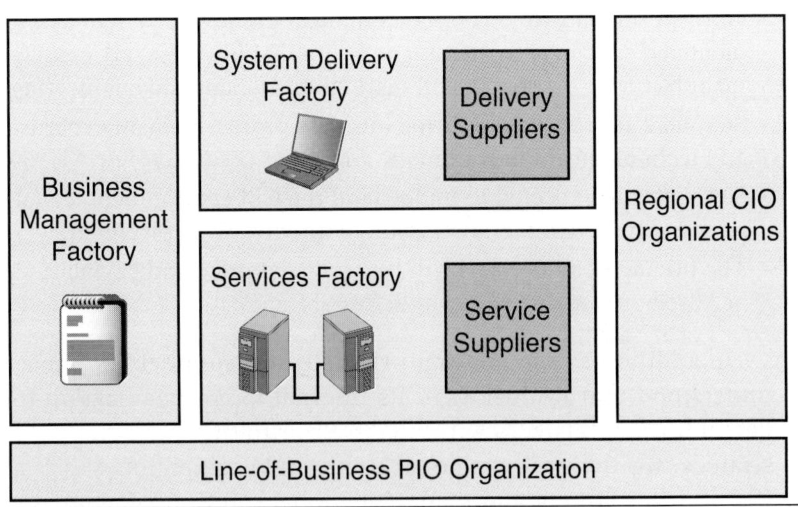

FIGURE 7.3
IS&S Virtual Factory Structure

In addition to the three factories, IS&S leadership also includes regional CIO organizations. The CIO organizations align with the region-based GM business organizations in North America, Latin America-Africa-Middle East, Asia Pacific, and Europe. They ensure that the needs of the regional business units are understood and that IT strategies and plans align with regional business objectives.

To ensure that IS&S is always aligned to actual business activities, Process Information Officers (PIOs) are a critical part of the leadership matrix and report directly to the global CIO. The PIO organizations are aligned with the GM business process functions and have global responsibility for the IT needs and strategy for the business process. There are separate PIO organizations for each of the following business process areas: Product Development, Manufacturing and Quality, Purchasing and Supply Chain, Sales-Service and Marketing, Business Services, and OnStar. Each PIO aligns with a senior business process officer and coordinates the IT strategy for the global process area. PIO organizations are the focal point for aligning with the business and driving innovation for the GM business areas. Each PIO organization contains a delivery center, which participates in SDF, and these PIO delivery centers are responsible for the delivery of all projects to the business.

The IS&S structure of PIO, CIO, and factory organizations provides GM with many benefits. For instance, this structure provides clear lines of governance for global IS&S and within each factory. In addition, the factories clearly identify responsibilities and interface touch points through established standardized processes within themselves and among each other, and the interfactory processes streamline the effort to move among factories, yet also provide natural quality and coordination checks for projects and operations. Also, the PIO and CIO organizations bring line-of-business and regional business process alignment to all initiatives; this representation ensures coordination of global strategies with regional priorities and time frames. And finally, governance and technology issues are resolved swiftly via weekly global meetings of the senior IS&S executives and corresponding meetings of the executives within each factory.

System Delivery Factory: An Acquisition Organization

This case study is focused on the work within the SDF of IS&S, which is responsible for delivering new capabilities to the GM business. The SDF delivers new capabilities to the business by partnering with the business, developing strategies, identifying and specifying projects, and then sourcing the development and deployment with fixed-price projects from suppliers. To accomplish these goals, the SDF has created standard organizational, governance, and project-execution processes that align with CMMI-ACQ.

The organizational structure of the SDF consists of the PIO organizations and a Chief Systems & Technology Office (CS&TO) organization (see Figure 7.4). The PIO organizations align with business areas to understand their needs, deliver systems, and help drive innovation within the business. CS&TO coordinates across PIO areas to drive IT strategy, standardization, and innovation across the enterprise through collaboration across the PIO areas and the business units.

The PIO organizations have the responsibility of partnering with the business to drive innovation and efficiency. They do this by developing new systems, enhancing existing systems, and streamlining the IT landscape for their respective business units. To accomplish these objectives, each PIO organizes resources by the following critical functions: Strategy, Architecture, Delivery Center, and Sustain. The Strategy function works with the line-of-business and leading technology partners to develop IT strategies and plans that align with business goals. The Architecture function develops the overriding systems architecture for the line of business, develops high-level architectures for projects, and collaborates with CS&TO to develop the enterprise architecture for the entire GM enterprise. The Delivery Center function is responsible for the delivery of all projects. This includes project management, business modeling, requirements development, quality assurance, deployment, and Project Management Organization (PMO) support. The Sustain function provides minor enhancements to systems once they are in production.

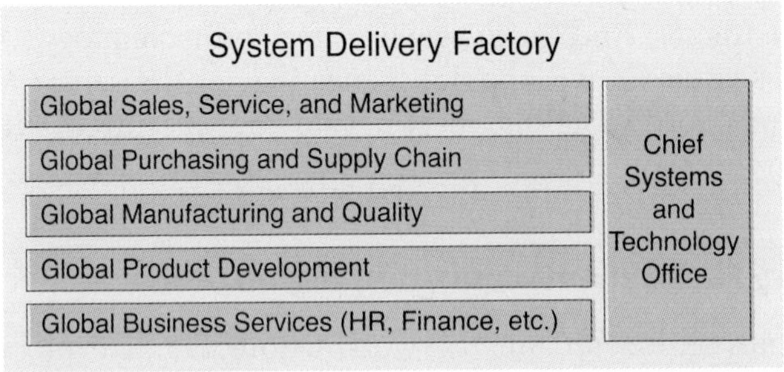

FIGURE 7.4
System Delivery Factory

The CS&TO organization is led by the Chief Technology Officer (CTO) for GM and has three primary functions relevant to the CMMI-ACQ model: Process and Program Management, Systems Engineering, and Emerging Technologies. The Process and Program Management function collaborates with the PIO organizations for development and improvement of all processes, tools, and support systems for the delivery center. The Systems Engineering function collaborates with PIO areas to develop the enterprise architecture, maintain and improve technology standards, and identify cross-PIO technology synergies. The Emerging Technologies laboratory serves as a focal point for innovation and new technology across IS&S. Each of these functional areas within CS&TO has an executive steering council that includes members from the PIO organizations. This ensures that process and technology standards always align with the needs of the organizations that deliver systems to the business.

Governance of the System Development Factory

The primary purposes of governance in the SDF are to provide clear process and technology standards, continually improve standardized work within the delivery centers, and gain operational efficiency by identifying synergies with the factory. In addition to these goals, the governance must be nimble, quickly respond to issues, and capitalize on opportunities. GM realized that proper governance must provide the proper balance of strategic and operational objectives and ensure that governance is developed and agreed to by practitioners across the factory. To accomplish this, GM developed a structure that is led by the CS&TO organization and has executive representation from each of the PIO areas. Governance meetings are held every week, and all meetings use appropriate technology to ensure global involvement.

The primary governance structure consists of two executive councils: the System Factory Management Council (SFMC) and the Joint Architecture Management Council (JAMC). The SFMC is responsible for developing the strategy for IS&S delivery processes, institutionalizing program management, and improving the operations of the factory. The JAMC is responsible for approving IT standard components and setting technical direction for IT solutions at GM. Each council meets on a weekly basis so that process and technical issues can be addressed and communicated in a timely manner.

The members of the councils consist of executives from each of the PIO areas and CS&TO. Members of the CIO teams often attend to ensure that regional viewpoints are represented. Although the JAMC and SFMC are separate councils to address process and technology, there is partial overlap of staff members between the two councils to ensure continuity and alignment. The two council meetings are held back to back, and joint meetings are often held to address topics that involve both process and technology.

Operationally, the SFMC and JAMC strive to keep the pace of the meetings brisk and focused to make efficient use of the council's time. When initiatives require extensive research or process, the council members form small work teams to develop solutions and recommendations. These work teams are usually led by one of the council members, and the PIO organizations provide staff members to participate. Typical topics addressed by work teams include process improvement issues, new-technology evaluations, and improvement of interfaces with other factory processes. The teams are given a high-level objective as well as the freedom to find the right solution for GM. This approach ensures that all areas can participate in initiatives and provides the IS&S staff with the opportunity to work on cross-functional teams and gain exposure to other executives.

Each factory in IS&S benefits from the adoption of CMMI-ACQ, but the SDF is the main engine that drives new capability to the business. By aligning the people and processes to the model, the SDF has become a more mature acquisition organization. The next section describes how GM has built the right capabilities internally to deliver systems to the business through partnering with world-class IT suppliers.

Aligning the GM System Delivery Process to CMMI-ACQ

GM realized that proper implementation of CMMI-ACQ meant internalizing the model, developing a deep understanding of the authors' intent when they wrote the practices, and designing an implementation that aligns with the culture of GM. When developing the process, the SDF had to ensure that the practices were translated into work steps that could be followed by GM personnel globally. Due to the complexity of the organization, significant thought was given to how the implementation of these practices impacted organizational processes, related structures, and contracts. Aligning these structural elements was a significant organizational and process design challenge. One of the first steps in addressing this challenge was to clearly identify which parts of the delivery process were the responsibility of GM and which parts would be the responsibility of the supplier. Figure 7.5 shows the conceptual architecture of the high-level

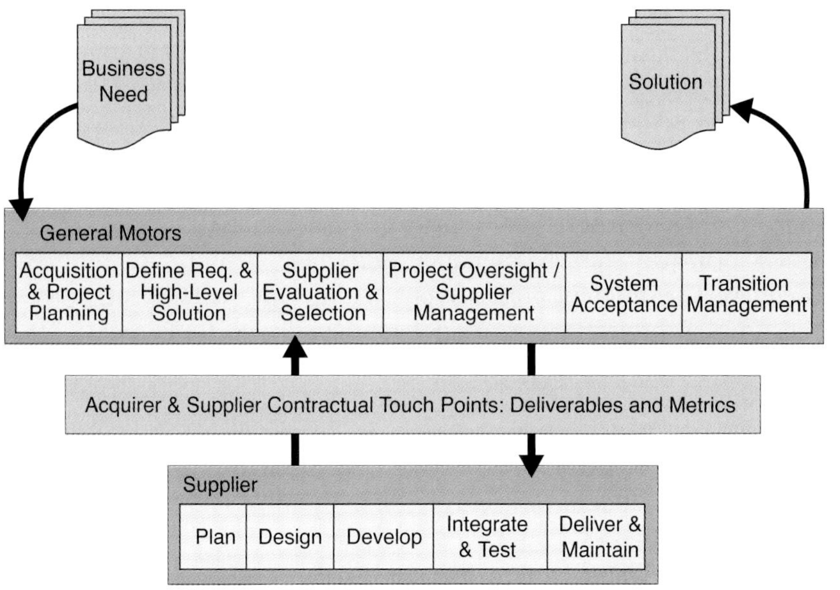

FIGURE 7.5
GM Process and Supplier Process

process. Following this process, consistent with the guiding principles, GM remains accountable to the business, develops the requirements, and retains project management responsibilities. The supplier develops the solution using its own methodology and delivers well-defined deliverables, metrics, and status to GM through standardized interfaces.

Based on this process vision, GM's process development team designed a process architecture that had at its foundation a series of "rules" known as *standardized work*. These standardized work rules were approved by the highest levels of IT management at the company. Global training sessions were provided to all IS&S employees and suppliers to ensure a consistent understanding and interpretation of these work rules. The standardized work rules provided boundaries and constraints that cross-functional teams used to develop processes for project teams to execute. The resultant processes were part of GM's IT delivery framework called the System Delivery Process (SDP).

The SDP supports different project types through appropriate levels of process and oversight based on the size, complexity, and criticality of the project. The project teams select the project type using predefined criteria published in the SDP with assistance from the project management office and lead architect. The project type selected by most significant GM projects is the Standard type. Standard projects start with the full framework and tailor that framework to define the project's unique process. Each phase of the SDP framework has activities, templates, and examples to help with project execution. The other project types include Express and Express-Lite. Express projects start with a smaller set of processes and are tailored accordingly to meet their project needs. Express-Lite projects are used primarily for maintenance and have appropriate processes defined. The different project types, along with the tailoring process, ensure that project teams are not burdened with unnecessary overhead and that management has oversight and insight into project activities.

The Standard project type consists of six phases: Plan, Define, Construct, Test, Deploy, and Close. Depending on the complexity of the project, Standard projects are often planned and executed using two "super" phases: Plan/Define and Construct to Close (see Figure 7.6). During Plan/Define, GM establishes a priority for the project, assigns GM resources, and understands the business needs and impacts. Then GM develops the requirements and technical strategy for the project before approaching a supplier. GM may utilize suppliers to provide specific expertise and additional bandwidth during the Plan/Define phase. In these instances, GM remains accountable for the deliverables, and supplier personnel are managed by the GM project manager. In this instance, suppliers can be engaged on a time and materials basis because they are under direct supervision of a GM project manager. Before completion of the Define phase, the suppliers capable of delivering the systems are engaged to submit a fixed-price proposal based on a standard bid request process. The scope proposal includes all development, deployment, and transition work necessary to bring the system into the GM environment.

The Construct to Close phases (i.e., Construct, Test, Deploy, and Close) are much different from the Plan/Define phase. During these

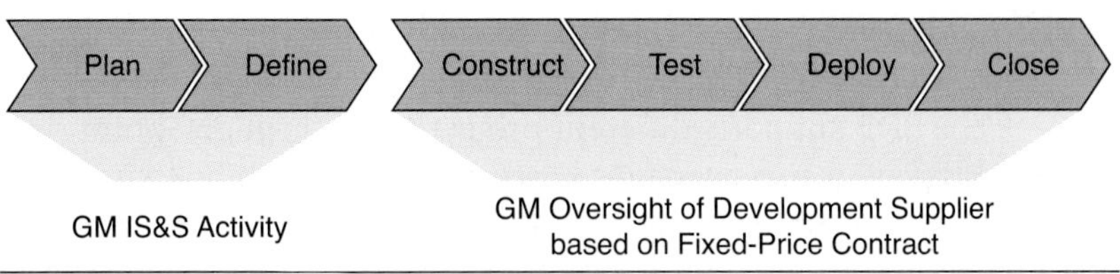

FIGURE 7.6
SDP Phase Overview

phases the GM activities focus on supplier management and oversight, as well as business relationship management. GM does not prescribe the supplier development methodology. GM engages only high-maturity development organizations and wants to ensure that these organizations fully leverage their development capabilities. Based on this philosophy, GM monitors progress and quality, but does not manage the tasks, resources, or environments used for development.

During the Construct phase, GM sets expectations for the supplier and requires the supplier to obtain the necessary environments and to design and develop the system. GM accepts the detailed system designs and test plans developed by the supplier. The supplier then constructs the system and demonstrates complete functionality to GM before leaving the Construct phase.

In the Test phase, the system is moved to the targeted hosting center and is placed into a pre-production environment. In this environment, tests are performed to verify the functionality, performance, scalability, and security of the system. The supplier is responsible for performing these tests and providing GM with the results. After these tests are accepted, the GM project manager will engage the business user for a User Acceptance Test. Once the business customer accepts the system, the supplier deploys the system in coordination with the business-driven training and process rollout.

GM expects suppliers to deliver high-quality systems into production. In accordance with this, suppliers provide GM with rolling 90-day warranties for all systems. The warranty begins when the systems are first deployed into production. During the warranty period, the supplier is responsible for addressing all high-severity defects encountered in the production environment, and the warranty period for the system is reset for an additional 90 days upon remediation of the defect.

In addition to the activities in each phase, recurring activities are defined in the SDP that describe how the project team periodically ensures that the project is executing according to plan (from both a GM and a supplier perspective) and that management is provided with appropriate updates. Standard metrics are collected and reported. Work products are baselined, changes are evaluated and decided upon, and auditors independent of the projects conduct process reviews to ensure that processes are being followed.

Figure 7.7 shows more details regarding the activities conducted in the execution of a GM Standard project.

System Delivery Process (SDP)

Plan	*Define*	*Construct*	*Test*	*Deploy*	*Close*
Initiate Project	Develop System Requirements	Conduct Joint GM/Performing Supplier Kick-Off	Accept Test Readiness	Verify Operational Readiness	Authorize De-Installation of Legacy System
Develop Process Design	Make Reuse / Buy / Build Decision	Accept Detailed Design	Accept Test Results	Authorize Promote to Production	Certify Project Completion
Develop Project Charter	Develop Architectural Design and IT BoM	Procure Additional External Services	Accept Site out Over and Back Out Steps	Analyze Deployment Results	
Develop Business Requirements	Develop Test Strategy	Accept Test Plans and Test Cases	Accept System Training		
Tailor SDP	Finalize Overall Estimate	Accept Site / Pilot Plans	Accept System		
Develop Initial Overall Estimate	Finalize Integrated Project Plan and Schedule				
Develop Integrated Project Plan and Schedule					

FIGURE 7.7
An Overview of the Standard SDP

The SDP was purposely developed to align with CMMI-ACQ. GM had to internalize the model and translate its intent into meaningful processes to ensure that the users of the SDP could relate to the terms in the way they have to execute. Before SDP could be deployed, it was reviewed by representatives from each business unit and geography described in the IS&S organizational structure earlier. The next section describes some of the CMMI-ACQ process areas and how GM implemented them at IS&S.

Realizing Value from the CMMI-ACQ at GM

GM IS&S recognizes the importance of each component of the CMMI-ACQ model. Certain process areas, however, are critical to the success of IT acquisition for GM. The sections that follow discuss these areas, the value they contribute to GM, and GM's implementation of their practices.

Acquisition Requirements Development

As GM aligned its processes with the CMMI-ACQ model and the new IT sourcing model, IS&S leadership recognized the criticality of developing effective requirements in collaboration with their GM business customers. Unclear or incorrect business and system requirements can compromise functionality and the business objective. Analysis of project history demonstrated that improper requirements definition and management were the major causes of project delays and cost overruns. With this understanding, it became a priority to define a robust requirements development process that aligns to the CMMI-ACQ model specific goal 1, "Develop Customer Requirements."

The process development team began by identifying the essential stakeholders and participants in requirements development. Roles were defined for a *requirements lead*, an organizational role responsible for requirements ownership throughout the project and oversight of requirements across multiple projects, and for a *requirements analyst* whose primary responsibility is requirements elicitation and documentation. Processes describing how these roles interact, and the deliverables they produce, were defined.

An essential objective of the requirements development process is to accurately capture the knowledge of GM business representatives. History has proven that the best technology in the world cannot compensate for a lack of understanding of business needs. IS&S requirements analysts have effectively utilized business process

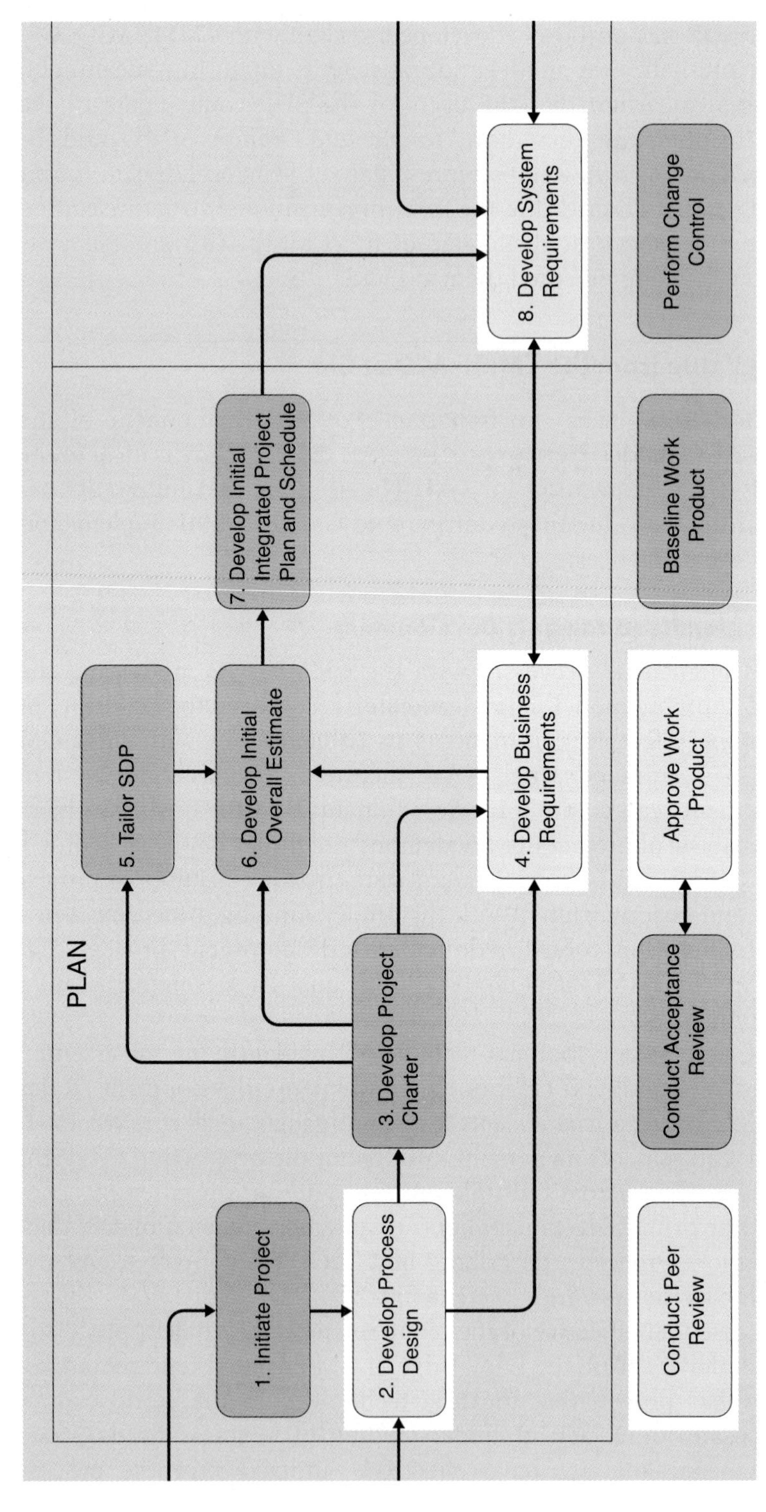

FIGURE 7.8
Requirements Process in SDP

analysis, early in the process, to understand the business situation and analyze the impacts that process and technology changes may have on it (see Figure 7.8).

Use cases are also developed to model system behavior under various business conditions. Each use case consists of a set of possible sequences of interactions among systems and users in a particular environment and related to a particular goal. The use cases must contain all system activities that have significance to the users. In business situations where requirements need even further clarification or are of particular significance to the users, visualization techniques are implemented.

Visualization is the process of presenting a prototype in a form that facilitates an understanding of data and system concepts that are not readily evident in typical textual descriptions. Visualization techniques have proven useful in establishing operational concepts and in validating requirements throughout the requirements lifecycle. A standard visualization tool set is utilized by requirements analysts to develop functional prototypes early in the project. These prototypes mimic the functionality of the proposed systems and are used to collaborate with the business customers, reach alignment, understand new business processes, and innovate on new concepts. The visualizations are also used with the business to clarify and validate requirements, elicit new requirements, and provide a working model of the key functionality of the system. The prototypes are further leveraged with GM development suppliers to ensure that they fully understand the requirements and functionality of the desired solution. Additionally, GM has found that visualizations provide a jump-start in the development of system training materials.

To further improve the efficiency of the requirements process, GM developed the concept of enterprise standard requirements. The genesis for standard requirements is the concept that many requirements are repeated by numerous projects throughout an organization. Within GM, standard requirements cover topics including security, privacy, globalization, regulatory compliance, and disaster recovery. The standard system requirement specification (SRS) was enhanced to include a section that identifies the standard requirements applicable to the project. The process team developed a questionnaire-based tool that guides the requirements team to determine which standard requirements apply to their project. A formal deviation process also was defined for projects to use when they identify that a standard requirement does not apply to a particular project.

Requirements are moved forward as an input to the contracting process once the project team and the business customer are confident that the requirements are accurate, complete, and prioritized. In the contracting process, requirements are allocated to one or more suppliers to achieve effective delivery and integration. Contracts with suppliers define not only their specific deliverables but also their integration activities with other suppliers. Linking the requirements development process directly to the contracting process helps GM align day-to-day work to specific goal 2 of Acquisition Requirements Development process area, "Develop Contractual Requirements."

GM's commitment to developing requirements capabilities is reinforced by a central Requirements team within CS&TO. A dedicated team with a full-time program manager oversees several initiatives annually to continuously improve the quality of requirements that GM elicits from its business customers and provides to its suppliers. The team also includes members, on a part-time basis, from each PIO organization and all key suppliers. Like other teams in GM, some team members are located in the United States and some are located in other regions. The team also has suppliers involved so that they can provide input to the processes; that is, training and other assets the team creates and makes available to the enterprise via the corporate intranet (see Figure 7.9).

The suppliers to GM can be thought of as the "customers" of requirements that GM produces. GM works with the suppliers to understand the information required to accurately price and respond to GM's project requests. Through collaborative efforts across organizational boundaries, the center of excellence team drives improved project performance by ensuring that the requirements at their foundation are effective for system delivery. Suppliers are provided input to the standard requirements, which are provided with each system requirements specification. They also participate in forums to discuss best practices in requirements, including use case development, visualization, and elicitation techniques. Through this ongoing dialog with suppliers, GM ensures that high-quality resources are provided when GM supplements its staff. This dialog also moves both sides forward toward a common understanding of effective requirements. This helps suppliers bid accurately on projects and deliver solutions that delight GM business customers.

The emphasis GM has placed on the importance of requirements has been well received by both internal resources and suppliers. Understanding the business situation helps project teams deliver appropriate technology to meet business needs, and visualization has

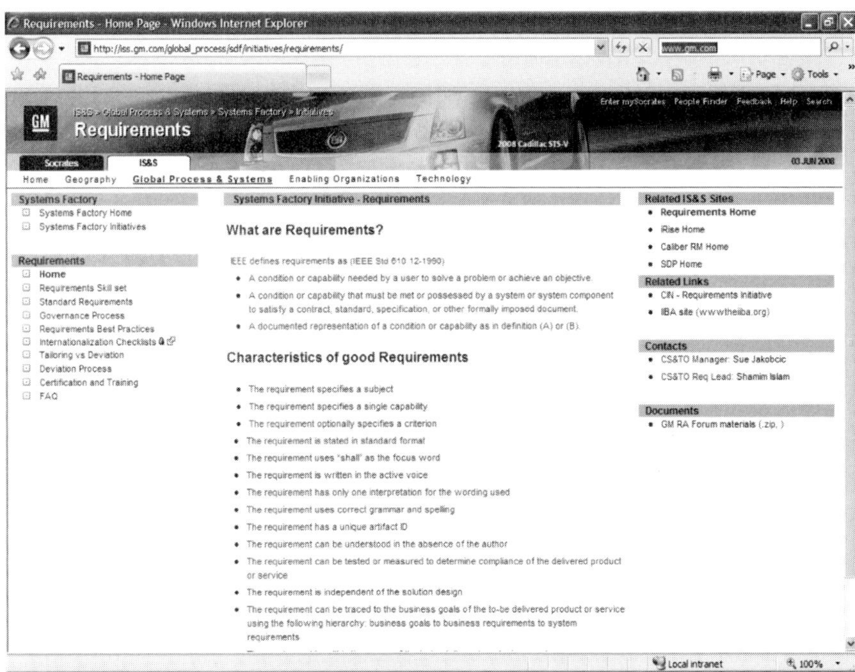

FIGURE 7.9
Requirements Intranet Site

brought that understanding to new levels of clarity for both the customer and the provider. Since project teams cross organizational boundaries, it is absolutely critical that projects develop accurate requirements. If requirements are ambiguous, changes to these requirements are very expensive since they may require contract changes. Identifying standard requirements has institutionalized consistency in critical areas and helped the project teams operate more efficiently. In the long run, GM's investment in the center of excellence and other requirements initiatives will continue to generate high returns through successful projects for GM.

Project Planning and Project Monitoring and Control

Project management for an acquisition organization is as important, if not more important, than project management in an organization where systems are developed internally. Project managers have to actively manage the commitments and tasks of the acquisition team in addition to understanding the true status of the supplier commitments. In organizations that acquire technology products and services, acquisition project managers must ensure that they actively manage the project and that they do not delegate management responsibilities to suppliers. It is only through active management that the acquisition project manager will identify project issues and be prepared to proactively take corrective action.

GM realizes that successful projects require a strong GM project manager who is accountable to the business customer and who will actively manage suppliers. GM project managers are trained on SDP and are careful that they manage suppliers to ensure that commitments and deliverables are fulfilled. They are equally careful that they do not manage the staff or tasks of the supplier.

Effective and efficient project management is critical to successful acquisition of technology. For GM projects to be successful, they must meet the goals of Project Planning and Project Monitoring and Control. To this end, the SDP clearly defines the GM IS&S project manager role, and the processes for developing a comprehensive, integrated project plan, with regular touch points for monitoring and controlling both GM and supplier activities. This GM IS&S project manager is accountable for delivery to the business customer and has to balance the amount of effort spent managing to achieve the appropriate amount of supplier oversight without performing the role for which the supplier is paid by GM.

During project planning, the project teams build a plan to realize the vision established during project funding. Initial planning steps ensure that the right resources, including systems engineers, requirements analysts, the PMO, and the business customer, are engaged to start the project. These steps include development of requirements, as described earlier, development of the acquisition strategy, and project estimation. The team also considers how the solution will be deployed and where it will be hosted.

GM's project managers and estimation experts use a standard estimation process to develop the project estimate (see Figure 7.10). The estimation process is used to estimate both GM and supplier activities. The standard process also provides a structured approach to estimating based on historical data, and four additional estimation techniques (function-point-based and use-case-based) can be added via tailoring to enhance the accuracy of the estimate. The foundation for, and critical input to, the estimate are the combination of business and system requirements along with the acquisition strategy, any of which can drive overall cost and effort and must be clear in order to engage suppliers.

Following GM's estimation, suppliers are engaged to propose solutions to meet their allocated requirements within the context of

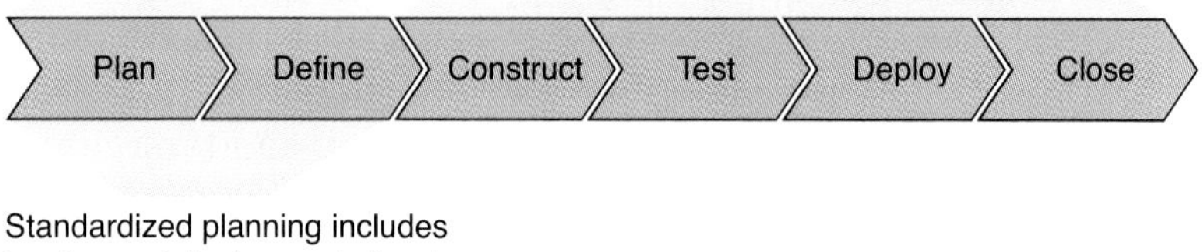

FIGURE 7.10
GM Project Management Focus in SDP

the project activities and deliverables. Multiple suppliers may be involved in the proposal process. For example, one supplier may perform software development while another assumes responsibility for sustaining the solution. GM ensures that a primary supplier is identified, and all of the parties must come to a consensus on the project parameters. When this is accomplished and the proposal is accepted, the GM project manager integrates the plans into one overall plan for project delivery. Then the project manager aligns the supplier project team with the project expectations.

The first step in bringing on board the supplier project team, which may or may not have been involved with the proposal process, is a meeting between the GM team and the supplier team. The overall plan is reviewed, and suppliers describe their tailored processes for the specific project. The team sets expectations for delivery and acceptance of work products and deliverables. The team also confirms expectations for metrics to be reported and periodic touch points.

As defined in the standard contracts, supplier project managers must meet with the GM IS&S project manager on a regular basis so that IS&S does not lose visibility and can help remove roadblocks. During project progress reviews, the team reviews the integrated plan and schedule, and issues may be escalated for GM resolution. If issues are raised, GM and the supplier determine the appropriate corrective action and manage it to closure. Risks are regularly reviewed and mitigated to maintain high, on-time delivery standards. GM project managers focus on actively managing the outcomes and deliverables of the suppliers, rather than monitoring and controlling the tasks themselves (see Figure 7.10).

With a wide variety of stakeholders to satisfy, from the business customer to other IS&S groups to suppliers, GM project managers must establish and maintain plans that communicate direction and provide a mechanism for tracking. The monitoring and control activity includes not only ensuring supplier oversight but also ensuring that GM resources are engaged and are meeting their commitments. Developing and executing processes that enable these activities across GM align IS&S to the Project Planning and Project Monitoring and Control process areas in CMMI-ACQ.

Integrated Project Management

When the GM team and the supplier team collaborate as described in the preceding section, the opportunity to deliver value to the business increases significantly. Additional benefits are achieved by incorporating practices from the CMMI-ACQ Integrated Project Management practice. Accordingly, GM has invested in processes and tools that drive integration and synergy. The processes enable projects to tailor the SDP to meet project-specific requirements, manage the project using an overall integrated plan, and ensure that relevant stakeholders are involved.

Project tailoring of the SDP is executed using a standard tailoring matrix. The matrix shows the standard processes that projects are expected to follow, as well as decisions the projects make to "tailor in" additional processes to ensure quality delivery or to "tailor out" processes that are not applicable to the unique aspects of the project. The PMO reviews the project tailoring to determine additional opportunities to deliver more efficiently or effectively based on the performance of other projects. The executive in charge of the delivery center then approves the tailoring.

Once tailoring is complete, the team develops the Integrated Project Plan (IPP), which integrates all of the other plans for the project. The IPP allows any stakeholder to quickly understand the project scope, resources, and timing. To ensure that this plan is developed consistently across all IS&S projects, a template is included in the SDP. The plan covers acquisition strategy, milestones, deliverables, quality assurance, configuration management, and many other critical areas. The IPP is developed in two phases: The first phase occurs before planning and requirements and the second phase occurs afterward. The IPP is then maintained throughout the life of the project.

GM provides a number of tools to project managers to assist in coordination of and collaboration with many stakeholders, and to provide consistency across projects. The GM SDP RASIC is one of these tools. The RASIC chart describes the roles of team members who are Responsible for executing and Approving the process. The chart also describes Support roles, and roles that should be Informed of status and completion and Consulted along the way. . The RASIC chart is a global standard for GM, and each project has individuals assuming these roles (see Figure 7.11 for an excerpt).

Name of Activity	*Develop Initial Intergated Project Plan*	*Prioritize System Requirements*	*Conduct Acceptance Review of System Test Results*
Business Project Champion	I	S	
Business SME	S	S	
CM Lead	S		
Integrator Application Architect		S	S
Integrator Infrastructure Architect		S	S
Integrator Program Management Office	S		
Integrator Quality Assurance	S		
Integrator Test Lead			S
Moderator			R
Performing Supplier—Development (PS-D)			C
Performing Supplier—Infrastructure (PS-I)	C	S	C
Performing Supplier—Sustain (PS-S)	C	S	S
Project Architect		S	S
Project Manager	R	A	A
Requirements Analyst	S	R	
Requirements Lead		C	
Senior Manager	A	I	I
Services Management	C	S	
Site Manager	C	S	I
Test Manager		S	S

FIGURE 7.11
SDP RASIC Excerpt

Project teams within GM are encouraged to reuse process assets when feasible, and to contribute to continuous improvement of common assets. Business units submit examples of best practices to the Integrator Project Management Office (IPMO). The IPMO coaches projects on best practices, and works with the corporate process team to incorporate these best practices into the SDP. Project team members may also provide process improvement ideas electronically, at any time, directly to the SDP continuous improvement team, which logs and tracks each proposal until it is implemented or declined.

Integrating all project plans into the IPP and establishing a standard RASIC chart positions GM project managers to successfully deliver projects. The project teams feed improvements back into the organizational process assets based on their experience using them. Together, these activities help GM to align its work to the goals of Integrated Project Management and to ensure that integrated GM and supplier teams continue to deliver successful projects with the available budget and time as specified in the supplier agreements.

Solicitation and Supplier Agreement Development

Relationships between acquirers and suppliers are complex, and the agreements between them, which can vary from company to company and region to region, add to the complexity. GM IS&S leveraged lessons learned by the GM business, and took significant steps to ensure that the supplier agreements would support the new IT sourcing model by enabling a cohesive working environment between the supplier and GM, and among suppliers.

IS&S analyzed the different types of sourcing arrangements that were in place and decided to capitalize on best practices from GM's supply chain organization. IS&S negotiated general service contracts (GSCs) with a select group of large, global IT companies capable of supporting the GM business. Each supplier is aligned to one or more of the major business processes supported by the IS&S PIO leaders. In exchange for a long-term contract with GM that allowed the suppliers to plan, learn, and staff accordingly, the suppliers are expected to provide business domain knowledge to the business unit they support. Identifying target suppliers and negotiating long-term GSCs provides significant efficiencies for GM and the supplier. It allows project request and response activities to focus on project deliverables and avoids project teams having to negotiate terms and conditions for each project.

The GM project team packages its requirements in an Information Technology Service Request (ITSR) for the supplier, which is very similar to a Request for Proposal (RFP), and the supplier team provides a response. The two teams then negotiate scope, effort, and timing, but do not have to negotiate rates or legal terms and conditions, which are already defined in the GSC. If the project has unique needs that the main supplier cannot meet, the project team may pursue new suppliers using a rigorous solicitation process.

Key to the sourcing model, the supplier agreements also define how suppliers must interact with other suppliers. For example, if one supplier develops a solution and another supplier has to support it, both suppliers must agree that the solution is ready for transition.

Clear, robust agreements between GM and its suppliers enable this complex internal and external resourced organization to deliver and support capabilities for the GM business. The contracts have been structured in a way that minimizes negotiations and allows teams to spend more time on solutions. These agreements not only set expectations about how suppliers will support GM, but also specify how suppliers interact with other suppliers. They also reference GM standards that suppliers will have to meet in order to deploy their solution in the GM environment.

Acquisition Technical Management

GM has partnered with technical resources from IT suppliers for many years. Throughout this time frame, GM has observed that there is often inconsistency regarding technical recommendations among suppliers, and often from within the same suppliers. Supplier architects may advocate particular vendors, product lines, or technologies that they are familiar with, rather than what is in the best interest of the customer. GM realized that in order to drive standardization and simplification, IS&S must drive the overall architecture of systems, and institute a strong governance process to determine which technology can be used in GM systems.

For GM to maintain control over the IS&S technical landscape, a corporate process was established to submit, review, and approve technology components. Once approved, the components become a part of GM IT Standards and are then eligible for inclusion in new solutions. The Standards group approves standard infrastructure (e.g., hardware, network, and supporting software), commercial-off-the-shelf (COTS) business applications, and technology platforms. Suppliers submit a *Bill-of-IT,* a list of the technology components to be used, that conforms to the established IT standards. The GM architect for the project (identified in the RASIC), with support from the Joint Architecture Management Council (JAMC) mentioned previously,

FIGURE 7.12
GM Architecture Principles

ensures that the solution makes sense for the GM environment (see Figure 7.12). Solutions not conforming to the standards must be validated and approved by a global, cross-functional committee. Technical reviews are conducted throughout the life of the project to ensure that solution designs are aligned with both functional and technical requirements.

In addition to project-level technical management, a corporate-level team of systems engineers looks for opportunities to leverage technologies across projects and business units. This team has successfully consolidated the number of systems GM utilizes globally. Continued success in this area allows the company to continue to reduce GM's budget for maintenance and operations, and to shift that spending instead to reinvest in delivering new capabilities to the GM business.

Acquisition Validation

To ensure that the solutions developed by the IT suppliers support the GM business as specified, validation steps have been incorporated throughout the project lifecycle (see Figure 7.13). GM validates supplier designs, tests, and deployment results. This validation occurs by accepting these and other supplier deliverables at predefined points in the project.

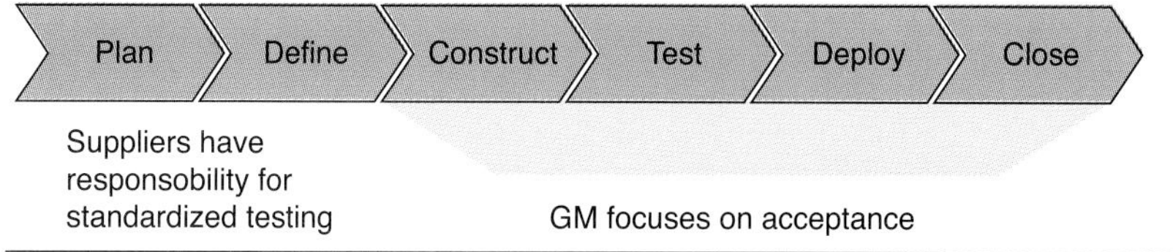

FIGURE 7.13
Ensuring Product Quality at GM

Each development project has a predefined set of deliverables. In the Construct, Test, and Deploy phases of the SDP, these deliverables are the responsibility of the supplier, and they include detailed solution design (within the constraints of IT standards), testing artifacts (including test plans, test cases, and test results), user acceptance and training, and deployment to one or more GM environments. For each deliverable, a standard set of acceptance criteria is provided to the supplier before work commences. The validation is not complete until each acceptance criterion has been met and confirmed by GM.

Acceptance review dates are scheduled based on supplier commitments to provide project deliverables and are documented in the integrated plan. In an acceptance review, the supplier provides context for the deliverable to the evaluating GM subject matter experts. The acceptance criteria are then used to determine whether the deliverable is ready. If the deliverable is ready, it is accepted and the supplier is approved for payment. If the deliverable is not ready, GM notes the criteria the deliverable failed to meet. The supplier resolves any defects and subsequent reviews occur until the deliverable is acceptable. GM suppliers demonstrate capability by delivering a high percentage of first-time acceptances across multiple projects.

A unique characteristic of user acceptance testing within GM is that both the system and the training materials are accepted. In addition to the system functionality itself, users must have whatever additional information they need to leverage the system prior to the supplier receiving full payment. The GM operations supplier responsible for supporting the new application also participates in the acceptance of user guides and related materials.

GM suppliers operate under fixed-price contracts, and are paid only after validation of their deliverables. Upon acceptance of a deliverable, contract management and finance representatives are notified and the supplier is allowed to invoice. Thus, acquisition validation at GM must be tightly aligned with the development and management of supplier agreements.

Agreement Management

Organizations that acquire rather than develop their IT products and services need to manage their agreements once they are established. Suppliers typically will not exceed their commitments, and it is up to the acquirer to ensure that the commitments are met.

At GM, project and contract managers collaborate to ensure that GSC requirements and ITSR requirements are met. Project managers assess and report supplier performance throughout project execution. Contract managers regularly summarize the results of project performance and customer feedback surveys and provide feedback to suppliers through a standard supplier score card. If inadequate performance is detected in either of these channels, a formal corrective action process remedies any issues and facilitates improvements needed to enhance future performance.

To ensure that solutions are sustainable, GM requires a 90-day warranty period for all new applications, commencing on the deployment of the application to its final environment. During this period, the supplier keeps the development team in place to resolve any issues. Warranties are extended for an additional 90 days if issues are discovered during the initial period.

GM manages supplier agreements through multiple channels. The project manager and contract manager both provide suppliers with regular feedback, and the 90-day warranty period is an incentive to ensure that defects are not brought into the GM environment.

Acquisition Verification

GM IS&S realizes that its own commitment to quality drives the eventual success of any project it conducts. GM deliverables must be accurate, and project stakeholders must commit to the deliverables, if the projects that produce them are going to be successful. To ensure this high level of quality and commitment, GM performs verification throughout the lifecycle of each project on the deliverables for which GM is responsible. GM also participates in verification of supplier deliverables when appropriate.

A project selects the deliverables to be verified during the tailoring process. For most deliverables that GM produces, a peer review is conducted with a standard checklist of criteria to ensure that reviewers use every opportunity to identify defects. For deliverables not undergoing a peer review, an inspection and approval process is often used.

The "peer review" process at IS&S is unique in comparison to most industry standards. IS&S uses peer reviews not only to receive feedback from peers in comparable roles, but also to gather feedback from stakeholders affected by the work product. For example, when a project peer reviews an SRS, requirements Subject Matter Experts SMEs are joined by test leads to ensure that the requirements are testable, and by the project architect to ensure that the requirements are clear for the solution architecture. By including these stakeholders earlier in the development lifecycle, GM teams are building commitment and consensus to the project approach. GM truly believes that the costs associated with involving stakeholders early in the process are much lower than the costs incurred when defects are identified later in the project lifecycle, when they are much more expensive to fix.

By definition, acquisition practices cross organizational boundaries as acquirers engage suppliers to develop their systems. Verification practices are critical to the success of the acquirer in engaging a supplier. These practices ensure that the right stakeholders are involved and aligned before the supplier is engaged. Verification also helps to prevent defects from being injected into the lifecycle before expensive processes such as contract changes have to be executed to fix the defects. These processes and others must be measured and analyzed to ensure that they are effective at meeting their objectives.

Measurement and Analysis

With an organization as large and complex as GM, there are many opportunities to measure and gather data. When suppliers are engaged, those opportunities increase exponentially as each supplier has metrics that it uses in addition to the metrics inside GM. At GM, measurements that are valuable and sustained over time are focused on measuring performance that will drive management objectives. GM is cautious to collect only those metrics that will be used and can be acted upon. Metric information can become stale as processes change. GM will not burden itself or its suppliers by collecting data that is not actionable.

GM currently gathers data and reports measures that drive the overall objectives of innovation, simplification, and cost reduction. Figure 7.14 highlights some of the unique measurement relationships that GM uses to track progress toward those goals.

IS&S projects at GM gather this data through global standard tools. Derived measures are reported in executive dashboards tailored to each executive's role. Some dashboards are regionally based (for a CIO in charge of one of GM's regions) and others are process area based (for a PIO that is in charge of a global process area).

Example Measurement Objectives	*Measurement Information Categories*	*Example Base Measures*	*Example Derived Measures*
Reduced number of systems	Architecture	Number of new systems in production; number of systems decommissioned	Percentage system reduction
Deliver business value	Schedule	Estimated and actual start and end dates by deliverable	Percentage of deliverables on time
Simplify IT environment	Bill-of-IT	Number of systems compliant with IT standards; total number of systems in production	Percentage of systems compliant with IT standards
Ensure customer satisfaction	Business value	Customer satisfaction survey score	Average satisfaction score by process area
Leverage suppliers	Quality delivery	Number of work products with first-time acceptance	Percentage of work products with first-time acceptance by supplier
Increase supplier performance	Supplier feedback	Business competency Quality (each ranking from 1 to 5)	Competency trend over time Quality over time

FIGURE 7.14
Example GM Measurement Relationships

Globally derived measures are regularly reported to the Group Vice President in charge of IS&S as well as to staff members for analysis and action.

Several of GM's business units have been gathering and reporting these measures for many years. They now have sufficient data to quantitatively manage critical processes, not only within GM but also to manage supplier processes. Some pieces of the SDP have been developed in a way that allows for these measures and high-maturity practices to be leveraged by those business units when they are appropriate for the project. GM will continue to evolve these measures and high-maturity practices where they will add the most business value.

The foundation for effective measurement and analysis is clear objectives. GM's management has been very clear about what it needs from IS&S in terms of innovation, cost reduction, and simplification. IS&S has adopted measures that help the project teams and support organizations focus on delivering on those objectives. Measurement and analysis has been a critical process for IS&S' success in the acquisition environment, and will continue to be improved over time to adapt to the changing needs of the business.

GM to CMMI-ACQ Practice Mapping

The CMMI-ACQ model contains many important concepts. GM needed to consider lessons learned from managing IT suppliers, the business environment, and project history to decide where focused efforts were required to achieve the most leverage from the model. GM's processes align to each process area of the CMMI-ACQ model, but history and vision have driven leadership to focus on the several process areas that were mentioned in the previous paragraphs. Figure 7.15 summarizes these process areas, the unique GM implementation, and the value that these implementations have institutionalized across IS&S.

Realizing the value in the processes was critical to success at GM. Just as critical to success is to deploy those processes globally to the extended IS&S team. Institutionalization around the world is the only way that IS&S will be successful, and the next section describes GM's approach to this tremendous organizational change.

Managing Process Deployment and Change

In an organization as large and complex as GM, making and sustaining significant operational change is very challenging. The new IS&S

CMMI-ACQ Process Area	*GM Implementation*	*GM Benefits*
Acquisition Requirements Development	• Standard requirements • Visualization	• Accurate supplier estimates • Better project execution
Acquisition Technical Management	• Standard Bill-of-IT • Governance structures	• Control over architecture • Simplification of environment
Project Planning	• Standard estimation tool • Supplier on-boarding	• Accurate estimation • Supplier alignment
Project Monitoring and Control	• Progress reviews • GM *and* supplier tracking	• Issue escalation and resolution
Integrated Project Management	• Standard tailoring matrix • Standard RASIC	• Projects move quickly • Clear line of responsibility
Acquisition Verification	• Peer review GM deliverables with wide range of stakeholders	• Plans and requirements are accurate before GM commits
Acquisition Validation	• Acceptance reviews • Standard acceptance criteria	• Suppliers know what to expect before payment
Solicitation and Supplier Agreement Development	• Master service contracts • IT service requests	• Less time negotiating, more time focused on delivery
Agreement Management	• Supplier score card • 90-day warranty period	• Consistent supplier feedback • No defects in production
Measurement and Analysis	• Measure customer satisfaction • Measure system reduction	• Ensure that business is satisfied • Sustain cost reduction

FIGURE 7.15
Summary of Realizing CMMI-ACQ Value for GM

business model would enable GM to leverage suppliers for innovative solutions that contributed to the GM business, but not unless it was well understood and embraced by the entire organization. To build these acquisition capabilities, GM had to deploy a comprehensive change management strategy, including communications, training, support, and continuous improvement.

The communications strategy involved informing IS&S employees and suppliers of their new roles and responsibilities. Target stakeholders varied from GM employees to GM agents (suppliers in GM roles) to developing suppliers to suppliers of IT system maintenance and support. To reach this wide variety of stakeholders, GM had to use several communication channels.

Town hall-style meetings, conducted live at GM's North American headquarters and broadcast via Webcast globally, informed GM employees about the new business model and the changes in their roles and responsibilities. These meetings were reinforced with in-person training sessions on standardized work (discussed earlier), which provides boundaries on the processes critical to the success of the new organizational model. GM continues to use town hall meetings to provide strategic information to the GM IS&S community.

Cross-functional teams, composed of GM business and IS&S resources, along with supplier resources, were formed to develop processes at the work instruction level. The results of their work were incorporated into new versions of the SDP and standard RASIC. On return to their respective parts of the extended organization, team participants served as change agents, addressing issues and answering questions regarding the new framework.

Development of the SDP was followed by a global deployment, organizational change, and training program (see Figure 7.16). The new version of SDP that supports CMMI-ACQ was introduced with a set of global "SDP Days." These were one-day seminars, held globally, that provided a high-level overview of the process and roles of the SDP. This was followed with role-based training courses, delivered in face-to-face environments by trainers with practical experience within and outside the GM environment. Training ranged from executive awareness sessions of a few hours, to multiday training that included individual and team exercises and exams. Training sessions were recorded and made available to new employees and supplier partners.

GM put SDP Coaches in place in each process area and geographic region to continue support of the user community. An SDP Coach serves as the local point of contact for questions regarding the

FIGURE 7.16
GM's Deployment of the SDP

SDP process, and works with project teams to better understand complex topics such as project tailoring and estimating. Coaches also serve as the distribution point for updates to the SDP and are responsible for disseminating changes to their organizations.

Most important to all of these communication vehicles was the ongoing support of the leadership team described in the IS&S overview earlier. The PIOs, CIOs, and other senior executives supported the overall vision. The SFMC and JAMC reinforced communications to project teams and worked together to resolve implementation issues. These IS&S leaders were responsible for the initial push to move the company to its third generation of IT sourcing and are still responsible today for making IS&S a high-performing IT organization.

As one of the largest companies in the world with a global presence, GM has significant experience in making sustainable changes on a large scale. Simply creating processes that align to CMMI-ACQ would not have been enough to institutionalize the vision that IS&S leadership had formed. Training, regular communications, and commitment from executives were necessary to move GM to a more mature "customer" of IT products and services.

Integrated Tools Enable High-Performance Acquisition

GM recognizes that to gain the full benefits of CMMI-ACQ, proper tools must be implemented to facilitate and automate process activities and provide management visibility. Based on its concept of standardized work, GM developed a framework depicting the functionality of tools required for acquisition organizations. This framework, known internally within GM as IT-ERP, reveals that the tools utilized by acquisition organizations can be quite different from those required by development organizations. The tools required in acquisition include requirements definition, architecture management, project management, contract management, and financial controls. The acquisition organization is not concerned with compliers, defect trackers, unit testers, or automated build tools.

GM performed a market analysis and consulted with several major tool vendors regarding their current tool offerings. The results indicated that currently, IT tool sets are targeted toward development organizations and not acquisition organizations. To compensate for this, GM has developed a hybrid approach to tools. It has developed a set of custom-built tools with basic support for support program and application management. It supplements these with requirements visualization, contracting, and architecture tools from various vendors. GM has found that tools from various sources can be difficult to integrate with each other and into an integrated process. The lack of tool integration can cause extra work for project teams and cause delays in properly monitoring and managing project progress and costs. GM is sharing its IT-ERP concept with tool vendors and encouraging them to develop tool sets focused on the acquisition model. GM will continue to monitor the market for integrated acquisition tool sets.

Conducting Appraisals to Drive Change

A benefit of using a standard capability maturity model versus a proprietary model is the suite of tools that typically accompany a standard. Such is the case with the CMMI Product Suite. A key component of the SEI's suite is the Standard CMMI Appraisal Method for Process Improvement (SCAMPI) appraisal method. GM used SCAMPI appraisals to benchmark its business units under the previous CMMI-DEV model, and wanted to continue to use them with CMMI-ACQ to help drive and measure business change.

GM conducted several pilot appraisals following the SCAMPI B and SCAMPI C methods. The appraisals were insightful and drove several improvements to the CMMI-ACQ model based on model change requests from appraisal team members. The appraisals were also valuable as the findings identified improvements for GM's SDPs, including the example in the next paragraph.

While reviewing Solicitation and Supplier Agreement Development, the appraisal team did not identify anything to prevent GM from meeting its stated CMMI-ACQ goals. However, the team did notice that the contract management and system delivery processes could be better integrated to support project execution. After additional analysis, the process improvement team made improvements to the integration by adding references to contract management information early in the SDP and encouraging project teams to reach out to suppliers earlier so that they would be ready to respond quickly to new ITSRs.

GM is defining its global appraisal strategy as the conclusion on the moratorium for SCAMPI A appraisal approaches. The business value of the appraisals must be weighed against the cost and effort they require, and leveraged accordingly. GM will continue to use appraisals to identify improvements such as the one listed here and drive consistency across the globe.

Aligning Supplier Relationships

To drive innovation that addresses business needs, suppliers have to be in lock step with GM so that IS&S can respond when the business requires new capabilities. As such, GM invests heavily in supplier relationships to ensure that GM and key suppliers remain aligned in terms of vision, processes, contracts, and people. Several activities reinforce these relationships.

Annually, GM has a strategic planning session off-site where executives from GM and executives from each supplier establish a common vision of the state of IT, the state of the industry, and where each is moving in the future. The session includes strategic collaboration discussions in which suppliers can describe how they will help GM with business and IT goals, and GM gives direction to suppliers on what they will need to be successful both in the short term and in the long term. The executives collaborate on strategies for key initiatives that will provide opportunities for both the acquirer and the suppliers to be successful.

There are also regular joint forums between acquirers and suppliers at the practitioner level. In addition to the requirements forums discussed earlier, there are project management forums that ensure alignment with GM and supplier project managers. Suppliers regularly participate in process improvement initiatives and sit on the SDP continuous improvement team.

Each key supplier has a GM executive as a mentor. The mentor is involved in a different business unit than the business unit the supplier supports, so the mentor does not have direct influence over contracting decisions. In this situation, mentors can provide candid advice to the supplier about how the supplier can improve performance and success at GM.

Supplier relationships are critical in an acquisition environment. Aligning suppliers with GM and each other is a constant challenge. By investing in forums for executives, project team roles, and process development roles, GM provides a number of opportunities to communicate and align. The relationships that are developed out of these opportunities help drive the combined team toward the overall objective of helping GM design, build, and sell more great cars and trucks.

Future Actions

GM IS&S has realized significant benefits from working with the SEI to develop and apply CMMI-ACQ and plans to continue to work with the SEI on further developments of the CMMI Product Suite. GM will also continue to make improvements to IS&S system delivery processes, ensuring the delivery of high-quality systems to the GM business.

The SDP team within IS&S is constantly monitoring the software engineering community and requesting feedback from its internal organization and supplier base. It uses this feedback to drive future versions of the SDP. At the time this case study was prepared, the SDP team was piloting a version of the SDP that integrated Iterative and Agile development techniques into the acquisition model. After thoroughly analyzing these methodologies and consulting with industry experts, GM has developed an approach that integrates best practices for Agile methodologies and fully aligns with the core principles of the third-generation IT sourcing strategy.

The modifications allow projects to continue to develop robust requirements and visualizations early in the lifecycle. These are used to agree on prioritization with the business and develop a strategy for incremental delivery that aligns with the business goals. With this information, suppliers can develop fixed-price proposals to develop the systems in accordance with the requirements and incremental strategy. At the start of each iteration, business users participate in requirements validation sessions to incorporate their learning from previous iterations. This approach is being piloted by several business units and a strategy for its global deployment is under development.

There are many opportunities to standardize, measure, control, and improve system delivery processes in an environment as complex as that of GM. GM will continue to work with the SEI to identify best practices and next practices that support IS&S in delivering systems to help the business build better cars and trucks. GM will also continue to invest in improvements to its people, processes, and tools to drive innovation.

Summary

The CMMI-ACQ model helps GM focus on the capabilities and processes it must excel at in an environment where all IT development and support is sourced. As a capability maturity model, CMMI-ACQ also provides a road map for continuous process improvement. Its design has a broad range of potential applications, as evidenced by its compatibility with the IS&S business model.

After an extensive change management program, IS&S now executes consistent processes, globally, in accordance with its standardized work. Mechanisms are in place to allow the continuous improvement of the SDP, including a governance structure and coaching program. There is a special focus on the areas in which GM must be particularly effective, including requirements development, project management, technical management, and supplier management.

GM has seen significant, beneficial results from the new IS&S business model and the adoption of CMMI-ACQ. The IT cost per vehicle at GM is now among the lowest in the industry. Some of the best IT companies in the world now work together, under the direction of GM, to deliver innovative solutions for the business. Process and technology improvements together have allowed GM IS&S to offer more capability to the business, more efficiently. These improvements have also propelled GM toward world leadership in transportation products and related services.

PART TWO

Generic Goals and Generic Practices, and the Process Areas

GENERIC GOALS AND GENERIC PRACTICES

Overview

This section describes, in detail, all CMMI generic goals and generic practices—model components that directly address process institutionalization.

The text of the generic goals and generic practices is not repeated in the process areas. As you address each process area, refer back to this section for details of all generic practices.

TIP

The generic goals and generic practices in the CMMI for Development model are repeated with each process area along with process-area-specific elaborations. This is not the case in CMMI-ACQ. Listing them only in this section means that you will need to refer to this section often for the application of generic goals and generic practices to each process area.

Process Institutionalization

Institutionalization is an important concept in process improvement. When mentioned in the generic goal and generic practice descriptions, institutionalization implies that the process is ingrained in the way the work is performed and there is commitment and consistency to performing the process.

An institutionalized process is more likely to be retained during times of stress. When the requirements and objectives for the process change, however, the implementation of the process may also need to change to ensure that it remains effective. The generic practices describe activities that address these aspects of institutionalization.

The degree of institutionalization is embodied in the generic goals and in the names of the processes that correspond to each goal as indicated in Table 8.1.

HINT

Consider institutionalization mismatches when working process issues that span multiple organizations. An acquirer that has institutionalized a "quantitatively managed" requirements process working with a supplier that has institutionalized a "managed" requirements process may need to pay attention to negotiating measurement definitions across the team.

TABLE 8.1 Generic Goals and Process Names

Generic Goal	*Progression of Processes*
GG 1	Performed process
GG 2	Managed process
GG 3	Defined process
GG 4	Quantitatively managed process
GG 5	Optimizing process

The progression of process institutionalization is characterized in the following descriptions of each process.

Performed Process

A performed process is a process that accomplishes the work necessary to produce work products. The specific goals of the process area are satisfied.

Managed Process

A managed process is a performed process that is planned and executed in accordance with policy; employs skilled people who have adequate resources to produce controlled outputs; involves relevant stakeholders; is monitored, controlled, and reviewed; and is evaluated for adherence to its process description. The process may be used by a project, group, or organizational function. Management of the process focuses on achieving the objectives established for the process, such as cost, schedule, and quality. The control provided by a managed process ensures that the established process is retained during times of stress.

The organization establishes requirements and objectives for the process. The status of the work products and delivery of the services are visible to management at defined points (e.g., at major milestones and completion of major tasks). Commitments are established among those performing the work and the relevant stakeholders and these commitments are revised as necessary. Work products are reviewed with relevant stakeholders and are controlled. The work products and services satisfy their specified requirements.

A critical distinction between a performed process and a managed process is the extent to which the process is managed. A managed process is planned (the plan may be part of a more encompassing plan) and the performance of the process is managed against the plan. Corrective actions are taken when the actual results deviate significantly from the plan. A managed process achieves the objectives of the plan and is institutionalized for consistent performance.

Defined Process

A defined process is a managed process that is tailored from the organization's set of standard processes according to the organization's tailoring guidelines; has a maintained process description; and contributes work products, measures, and other process improvement information to the organizational process assets.

The organizational process assets are artifacts that relate to describing, implementing, and improving processes. These artifacts are assets because they are developed or acquired to meet the business objectives of the organization, and they represent investments by the organization that are expected to provide current and future business value.

The organization's set of standard processes, which are the basis of the defined process, are established and improved over time. Standard processes describe fundamental process elements that are expected in defined processes. Standard processes also describe relationships (e.g., the ordering and the interfaces) among these process elements. The organization-level infrastructure to support current and future use of the organization's set of standard processes is established and improved over time. (See the definition of "standard process" in the glossary.)

A project's defined process provides a basis for planning, performing, and improving the project's tasks and activities. A project may have more than one defined process (e.g., one for developing the product and another for testing the product).

A defined process clearly states the following:

- Purpose
- Inputs
- Entry criteria
- Activities
- Roles
- Measures
- Verification steps
- Outputs
- Exit criteria

A critical distinction between a managed process and a defined process is the scope of application of the process descriptions, standards, and procedures. For a managed process, the process descriptions, standards, and procedures are applicable to a particular project, group, or organizational function. As a result, the managed processes of two projects in one organization may be different.

Another critical distinction is that a defined process is described in more detail and is performed more rigorously than a managed process. This means that improvement information is easier to understand, analyze, and use. Finally, management of the defined process is based on the additional insight provided by an understanding of the interrelationships of the process activities and detailed measures of the process, its work products, and its services.

Quantitatively Managed Process

A quantitatively managed process is a defined process that is controlled using statistical and other quantitative techniques. The product quality, service quality, and process-performance attributes are measurable and controlled throughout the project.

Quantitative objectives are established based on the capability of the organization's set of standard processes; the organization's business objectives; and the needs of the customer, end users, organization, and process implementers, subject to the availability of resources. The people performing the process are directly involved in quantitatively managing the process.

Quantitative management is performed on the overall set of processes that produces a product. The subprocesses that significantly contribute to overall process performance are statistically managed. For these selected subprocesses, detailed measures of process performance are collected and statistically analyzed. Special causes of process variation are identified and, as appropriate, the source of the special cause is addressed to prevent its recurrence.

Quality and process-performance measures are incorporated into the organization's measurement repository to support future fact-based decision making.

Activities for quantitatively managing the performance of a process include the following:

- Identifying subprocesses to be brought under statistical management
- Identifying and measuring product and process attributes important to quality and process performance
- Identifying and addressing special causes of subprocess variation (based on the selected product and process attributes and subprocesses selected for statistical management)
- Managing each selected subprocess to bring its performance within natural bounds (i.e., making the subprocess performance statistically stable and predictable based on the selected product and process attributes)
- Predicting the ability of the process to satisfy established quantitative quality and process-performance objectives
- Taking appropriate corrective actions when the established quantitative quality and process-performance objectives will not be satisfied

Corrective actions include updating the objectives or ensuring that relevant stakeholders have a quantitative understanding of, and have agreed to, the performance shortfall.

A critical distinction between a defined process and a quantitatively managed process is the predictability of process performance. The term *quantitatively managed* implies using appropriate statistical and other quantitative techniques to manage the performance of one or more critical subprocesses so that the performance of the process can be predicted. A defined process provides only qualitative predictability.

Optimizing Process

An optimizing process is a quantitatively managed process that is adapted to meet current and projected business objectives. An optimizing process focuses on continually improving process performance through both incremental and innovative technological improvements. Process improvements that address common causes of process variation, root causes of defects, and other problems; and those that would measurably improve the organization's processes are identified, evaluated, and deployed, as appropriate. Improvements are selected based on a quantitative understanding of their expected contribution to achieving the organization's process improvement objectives versus the cost and impact to the organization.

Selected incremental and innovative technological process improvements are systematically managed and deployed into the organization. The effects of the deployed process improvements are measured and compared to quantitative process improvement objectives.

In an optimizing process, common causes of process variation are investigated to determine how to shift the mean or decrease the variation in quality and process performance. Changes that support the achievement of the organization's process improvement objectives are candidates for deployment.

A critical distinction between a quantitatively managed process and an optimizing process is that the optimizing process is continuously improved by addressing common causes of process variation. A quantitatively managed process is concerned with addressing special causes of process variation and providing statistical predictability of results. Although the process may produce predictable results, the results may be insufficient to achieve the organization's process improvement objectives.

Relationships among Processes

Generic goals evolve so that each goal provides a foundation for the next. Therefore, the following conclusions can be made.

- A managed process is a performed process.
- A defined process is a managed process.
- A quantitatively managed process is a defined process.
- An optimizing process is a quantitatively managed process.

Thus, applied sequentially and in order, the generic goals describe a process that is increasingly institutionalized from a performed process to an optimizing process.

Achieving GG 1 for a process area is equivalent to satisfying the specific goals of the process area.

Achieving GG 2 for a process area is equivalent to managing the performance of processes associated with the process area. There is a policy that indicates you will perform it. There is a plan for performing it. Resources are provided, responsibilities are assigned, training on how to perform it is available, selected work products from performing the process are controlled, and so on. In other words, the process is planned and monitored just like any project or support activity.

Achieving GG 3 for a process area assumes that an organizational standard process exists that can be tailored to create the process you will use. Tailoring might result in making no changes to the standard process. In other words, the process used and the standard process may be identical. Using the standard process "as is" is tailoring because the choice is made that no modification is required.

Each process area describes multiple activities, some of which are repeatedly performed. You may need to tailor the way one of these activities is performed to account for new capabilities or circumstances. For example, you may have a standard for developing or obtaining organizational training that does not consider Web-based training. When preparing to develop or obtain a Web-based course, you may need to tailor the standard process to account for the challenges and benefits of Web-based training.

Achieving GG 4 or GG 5 for a process area is conceptually feasible but may not be economical except, perhaps, in situations in which the product domain is stable for an extended period or in situations in which the process area or domain is a critical business driver.

Generic Goals and Generic Practices

This section describes all of the generic goals and generic practices as well as their subpractices, notes, examples, and references. The generic goals are organized in numerical order, GG 1 through GG 5. The generic practices are also organized in numerical order under the generic goal they support.

As mentioned earlier in this chapter, the text of the generic practices is not repeated in the process areas; the text for each generic goal and generic practice is found only here.

GG 1 Achieve Specific Goals

The process supports and enables achievement of the specific goals of the process area by transforming identifiable input work products to produce identifiable output work products.

GP 1.1 Perform Specific Practices

Perform the specific practices of the process area to develop work products and provide services to achieve the specific goals of the process area.

The purpose of this generic practice is to produce the work products and deliver the services that are expected by performing the process. These practices may be done informally, without following a documented process description or plan. The rigor with which these practices are performed depends on the individuals managing and performing the work and may vary considerably.

GG 2 Institutionalize a Managed Process

The process is institutionalized as a managed process.

GP 2.1 Establish an Organizational Policy

Establish and maintain an organizational policy for planning and performing the process.

The purpose of this generic practice is to define the organizational expectations for the process and make these expectations visible to those in the organization who are affected. In general, senior management is responsible for establishing and communicating guiding principles, direction, and expectations for the organization.

Not all direction from senior management will bear the label *policy*. The existence of appropriate organizational direction is the expectation of this generic practice, regardless of what it is called or how it is imparted.

This policy establishes organizational expectations for planning and performing the process, including not only the elements of the process addressed directly by the acquirer, but also the interactions of the acquirer with suppliers.

TIP

Policy direction may come from multiple levels above the project. For example, in the DoD, policy is established by legislation, the Pentagon, senior acquisition executives, product center management, and others.

GP 2.2 Plan the Process

Establish and maintain the plan for performing the process.

The purpose of this generic practice is to determine what is needed to perform the process and achieve the established objectives, to prepare a plan for performing the process, to prepare a process description, and to get agreement on the plan from relevant stakeholders.

The practical implications of applying a generic practice vary for each process area.

For example, the planning described by this generic practice as applied to the Project Monitoring and Control process area may be carried out in full by the processes associated with the Project Planning process area. However, this generic practice, when applied to the Project Planning process area, sets an expectation that the project planning process itself be planned.

Therefore, this generic practice may either reinforce expectations set elsewhere in CMMI or set new expectations that should be addressed.

Refer to the Project Planning process area for more information about establishing and maintaining a project plan.

HINT

This practice does not require a separate plan for each process area. Consider incorporating process area planning requirements into existing project plans (e.g., systems engineering plan or program management plan).

Establishing a plan includes documenting both the plan and the process. Maintaining the plan includes updating it to reflect corrective actions or changes in requirements or objectives.

The plan for performing the process typically includes the following:

- Process description
- Standards and requirements for the work products and services of the process
- Objectives for the performance of the process (e.g., quality, time scale, cycle time, and resource usage)
- Dependencies among activities, work products, and services of the process
- Resources (including funding, people, and tools) needed to perform the process
- Assignment of responsibility and authority
- Training needed for performing and supporting the process
- Work products to be controlled and the level of control to be applied
- Measurement requirements to provide insight into the performance of the process, its work products, and its services
- Involvement of identified stakeholders
- Activities for monitoring and controlling the process
- Objective evaluation activities of the process
- Management review activities for the process and the work products

Subpractices

1. Define and document the plan for performing the process.
   This plan may be a stand-alone document, a plan embedded in a more comprehensive document, or a plan distributed across multiple documents. In the case of a plan being distributed across multiple documents, ensure that a coherent picture of who does what is preserved. Documents may be hardcopy or softcopy.
2. Define and document the process description.
   The process description, which includes relevant standards and procedures, may be included as part of the plan for performing the process or may be referenced in the plan.
3. Review the plan with relevant stakeholders and get their agreement.
   This review includes ensuring that the planned process satisfies the applicable policies, plans, requirements, and standards to provide assurance to relevant stakeholders.
4. Revise the plan as necessary.

GP 2.3 Provide Resources

Provide adequate resources for performing the process, developing the work products, and providing the services of the process.

The purpose of this generic practice is to ensure that resources necessary to perform the process as defined by the plan are available when they are needed. Resources include adequate funding, appropriate physical facilities, skilled people, and appropriate tools.

The interpretation of the term *adequate* depends on many factors and can change over time. Inadequate resources may be addressed by increasing resources or by removing requirements, constraints, and commitments.

HINT

In addition to a skilled staff, consider other resource needs of the project team and suppliers throughout the lifecycle. Examples include collaboration environments for "system of systems" acquisition, tools for engineering analysis and decision making, test beds or simulators, access to operational data or environments, benchmark data, and access to targeted "experts" in areas of high risk.

GP 2.4 Assign Responsibility

Assign responsibility and authority for performing the process, developing the work products, and providing the services of the process.

The purpose of this generic practice is to ensure there is accountability for performing the process and achieving the specified results throughout the life of the process. The people assigned must have the appropriate authority to perform their assigned responsibilities.

Responsibility can be assigned using detailed job descriptions or in living documents, such as the plan for performing the process. Dynamic assignment of responsibility is another legitimate way to perform this generic practice, as long as the assignment and acceptance of responsibility are ensured throughout the life of the process.

HINT

Don't pass the buck to your suppliers. Acquirers must assume responsibility for executing important processes such as managing risk, analyzing measurement indicators, making important trade-study decisions, and managing customer requirements and expectations.

HINT

Consider sharing training opportunities for project-specific needs across the acquirer, supplier, and end-user teams.

Subpractices

1. Assign overall responsibility and authority for performing the process.
2. Assign responsibility and authority for performing the tasks of the process.
3. Confirm that the people assigned to the responsibilities and authorities understand and accept them.

GP 2.5 Train People

Train the people performing or supporting the process as needed.

The purpose of this generic practice is to ensure that the people have the necessary skills and expertise to perform or support the process.

Appropriate training is provided to the people who will be performing the work. Overview training is provided to orient people who interact with those performing the work.

> Examples of methods for providing training include self-study; self-directed training; self-paced, programmed instruction; formalized on-the-job training; mentoring; and formal and classroom training.

Training supports the successful performance of the process by establishing a common understanding of the process and by imparting the skills and knowledge needed to perform the process.

Experience (e.g., participation in a project with responsibility for managing some acquisition processes) may be substituted for training.

The acquisition organization should conduct a training needs analysis to understand its process training needs at both the organization and project levels. Then, appropriate training vehicles can be identified and provided to minimize process-performance-related risks.

Refer to the Organizational Training process area for more information about training the people performing or supporting the process.

GP 2.6 Manage Configurations

Place designated work products of the process under appropriate levels of control.

The purpose of this generic practice is to establish and maintain the integrity of designated work products of the process (or their descriptions) throughout their useful life.

Designated work products are identified in the plan for performing the process, along with a specification of the appropriate level of control.

Different levels of control are appropriate for different work products and for different points in time. For some work products, it may be sufficient to maintain version control (i.e., the version of the work product in use at a given time, past or present, is known and changes are incorporated in a controlled manner). Version control is usually under the sole control of the work product owner (which may be an individual, a group, or a team).

Sometimes it may be critical that work products be placed under formal or baseline configuration management. This type of control includes defining and establishing baselines at predetermined points. These baselines are formally reviewed and agreed on and serve as the basis for further development of designated work products.

Refer to the Configuration Management process area for more information about placing work products under configuration management.

Additional levels of control between version control and formal configuration management are possible. An identified work product may be under different levels of control at different points in time.

The acquirer is responsible for establishing and maintaining baselines and ensuring designated acquirer work products and supplier deliverables are placed under appropriate levels of control.

HINT

Pay special attention to the configuration management of program documentation and products when moving from one phase of the program to another, especially if there is a hand-off of system development or maintenance responsibility from supplier to supplier or to an internal maintenance group.

Examples of acquirer work products and supplier deliverables placed under control include the following:

- Project plans
- Solicitation packages
- Measures
- Product documentation

GP 2.7 Identify and Involve Relevant Stakeholders

Identify and involve the relevant stakeholders of the process as planned.

The purpose of this generic practice is to establish and maintain the expected involvement of stakeholders during the execution of the process.

Involve relevant stakeholders as described in an appropriate plan for stakeholder involvement. Involve stakeholders appropriately in activities such as the following:

- Planning
- Decisions
- Commitments
- Communication
- Coordination
- Reviews
- Appraisals
- Requirements definitions
- Resolution of problems/issues

Refer to the Project Planning process area for more information about planning for stakeholder involvement.

HINT

Use surrogates when the relevant stakeholder group is too large. For example, stakeholders for review and acceptance of an environmental impact statement may include the entire population of a given area, so a representative subgroup may be needed to make involving them practical.

To plan stakeholder involvement, ensure that sufficient stakeholder interaction necessary to accomplish the process occurs, while avoiding excessive numbers of stakeholders that could impede process execution.

Examples of stakeholders that might serve as relevant stakeholders for acquisition tasks, depending on context, include the acquirer, customers, suppliers, end users, support personnel, other projects, and government regulators.

Subpractices

1. Identify stakeholders that are relevant to the process and plan their appropriate involvement.

   Relevant stakeholders are identified among suppliers of inputs to, users of outputs from, and performers of activities within the process. Once relevant stakeholders are identified, the appropriate level of their involvement in process activities is planned.
2. Share these identifications with project planners or other planners, as appropriate.
3. Involve relevant stakeholders as planned.

GP 2.8 MONITOR AND CONTROL THE PROCESS

Monitor and control the process against the plan for performing the process and take appropriate corrective action.

The purpose of this generic practice is to perform the direct day-to-day monitoring and controlling of the process. Appropriate visibility into the process is maintained so that appropriate corrective action can be taken when necessary. Monitoring and controlling the process involves measuring appropriate attributes of the process or work products produced by the process.

Refer to the Project Monitoring and Control process area for more information about monitoring and controlling the project and taking corrective action.

Refer to the Measurement and Analysis process area for more information about measurement.

HINT

Use this practice to determine the effectiveness of your processes. A SCAMPI appraisal team may not be able to assess process effectiveness, but it will check to see whether *you* can judge adequacy and are making adjustments accordingly.

The project collects and analyzes measurements from the acquirer and from the supplier to effectively monitor and control the project.

Subpractices

1. Measure actual performance against the plan for performing the process.

   Measurements are collected from the process, its work products, and its services.
2. Review accomplishments and results of the process against the plan for performing the process.
3. Review activities, status, and results of the process with the immediate level of management responsible for the process and identify issues. Reviews are intended to provide the immediate level of management with appropriate visibility into the process. The reviews can be both periodic and event-driven.
4. Identify and evaluate effects of significant deviations from the plan for performing the process.
5. Identify problems in the plan for performing the process and in the execution of the process.
6. Take corrective action when requirements and objectives are not being satisfied, when issues are identified, or when progress differs significantly from the plan for performing the process.

   There are inherent risks that should be considered before corrective action is taken.

Corrective action may include the following:
- Taking remedial action to repair defective work products or services
- Changing the plan for performing the process
- Adjusting resources, including people, tools, and other resources
- Negotiating changes to established commitments
- Securing change to requirements and objectives that must be satisfied
- Terminating the effort

7. Track corrective action to closure.

GP 2.9 Objectively Evaluate Adherence

Objectively evaluate adherence of the process against its process description, standards, and procedures, and address noncompliance.

The purpose of this generic practice is to provide credible assurance that the process is implemented as planned and adheres to its process description, standards, and procedures. This generic practice is implemented, in part, by evaluating selected work products of the process. (See the definition of "objectively evaluate" in the glossary.)

Refer to the Process and Product Quality Assurance process area for more information about objectively evaluating adherence.

TIP

Most acquirers don't use an independent quality assurance (QA) function to objectively evaluate process and product quality. In these situations, using objective criteria to evaluate quality and allowing for escalation of issues without retribution becomes even more critical.

People not directly responsible for managing or performing the activities of the process typically evaluate adherence. In many cases, adherence is evaluated by people in the organization but external to the process or project or by people external to the organization. As a result, credible assurance of adherence can be provided even in times when the process is under stress (e.g., when the effort is behind schedule or over budget).

GP 2.10 Review Status with Higher Level Management

Review the activities, status, and results of the process with higher-level management and resolve issues.

HINT

Some acquisition projects have multiple reporting paths. Make explicit who is considered "higher-level management."

HINT

Not every process area will be included in each review with senior management. Establish a strategic rhythm for reviews that includes examination of high-risk areas as well as regular health checks on process execution.

The purpose of this generic practice is to provide higher-level management with appropriate visibility into the process.

Higher-level management includes those levels of management in the organization above the immediate level of management responsible for the process. In particular, higher-level management includes senior management. These reviews are for managers who provide the policy and overall guidance for the process and not for those who perform the direct day-to-day monitoring and controlling of the process.

Different managers have different needs for information about the process. These reviews help ensure that informed decisions on the planning and performing of the process can be made. Therefore, these reviews are both periodic and event-driven.

Proposed changes to commitments to be made external to the organization (e.g., changes to supplier agreements) are typically reviewed with higher-level management to obtain their concurrence with the proposed changes.

GG 3 Institutionalize a Defined Process

The process is institutionalized as a defined process.

GP 3.1 Establish a Defined Process

Establish and maintain the description of a defined process.

The purpose of this generic practice is to establish and maintain a description of the process that is tailored from the organization's set of standard processes to address the needs of a specific situation. The organization should have standard processes that cover the process area and have guidelines for tailoring these standard processes to meet the needs of a project or organizational function. With a defined process, variability in how the processes are performed across the organization is reduced and process assets, data, and learning can be effectively shared.

HINT

Don't go overboard. Use lightweight descriptions that are usable by project team members. Incorporate these descriptions (directly or by reference) into program plans (e.g., systems engineering plan and program management plan).

Refer to the Organizational Process Definition process area for more information about the organization's set of standard processes and tailoring guidelines.

Refer to the Integrated Project Management process area for more information about establishing and maintaining the project's defined process.

The descriptions of defined processes provide the basis for planning, performing, and managing activities, work products, and services associated with the process.

Subpractices

1. Select from the organization's set of standard processes those processes that best meet the needs of the project or organizational function.
2. Establish the defined process by tailoring the selected processes according to the organization's tailoring guidelines.
3. Ensure that the organization's process objectives are appropriately addressed in the defined process.
4. Document the defined process and records of tailoring.
5. Revise the description of the defined process as necessary.

GP 3.2 Collect Improvement Information

Collect work products, measures, measurement results, and improvement information derived from planning and performing the process to support the future use and improvement of the organization's processes and process assets.

HINT

Periodically review whether the information provided to the organization is still relevant and useful and adjust your collection practices as needed. Often, metrics used and measurements gathered will change as the organization's proficiency in quantitative management increases.

The purpose of this generic practice is to collect information and artifacts derived from planning and performing the process. This generic practice is performed so that information and artifacts can be included in organizational process assets and made available to those who are (or who will be) planning and performing the same or similar processes. The information and artifacts are stored in the organization's measurement repository and the organization's process asset library.

Examples of relevant information include the effort expended for various activities, defects injected or removed in a particular activity, and lessons learned.

Refer to the Organizational Process Definition process area for more information about incorporating the work products, measures, measurement results, and improvement information into the organization's measurement repository and process asset library.

Refer to the Integrated Project Management process area for more information about contributing work products, measures, measurement results, and documented experiences to organizational process assets.

Subpractices

1. Store process and product measures and measurement results in the organization's measurement repository.

   The process and product measures are primarily those defined in the common set of measures for the organization's set of standard processes.
2. Submit documentation for inclusion in the organization's process asset library.
3. Document lessons learned from the process for inclusion in the organization's process asset library.
4. Propose improvements to organizational process assets.

GG 4 INSTITUTIONALIZE A QUANTITATIVELY MANAGED PROCESS

The process is institutionalized as a quantitatively managed process.

GP 4.1 ESTABLISH QUANTITATIVE OBJECTIVES FOR THE PROCESS

Establish and maintain quantitative objectives for the process, which address quality and process performance, based on customer needs and business objectives.

The purpose of this generic practice is to determine and obtain agreement from relevant stakeholders about quantitative objectives for the process. These quantitative objectives can be expressed in terms of product quality, service quality, and process performance.

Refer to the Quantitative Project Management process area for more information about establishing quantitative objectives for subprocesses of the project's defined process.

These quantitative objectives may be specific to the process or they may be defined for a broader scope (e.g., for a set of processes). In the latter case, these quantitative objectives may be allocated to some of the included processes.

These quantitative objectives are criteria used to judge whether the products, services, and process performance will satisfy the customers, end users, organization management, and process implementers. These quantitative objectives go beyond the traditional end-product objectives. They also cover intermediate objectives used to manage the achievement of the objectives over time. They reflect, in part, the demonstrated performance of the organization's set of standard processes. These quantitative objectives should be set to values that are likely to be achieved when the processes or subprocesses involved are stable and within their natural bounds.

HINT

When establishing quantitative objectives for a process, understanding the "voice of the process" helps you understand how likely you are to satisfy the "voice of the customer."

Subpractices

1. Establish quantitative objectives that pertain to the process.
2. Allocate quantitative objectives to the process or its subprocesses.

GP 4.2 Stabilize Subprocess Performance

Stabilize the performance of one or more subprocesses to determine the ability of the process to achieve the established quantitative quality and process-performance objectives.

The purpose of this generic practice is to stabilize the performance of one or more subprocesses of the defined process, which are critical contributors to overall performance, using appropriate statistical and other quantitative techniques. Stabilizing selected subprocesses supports predicting the ability of the process to achieve the established quantitative quality and process-performance objectives.

Refer to the Quantitative Project Management process area for more information about selecting subprocesses for statistical management, monitoring the performance of subprocesses, and other aspects of stabilizing subprocess performance.

A stable subprocess shows no significant indication of special causes of process variation. Stable subprocesses are predictable within the limits established by natural bounds of the subprocess. Variations in the stable subprocess are changes due to a common cause system.

Predicting the ability of the process to achieve the established quantitative objectives requires a quantitative understanding of the contributions of the subprocesses that are critical to achieving these objectives and establishing and managing against interim quantitative objectives over time.

Selected process and product measures and measurement results are incorporated into the organization's measurement repository to support process-performance analysis and future fact-based decision making.

HINT

Consult statistical process control experts who are familiar with CMMI when selecting subprocesses to statistically manage.

Subpractices

1. Statistically manage the performance of one or more subprocesses that are critical contributors to the overall performance of the process.
2. Predict the ability of the process to achieve its established quantitative objectives considering the performance of the statistically managed subprocesses.
3. Incorporate selected process-performance measurement results into the organization's process-performance baselines.

GG 5 INSTITUTIONALIZE AN OPTIMIZING PROCESS

The process is institutionalized as an optimizing process.

GP 5.1 ENSURE CONTINUOUS PROCESS IMPROVEMENT

Ensure continuous improvement of the process in fulfilling the relevant business objectives of the organization.

The purpose of this generic practice is to select and systematically deploy process and technology improvements that contribute to meeting established quality and process-performance objectives.

Refer to the Organizational Innovation and Deployment process area for more information about selecting and deploying incremental and innovative improvements that measurably improve the organization's processes and technologies.

Optimizing processes to be agile and innovative depends on the participation of an empowered work force aligned with the organization's business values and objectives. The organization's ability to rapidly respond to changes and opportunities is enhanced by finding ways to accelerate and share learning. Improvement of the processes is inherently part of everyone's role, resulting in a cycle of continual improvement.

Subpractices

1. Establish and maintain quantitative process improvement objectives that support the organization's business objectives.

   The quantitative process improvement objectives may be specific to an individual process or they may be defined for a broader scope (i.e., for a set of processes), with individual processes contributing to achieving these objectives. Objectives that are specific to an individual process are typically allocated from quantitative objectives established for a broader scope.

   These process improvement objectives are primarily derived from the organization's business objectives and from a detailed understanding of process capability. These objectives are the criteria used to judge whether process performance is quantitatively improving the organization's ability to meet its business objectives. These process improvement objectives are often set to values beyond current process performance, and both incremental and innovative technological improvements may be needed to achieve these objectives. These objectives may also be revised frequently to continue to drive the improvement of the process (i.e., when an objective is achieved, it may be set to a new value that is again beyond the new process performance).

   These process improvement objectives may be the same as, or a refinement of, objectives established in the Establish Quantitative Objectives for the Process generic practice, as long as they can serve as both drivers and criteria for successful process improvement.

2. Identify process improvements that will likely result in measurable improvements to process performance.

   Process improvements include both incremental changes and innovative technological improvements. Innovative technological improvements are typically pursued as efforts that are separately planned, performed, and managed. Piloting is often performed. These efforts often target process factors that a process-performance analysis has determined to be key to significant measurable improvement.

3. Define strategies and manage the deployment of selected process improvements based on quantified expected benefits, estimated costs and impacts, and measured change to process performance.

   The costs and benefits of these improvements are estimated quantitatively, and actual costs and benefits are measured. Benefits are primarily considered relative to the organization's quantitative process improvement objectives. Improvements are made to both the organization's set of standard processes and defined processes.

HINT

At capability level 4, you establish quantitative objectives based on the "voice of the process" and the "voice of the customer" (e.g., fewer than 3.6 defects per engineering change proposal). At capability level 5, you establish quantitative *improvement* objectives (e.g., decrease engineering change proposal defects by 50 percent).

Managing the deployment of process improvements includes piloting changes and implementing adjustments as appropriate, addressing potential and real barriers to deployment, minimizing disruption to ongoing efforts, and managing risks.

GP 5.2 *CORRECT ROOT CAUSES OF PROBLEMS*

Identify and correct the root causes of defects and other problems in the process.

X-REF

Although an Ishikawa diagram (i.e., fishbone diagram) is a common tool for simple root cause analysis, most defects or problems require more in-depth analysis. Consider tools such as the *Current Reality Tree* from the Theory of Constraints. For more information, visit the Goldratt Institute at www.goldratt.com/.

The purpose of this generic practice is to analyze defects and other problems encountered in a quantitatively managed process, to correct the root causes of these types of defects and problems, and to prevent these defects and problems from occurring in the future.

Refer to the Causal Analysis and Resolution process area for more information about identifying and correcting root causes of selected defects. Even though the Causal Analysis and Resolution process area has a project context, it can be applied to processes in other contexts as well.

Root cause analysis can be applied beneficially to processes that are not quantitatively managed. However, the focus of this generic practice is to act on a quantitatively managed process, though the final root causes may be found outside of that process.

Applying Generic Practices

This section helps you to better understand the generic practices and provides information to help you interpret and apply generic practices in your organization.

Generic practices are model components applicable to all process areas. Think of generic practices as reminders. They remind you to do things right, and they are expected model components.

For example, when you are achieving the specific goals of the Project Planning process area, you are establishing and maintaining a plan that defines project activities. One of the generic practices that applies to the Project Planning process area is "Establish and maintain the plan for performing the process" (GP 2.2). When applied to this process area, this generic practice reminds you to plan the activities involved in creating the plan for the project.

When you are satisfying the specific goals of the Organizational Training process area, you are developing the skills and knowledge of people in your project and organization so that they can perform their roles effectively and efficiently. When applying the same generic practice (GP 2.2) to the Organizational Training process area, this generic practice reminds you to plan the activities involved in developing the skills and knowledge of people in the organization.

Process Areas That Support Generic Practices

Although generic goals and generic practices are the model components that directly address the institutionalization of a process across the organization, many process areas likewise address institutionalization by supporting the implementation of generic practices. Knowing these relationships will help you effectively implement generic practices.

Such process areas contain one or more specific practices that, when implemented, may also fully implement a generic practice or generate a work product that is used in the implementation of a generic practice.

An example is the Configuration Management process area and GP 2.6, "Place designated work products of the process under appropriate levels of control." To implement the generic practice for one or more process areas, you might choose to implement the Configuration Management process area, in full or in part, to implement the generic practice.

Another example is the Organizational Process Definition process area and GP 3.1, "Establish and maintain the description of a defined process." To implement this generic practice for one or more process areas, you should first implement the Organizational Process Definition process area, in full or in part, to establish the organizational process assets that are needed to implement the generic practice.

Table 8.2 describes (1) the process areas that support the implementation of generic practices and (2) the recursive relationships between generic practices and their closely related process areas. Both types of relationships are important to remember during process improvement to take advantage of the natural synergies that exist between the generic practices and their related process areas.

TABLE 8.2 Generic Practice and Process Area Relationships

Generic Practice	*Roles of Process Areas in Implementation of the Generic Practice*	*How the Generic Practice Recursively Applies to Its Related Process Area(s)*[1]
GP 2.2 Plan the Process	**Project Planning:** The project planning process can implement GP 2.2 in full for all project-related process areas (except for Project Planning itself).	GP 2.2 applied to the project planning process can be characterized as "plan the plan" and covers planning project planning activities.
GP 2.3 Provide Resources GP 2.4 Assign Responsibility	**Project Planning:** The part of the project planning process that implements Project Planning SP 2.4, "Plan the Project's Resources," supports the implementation of GP 2.3 and GP 2.4 for all project-related process areas (except perhaps initially for Project Planning itself) by identifying needed project resources to ensure that the proper staffing, facilities, equipment, and other assets needed by the project are secured.	
GP 2.5 Train People	**Organizational Training:** The organizational training process supports the implementation of GP 2.5 as applied to all process areas by making the training that addresses strategic or organization-wide training needs available to those who will perform or support the process. **Project Planning:** The part of the project planning process that implements Project Planning SP 2.5, "Plan Needed Knowledge and Skills," together with the organizational training process, support the implementation of GP 2.5 in full for all project-related process areas.	GP 2.5 applied to the organizational training process covers training for performing organizational training activities, which addresses the skills required to manage, create, and accomplish the training.
GP 2.6 Manage Configurations	**Configuration Management:** The configuration management process can implement GP 2.6 in full for all project-related process areas as well as some of the organizational process areas.	GP 2.6 applied to the configuration management process covers change and version control for work products produced by configuration management activities.

1. When the relationship between a generic practice and a process area is less direct, the risk of confusion is reduced; therefore, we do not describe all recursive relationships in the table (e.g., for generic practices 2.3, 2.4, and 2.10).

TABLE 8.2 Generic Practice and Process Area Relationships *(Continued)*

Generic Practice	*Roles of Process Areas in Implementation of the Generic Practice*	*How the Generic Practice Recursively Applies to Its Related Process Area(s)*
GP 2.7 Identify and Involve Relevant Stakeholders	**Project Planning:** The part of the project planning process that implements Project Planning SP 2.6, "Plan Stakeholder Involvement," can implement the stakeholder identification part (first two subpractices) of GP 2.7 in full for all project-related process areas. **Project Monitoring and Control:** The part of the project monitoring and control process that implements Project Monitoring and Control SP 1.5, "Monitor Stakeholder Involvement," can support implementing the third subpractice of GP 2.7 for all project-related process areas. **Integrated Project Management:** The part of the integrated project management process that implements Integrated Project Management SP 2.1, "Manage Stakeholder Involvement," can support implementing the third subpractice of GP 2.7 for all project-related process areas.	GP 2.7 applied to the project planning process covers the involvement of relevant takeholders in project planning activities. GP 2.7 applied to the project monitoring and control process covers the involvement of relevant stakeholders in project monitoring and control activities. GP 2.7 applied to the integrated project management process covers the involvement of relevant stakeholders in integrated project management activities.
GP 2.8 Monitor and Control the Process	**Project Monitoring and Control:** The project monitoring and control process can implement GP 2.8 in full for all project-related process areas. **Measurement and Analysis:** For all processes, not just project-related processes, the Measurement and Analysis process area provides general guidance about measuring, analyzing, and recording information that can be used in establishing measures for monitoring actual performance of the process.	GP 2.8 applied to the project monitoring and control process covers the monitoring and control of the project's monitor and control activities.
GP 2.9 Objectively Evaluate Adherence	**Process and Product Quality Assurance:** The process and product quality assurance process can implement GP 2.9 in full for all process areas (except perhaps for Process and Product Quality Assurance itself).	GP 2.9 applied to the process and product quality assurance process covers the objective evaluation of quality assurance activities.

Continues

TABLE 8.2 Generic Practice and Process Area Relationships *(Continued)*

Generic Practice	*Roles of Process Areas in Implementation of the Generic Practice*	*How the Generic Practice Recursively Applies to Its Related Process Area(s)*
GP 2.10 Review Status with Higher Level Management	**Project Monitoring and Control:** The part of the project monitoring and control process that implements Project Monitoring and Control SP 1.6, "Conduct Progress Reviews," and SP 1.7, "Conduct Milestone Reviews," supports the implementation of GP 2.10 for all project-related process areas, perhaps in full, depending on higher-level management involvement in these reviews.	
GP 3.1 Establish a Defined Process	**Integrated Project Management:** The part of the integrated project management process that implements Integrated Project Management SP 1.1, "Establish the Project's Defined Process," can implement GP 3.1 in full for all project-related process areas. **Organizational Process Definition:** For all processes, not just project-related processes, the organizational process definition process establishes the organizational process assets needed to implement GP 3.1.	GP 3.1 applied to the integrated project management process covers establishing defined processes for integrated project management activities.
GP 3.2 Collect Improvement Information	**Integrated Project Management:** The part of the integrated project management process that implements Integrated Project Management SP 1.7, "Contribute to Organizational Process Assets," can implement GP 3.2 in part or full for all project-related process areas. **Organizational Process Focus:** The part of the organizational process focus process that implements Organizational Process Focus SP 3.4, "Incorporate Experiences into Organizational Process Assets," can implement GP 3.2 in part or full for all process areas. **Organizational Process Definition:** For all processes, the organizational process definition process establishes the organizational process assets needed to implement GP 3.2.	GP 3.2 applied to the integrated project management process covers collecting improvement information derived from planning and performing integrated project management activities.

TABLE 8.2 Generic Practice and Process Area Relationships *(Continued)*

Generic Practice	*Roles of Process Areas in Implementation of the Generic Practice*	*How the Generic Practice Recursively Applies to Its Related Process Area(s)*
GP 4.1 Establish Quantitative Objectives for the Process	**Quantitative Project Management:** The part of the quantitative project management process that implements Quantitative Project Management SP 1.1, "Establish the Project's Objectives," supports the implementation of GP 4.1 for all project-related process areas by providing objectives from which the objectives for each particular process can be derived. If these objectives become established as part of implementing subpractices 5 and 8 of Quantitative Project Management SP 1.1, then the quantitative project management process implements GP 4.1 in full. **Organizational Process Performance:** The part of the organizational process-performance process that implements Organizational Process Performance SP 1.3, "Establish Quality and Process-Performance Objectives," supports the implementation of GP 4.1 for all process areas.	GP 4.1 applied to the quantitative project management process covers establishing quantitative objectives for quantitative project management activities. GP 4.1 applied to the organizational process-performance process covers establishing quantitative objectives for organizational process-performance activities.
GP 4.2 Stabilize Subprocess Performance	**Quantitative Project Management:** The part of the quantitative project management process that implements Quantitative Project Management SG 2, "Statistically Manage Subprocess Performance," can implement GP 4.2 in full for all project-related process areas to which a statistically managed subprocess can be mapped. **Organizational Process Performance:** For all processes, not just project-related processes, the organizational process-performance process establishes organizational process assets that may be needed to implement GP 4.2.	GP 4.2 applied to the quantitative project management process covers stabilizing selected subprocesses of quantitative project management activities.
GP 5.1 Ensure Continuous Process Improvement	**Organizational Innovation and Deployment:** The organizational innovation and deployment process can implement GP 5.1 in full for all process areas providing that quality and process-performance objectives for the organization have been defined. (The latter would be the case, say, if the Organizational Process Performance process area has been implemented.)	GP 5.1 applied to the organizational innovation and deployment process covers ensuring continuous process improvement of organizational innovation and deployment activities.

Continues

TABLE 8.2 Generic Practice and Process Area Relationships *(Continued)*

Generic Practice	*Roles of Process Areas in Implementation of the Generic Practice*	*How the Generic Practice Recursively Applies to Its Related Process Area(s)*
GP 5.2 Correct Root Causes of Problems	**Causal Analysis and Resolution:** The causal analysis and resolution process can implement GP 5.2 in full for all project-related process areas.	GP 5.2 applied to the causal analysis and resolution process covers identifying root causes of defects and other problems in causal analysis and resolution activities.

Given the dependencies that generic practices have on these process areas, and given the more holistic view that many of these process areas provide, these process areas are often implemented early, in whole or in part, before or concurrent with implementing the associated generic practices.

There are also a few situations in which the result of applying a generic practice to a particular process area would seem to make a whole process area redundant, but in fact, it does not. It may be natural to think that applying GP 3.1, "Establish a Defined Process," to the Project Planning and Project Monitoring and Control process areas yields the same effect as the first specific goal of Integrated Project Management, "Use the Project's Defined Process."

Although it is true that there is some overlap, the application of the generic practice to these two process areas provides defined processes covering project planning and project monitoring and control activities. These defined processes do not necessarily cover support activities (such as configuration management), other project management processes (such as integrated project management), or the acquisition processes. In contrast, the project's defined process, provided by the Integrated Project Management process area, covers all appropriate processes.

AGREEMENT MANAGEMENT
An Acquisition Process Area at Maturity Level 2

AM

Purpose

The purpose of Agreement Management (AM) is to ensure that the supplier and the acquirer perform according to the terms of the supplier agreement.

TIP

AM helps to prevent problems, such as suppliers that can't meet requirements, by providing a proactive approach to supplier management and visibility into supplier activities. Although the goal of AM is effective performance by both parties to the agreement, acquirers will be successful in satisfying the goal by performing all of the elements for which they are accountable and taking appropriate corrective actions if the supplier fails to meet the terms of the agreement.

Introductory Notes

The Agreement Management process area involves the following activities:

- Executing the supplier agreement
- Monitoring supplier processes
- Accepting the delivery of acquired products
- Managing supplier invoices

The legal nature of many acquirer–supplier agreements makes it imperative that the project management team is acutely aware of the legal implications of actions taken when managing the acquisition of products or services.

The supplier agreement is the basis for managing the relationship with the supplier, including resolving issues. It defines the mechanisms that allow the acquirer to oversee the supplier's activities and evolving products and to verify compliance with supplier agreement requirements. It is also the vehicle for a mutual understanding between the acquirer and supplier. When the supplier's performance, processes, or products fail to satisfy established criteria as outlined in the supplier agreement, the acquirer may take corrective action.

TIP

Well-executed SSAD processes provide significant leverage to success in AM.
Often, suppliers have "capture teams" that are different from the team actually assigned to perform the work. So AM may involve different personnel than SSAD and have unique challenges for the acquirer–supplier relationship.

Related Process Areas

Refer to the Project Monitoring and Control process area for more information about monitoring projects and taking corrective action.

Refer to the Measurement and Analysis process area for more information about specifying, analyzing, and reporting measures and how measurement data are analyzed and reported.

Refer to the Solicitation and Supplier Agreement Development process area for more information about establishing and maintaining the supplier agreement.

Refer to the Acquisition Validation process area for more information about validating products.

Refer to the Acquisition Technical Management process area for more information about evaluating supplier deliverables.

Specific Goal and Practice Summary

SG 1 Satisfy Supplier Agreements
- SP 1.1 Execute the Supplier Agreement
- SP 1.2 Monitor Selected Supplier Processes
- SP 1.3 Accept the Acquired Product
- SP 1.4 Manage Supplier Invoices

Specific Practices by Goal

SG 1 SATISFY SUPPLIER AGREEMENTS

The terms of the supplier agreement are met by both the acquirer and the supplier.

SP 1.1 EXECUTE THE SUPPLIER AGREEMENT

Perform activities with the supplier as specified in the supplier agreement.

This specific practice covers internal and external communication as well as the use of information by the acquirer and supplier regarding the relationship, performance, results, and impact to the business. The acquirer manages the relationship with the supplier to maintain effective communication on key issues (e.g., changes in the acquirer's business), new supplier products and technologies, and changes in the organizational structure.

Refer to the Project Monitoring and Control process area for more information about monitoring projects and taking corrective action.

Typical Work Products

1. Integrated list of issues
2. Supplier project progress and performance reports
3. Supplier review materials and reports
4. Action items tracked to closure
5. Records of product and document deliveries

Typical Supplier Deliverables

1. Supplier project progress and performance reports
2. Corrective action results for supplier issues
3. Correspondence with the acquirer

Subpractices

1. Monitor supplier project progress and performance (e.g., schedule, effort, and cost) as defined in the supplier agreement.
2. Conduct management reviews with the supplier as specified in the supplier agreement.

   Reviews cover both formal and informal reviews and include the following steps:

   - Preparing for the review
   - Ensuring that relevant stakeholders participate
   - Conducting the review
   - Identifying, documenting, and tracking all action items to closure
   - Preparing and distributing to the relevant stakeholders a summary report of the review

TIP

The purpose of a *management review* is to monitor the supplier's progress against the plan and identify and resolve issues (usually risks).

Management reviews typically include the following:
- Reviewing critical dependencies
- Reviewing project risks involving the supplier
- Reviewing schedule and budget

Refer to the Project Monitoring and Control process area for more information about conducting project milestone reviews.

Refer to the Acquisition Technical Management process area for more information about conducting technical reviews.

3. Identify issues and determine corrective actions necessary to resolve and track them to closure.

   Refer to the Manage Corrective Action to Closure specific goal in the Project Monitoring and Control process area for more information about tracking corrective actions to closure.

Unresolved issues escalate through the appropriate management chain according to the organization's issue resolution process.

4. Use the results of reviews to improve the supplier's performance and to establish and nurture long-term relationships with preferred suppliers.

   The acquirer's evaluation of supplier performance is carried out primarily to confirm the supplier's competency or lack of competency relative to performing similar work on the project or other projects.

5. Monitor risks involving the supplier and take corrective action as necessary.

   Refer to the Project Monitoring and Control process area for more information about monitoring project risks.

TIP

Just as peer reviews provide secondary benefits, so do reviews conducted with the supplier.

SP 1.2 MONITOR SELECTED SUPPLIER PROCESSES

Select, monitor, and analyze supplier processes.

HINT

Select the processes in which work products will be monitored and evaluated to obtain visibility into supplier progress and performance and to identify and mitigate risks.

When there must be tight alignment between supplier and acquirer processes, the acquirer should monitor these processes to help prevent interface problems.

Selecting processes for monitoring involves considering the impact of the supplier's processes on the project. On larger projects with significant subcontracts for development of critical components, monitoring key processes is expected. For less critical components, the selection process may determine that monitoring is not appropriate. Between these extremes, the overall risk should be considered when selecting processes to be monitored.

TIP

Monitoring is a cost to both parties, so which processes to monitor depends on which ones provide the most insight into supplier activities, pose the most risk, and provide an early indication of problems. In cases of low risk, process monitoring may be relatively informal.

Monitoring, if not performed with adequate care, can at one extreme be invasive and burdensome, or at the other extreme be uninformative and ineffective. The acquirer decides on the necessary level of monitoring depending on the level of risk if the supplier's process is not performed correctly. Monitoring activities can range from reviewing supplier-supplied process data to on-site appraisals of the supplier's processes [SEI 2007].

Analyzing selected processes involves taking the data obtained from monitoring the processes and analyzing them to determine whether there are serious issues.

Typical Work Products

1. List of processes selected for monitoring or rationale for nonselection
2. Activity reports
3. Performance reports
4. Performance curves
5. Discrepancy reports

Typical Supplier Deliverables

1. Supplier process quality assurance reports

Subpractices

1. Identify supplier processes critical to the success of the project.
2. Monitor selected supplier processes for compliance with requirements of the agreement.
3. Analyze results of monitoring selected processes to detect issues as early as possible that may affect the supplier's ability to satisfy requirements of the agreement.

   Trend analysis can rely on internal and external data.

SP 1.3 Accept the Acquired Product

This practice involves ensuring that the acquired product meets all requirements and that customers concur before acceptance of the product. The acquirer ensures that all acceptance criteria have been satisfied and that all discrepancies have been corrected. Requirements for formal deliverable acceptance and how to address nonconforming deliverables are usually defined in the supplier agreement. The acquirer should be prepared to exercise all remedies if the supplier fails to perform.

TIP

Ensure that the supplier agreement is satisfied before accepting the acquired product.

The acquirer, usually through its authorized supplier agreement administrator, provides the supplier with formal written notice that supplier deliverables have been accepted or rejected.

TIP

Sometimes the operational need is so great that a conditional acceptance is granted before the supplier agreement is fully satisfied. In these cases, the acquirer must proactively manage the "punch list" of outstanding items or discrepancies to ensure that the agreement is satisfied.

Typically, an authorized representative of the acquirer assumes ownership of existing identified supplier products or deliverables tendered, or approves services rendered, as partial or complete performance of the supplier agreement.

The acquirer has defined how this product or service will make the transition to operations and support in the transition to operations and support plan. Transition to operations and support activities are monitored by the acquirer.

Refer to the Plan Transition to Operations and Support specific practice in the Project Planning process area for more information about planning for the transition of the accepted product or service.

Refer to the Monitor Transition to Operations and Support specific practice in the Project Monitoring and Control process area for more information about monitoring transition activities.

Typical Work Products

1. Stakeholder approval reports
2. Discrepancy reports
3. Product acceptance review report with approval signatures

Typical Supplier Deliverables

1. Work products as defined in the supplier agreement
2. Services as defined in the supplier agreement

Subpractices

X-REF

Acceptance procedures, reviews, and tests are also covered in AVAL, so consult that process area's practices for more information about establishing the appropriate environment, procedures, and criteria for validation (and thus for accepting the acquired product).

1. Review the validation results, reports, logs, and issues for the acquired product.

   Refer to the Acquisition Validation process area for more information about validating products.

2. Review supplier verification results, reports, logs, and issues for the acquired product.
3. Confirm that all contractual requirements for the acquired product are satisfied.

   This subpractice may include confirming that appropriate license, warranty, ownership, usage, and support or maintenance agreements are in place and all supporting materials are received.

HINT

Be sure to address proprietary issues related to the acquired product before accepting it.

4. Confirm that all discrepancies have been corrected and all acceptance criteria have been satisfied.
5. Communicate to appropriate stakeholders that the supplier agreement has been satisfied.

   The acquirer, usually through its authorized supplier agreement or contract administrator, provides the supplier with formal written notice that the supplier agreement has been satisfied so the supplier can be paid and the supplier agreement closed.

6. Communicate to relevant stakeholders the product's readiness for transition to operations and support.

SP 1.4 Manage Supplier Invoices

Manage invoices submitted by the supplier.

X-REF

This practice may be executed by a support function outside the control of the project team. However, slow or missed payments pose a risk to the project and must be on the project's radar screen.

The intent of this practice is to ensure that payment terms defined in the supplier agreement are met and that supplier compensation is linked to supplier progress, as defined in the supplier agreement. This practice covers invoices for any type of charge (e.g., one-time, monthly, deliverable-based, pass-through). It covers invoice errors or issues, changes to invoices, billing errors, and withholding disputed charges consistent with the terms and conditions of the supplier agreement. The acquirer must also ensure that appropriate financial and invoice management controls are in place.

When accepting supplier deliverables, final payment should not be made to the supplier until it has been certified that all supplier deliverables meet contractual requirements and all acceptance criteria have been satisfied. When acceptance criteria have not been satisfied, the provisions of the supplier agreement may be exercised.

Typical Work Products

1. Invoices approved for payment

Typical Supplier Deliverables

1. Invoices

Subpractices

1. Receive invoices.
2. Review invoices and related supporting material.

Examples of areas of review for invoices and related support material include the following:

- Volumes for variable charges
- Pass-through expenses
- Regulatory commitments related to payments
- Purchases made by the supplier on behalf of the acquirer

3. Resolve errors and manage issues with the supplier as required.
4. Approve invoices.

ACQUISITION REQUIREMENTS DEVELOPMENT

An Acquisition Process Area at Maturity Level 2

Purpose

The purpose of Acquisition Requirements Development (ARD) is to develop and analyze customer and contractual requirements.

X-REF

REQM addresses managing requirements once they have been developed.

Introductory Notes

This process area describes two types of requirements: customer requirements, which address the needs of relevant stakeholders for which one or more products and services will be acquired, and contractual requirements, which are the requirements to be addressed through the acquirer's relationship with suppliers and other appropriate organizations. Both sets of requirements must address needs relevant to later product lifecycle phases (e.g., operation, maintenance, support, and disposal) and key product attributes (e.g., safety, reliability, and maintainability).

TIP

Customer needs can prescribe particular solutions (e.g., a particular service-oriented architecture to facilitate interoperability) in addition to describing the problem to be solved.

In some acquisitions, the acquirer assumes the role of overall systems engineer, architect, or integrator for the product. In these acquisitions, the Requirements Development process area of CMMI-DEV should be used. Requirements Development in CMMI-DEV includes additional information helpful in these situations, including deriving and analyzing requirements at successively lower levels of product definition (e.g., establishing and maintaining product component requirements).

HINT

Significant changes to requirements may occur during different phases in the project lifecycle. It may be useful to think about your acquisition strategy differently (e.g., evolutionary or incremental approaches), especially if the project lifecycle is lengthy.

Requirements are the basis for the selection and design or configuration of the acquired product. The development of requirements includes the following activities:

- Elicitation, analysis, and validation of stakeholder needs, expectations, constraints, and interfaces to obtain customer requirements that constitute an understanding of what will satisfy stakeholders

- Development of the lifecycle requirements of the product (e.g., development, maintenance, transition to operations, decommissioning)
- Establishment of contractual requirements consistent with customer requirements to a level of detail that is sufficient to be included in the solicitation package and supplier agreement
- Development of the operational concept
- Analysis of needs and requirements (for each product lifecycle phase), the operational environment, and factors that reflect overall customer and end user needs and expectations for attributes such as safety, security, and affordability

The requirements included in the solicitation package form the basis for evaluating proposals by suppliers and for further negotiations with suppliers and communication with the customer. The contractual requirements for the supplier are baselined in the supplier agreement.

Requirements are refined throughout the project lifecycle. Design decisions, subsequent corrective actions, and feedback during each phase of the project's lifecycle are analyzed for their impact on contractual requirements.

TIP

As long as they continue to be maintained, requirements provide stakeholders a common understanding of the product or service as it evolves through the life of the acquisition project.

Requirements analyses aid understanding, defining, and selecting requirements at all levels from competing alternatives. Analyses occur recursively at successively more detailed levels until sufficient detail is available to produce contractual requirements and to further refine these, if necessary, while the supplier builds or configures the product.

X-REF

Requirements validation is addressed in ARD because it is critical to align project and customer expectations. However, the practices in AVAL provide additional insight into how the ARD validation activities can be performed.

Involvement of relevant stakeholders in both requirements development and analyses gives them visibility into the evolution of requirements. Participation continually assures stakeholders that requirements are being properly defined.

The Acquisition Requirements Development process area includes three specific goals. The Develop Customer Requirements specific goal addresses eliciting and defining a set of customer requirements. The Develop Contractual Requirements specific goal addresses defining contractual requirements that are based on customer requirements and are included in the solicitation package and supplier agreement. The specific practices of the Analyze and Validate Requirements specific goal support the development of the requirements in the first two specific goals. The specific practices associated with this specific goal cover analyzing and validating requirements with respect to the acquirer's intended environment.

Related Process Areas

Refer to the Requirements Management process area for more information about managing requirements and changes, obtaining agreement with the requirements provider, obtaining commitments with those implementing the requirements, and maintaining traceability.

Refer to the Solicitation and Supplier Agreement Development process area for more information about developing solicitation packages and supplier agreements.

Refer to the Acquisition Technical Management process area for more information about confirming that the resulting product meets contractual requirements.

Refer to the Acquisition Validation process area for more information about validating the acquired product or service against stakeholder needs, expectations, constraints, and interfaces.

Refer to the Risk Management process area for more information about identifying and managing risks that are related to requirements.

Specific Goal and Practice Summary

SG 1 Develop Customer Requirements
- SP 1.1 Elicit Stakeholder Needs
- SP 1.2 Develop and Prioritize Customer Requirements

SG 2 Develop Contractual Requirements
- SP 2.1 Establish Contractual Requirements
- SP 2.2 Allocate Contractual Requirements

SG 3 Analyze and Validate Requirements
- SP 3.1 Establish Operational Concepts and Scenarios
- SP 3.2 Analyze Requirements
- SP 3.3 Analyze Requirements to Achieve Balance
- SP 3.4 Validate Requirements

Specific Practices by Goal

SG 1 Develop Customer Requirements

Stakeholder needs, expectations, constraints, and interfaces are collected and translated into customer requirements.

Stakeholders (e.g., customers, end users, suppliers, testers, integrators, maintainers, operators, supplier agreement management personnel, manufacturers, and logistics support personnel) are sources of requirements. Their needs, expectations, constraints, interfaces, operational concepts, and product concepts are analyzed, harmonized, refined, and elaborated for translation into a set of customer requirements.

TIP

Stakeholder needs are rarely communicated fully in an official document. They are communicated in documentation, conversations, meetings, demonstrations, and so on. Therefore, this information must be translated into requirements that the project and the customer can agree to.

HINT

Pay particular attention to nonfunctional requirements or other architecturally significant quality attributes or "ilities" (e.g., security, interoperability, maintainability, extendability, and performance).

X-REF

For help in facilitating the discovery of quality attributes, see "Quality Attribute Workshops, Third Edition," at www.sei.cmu.edu/publications/documents/03.reports/03tr016.html.

Frequently, stakeholder needs, expectations, constraints, and interfaces are poorly identified or conflicting. Since these needs, expectations, constraints, and interfaces must be clearly identified and understood throughout the project lifecycle, an iterative process is used throughout the life of the project to accomplish this objective. To facilitate the required interaction, relevant stakeholders are frequently involved throughout the project lifecycle to communicate their needs, expectations, and constraints, and to help resolve conflicts. Environmental, legal, and other constraints should be considered when creating and evolving the set of requirements for acquiring products or services.

HINT

Rarely do customers know exactly what they want. Plan to use an iterative process to learn the requirements for the product or service to be acquired.

SP 1.1 ELICIT STAKEHOLDER NEEDS

Elicit stakeholder needs, expectations, constraints, and interfaces for all phases of the product lifecycle.

Eliciting goes beyond collecting needs by proactively identifying additional needs not explicitly provided by stakeholders. Relevant stakeholders who represent all phases of the product lifecycle in the acquirer's intended environment should include business as well as technical functions. Using this approach, needs for all product-related lifecycle processes are considered concurrently with concepts for acquired products.

An analysis of business processes is a common source of stakeholder needs, expectations, constraints, and interfaces. Additional needs typically address project lifecycle activities and their impact on the product.

TIP

In the case of acquiring product lines or product families, SP 1.1 is sometimes implemented across the product line or product family. A special infrastructure project may establish core assets used in developing each product in the family. In such an organization, requirements come from the organization, the individual acquisition programs, and the core asset development project.

X-REF

For more information on acquiring products and services in a product line environment, see "Acquisition Organizations and Product Lines" at www.sei.cmu.edu/productlines/acquisition.html.

Examples of techniques to elicit needs from stakeholders include the following:

- Questionnaires and interviews
- Operational scenarios obtained from end users
- Operational walkthroughs and end-user task analyses
- Prototypes and models
- Observation of existing products, environments, and workflow patterns
- Technology demonstrations
- Interim project reviews
- Brainstorming
- Quality Function Deployment
- Market surveys
- Extraction from sources such as business process documents, standards, or specifications
- Use cases
- Business case analyses
- Reverse engineering (for legacy products)

Examples of sources of requirements that might not be identified by the customer include the following:

- Government regulations
- Policies and standards
- Technology
- Legacy products or product components (for reuse)

HINT

Ask what the product must do and how it will behave. Also determine what is required to produce it (if it is a physical product), license it, install it, train end users, maintain it, migrate to new versions, support its use, retire it, and dispose of it.

Never underestimate the value of reviewing other sources of requirements. A large number of acquisition projects fail because one or more sources of requirements were not considered.

Typical Work Products

1. Stakeholder needs, expectations, constraints, and interfaces

Subpractices

1. Engage relevant stakeholders using methods for eliciting needs, expectations, constraints, and external interfaces.

SP 1.2 Develop and Prioritize Customer Requirements

Transform stakeholder needs, expectations, constraints, and interfaces into prioritized customer requirements.

The customer typically describes requirements as capabilities expressed in broad operational terms concerned with achieving a desired effect under specified standards and regulations. Customer requirements may also include needs, expectations, constraints, and interfaces with regard to verification and validation. Inputs from the customer and other stakeholders must be aligned to the organization's strategy. Missing information must be obtained and conflicts must be resolved as customer requirements are developed and prioritized.

Customer requirements may also exist as an output of another project's activities such as a previous project that delivered the initial capability.

Examples of factors to consider when expressing customer requirements include the following:

- Key characteristics (attributes) of the desired capability with appropriate parameters and measures
- Obstacles to overcome to achieve the capability
- Competitive gap between the existing and the desired capability
- Supportability of the desired capability
- Level of detail of customer requirements that does not prejudice decisions in favor of a particular means of implementation, but are specific enough to evaluate alternative approaches to implement the capability

Typical Work Products

1. Prioritized customer requirements
2. Customer constraints on the conduct of verification
3. Customer constraints on the conduct of validation

Subpractices

1. Translate stakeholder needs, expectations, constraints, and interfaces into documented customer requirements.
2. Establish and maintain a prioritization of customer requirements.

   Having prioritized customer requirements guides the acquirer in determining project scope and which requirements and requirements changes to include in supplier agreements. This prioritization ensures that requirements critical to the customer and other stakeholders are addressed quickly.

   Determining priorities and resolving conflicts among them can be addressed when eliciting stakeholder needs, as described in the previous specific practice.
3. Define constraints for verification and validation.

SG 2 DEVELOP CONTRACTUAL REQUIREMENTS

Customer requirements are refined and elaborated into contractual requirements.

Customer requirements are analyzed in conjunction with the development of the operational concept to derive more detailed and precise sets of requirements, called contractual requirements, to be included in the solicitation package for potential suppliers and eventually in the supplier agreement. The level of detail of contractual requirements is based on the acquisition strategy and project characteristics.

Contractual requirements arise from constraints, consideration of issues implied but not explicitly stated in the customer requirements baseline, and factors introduced by design constraints and supplier capabilities. Contractual requirements include both requirements documented in contracts between an acquirer and supplier and requirements addressed through formal agreements between the acquirer and other organizations (e.g., partners, subcontractors, government agencies, and internal organizational units). (See the definition of "contractual requirements" in the glossary.) Requirements are reexamined throughout the project lifecycle.

The requirements are allocated to supplier deliverables. The traceability across levels of requirements and supplier deliverables is documented.

Refer to the Maintain Bidirectional Traceability of Requirements specific practice of the Requirements Management process area for more information about maintaining bidirectional traceability.

SP 2.1 Establish Contractual Requirements

Establish and maintain contractual requirements that are based on customer requirements.

Customer requirements may be expressed in the customer's terms and may be nontechnical descriptions. Contractual requirements are the expression of these requirements in technical terms that can be used for design decisions.

In addition to technical requirements (e.g., requirements specifying interfaces with other products or applications, functional requirements and their validation, technical performance measures, and verification requirements such as product acceptance criteria), contractual requirements cover nontechnical stakeholder needs, expectations, constraints, and interfaces.

HINT

Translating requirements (i.e., from customer to contractual) introduces opportunities for misinterpretation and risk. Spend extra time ensuring that the contractual requirements reflect the customer need.

Examples of nontechnical requirements include the following:

- Frequency and format of supplier reviews
- Supplier reports and other communication
- Availability of support to meet levels of the business process or product performance
- Warranty of products provided by a supplier
- Logistics support that sustains both short- and long-term readiness
- Minimal total lifecycle cost to own and operate (i.e., minimal total ownership cost)
- Maintenance concepts that optimize readiness while drawing on both acquirer and supplier sources
- Data management and configuration management that facilitates cost-effective product support throughout the product's use by the acquirer

Refer to the Requirements Management process area for more information about managing changes to requirements.

TIP

The modification of requirements due to approved requirement changes is covered by the *maintain* function of this specific practice, whereas the administration of requirement changes is covered by the REQM process area.

Typical Work Products

1. External interface requirements
2. Contractual requirements
3. Contractual requirements priorities

Subpractices

1. Develop functional and performance requirements necessary for the determination of alternative solutions and the development of the product by the supplier.

   Priorities may be assigned to product requirements to provide a basis for future requirements tradeoffs should this become necessary. Acquirers may assign priorities using categories such as Essential, Important, or Desirable.

2. Develop interface requirements of the acquired product to other products in the intended environment.

   Requirements for interfaces are defined in terms of origination, destination, stimulus, data characteristics for software, and electrical and mechanical characteristics for hardware.

3. Develop design constraints necessary for the determination of alternative solutions and the development of the product by the supplier.

   Design constraints express the qualities and technical performance that are critical to the success of the product in its intended operational environment. They account for customer requirements relative to product interoperability, implications from the use of commercial-off-the-shelf (COTS) products, safety, security, durability, and other mission-critical concerns.

   To achieve high levels of reuse and interoperability, acquirers may establish common design constraints for products or product families that can be deployed in one or more domains. Alternatively, acquirers may accelerate the development of technical requirements and design constraints by reusing shared or common constraints or requirements and their associated test cases from previous acquisitions or leverage the supplier's previous product developments.

4. Develop requirements for verification and validation of the product to be developed by the supplier.

   Requirements for verification and validation typically include types and coverage of testing and review to be carried out in the supplier's and acquirer's environments.

Testing requirements may include mirroring the production environment of the acquirer, the type of test data to be used, and simulated testing of interfaces with other products.

TIP

Identifying the interfaces for which requirements will be developed is not a one-time event, but continues for as long as new interfaces are established.

HINT

Recognize that if multiple systems are being developed to provide the needed capability, the interfaces may change as the systems evolve.

TIP

Previous acquisitions may have had somewhat different needs to fulfill, so requirements and test cases to be reused may need to be analyzed and possibly modified for the current acquisition.

TIP

If the satisfaction of a requirement cannot be ensured through some verification process, the requirements should be restated or eliminated.

5. Establish and maintain relationships among the requirements under consideration during change management and requirements allocation.

   Relationships between requirements can affect evaluating the impact of requirements changes. Expected requirements volatility is a key factor in anticipating scope changes and supporting the acquirer's selection of the appropriate acquisition type.
6. Identify nontechnical requirements.

   Contractual requirements consist of both technical and nontechnical requirements. Examples of nontechnical requirements are listed in the example box in this specific practice.
7. Establish and maintain a prioritization of contractual requirements.

   Priority can be based on a combination of several factors that include customer desires, costs, time frame for when the capabilities are needed, and length of time to satisfy a particular requirement.

   When cost estimates can be determined for contractual requirements, their priority and costs can be used to guide contract and budget negotiations and to determine which changes should be made to the contract.

   Priority may also help when developing a release strategy (e.g., first release only addresses high-priority requirements; lower-priority requirements are deferred to a later release or maintenance phase).

   Refer to the Project Planning process area for more information about establishing an acquisition strategy and estimating costs associated with requirements.

TIP

Sometimes an insignificant requirements change can greatly improve the merits of a COTS-based solution, especially with regard to cost and schedule risks. However, the use of COTS may constrain the overall solution's performance and the support that can be offered later in the product's life. A relationship with a vendor may need to be maintained.

X-REF

See www.sei.cmu.edu/cbs/index.html for more information about using COTS.

ARD

TIP

Sometimes a higher-level requirement specifies performance that is satisfied by multiple supplier deliverables or even across multiple supplier teams. The allocation of a higher-level requirement to supplier deliverables is not necessarily fixed. Often, a provisional allocation of a higher-level requirement to a supplier is made, but is later revised to account for the unique or emerging capabilities of individual suppliers, teams, or new COTS products.

SP 2.2 Allocate Contractual Requirements

Allocate contractual requirements to supplier deliverables.

Contractual requirements are allocated, as appropriate, to supplier deliverables. The requirements for each supplier deliverable are documented. In some cases, technical requirements are allocated to third-party products that must be used by the supplier (e.g., COTS products).

Typical Work Products

1. Requirement allocation sheets

Subpractices

1. Allocate requirements to supplier deliverables.
2. Allocate design constraints to supplier deliverables.
3. Document relationships among allocated requirements and design constraints.

HINT

Pay close attention to integration issues when you allocate contractual requirements to multiple suppliers. You unknowingly may end up as the product integrator.

Relationships include dependencies (i.e., a change in one requirement may affect other requirements).

4. Allocate requirements to suppliers.

   In situations where multiple suppliers are involved in developing the technical solution, different products or product components may be allocated to different suppliers.

TIP

The purpose of requirements validation is to ensure that you have a clear understanding of what the customer wants and needs. Often, this understanding evolves over time and requires a series of requirements validation activities.

SG 3 ANALYZE AND VALIDATE REQUIREMENTS

Requirements are analyzed and validated.

Analyses are performed to determine the impact the intended operational environment will have on the ability to satisfy stakeholder needs, expectations, constraints, and interfaces. Considerations such as feasibility, mission needs, cost constraints, potential market size, and acquisition strategy must all be taken into account, depending on the product context.

The objectives of these analyses are (1) to determine candidate requirements for product concepts that will satisfy stakeholder needs, expectations, constraints, and interfaces and (2) to translate these concepts into requirements. In parallel with these activities, the parameters to be used to evaluate the effectiveness of the product are determined based on customer input and the preliminary product concept.

Requirements are validated to increase the probability that the resulting product will perform as intended in the acquirer's environment.

TIP

Requirements analyses examine requirements from different perspectives (e.g., feasibility, cost, and risk) and using different abstractions (e.g., functional, data flow, entity relationship, state diagrams, and temporal).

HINT

Identify technical performance measures and other measures that help in assessing or predicting performance, usability, cost, schedule, risk, and so forth. Use them to state contractual requirements, establish quality objectives, evaluate progress, manage risk, and conduct trade studies. They provide a data-driven approach to engineering the product.

SP 3.1 ESTABLISH OPERATIONAL CONCEPTS AND SCENARIOS

Establish and maintain operational concepts and associated scenarios.

Operational concepts or concepts of operations is an overall description of the problem to be solved in operational terms and the way in which the product to be acquired is intended to be used or operated, deployed, supported (including maintenance and sustainment), and disposed. The acquirer explicitly accounts for design constraints.

For example, the operational concept for a satellite-based communications product is quite different from one based on landlines.

In contrast, an operational scenario is a description of a sequence of events that might occur in the use of the product to be acquired, and makes explicit some stakeholder needs. Typically, operational scenarios are derived from business process descriptions and operational concepts.

X-REF

For more information about technical performance parameters, see "Using Capability Maturity Model Integration (CMMI) to Improve Earned Value Management" (www.sei.cmu.edu/publications/documents/02.reports/02tn016.html).

Operational concepts and scenarios can assist in the elicitation of needs and the analysis and refinement of requirements. Operational concepts and scenarios can be further refined as solution decisions are made and more detailed requirements are developed. They are evolved to facilitate the validation of technical solutions delivered by the supplier.

Typical Work Products

1. Operational, maintenance, support, and disposal concepts
2. Use cases
3. New requirements

Subpractices

1. Develop operational concepts and scenarios that include functionality, performance, maintenance, support, and disposal, as appropriate.
2. Define the environment in which the product will operate, including boundaries and constraints.
3. Review operational concepts and scenarios to refine and discover requirements.

   Operational concept and scenario development is an iterative process. Reviews should be held periodically to ensure that the operational concepts and scenarios agree with the requirements. The review may be in the form of a walkthrough.
4. Develop a detailed operational concept, as candidate solutions are identified and product and product component solutions are selected by the supplier, that defines the interaction of the product, the end user, and the environment, and that satisfies operational, maintenance, support, and disposal needs.

HINT

Think of an operational concept as a *picture* that portrays the product, end user, and other entities in the intended environment. Think of an operational scenario as a *story* describing a sequence of events and end-user and product interactions. An operational concept provides a context for developing or evaluating a set of scenarios.

TIP

Operational concepts and scenarios are a way to demonstrate or bring to life what the requirements are trying to capture.

TIP

Functionality is typically documented using diagrams and descriptions. The diagrams provide a high-level picture of the overall functionality, whereas the descriptions provide the details.

SP 3.2 Analyze Requirements

Analyze requirements to ensure they are necessary and sufficient.

As contractual requirements are defined, their relationship to customer requirements must be understood. In light of the operational concepts and scenarios, the contractual requirements are analyzed to determine whether they are necessary and sufficient to meet customer requirements. The analyzed requirements then provide the basis for more detailed and precise requirements throughout the project lifecycle.

One of the other actions is the determination of which key requirements will be used to track technical progress. For instance, the weight of a product or size of a software product may be monitored through development based on its risk.

TIP

One senior DoD program manager on a 7-million-line code development project mused, "We need to find a way to suppress our appetite. We're developing millions of lines of code for functionality that will never be used." Although "gold plating" or overpromising may be a good way to justify a project early on, eventually the products need to be built in a reasonable amount of time.

Refer to the Acquisition Technical Management process area for more information about tracking technical progress and technical performance measures.

Typical Work Products

1. Requirements defects reports
2. Proposed requirements changes to resolve defects
3. Key requirements
4. Technical performance measures

Subpractices

1. Analyze stakeholder needs, expectations, constraints, and external interfaces to remove conflicts and to organize into related subjects.
2. Analyze requirements to determine whether they satisfy higher-level requirements.
3. Analyze requirements to ensure that they are complete, feasible, realizable, and verifiable.
4. Analyze and propose the allocation of requirements to supplier deliverables.
5. Identify key requirements that have a strong influence on cost, schedule, functionality, risk, or performance.
6. Identify technical performance measures to be tracked during the acquisition.

   Technical performance measures are precisely defined measures based on a product requirement, product capability, or some combination of requirements and/or capabilities. Technical performance measures are chosen to monitor requirements and capabilities that are considered key factors in a product's performance. Data for technical performance measures are provided by the supplier as specified in the supplier agreement.

   Refer to the Measurement and Analysis process area for more information about specifying measures.

7. Analyze operational concepts and scenarios to refine customer needs, constraints, and interfaces and to discover new requirements.

   This analysis may result in more detailed operational concepts and scenarios as well as support the derivation of new requirements.

TIP

Requirements analyses help to answer questions such as whether all requirements are necessary, whether any are missing, whether they are consistent with one other, and whether they can be implemented and verified.

SP 3.3 ANALYZE REQUIREMENTS TO ACHIEVE BALANCE

Analyze requirements to balance stakeholder needs and constraints.

Stakeholder needs and constraints can address cost, schedule, performance, functionality, reusable components, maintainability, or risk.

Requirements are analyzed to determine whether they reflect an appropriate balance among cost, schedule, performance, and other factors of interest to relevant stakeholders. Models and simulations can be used to estimate the impacts that requirements will have on these factors. By involving stakeholders from different phases of the product's lifecycle in analyzing these impacts, risks can be determined. If the risks are considered unacceptable, the requirements may be revised or reprioritized to improve the balance of cost, schedule, and performance.

X-REF

When analyzing requirements, look at some of the characteristics described in REQM SP 1.1 subpractice 2 to understand the many factors that can be considered.

TIP

The relationships among customer and contractual requirements are investigated and recorded (see REQM SP 1.4).

Typical Work Products

1. Assessment of risks related to requirements

Subpractices

1. Use proven models, simulations, and prototyping to analyze the balance of stakeholder needs and constraints.

   Results of analyses can be used to reduce the cost of the product and the risk in acquiring and using the product.
2. Perform a risk assessment on requirements and design constraints.

   Refer to the Risk Management process area for more information about performing a risk assessment on customer and contractual requirements and design constraints.
3. Examine product lifecycle concepts for impacts of requirements on risks.

HINT

As conflicts are removed, inform the relevant stakeholders of changes that affect the requirements they provided.

TIP

In these subpractices, you determine whether the requirements serve as an adequate basis for product development and how to track progress in achieving key requirements.

SP 3.4 Validate Requirements

Validate requirements to ensure the resulting product performs as intended in the user's environment.

Requirements validation is performed early in the acquisition with end users or their representatives to gain confidence that the requirements are capable of guiding a development that results in successful final validation. This activity should be integrated with risk management activities. Mature organizations typically perform requirements validation in a more sophisticated way using multiple techniques and broaden the basis of the validation to include other stakeholder needs and expectations. These organizations typically perform analyses, prototyping, and simulations to ensure that requirements will satisfy stakeholder needs and expectations.

Examples of techniques used for requirements validation include the following:

- Analysis
- Simulations
- Prototyping
- Demonstrations

Typical Work Products

1. Records of analysis methods and results

Typical Supplier Deliverables

1. Requirements and validation methods (e.g., prototypes and simulations)

Subpractices

1. Analyze the requirements to determine the risk that the resulting product will not perform appropriately in its intended-use environment.
2. Explore the adequacy and completeness of requirements by developing product representations (e.g., prototypes, simulations, models, scenarios, and storyboards) and by obtaining feedback about them from relevant stakeholders.

   Refer to the Acquisition Validation process area for more information about preparing for and performing validation on products and product components.

3. Assess product and product component solutions as they are developed by the supplier in the context of the validation environment to identify issues and expose unstated needs and customer requirements.

TIP

Requirements validation in this SP focuses on the adequacy and completeness of the requirements. *Product and service validation* in AVAL focuses on predicting at multiple points in development how well the product or service will satisfy user needs.

ACQUISITION TECHNICAL MANAGEMENT

An Acquisition Process Area at Maturity Level 3

Purpose

The purpose of Acquisition Technical Management (ATM) is to evaluate the supplier's technical solution and to manage selected interfaces of that solution.

TIP

The focus of ATM is on the suppliers' products as they evolve into a usable solution and the focus of AVER is on the acquirer's work products.

Introductory Notes

The Acquisition Technical Management process area focuses on the following:

- Conducting technical reviews of the supplier's technical solution
- Analyzing the development and implementation of the supplier's technical solution to confirm technical progress criteria or contractual requirements are satisfied
- Managing selected interfaces

TIP

Many problems encountered in the integration of product or service components or the product or service transition to operations is due to interface incompatibilities. Therefore, ATM covers interface management.

Typically, these activities interactively support one another to gauge technical progress and allow effective management of project technical risks. Different levels of detailed analysis, depending on the development progress and insight required, may be needed to conduct technical reviews to the acquirer's satisfaction. Prototypes, simulations, and technology demonstrations created by the supplier may be used as a means of gaining knowledge to manage selected interfaces.

In some acquisitions, the acquirer assumes the role of overall systems engineer, architect, or integrator for the product. In these acquisitions, the Technical Solution process area of CMMI-DEV should be used. Technical Solution in CMMI-DEV includes additional information about designing, developing, and implementing solutions, including the design approaches, design concepts, and alternative solutions for which an acquirer may have varying degrees of responsibility.

HINT

It is not enough to consider product functionality and behavior in the intended operational environment when evaluating a solution. Ask questions about other phases in the life of the product, including whether the solution can be manufactured; whether it is easy to test, install, repair, migrate to new versions or platforms, and support; and what the costs and legal implications will be.

X-REF

ATM is driven by the contractual requirements established by ARD, which are managed by REQM. The technical management in ATM has to coordinate with the supplier agreement management in AM. The processes associated with these process areas interact significantly to accomplish their purposes.

TIP

SG 1 and SG 2 of ATM apply at any phase in the lifecycle of a product or service if a supplier is delivering a technical solution to meet contractual requirements in a supplier agreement.

Acquisition Technical Management activities involve measuring technical progress and the effectiveness of plans and requirements. Activities include those associated with technical performance measurement and the conduct of technical reviews. A structured review process should demonstrate and confirm completion of required accomplishments and exit criteria as defined in project planning and technical plans (e.g., the Systems Engineering Management Plan). Acquisition Technical Management activities discover deficiencies or anomalies that often result in corrective action.

Acquisition Technical Management should be performed with other technical and agreement management processes, such as requirements management, risk management, configuration management, data management, and agreement management.

Related Process Areas

Refer to the Acquisition Requirements Development process area for more information about allocating requirements, establishing an operational concept, specifying technical performance measures, and defining interface requirements.

Refer to the Decision Analysis and Resolution process area for more information about establishing evaluation criteria and selecting alternatives based on those criteria.

Refer to the Requirements Management process area for more information about managing requirements.

Refer to the Risk Management process area for more information about managing risks.

Refer to the Configuration Management process area for more information about managing configuration items.

Refer to the Plan Data Management specific practice of the Project Planning process area for more information about managing data.

Refer to the Agreement Management process area for more information about managing the supplier agreement.

Specific Goal and Practice Summary

SG 1 Evaluate Technical Solutions
- SP 1.1 Select Technical Solutions for Analysis
- SP 1.2 Analyze Selected Technical Solutions
- SP 1.3 Conduct Technical Reviews

SG 2 Perform Interface Management
- SP 2.1 Select Interfaces to Manage
- SP 2.2 Manage Selected Interfaces

Specific Practices by Goal

SG 1 Evaluate Technical Solutions

Supplier technical solutions are evaluated to confirm that contractual requirements continue to be met.

Technical reviews (or architectural evaluations) are performed throughout the project lifecycle to gain confidence that the requirements, architecture, and supplier technical solutions are capable of guiding a development that results in a product or service that provides the required capability. This activity should be integrated with risk management activities. Mature organizations typically perform technical reviews using different proven techniques depending on the type of review. They broaden the basis of the review to include other stakeholder needs, expectations, and constraints.

Refer to the Establish the Acquisition Strategy specific practice in the Project Planning process area for more information about specifying technical performance measures and their threshold values.

This specific goal focuses on the following:

- Selecting supplier technical solutions (i.e., preliminary designs, detailed designs, and design implementations) based on sound decision-making criteria
- Analyzing selected supplier technical solutions
- Conducting technical reviews using results of the analysis

ATM

SP 1.1 Select Technical Solutions for Analysis

Select supplier technical solutions to be analyzed and analysis methods to be used.

TIP

DAR supports the selection of supplier technical solutions for analysis.

The supplier technical solutions are typically in one of the following three stages:

- Candidate solutions (i.e., *design approaches, design concepts,* or *preliminary designs*) that potentially satisfy an appropriate set of allocated requirements
- Detailed designs for selected solutions (i.e., containing all the information needed to manufacture, code, or otherwise implement the design as a product or product component)
- Implemented designs (i.e., the product or service)

TIP

It is best to evaluate a range of candidate solutions. Input from stakeholders with diverse skills and backgrounds can help teams identify and address assumptions, constraints, and biases that may be exhibited in the supplier's candidate designs. Also, consider the "ilities" addressed in the contractual requirements (e.g., usability, reliability, maintainability, interoperability, and security). When you consider the successful products or services you have acquired, ask what made them successful. Was it features, usability, cost, customer support, response time, reliability, and so forth? These characteristics were achieved through careful evaluation of technical solutions.

TIP

Complexity is a "double-edged sword." Sometimes today's high-performance solution becomes tomorrow's high-maintenance solution.

HINT

When evaluating a supplier's alternative solution, treat its components together, not individually. For example, do not rush to evaluate a promising COTS component or new technology without considering the impacts and risks.

HINT

Consider the entire life of the product when evaluating a technical solution to ensure that it will have the desired versatility and market endurance.

Depending on where in the acquisition lifecycle the highest risks occur, the acquirer selects supplier technical solutions for analysis to reduce those risks. Analysis methods are selected based on the type of technical solution being analyzed.

For example, in the implementation phase of the supplier technical solution, the acquirer may examine a product to determine if it is ready for production and if the supplier has accomplished adequate production planning. The analysis would determine if production or production preparations incur unacceptable risks that might compromise schedule, performance, cost, or other established objectives. The acquirer might evaluate the full, production-configured product to determine if it correctly and completely implements all contractual requirements. The acquirer could also determine whether the traceability of the final contractual requirements to the final production-configured product has been maintained.

The acquirer may want to select interfaces for analysis to help decide which interfaces require acquirer management. (See specific goal 2 of this process area.)

Typical Work Products

1. Criteria used for selecting supplier technical solutions for analysis
2. Lists of supplier technical solutions selected for analysis
3. Analysis methods for each selected supplier solution

Typical Supplier Deliverables

1. List of supplier deliverables

Subpractices

1. Select criteria for determining which supplier technical solutions to analyze.

   Refer to the Decision Analysis and Resolution process area for more information about establishing evaluation criteria used in making decisions.

2. Identify supplier technical solutions for analysis.

Supplier technical solutions that are typically analyzed by the acquirer include the following:

- Supplier-derived product and product component requirements, architectures, and designs
- Product interface descriptions
- Products and product components
- Operations manuals
- Plans for training the operations staff

3. Identify the requirements to be satisfied by each selected technical solution.

   A traceability matrix is a useful tool for identifying requirements for each selected technical solution, as it typically includes information that relates requirements to work products. When identifying requirements for each selected technical solution, consult the appropriate traceability matrix.

   Refer to the Maintain Bidirectional Traceability of Requirements specific practice in the Requirements Management process area for more information about tracing requirements to work products.

4. Identify the analysis methods to be used for each selected technical solution.

Examples of techniques used for analysis include the following:

- Simulations
- Architectural prototyping
- Demonstrations

5. Include analysis methods and review activities in the project plan.

   Refer to the Project Planning process area for more information about planning the technical aspects of the project.

TIP

Criteria for selection can include the impact of the technical solution on cost, schedule, performance, and risk. How these criteria are defined in detail, however, depends on the requirements. Screening criteria may involve setting thresholds for selected quality attributes (e.g., response time) that must be met by technical solutions.

TIP

It may be possible to exploit a technology not available to competitors.

HINT

Explore the use of COTS (or open source or new technology) by the supplier early in technical evaluations because to use COTS effectively, you may need to consider changes to requirements. Fully understand the tradeoffs of such requirements and designs early, before committing to (and putting under contract) a particular development approach.

SP 1.2 Analyze Selected Technical Solutions

Analyze selected supplier technical solutions.

Depending on the type of technical solution being analyzed (i.e., preliminary design, detailed design, or design implementation), the results of the analysis are provided to the technical review described in the next specific practice.

For example, the acquirer should assess the design as it matures in the context of the requirements to identify issues and expose unstated needs and customer requirements.

The acquirer should select a supplier's design to analyze by exploring the adequacy and completeness of that design by reviewing product representations (e.g., prototypes, simulations, models, scenarios, and storyboards) and by obtaining feedback about them from relevant stakeholders.

The acquirer should confirm the following.

- The selected design adheres to applicable design standards and criteria.

X-REF

For more information regarding principles, methods, and techniques for creating systems from COTS products, see the SEI Web site at www.sei.cmu.edu/cbs/.

- The design adheres to allocated requirements.
- The resulting product will perform appropriately in its intended-use environment.

During design implementation, the supplier implements the design reviewed and analyzed by the acquirer by developing product components, integrating those components, conducting unit and integration testing of the product, and developing end-user documentation.

A successful analysis of the supplier's implementation is predicated on the acquirer's determination that the requirements are fully met in the final production configuration, that the production capability forms a satisfactory basis for proceeding into pilots or full-rate production, and that the product is ready to be brought into the acquirer environment for further integration and acceptance testing.

Examples of success criteria for the analysis of the supplier's design implementation include the following.

- The product baseline enables hardware fabrication and software coding to proceed with proper configuration management.
- Adequate production processes and measures are in place for the project to succeed.
- Risks are managed effectively.
- The detailed design is producible within the production budget.

The acquirer may require delivery of verification results from the supplier of the technical solution, as applicable. The suppliers may conduct verifications in an iterative fashion, concurrently with the acquirer's technical analyses, or the supplier may be required to conduct follow-on verifications of technical solutions.

Typical expectations for verification addressed by the supplier agreement include the following:

- List of deliverables and other work products that must be verified by the supplier
- Applicable standards, procedures, methods, tools
- Criteria for verification of supplier work products
- Measurements to be collected and provided by the supplier with regard to verification activities
- Reviews of supplier verification results and corrective actions with the acquirer

HINT

To gain the insight needed to fully evaluate supplier solutions, you may need to refine operational concepts and scenarios to understand the implications of each alternative solution. Also, you may need to develop scenarios for other phases of the product lifecycle.

X-REF

ARD SP 3.1 establishes and maintains the operational concepts and scenarios.

HINT

A design is a document used by stakeholders over the life of the product, and thus must communicate clearly and accommodate change. Consider this when selecting criteria to be used in evaluating the value of a design.

TIP

Documentation can be treated as a type of product component for which a solution may be selected, designed, and implemented. There are design and implementation methods and standards for documentation.

Examples of considerations for follow-on verifications of technical solutions include the following.

- During the production stage of the project, there are changes in either materials or manufacturing processes.
- Production start-up or restart occurs after a significant shutdown period.
- Production starts up with a new supplier.
- A manufacturing site has relocated.

The acquirer should also confirm that sufficient end-user documentation has been developed and is in alignment with the tested implementation. The supplier may develop preliminary versions of the installation, operations, and maintenance documentation in early phases of the project lifecycle for review by acquirer and relevant stakeholders.

TIP

Installers, operators, end users, and maintainers may have different documentation needs that may be addressed in different documents.

Documentation assists product maintenance and support later in the life of the product.

Typical Work Products

1. Record of analysis
2. Results of analysis

Typical Supplier Deliverables

1. Alternative solutions
2. Product architecture
3. Product component designs
4. Unit and integration test results
5. Verification results

Subpractices

1. Confirm that the selected technical solution adheres to applicable standards and criteria.
2. Confirm that the selected technical solution adheres to allocated requirements.
3. Use analysis results to compare actual performance measurements to specified thresholds of technical performance measures.

   Refer to the Measurement and Analysis process area for more information about technical performance measures.

4. Conduct technical interchange meetings as necessary.
   Technical interchange meetings are scheduled meetings between the supplier and acquirer to discuss technical progress. These meetings are less formal than the event-driven technical reviews in the next specific practice.

HINT

No solution will rank best for every criterion used. Instead, analyze a solution's ability to provide a balanced approach to cost, schedule, performance, and risks across the product lifecycle.
Following the evaluation, you may conclude that the selection criteria were not complete or detailed enough to adequately assess the ability of the solution to meet the entrance criteria for the technical review. If so, you may need to iterate through SP 1.1 and 1.2.

5. Confirm that the selected technical solution is sufficiently analyzed and meets entrance criteria to begin technical review.
6. Review critical verification results and data from verifications conducted by the supplier.

SP 1.3 Conduct Technical Reviews

Conduct technical reviews with the supplier as defined in the supplier agreement.

Technical reviews are used by the acquirer to confirm that products and services being developed or produced by suppliers meet user needs and requirements.

Technical reviews should have the following characteristics:

- Conducted when the technical solution under development satisfies review entry criteria (i.e., event-driven, not schedule-driven)
- At a minimum, conducted at the transition from one acquisition phase to the next and at major transition points of technical effort
- Have their processes and requirements addressed in and required by the supplier agreement

TIP

The purpose of a *technical review* is to review the supplier's technical progress and identify and resolve issues.

Typically, the project's technical plan (e.g., the systems engineering management plan) documents the timing, conduct, entrance criteria, and success or exit criteria used for technical reviews.

Refer to the Project Planning process area for more information about planning the technical aspects of the project.

Technical reviews typically include the following activities:

- Reviewing the supplier's technical activities and verifying that the supplier's interpretation and implementation of requirements are consistent with the acquirer's interpretation
- Ensuring that technical commitments are being met and that technical issues are communicated and resolved in a timely manner
- Obtaining technical information about the supplier's products
- Providing the supplier with insight into customer and end-user expectations and requirements
- Providing appropriate technical information and support to the supplier

Examples of technical reviews that can be conducted include the following:

- Initial Technical Review (ITR)
- Alternative System Review (ASR)
- Integrated Baseline Review (IBR)
- Technology Readiness Assessment (TRA)
- System Requirements Review (SRR)
- System Functional Review (SFR)
- Preliminary Design Review (PDR)
- Critical Design Review (CDR)
- Test Readiness Review (TRR)
- System Verification Review (SVR)
- Production Readiness Review (PRR)
- Operational Test Readiness Review (OTRR)
- Physical Configuration Audit (PCA)

Typical Work Products

1. Review schedule
2. Entry and exit criteria
3. Review results
4. Documented issues (e.g., issues with customer requirements, product and product component requirements, product architecture, and product design)

Typical Supplier Deliverables

1. Progress reports and process, product, and service-level measurements
2. Technical performance measurements
3. Review materials and reports
4. Action items tracked to closure
5. Documentation of product and document deliveries

Subpractices

1. Identify participants for the technical review.
2. Conduct the technical review.
3. Analyze and record results of the review.
4. Use the results of technical reviews to improve the supplier's technical solution.

   The results of some reviews may require changes to the supplier agreement.

TIP

Involving relevant stakeholders (engineers, technical writers, QA personnel, etc.) in evaluating a supplier's technical solution can reduce the number of serious issues that must be resolved by participating in reviews of the supplier's technical solutions. In these reviews, issues affecting installation, operation, and so on can be identified and resolved.

HINT

You may want to examine the rationale for a particular technical review result when you later learn that a promising technology or COTS component is now available. It may be unnecessary to interrupt product development to explore the implications if they were already explored earlier and records were maintained.

Refer to the Solicitation and Supplier Agreement Development process area for more information about establishing and maintaining the supplier agreement.

SG 2 Perform Interface Management

Selected interfaces are managed.

Many integration and transition problems arise from unknown or uncontrolled aspects of both internal and external interfaces. Effective management of interface requirements, specifications, and designs helps to ensure implemented interfaces are complete and compatible.

The supplier is responsible for managing the interfaces of the product or service it is developing. However, the acquirer identifies those interfaces, particularly external interfaces, that it will manage as well.

SP 2.1 Select Interfaces to Manage

Select interfaces to manage.

The interfaces considered for selection include all interfaces with other products and services in the operations and support environment as well as environments for verification and validation and services that support those environments. The acquirer should review all supplier interface data for completeness to substantiate the complete coverage of all interfaces when making the selection.

Typical Work Products

1. Criteria to be used in selecting acquirer-managed interfaces
2. Categories of interfaces
3. List of interfaces per category

Typical Supplier Deliverables

1. Interface description documents
2. Categories of interfaces
3. List of interfaces per category
4. Mapping of interfaces to product components and the product integration environment
5. Interface design specifications
6. Interface control documents
7. Interface specification criteria

TIP

Overlooked or incompletely described interfaces are risks to be identified and managed (RSKM). The realization of these risks may lead to safety recalls and can prove very costly. Interface management may sometimes follow a formal evaluation (DAR) process: Establish criteria for correctness of an interface (based in part on interface requirements), evaluate alternatives, and so on.

HINT

Where possible, reach early agreement with the supplier on interface design. For some external interfaces, agreement must also be reached by the acquirers or owners of the other interfacing products or services. Lack of agreement leads to wasted time, as assumptions made by the teams on each side of an interface must be validated. Project costs may increase and the schedule may slip.

TIP

You can use a formal evaluation (DAR) process to select the interfaces to manage. Criteria for selection can include the impact of the interface on cost, schedule, performance, and risk.

TIP

Interface control documents define interfaces in terms of data items passed, protocols used for interaction, and so on. These documents are particularly useful in controlling products and product components being built by different teams.

Subpractices

1. Select the criteria to be used for determining which interfaces the acquirer should manage.

   Refer to the Decision Analysis and Resolution process area for more information about establishing evaluation criteria used in making decisions.

2. Identify interfaces that are candidates for acquirer management.

> Example criteria for interfaces that typically are the focus of the acquirer's management include the following.
> - The interface spans organizational boundaries.
> - The interface is mission-critical.
> - The interface is difficult or complex to manage.
> - Capability, interoperability, or efficiency issues are associated with the interface.
> - The interface impacts multiple acquisition projects.

3. Review identified interfaces against the selection criteria.
4. Include acquirer-managed interfaces in the project plan.

X-REF

Requirements for the interfaces are developed in ARD. The acquirer should pay special attention to those interfaces that were particularly important to the stakeholders.

X-REF

It may be prudent to mitigate risks by establishing integrated teams across related acquisition programs when final capabilities require effective interfaces between or among programs. IPM SP 1.6 provides guidance for such teams.

HINT

Manage interfaces early in the project to help prevent inconsistencies from arising.

SP 2.2 MANAGE SELECTED INTERFACES

Manage selected interfaces.

Managing interfaces includes the maintenance of the consistency of the interfaces throughout the life of the product and the resolution of conflict, noncompliance, and change issues. In a system of systems environment, the management of interfaces between products or services acquired from suppliers and other systems within the system of systems is critical for success of the project.

Refer to the Acquisition Requirements Development process area for more information about establishing and maintaining interface requirements.

Refer to the Requirements Management process area for more information about managing changes to interface requirements.

Refer to the Configuration Management process area for more information about managing changes to interface descriptions (i.e., specifications) as configuration items so that stakeholders can be made aware of the current state of the interfaces.

Interface changes are documented, maintained, and readily accessible.

HINT

To know which interfaces to manage, the acquirer should include in the supplier agreement a relationship table, prepared by the supplier, which identifies interfaces among product components (and among product components and the environment). The acquirer should also prepare a relationship table for the external interfaces if the acquired product or service will become part of a system of systems. The ultimate objective is to achieve coverage of all interfaces and ensure completeness.

TIP

An API is the interface that a computer system, library, or application provides to allow other computer programs to make requests for service and/or exchange data.

TIP

A repository for interface data provides access to interface descriptions so that deviations from these definitions are less likely.

X-REF

Interface descriptions are typically placed under configuration management (see GP 2.6) so that changes in status are recorded and communicated (see CM SP 3.1).

TIP

Interface data is all the data associated with product and product component interfaces, including requirements, designs, and interface descriptions.

TIP

These tests may include tests for interface compatibility, tests of how well the assembled product components interoperate, and tests involving end users. Interfaces with environments such as product integration or assembly, verification, and validation environments, as well as operational, maintenance, and support environments, should be addressed.

TIP

These reviews should be *periodic* to ensure that consistency is maintained between interface descriptions and product components (see subpractice 3) and that new interfaces are not overlooked.

Typical Work Products

1. Table of relationships among the supplier's product or service and the external environment
2. Updated interface description or agreement

Typical Supplier Deliverables

1. Table of relationships among the product components and the external environment (e.g., main power supply, fastening product, and computer bus system)
2. Reports from interface control working group meetings
3. Action items for updating interfaces
4. Application program interface (API)

Subpractices

1. Review and analyze selected interface definitions and designs.
2. Confirm that interface descriptions adhere to allocated requirements.
3. Confirm the compatibility of selected interfaces throughout the life of the product or service.

   Confirm that interface descriptions adhere to applicable standards, criteria, and interface requirements between the supplier's product and acquirer's intended environment.
4. Verify that interfaces have been sufficiently tested by the supplier.
5. Verify that issues identified during testing have been resolved appropriately, with product revisions, if necessary.
6. Resolve conflict, noncompliance, and change issues for the selected interfaces.
7. Periodically review the adequacy of interface descriptions.

   Once established, interface descriptions must be periodically reviewed to ensure there is no deviation between existing descriptions and the products being developed, processed, produced, or bought.

   The interface descriptions should be reviewed with relevant stakeholders to avoid misinterpretations, reduce delays, and prevent the development of interfaces that do not work properly.

ACQUISITION VALIDATION

An Acquisition Process Area at Maturity Level 3

Purpose

The purpose of Acquisition Validation (AVAL) is to demonstrate that an acquired product or service fulfills its intended use when placed in its intended environment.

TIP

Validation is a series of activities in which supplier solutions (requirements, designs, prototypes, models, products, etc.) are evaluated against criteria designed to increase the likelihood that the delivered product or service will be operationally acceptable.

Introductory Notes

Validation demonstrates that the acquired product or service, as provided, will fulfill its intended use. In other words, validation ensures that the acquired product or service meets stakeholders' needs and customer requirements.

Validation activities are performed early and incrementally throughout the project lifecycle. These activities can be applied to all aspects of the product and its components in any of their intended environments, such as operations, training, manufacturing, maintenance, and support services. (Throughout the process areas, where we use the phrase *product and product component,* the intended meaning encompasses services and their components.)

The product or product components that are selected to be validated by the acquirer vary depending on project attributes. Methods used to conduct validation also can be applied to selected acquirer work products (e.g., customer requirements) and supplier deliverables (e.g., prototypes, simulations, and demonstrations). Method selection is based on which methods best predict how well the acquired product or service will satisfy stakeholder needs.

TIP

Validation activities can be applied to all aspects of the product or service in any of its intended environments, such as operations, training, manufacturing, maintenance, and disposal.

Whenever possible, validation should be conducted using the product or product component operating in its intended environment. Either the entire environment or part of it can be used.

When validation issues are identified, these issues are referred to processes associated with the Acquisition Requirements Development or Project Monitoring and Control process areas for resolution.

HINT

If you wait until the acceptance test to find issues, you may be in big trouble with your customers and end users.

HINT

A well-verified work product should be used in validation; otherwise, you may lose valuable time with disruptions or rediscovering requirements you already knew. Conversely, validation helps you to uncover missing needs that you can incorporate into requirements.

X-REF

ARD addresses requirements validation. Requirements validation determines the adequacy and completeness of the requirements.

TIP

Early AVAL activities may lead to clarification of requirements passed to the supplier. Additional activities may also be demanded of the acquisition organization after acceptance from the supplier and before fully satisfying the end user.

The specific practices of this process area build on each other in the following way.

- The Select Products for Validation specific practice enables the identification of the product or product component to be validated and methods to be used to perform the validation.
- The Establish the Validation Environment specific practice enables the determination of the environment to be used to carry out the validation.
- The Establish Validation Procedures and Criteria specific practice enables the development of validation procedures and criteria that are aligned with the characteristics of selected products, customer constraints on validation, methods, and the validation environment.
- The Perform Validation specific practice enables the performance of validation according to methods, procedures, and criteria.
- The Analyze Validation Results specific practice enables the analysis of validation results against criteria.

Related Process Areas

Refer to the Acquisition Requirements Development process area for more information about requirements validation.

Refer to the Agreement Management process area for more information about accepting the acquired product or service.

Refer to the Acquisition Technical Management process area for more information about evaluating supplier work products.

Specific Goal and Practice Summary

SG 1 Prepare for Validation
- SP 1.1 Select Products for Validation
- SP 1.2 Establish the Validation Environment
- SP 1.3 Establish Validation Procedures and Criteria

SG 2 Validate Selected Products and Product Components
- SP 2.1 Perform Validation
- SP 2.2 Analyze Validation Results

Specific Practices by Goal

SG 1 PREPARE FOR VALIDATION

Preparation for validation is conducted.

Validation preparation activities include selecting products and product components for validation and establishing and maintaining the validation environment, procedures, and criteria. Items selected for validation may include only the product or it may include appropriate levels of product components used to build the product. Any product or product component may be subject to validation, including replacement, maintenance, and training products, to name a few.

The environment required to validate the product or product component is prepared. The environment may be purchased or may be specified, designed, and built. Environments used for verification may be considered in collaboration with the validation environment to reduce cost and improve efficiency or productivity.

HINT

Any product or product component can benefit from validation. What you select to validate should depend on the issues relating to user needs that pose the highest risk to project success and available resources.

TIP

Integration tests can address validation-type activities (with an end user present to evaluate the integrated product under different scenarios). Thus, for some product components, product integration, verification, and validation activities may be addressed together. Stakeholders may come from the customer community, other acquisition organizations needing functionality for their systems, and the suppliers covered by the acquisition agreement.

AVAL activities should be designed to reduce interference with supplier and end-user performed activities and to reduce duplication of the validation efforts.

Expectations for validation which are typically included in the supplier agreement include the following:

- List of acquired products to be validated by the acquirer before formal acceptance
- List of products to be validated with customers, users, or other stakeholders by the supplier and applicable validation standards, procedures, methods, tools, and criteria, if any
- Measurements to be collected and provided by the supplier with regard to validation activities
- Supplier roles in product and product component validation
- Validation environments to be used by the acquirer
- Validation procedures to be developed and criteria to be used for validation

SP 1.1 SELECT PRODUCTS FOR VALIDATION

Select products and product components to be validated and validation methods to be used.

Products and product components are selected for validation based on their relationship to user needs. For each product or product component, the scope of the validation (e.g., operational behavior, maintenance, training, and user interface) should be determined.

TIP

Validation can be an expensive activity. It takes good judgment to select (and limit) what to validate. Less formal and more frequent "customer use checks" can augment the more formal validation effort.

HINT

When you seek to validate a product component that has not yet been built, consider developing a prototype based on the component's requirements and design. The timely end-user feedback you obtain may more than compensate for the expense of the validation exercise.

X-REF

Customer constraints on the conduct of validation are described as part of the development of customer requirements in ARD SP 1.2. Design constraints are described in ARD SG 2 and SG 3.

HINT

The product (or prototype) may need special interfaces and functionality to properly interact with elements of the validation environment (e.g., data recording equipment). Develop these requirements and incorporate them with other product requirements.

TIP

Because validation generally involves stakeholders external to the project, it is important early in the project to identify and communicate with them about validation methods so that appropriate preparations can begin.

Examples of products and product components that can be validated include the following:

- Customer requirements and design constraints
- Acquired products and product components (e.g., system, hardware units, software, service documentation)
- User manuals
- Training materials
- Process documentation

Validation methods should be selected early in the life of the project so they are clearly understood and agreed to by relevant stakeholders.

Validation methods address the development, maintenance, support, and training for the product or product components, as appropriate.

Examples of validation methods include the following:

- Discussions with users, perhaps in the context of a formal review
- Prototype demonstrations
- Functional demonstrations (e.g., system, hardware units, software, service documentation, and user interfaces)
- Pilots of training materials
- Tests of products and product components by end users and other relevant stakeholders

Typical Work Products

1. Lists of products and product components selected for validation
2. Validation methods for each product or product component
3. Requirements for performing validation for each product or product component
4. Validation constraints for each product or product component

Subpractices

1. Identify the key principles, features, and phases for product or product component validation throughout the life of the project.
2. Determine the customer requirements to be validated.

   The product or product component must be maintainable and supportable in its intended operational environment. This specific practice also addresses the actual maintenance, training, and support services that may be delivered with the product.
3. Select the product and product components to be validated.

4. Select the evaluation methods for product or product component validation.
5. Review the validation selection, constraints, and methods with relevant stakeholders.

SP 1.2 Establish the Validation Environment

Establish and maintain the environment needed to support validation.

The requirements for the validation environment are driven by the product or service selected, type of work products (e.g., design, prototype, and final version), and validation methods. These selections may yield requirements for the purchase or development of equipment, software, or other resources. The validation environment may include the reuse of existing resources. In this case, arrangements for the use of these resources must be made.

Example types of elements in a validation environment include the following:

- Test tools interfaced with the product being validated (e.g., scope, electronic devices, and probes)
- Temporary embedded test software
- Recording tools for dump or further analysis and replay
- Simulated subsystems or components (e.g., software, electronics, or mechanics)
- Simulated interfaced systems (e.g., a dummy warship for testing a naval radar)
- Real interfaced systems (e.g., aircraft for testing a radar with trajectory tracking facilities)
- Facilities and customer-supplied products
- Skilled people to operate or use all the preceding elements
- Dedicated computing or network test environment (e.g., pseudo-operational telecommunications-network test bed or facility with actual trunks, switches, and systems established for realistic integration and validation trials)

Early selection of products or product components to be validated, work products to be used in validation, and validation methods is needed to ensure that the validation environment will be available when necessary.

The validation environment should be carefully controlled to provide for replication, results analysis, and revalidation of problem areas.

HINT

Items selected for validation might be shown as *a table* with columns identifying items to be validated, issues to be investigated, related requirements and constraints, and validation methods. The table might also list the work products to be verified by the supplier (under VER in CMMI-DEV), those to be verified by the acquisition organization (under AVER in this model), and the verification methods to be used. Using one table to address all of these work products for verification and validation may lead you to discover opportunities to combine verification and validation efforts.

TIP

Validation is not applied only to discover missing functionality and is not limited to the end-user operational environment. Other features, environments, and categories of user needs should be considered.

HINT

How might a "shrink-wrapped" product be validated? You can observe users with a prototype in their operational environment; bring users to a special testing laboratory; or release a beta version for end-user testing and feedback.

HINT

Preparing for and conducting validation requires coordination with many external groups. Obtain commitment from these groups to support the planned validation efforts.

Typical Work Products

1. Validation environment

Subpractices

1. Identify requirements for the validation environment.
2. Identify customer-supplied products.
3. Identify reuse items.
4. Identify validation equipment and tools.
5. Identify validation resources that are available for reuse and modification.
6. Plan the availability of resources in detail.

TIP

When validation environments are shared across multiple programs such as ranges or high-fidelity test beds, the acquirer must proactively plan for the use, evolution, and control of these environments.

TIP

Because validation resembles a controlled experiment and because of the need for fidelity with the operational environment, many tools, simulations, computers, networks, and skilled people may need to be involved. Thus, validation planning may itself be challenging.

SP 1.3 Establish Validation Procedures and Criteria

Establish and maintain procedures and criteria for validation.

Validation procedures and criteria are defined to ensure the product or product component will fulfill its intended use when placed in its intended environment. Acceptance test cases and procedures may be used for validation procedures.

The validation procedures and criteria include validation of maintenance, training, and support services.

These procedures also address the validation of requirements and the acquired product or service throughout the project lifecycle. Typically, formal acceptance testing procedures and criteria are established to ensure the delivered product or service meets stakeholder needs before it is deployed in the intended environment.

The validation procedures and criteria applicable to the supplier are typically referenced in the solicitation package and supplier agreement.

TIP

This practice helps to answer questions such as how you will exercise the product prototype to better understand a particular issue (validation procedures) and how you will know whether the performance is acceptable (validation criteria).

Examples of sources for validation criteria include the following:
- Business process descriptions
- Customer requirements
- Customer acceptance criteria
- Standards

Typical Work Products

1. Validation procedures
2. Validation criteria

3. Test and evaluation procedures for maintenance, training, and support

Subpractices

1. Review the requirements to ensure that issues affecting validation of the acquired product or service are identified and resolved.
2. Document the environment, operational scenario, procedures, inputs, outputs, and criteria for the validation of the acquired product or service.
3. Assess the product or service as it matures in the context of the validation environment to identify validation issues.

SG 2 VALIDATE SELECTED PRODUCTS AND PRODUCT COMPONENTS

Selected products and product components are validated to ensure they are suitable for use in their intended operating environment.

The validation methods, procedures, criteria, and the environment are used to validate the selected products and product components and associated maintenance, training, and support services. Validation activities are performed throughout the project lifecycle.

Validation activities are performed by the acquirer, the supplier, or both parties in accordance with the supplier agreement.

SP 2.1 PERFORM VALIDATION

Perform validation on selected products and product components.

To be acceptable to stakeholders, a product or product component must perform as expected in its intended operational environment.

Validation activities are performed and the resulting data are collected according to established methods, procedures, and criteria.

The as-run validation procedures should be documented and the deviations occurring during the execution should be noted, as appropriate.

HINT

The bottom line is to determine whether the product will perform as expected.

TIP

The validation environment may support the automatic collection of much of the data.

Typical Work Products

1. Validation reports
2. Validation results
3. Validation cross-reference matrix
4. As-run procedures log
5. Operational demonstrations

HINT

Validation activities are expensive and it is important to maximize learning. Therefore, analyzing the results of validation activities may help you to discover missing requirements, features in the product that delight the customer, lingering issues, and risks. In a system-of-systems environment, results may also suggest needed changes in adjacent systems to maximize the capability being delivered.

SP 2.2 Analyze Validation Results

Analyze results of validation activities.

The data resulting from validation tests, inspections, demonstrations, or evaluations are analyzed against defined validation criteria. Analysis reports indicate whether needs were met. In the case of deficiencies, these reports document the degree of success or failure and categorize probable causes of failure. The collected test, inspection, or review results are compared with established acceptance criteria to determine whether to proceed or to address requirements or design issues with the supplier.

Analysis reports or as-run validation documentation may also indicate that bad test results are due to a validation procedure problem or a validation environment problem.

Typical Work Products

1. Validation deficiency reports
2. Validation issues
3. Procedure change request

Subpractices

1. Compare actual results to expected results.
2. Based on the established validation criteria, identify products and product components that do not perform suitably in their intended operating environments, or identify problems with methods, criteria, or the environment.
3. Analyze validation data for defects.
4. Record results of the analysis and identify issues.
5. Use validation results to compare actual measurements and performance to the intended use or operational need.
6. Identify, document, and track action items to closure for work products that do not pass their validation.

   Refer to the Project Monitoring and Control process area for more information about tracking action items.

HINT

If requirements are missing, you must revisit your acquisition processes. If there are problems with the validation methods, environment, procedures, or criteria, you must revisit project activities that correspond to the specific practices of SG 1.

ACQUISITION VERIFICATION

An Acquisition Process Area at Maturity Level 3

Purpose

The purpose of Acquisition Verification (AVER) is to ensure that selected work products meet their specified requirements.

TIP

AVER involves ensuring that the evolving work products of the acquisition project meet specified requirements for those products. The work products covered by AVER are those "owned" by the acquisition organization, not those "owned" by the supplier. The suppliers' verification activities with their work products are covered by VER in the CMMI-DEV model and remain the responsibility of the supplier.

Introductory Notes

Acquisition verification addresses whether acquirer work products properly reflect specified requirements.

The Acquisition Verification process area involves the following activities:

- Preparing for verification
- Performing verification
- Identifying corrective action

Verification is inherently an incremental process because it occurs throughout the acquisition of the product or service, beginning with verification of requirements and plans, progressing through the verification of evolving work products such as design and test results, and culminating in the verification of the completed product.

X-REF

The acquirer reviews the supplier verification activities and evaluates the results in ATM. Verification expectations of the supplier should be covered in the supplier agreement in SSAD.

The specific practices of this process area build on each other in the following way:

X-REF

Managing corrective action to closure is addressed in PMC SG 2.

- The Select Work Products for Verification specific practice enables the identification of work products to be verified, methods to be used to perform the verification, and documented requirements to be satisfied by each selected work product.
- The Establish the Verification Environment specific practice enables the selection or creation of the environment to be used to carry out the verification.

- The Establish Verification Procedures and Criteria specific practice enables the development of verification procedures and criteria that are aligned with selected work products, requirements, methods, and characteristics of the verification environment.
- The Prepare for Peer Reviews, Conduct Peer Reviews, and Analyze Peer Review Data specific practices enable the performance of peer reviews, an important type of verification that is a proven mechanism for effective defect removal.
- The Perform Verification specific practice enables the conduct of verification according to available methods, procedures, and criteria.
- The Analyze Verification Results specific practice enables analysis of verification results against established criteria.

TIP

Peer reviews also focus on getting the work product "right" and on obtaining the data necessary to prevent defects and improve the process.

Related Process Areas

Refer to the Acquisition Validation process area for more information about confirming that a product or product component fulfills its intended use when placed in its intended environment.

Refer to the Acquisition Requirements Development process area for more information about generating and developing customer and contractual requirements.

Refer to the Acquisition Technical Management process area for more information about evaluating supplier work products.

Refer to the Requirements Management process area for more information about managing requirements.

X-REF

Many books and other sources describe testing and peer reviews (sometimes known as inspections). For a summary of software testing principles and terminology, see the entry for "Software Testing" on the Wikipedia site, www.wikipedia.org. Understand that supplier wok product verification activities are governed by the supplier agreement (SSAD), reviewed and evaluated in ATM, but conducted using VER practices in CMMI-DEV. For complex systems that demand access to environments controlled by the acquirer or customer, collaborative approaches to verification may be essential.

Specific Goal and Practice Summary

SG 1 Prepare for Verification
- SP 1.1 Select Work Products for Verification
- SP 1.2 Establish the Verification Environment
- SP 1.3 Establish Verification Procedures and Criteria

SG 2 Perform Peer Reviews
- SP 2.1 Prepare for Peer Reviews
- SP 2.2 Conduct Peer Reviews
- SP 2.3 Analyze Peer Review Data

SG 3 Verify Selected Work Products
- SP 3.1 Perform Verification
- SP 3.2 Analyze Verification Results

Specific Practices by Goal

SG 1 Prepare for Verification

Preparation for verification is conducted.

Up-front preparation is necessary to ensure that verification provisions are embedded in contractual requirements, constraints, plans, and schedules. Verification includes the selection, inspection, testing, analysis, and demonstration of acquirer work products.

Verification methods include, but are not limited to, inspections, peer reviews, audits, walkthroughs, analyses, simulations, testing, and demonstrations. Practices related to peer reviews as a verification method are included in specific goal 2.

Preparation for verification includes the definition of support tools, test equipment and software, simulations, prototypes, and facilities.

SP 1.1 Select Work Products for Verification

Select work products to be verified and verification methods to be used.

Acquirer work products are selected based on their contribution to meeting project objectives and requirements, and to addressing project risks.

> Typical verification activities include the review of the solicitation package, supplier agreements and plans, requirements documents, design constraints developed by the acquirer, and other acquirer-developed work products.

Selection of verification methods typically begins with the definition of requirements to ensure that the requirements are verifiable. Reverification should be addressed by verification methods to ensure that rework performed on work products does not cause unintended defects. Suppliers should be involved in this selection to ensure that the project's methods are appropriate for the supplier's environment.

HINT

Identify which work products put the project at the highest risk. These work products are often the required elements that must be shared with the supplier and confirmed with the customer.

HINT

Don't forget to verify work products important to all phases of the product lifecycle, such as maintenance documentation, installation services, and operator training. Often, these are the responsibility of the acquisition organization under an agreement with the customer rather than provided by the suppliers under the agreements the acquirer administers with them.

TIP

Reverification is not called out separately in this process area, since it is actually an iteration of the verification process. However, reverification should be considered when planning verification activities. For example, when fixing a requirements defect, the project team will need to inspect (reverify) other acquisition documents such as systems engineering plans, test plans, transition plans, and so forth to ensure that the project baselines remain consistent.

HINT

Work products that have been "reworked" need to be reverified.

TIP

Methods used for each work product may be shown in a *table* with columns identifying the work product to be verified, requirements to be satisfied, and verification methods to be used. As mentioned in AVAL, some activities across the various agreements with customers and suppliers may allow a combination of verification and validation activities for synergy.

Typical Work Products

1. Lists of work products selected for verification
2. Verification methods for each selected work product

Subpractices

1. Identify acquirer work products for verification.
2. Identify requirements to be satisfied by each selected work product.

   A traceability matrix is a useful tool for identifying requirements for each selected work product, as it typically includes information that relates requirements to work products. When identifying requirements for each selected work product, consult the traceability matrix maintained as part of managing requirements for the project.

   Refer to the Maintain Bidirectional Traceability of Requirements specific practice in the Requirements Management process area for more information about tracing requirements to work products.

TIP

By incorporating such a table into the project plan (perhaps by reference), resources can be provided and commitments made to perform the appropriate verification activities.

3. Identify verification methods available for use.
4. Define verification methods to be used for each selected work product.
5. Identify verification activities and methods to be used in the project plan.

   Refer to the Project Planning process area for more information about coordinating with project planning.

SP 1.2 *Establish the Verification Environment*

TIP

Some work products and verification methods may require special facilities and tools. These should be identified and obtained in advance.

TIP

In the case of peer reviews, a co-located team might meet in a room where the document being peer-reviewed can be displayed. Remote team members might participate through teleconferencing and use a Web-based collaboration tool that allows them to see the document while hearing the discussion.

Establish and maintain the environment needed to support verification.

An environment must be established to enable verification to take place. The type of environment required depends on the work products selected for verification and the verification methods used. A peer review may require little more than a package of materials, reviewers, and a room. A product test may require simulators, emulators, scenario generators, data reduction tools, environmental controls, and interfaces with other systems.

The verification environment may be acquired, developed, reused, modified, or a combination of these, depending on the needs of the project.

Typical Work Products

1. Verification environment

Subpractices

1. Identify verification environment requirements.
2. Identify verification resources that are available for reuse or modification.
3. Identify verification equipment and tools.
4. Acquire verification support equipment and an environment (e.g., test equipment and software).

SP 1.3 Establish Verification Procedures and Criteria

Establish and maintain verification procedures and criteria for the selected work products.

Verification criteria are defined to ensure that work products meet their requirements.

Examples of sources for verification criteria include the following:
- Standards
- Organizational policies
- Types of work products
- Proposals and agreements

Typical Work Products

1. Verification procedures
2. Verification criteria

Subpractices

1. Generate a set of comprehensive, integrated verification procedures for work products and commercial off-the-shelf products, as necessary.

TIP

The organization's information technology (IT) or facilities group, or perhaps other projects, might have some of the verification resources that a project might need. In some cases, domain-specific models, simulators, environmental labs, or antenna ranges are common resources used by multiple projects and must be reserved for use and should be verified as adequate for use.

HINT

The bottom line is to determine verification methods, environments, and procedures as early in the project as is practical.

TIP

In the case of engineering artifacts (e.g., architectures, designs, and implementations), the primary source for verification criteria is likely to be the requirements assigned to the work product being verified. The acquiring organization may need to verify that the customer's environment can actually support the system being acquired from the supplier.

HINT

Remember to establish comprehensive verification procedures and criteria for nondevelopmental items (such as off-the-shelf products or acquirer-furnished equipment) that subject the project to moderate or high risk.

HINT

Often, there isn't a single right result but a range of results that might be acceptable. In such instances, specify how much variability from the expected answer is still acceptable.

TIP

Peers are generally coworkers from your project that have interest in the item under peer review. Peer review participants should generally not include your management because that could restrain open and beneficial dialog. It may even be valuable to consider peers outside the project as suitable participants for specific items under review.
The intent is for the acquisition project to use peer reviews on selected products (e.g., solicitation documents, systems engineering plans, test plans) they produce internally to find and remove defects and to ensure compliance to acquisition standards. Many work products produced by the acquisition project set the stage for project success and are critical to supplier performance.
Peer reviews provide opportunities to learn and share information across the team.

HINT

Use peer reviews not just for contractual artifacts but also for project management artifacts (e.g., plans), process management artifacts (e.g., process descriptions), and support artifacts (e.g., measure definitions).

2. Develop and refine verification criteria as necessary.
3. Identify the expected results, tolerances allowed, and other criteria for satisfying the requirements.
4. Identify equipment and environmental components needed to support verification.

SG 2 Perform Peer Reviews

Peer reviews are performed on selected work products.

Peer reviews are an important part of verification and are a proven mechanism for effective defect removal. An important corollary is to develop an understanding of work products and the processes that produced them to help prevent defects and identify opportunities.

Peer reviews are applied to acquirer-developed work products. These reviews involve a methodical examination of work products by the acquirer's peers to identify defects for removal and to recommend other changes that are needed. Example work products to be peer-reviewed include the solicitation package and the supplier agreement.

SP 2.1 Prepare for Peer Reviews

Prepare for peer reviews of selected work products.

Preparation activities for peer reviews typically include identifying the staff to be invited to participate in the peer review of each work product; identifying key reviewers who must participate in the peer review; preparing and updating materials to be used during peer reviews, such as checklists and review criteria; and scheduling peer reviews.

Typical Work Products

1. Peer review schedule
2. Selected work products to be reviewed

Subpractices

1. Determine the type of peer review to be conducted.
2. Establish and maintain checklists to ensure that work products are reviewed consistently.
3. Distribute the work product to be reviewed and related information to participants early enough to enable them to adequately prepare for the peer review.
4. Assign roles for the peer review, as appropriate.

SP 2.2 Conduct Peer Reviews

Conduct peer reviews of selected work products and identify issues resulting from these reviews.

One of the purposes of conducting a peer review is to find and remove defects early. Peer reviews are performed incrementally as work products are being developed. These reviews are structured and are not management reviews.

Typical Work Products

1. Peer review results
2. Peer review issues
3. Peer review data

Subpractices

1. Perform the assigned roles in the peer review.
2. Identify and document defects and other issues in the work product.
3. Record results of the peer review, including action items.
4. Collect peer review data.

   Refer to the Measurement and Analysis process area for more information about data collection.

5. Identify action items and communicate issues to relevant stakeholders.
6. Conduct an additional peer review if needed.

SP 2.3 Analyze Peer Review Data

Analyze data about the preparation, conduct, and results of the peer reviews.

Refer to the Measurement and Analysis process area for more information about obtaining and analyzing data.

Typical Work Products

1. Peer review data
2. Peer review action items

Subpractices

1. Record data related to the preparation, conduct, and results of peer reviews.
2. Analyze the peer review data.

TIP

Easily overlooked, training improves the effectiveness of peer reviews.

X-REF

Peer reviews are used extensively in software development projects to great success. The principles can be easily applied in other environments (e.g., systems engineering, acquisition, and operations). For a historical perspective of peer review principles and terminology, see the entry for "Software Inspections" on the Wikipedia site, www.wikipedia.org.

HINT

A checklist identifies the classes of defects that commonly occur for a type of work product. By using the checklist, you're less likely to overlook certain classes of defects. Also, some classes of defects might be assigned to different peer review participants, helping to ensure adequate coverage of the checklist.

TIP

A classic problem that arises in low-maturity organizations is that participants skip preparation when under schedule pressure. One way to address this is to incorporate the peer review schedule into the acquisition project plans and schedule to help ensure adequate allocation of time. Another way is to postpone the peer review if participants have not prepared.

HINT

To maximize the effectiveness of the peer review, participants need to prepare prior to the meeting.

SG 3 VERIFY SELECTED WORK PRODUCTS

Selected work products are verified against their specified requirements.

Verification methods, procedures, criteria, and the environment are used to verify selected work products and associated maintenance, training, and support services. Verification activities should be performed throughout the project lifecycle. Practices related to peer reviews as a verification method are included in specific goal 2.

SP 3.1 PERFORM VERIFICATION

Perform verification on selected work products.

Verifying work products incrementally promotes early detection of problems and can result in the early removal of defects. The results of verification save the considerable cost of fault isolation and rework associated with troubleshooting problems.

Typical Work Products

1. Verification results
2. Verification reports
3. Demonstrations
4. As-run procedures log

Subpractices

1. Perform the verification of selected work products against their requirements.
2. Record the results of verification activities.
3. Identify action items resulting from the verification of work products.
4. Document the "as-run" verification method and deviations from available methods and procedures discovered during its performance.

SP 3.2 ANALYZE VERIFICATION RESULTS

Analyze results of all verification activities.

Actual results must be compared to established verification criteria to determine acceptability.

The results of the analysis of verification results are recorded as evidence that verification was conducted. The acquirer might consult

TIP

The ratio often reported that compares the cost to find a defect late in the project to the cost to find a defect early in the project is 100:1.

HINT

Provide a nonthreatening environment so that open discussions can occur. Once you start to include nonpeers (e.g., management, customers, and suppliers) in peer reviews, the effectiveness of peer reviews decreases dramatically.

HINT

During peer review training, train the staff in all of the roles necessary to conduct the peer reviews. These roles can vary from one peer review to the next.

TIP

Defects and issues are often recorded in a *table* with columns for such things as location of defect, defect description (including type and origin), discussion, and action items.

TIP

The analysis can help us answer questions such as what types of defects we are encountering, their severity, in which phases they are being injected and detected, the peer review "yield" (percent of defects detected), the review rate (pages per hour), and the cost (or hours expended) per defect found.

supplier work product verification results and reports to conduct verification activities of acquirer work products.

Refer to the Acquisition Technical Management process area for more information about evaluating supplier work products and reviewing verification results.

For each work product, all available verification results are incrementally analyzed and corrective actions are initiated to ensure that documented requirements have been met. Corrective actions are typically integrated into project monitoring activities. Since a peer review is one of several verification methods, peer review data should be included in this analysis activity to ensure that verification results are analyzed sufficiently.

Analysis reports or "as-run" method documentation may also indicate that bad verification results are due to method problems, criteria problems, or a verification environment problem.

Refer to the Project Monitoring and Control process area for more information about corrective actions.

Typical Work Products

1. Analysis report (e.g., statistics on performance, causal analysis of nonconformances, comparison of the behavior between the real product and models, and trends)
2. Trouble reports
3. Change requests for verification methods, criteria, and the environment

Typical Supplier Deliverables

1. Verification results
2. Verification reports

Subpractices

1. Compare actual results to expected results.
2. Based on the established verification criteria, identify products that do not meet their requirements or identify problems with methods, procedures, criteria, and the verification environment.
3. Analyze the defect data.
4. Record all results of the analysis in a report.
5. Provide information on how defects can be resolved (including verification methods, criteria, and verification environment) and formalize it in a plan.

X-REF

Some acquisition projects conduct "murder boards" on critical acquisition work products such as a Request for Proposal (RFP) or Statement of Work (SOW). A murder board is a comprehensive, line-by-line walkthrough of a document by all relevant stakeholders.
For more information on murder boards, see *A Survival Guide for Project Managers* by James Taylor (AMACOM).

HINT

Sometimes the verification procedure cannot be run as defined (e.g., incorrect assumptions were made as to the nature of the work product or verification environment). If so, record any deviations.

TIP

Analysis helps to identify areas (or risks) on which to focus limited resources.

HINT

When piloting a new verification tool, analyze results to help identify ways to adjust the process or tool to increase the effectiveness of verification activities.

TIP

The verification criteria established in SP 1.3 play an important role in determining where problems are.

CAUSAL ANALYSIS AND RESOLUTION

A Support Process Area at Maturity Level 5

Purpose

The purpose of Causal Analysis and Resolution (CAR) is to identify causes of defects and other problems and take action to prevent them from occurring in the future.

TIP

Although this process area is commonly used for defects, you also can use it for problems such as schedule overruns and inadequate response times that may not be considered defects.

Introductory Notes

The Causal Analysis and Resolution process area involves the following activities:

- Identifying and analyzing causes of defects and other problems
- Taking actions to remove causes and prevent the occurrence of those types of defects and problems in the future

Causal analysis and resolution improves quality and productivity by preventing the introduction of defects into a product. Reliance on detecting defects after they have been introduced is not cost-effective. It is more effective to prevent defects from being introduced by integrating causal analysis and resolution activities into each phase of the project.

HINT

Integrating CAR activities into each project phase will help prevent many defects from being introduced and is thus important to successful implementation of this process area.

Since similar defects and problems may have been previously encountered on other projects or in earlier phases or tasks of the current project, causal analysis and resolution activities are a mechanism for communicating lessons learned among projects.

Types of defects and other problems encountered are analyzed to identify trends. Based on an understanding of the defined process and how it is implemented, root causes of defects and future implications of defects are determined.

Causal analysis may also be performed on problems unrelated to defects. For example, causal analysis may be used to improve coordination and cycle time with one supplier or multiple suppliers.

HINT

You also can apply causal analysis to problems of concern to senior management.

HINT

It is impractical to analyze *all* defects and problems; instead, focus on defects and problems that have the largest risk or impact.

When it is impractical to perform causal analysis on all defects, defect targets are selected by tradeoffs on estimated investments and estimated returns of quality, productivity, and cycle time.

A measurement process should already be in place. Already defined measures can be used, though in some instances new measures may be needed to analyze the effects of the process change.

Refer to the Measurement and Analysis process area for more information about establishing objectives for measurement and analysis, specifying measures and analyses to be performed, obtaining and analyzing measures, and reporting results.

Causal Analysis and Resolution activities provide a mechanism for projects to evaluate their processes at the local level and look for improvements that can be implemented.

TIP

Unlike OID, which looks at many sources to trigger improvement activities, CAR is triggered by actual defects or problems that have been reported.

Causal Analysis and Resolution activities also include the evaluation of acquirer processes that interface with supplier processes, as appropriate. A jointly performed causal analysis may lead to such improvement actions as the supplier improving its processes to more effectively execute in the context of the project or the acquirer improving its supplier interfaces.

When improvements are judged to be effective, the information is extended to the organizational level.

Refer to the Organizational Innovation and Deployment process area for more information about improving organizational level processes through proposed improvements and action proposals.

TIP

Successful implementation of CAR requires significant management commitment and process maturity to ensure that defect and problem data is consistently recorded, causal analysis meetings are adequately supported, and CAR activities are consistently performed across the organization.

The informative material in this process area is written assuming that the specific practices are applied to a quantitatively managed process. The specific practices of this process area may be applicable, but with reduced value, if this assumption is not met.

See the definitions of "stable process" and "common cause of process variation" in the glossary.

Related Process Areas

Refer to the Quantitative Project Management process area for more information about analyzing process performance and determining process capability.

Refer to the Organizational Innovation and Deployment process area for more information about the selection and deployment of improvements to organizational processes and technologies.

Refer to the Measurement and Analysis process area for more information about establishing objectives for measurement and analysis, specifying the measures and analyses to be performed, obtaining and analyzing measures, and reporting results.

Specific Goal and Practice Summary

SG 1 Determine Causes of Defects
- SP 1.1 Select Defect Data for Analysis
- SP 1.2 Analyze Causes

SG 2 Address Causes of Defects
- SP 2.1 Implement Action Proposals
- SP 2.2 Evaluate the Effect of Changes
- SP 2.3 Record Data

Specific Practices by Goal

SG 1 Determine Causes of Defects

Root causes of defects and other problems are systematically determined.

A root cause is a source of a defect, such that if it is removed, the defect is decreased or removed.

SP 1.1 Select Defect Data for Analysis

Select defects and other problems for analysis.

HINT

Let your data help you determine which defects, if corrected, will realize the most benefit to your organization. Of course, this approach assumes that you have useful and valid data.

Typical Work Products

1. Defect and problem data selected for further analysis

Subpractices

1. Gather relevant defect or problem data.

TIP

A successful implementation of CAR requires a mature approach to measurement and analysis and the handling of defect and problem data.

Examples of relevant defect data include the following:
- Defects reported by the customer
- Defects reported by end users
- Defects reported by the supplier

Examples of relevant problem data include the following:
- Project management problem reports requiring corrective action
- Process capability problems
- Process duration measurements
- Earned value measurements by process (e.g., cost performance index)
- Resource throughput, utilization, or response time measurements

TIP

It is often impossible to look at every defect. Therefore, you should establish criteria to help you prioritize and categorize defects and problems.

TIP

For more information on analyzing and categorizing defects, consult references on Six Sigma. An example method is Orthogonal Defect Classification, which provides standard taxonomies for classifying defects and their resolution.

Refer to the Quantitative Project Management process area for more information about statistical management.

2. Determine the defects and other problems to be analyzed further.

   When determining which defects to analyze further, consider the impact of the defects, their frequency of occurrence, the similarity between defects, the cost of analysis, the time and resources needed, the safety considerations, etc.

Examples of methods for selecting defects and other problems include the following:

- Pareto analysis
- Histograms
- Process capability analysis

SP 1.2 Analyze Causes

HINT

To identify actions that address a defect or problem, you need to understand its root causes.

TIP

An action proposal typically documents the defect or problem to be resolved, when it was introduced and detected, its causes, and specific actions that, when taken, will prevent it from reoccurring.

X-REF

Action proposals are prioritized, selected, and implemented in specific goal (SG) 2.

Perform causal analysis of selected defects and other problems and propose actions to address them.

The purpose of this analysis is to develop solutions to identified problems by analyzing relevant data and producing action proposals for implementation.

Typical Work Products

1. Action proposal
2. Root cause analysis results

Typical Supplier Deliverables

1. Root cause analysis results
2. Recommended action proposals

Subpractices

1. Conduct causal analysis with those responsible for performing the task.

   Causal analysis is performed, typically in meetings, with those who understand the selected defect or problem under study. Those who have the best understanding of the selected defect are typically those responsible for performing the task.

Examples of when to perform causal analysis include the following:

- When a stable subprocess does not meet its specified quality and process-performance objectives
- When more defects than anticipated escape from earlier phases to the current phase
- When a work product exhibits an unexpected deviation from its requirements

Refer to the Quantitative Project Management process area for more information about achieving the project's quality and process-performance objectives.

2. Analyze selected defects and other problems to determine their root causes.

   Depending on the type and number of defects, it may make sense to first group the defects before identifying their root causes.

Examples of methods to determine root causes include the following:

- Cause-and-effect (fishbone) diagrams
- Check sheets

3. Group selected defects and other problems based on their root causes.

Examples of cause groups, or categories, include the following:

- Inadequate training and skills
- Inadequate resource allocation
- Breakdown of communication
- Not accounting for all details of a task
- Making mistakes in manual procedures (e.g., typing)
- Process deficiency
- Incomplete, ambiguous, or unclear contractual requirements
- Ineffective management of changes to the supplier agreement

4. Propose and document actions to be taken to prevent the future occurrence of similar defects or other problems.

TIP

There are secondary benefits to causal analysis meetings. Participants develop an appreciation for how upstream activities affect downstream activities, as well as a sense of responsibility and accountability for problems that might otherwise remain unaddressed.

TIP

By grouping defects together, it is often easier to identify the root cause, rather than just the symptoms that mask it.

TIP

You develop cause-and-effect diagrams using iterative brainstorming (i.e., the "Five Whys"). This process terminates when it reaches root causes outside the experience of the group or outside the control of its management.

Examples of proposed actions include changes to the following:

- The process in question
- Training
- Tools
- Methods
- Communication
- Work products

Examples of actions include the following:

- Providing training in common problems and techniques for preventing them
- Changing a process so that error-prone steps do not occur
- Automating all or part of a process
- Reordering process activities
- Adding process steps to prevent defects, such as task kickoff meetings to review common defects and actions to prevent them

An action proposal usually documents the following:

- Originator of the action proposal
- Description of the problem
- Description of the defect cause
- Defect cause category
- Phase when the problem was introduced
- Phase when the defect was identified
- Description of the action proposal
- Action proposal category

TIP

The real focus of this goal is defect and problem prevention. Defect and problem detection is addressed in real time by verification, validation, and project monitoring activities.

SG 2 ADDRESS CAUSES OF DEFECTS

Root causes of defects and other problems are systematically addressed to prevent their future occurrence.

Projects operating according to a well-defined process systematically analyze where in the operation problems still occur and implement process changes to eliminate root causes of selected problems.

SP 2.1 IMPLEMENT ACTION PROPOSALS

Implement selected action proposals developed in causal analysis.

Action proposals describe tasks necessary to remove root causes of analyzed defects or problems and avoid their reoccurrence.

Only changes that prove to be of value should be considered for broad implementation.

Typical Work Products

1. Action proposals selected for implementation
2. Improvement proposals

Typical Supplier Deliverables

1. Improvement proposals

Subpractices

1. Analyze action proposals and determine their priorities.

   Criteria for prioritizing action proposals include the following:

   - Implications of not addressing the defects
   - Cost to implement process improvements to prevent the defects
   - Expected impact on quality
2. Select action proposals to be implemented.
3. Create action items for implementing the action proposals.

Examples of information provided in an action item include the following:

- Person responsible for implementing it
- Description of the areas affected by it
- People who are to be kept informed of its status
- Next date that status will be reviewed
- Rationale for key decisions
- Description of implementation actions
- Time and cost required to identify the defect and correct it
- Estimated cost of not fixing the problem

To implement action proposals, the following tasks must be done.

- Make assignments.
- Coordinate the people doing the work.
- Review the results.
- Track action items to closure.

Experiments may be conducted for particularly complex changes.

Examples of experiments include the following:

- Using a temporarily modified process
- Using a new tool

TIP

When changes are piloted, measure the results of those changes to determine their value, and whether they should be considered for similar projects.

X-REF

For more information on designing experiments to understand the impact of certain changes, consult a good reference on Six Sigma and Experimental Design.

TIP

Subpractice 4 focuses on the project; subpractice 5 focuses on the organization.

HINT

When a resolution has more general applicability, don't document the resolution in a lessons learned document; instead document it in an improvement proposal.

X-REF

For more information about improvement proposals, see OPF SP 2.4.

HINT

Use the measures associated with a process or subprocess (perhaps supplemented by other measures) to evaluate the effect of changes. If the change affects a subprocess being statistically managed, recalculate the natural limits to obtain insight into the effects of the change.

Action items may be assigned to members of the causal analysis team, members of the project team, or other members of the organization.

4. Identify and remove similar defects that may exist in other processes and work products.
5. Identify and document improvement proposals for the organization's set of standard processes.

   Refer to the Organizational Innovation and Deployment process area for more information about the selection and deployment of improvement proposals for the organization's set of standard processes.

SP 2.2 Evaluate the Effect of Changes

Evaluate the effect of changes on process performance.

Refer to the Quantitative Project Management process area for more information about analyzing process performance, stabilizing selected subprocesses, and determining their capability to achieve objectives.

Once the changed process is deployed across the project, the effect of changes must be evaluated to gather evidence that the process change corrected the problem and improved performance.

Typical Work Products

1. Measures of performance and performance change

Typical Supplier Deliverables

1. Base and derived supplier measurements

Subpractices

1. Measure the change in performance of the project's defined process or of subprocesses, as appropriate.

   This subpractice determines whether the selected change has positively influenced process performance and by how much.
2. Measure the capability of the project's defined process or of subprocesses, as appropriate.

   This subpractice determines whether the selected change has positively influenced the ability of the process to meet its quality and process-performance objectives, as determined by relevant stakeholders.

An example of a change in the capability of the project's defined change management process would be a change in the ability of the process to stay within its process-specification boundaries. This change in capability can be statistically measured by calculating and comparing the range of time taken for processing a change request before and after the improvement has been made.

SP 2.3 Record Data

Record causal analysis and resolution data for use across the project and organization.

Data are recorded so that other projects and organizations can make appropriate process changes and achieve similar results.

Record the following:

- Data on defects and other problems that were analyzed
- Rationale for decisions
- Action proposals from causal analysis meetings
- Action items resulting from action proposals
- Cost of analysis and resolution activities
- Measures of changes to the performance of the defined process resulting from resolutions

HINT

It is often too costly to correct every defect or problem. Collect data to know that you are improving project performance relative to your business objectives and to prevent selected defects from reoccurring.

Typical Work Products

1. Causal analysis and resolution records

CONFIGURATION MANAGEMENT

A Support Process Area at Maturity Level 2

CM

Purpose

The purpose of Configuration Management (CM) is to establish and maintain the integrity of work products using configuration identification, configuration control, configuration status accounting, and configuration audits.

TIP

Since this is a Support process area, it is up to the acquisition project and organization to decide which customer, acquirer, or delivered supplier work products are subject to CM and the level of control needed for each.

Introductory Notes

The Configuration Management process area involves the following activities:

- Identifying the configuration of selected work products that compose baselines at given points in time
- Controlling changes to configuration items
- Building or providing specifications to build work products from the configuration management system
- Maintaining the integrity of baselines
- Providing accurate status and current configuration data to developers, end users, and customers

TIP

The CM system should capture enough information to identify and maintain work products after those who have developed them have left the project.

The work products placed under configuration management include the products that are delivered to the customer, designated internal work products, acquired products, tools, and other items used in creating and describing these work products. (See the definition of "configuration management" in the glossary.)

Acquired products may need to be placed under configuration management by both the supplier and the acquirer. Provisions for conducting configuration management should be established in supplier agreements. Methods to ensure that data are complete and consistent should be established and maintained.

The configuration management approach depends on acquisition factors such as acquisition approach, number of suppliers, design responsibility, support concept, and associated costs and risks. In any case, configuration management involves interaction between the acquirer and supplier.

TIP

During transition to operations and support, the acquisition project should ensure that the configuration of delivered products as well as items required to support the delivered products (e.g., support or test environments, requirements, architecture, and design artifacts) are maintained.

Planning for managing configuration items, including during the transition to operations and support, is addressed as part of project planning and supplier agreement development to avoid unexpected costs for both the acquirer and supplier. Project plans and supplier agreements should make provisions for managing configuration items within and across project teams and the infrastructure required to manage configuration items among the acquirer, supplier, operational users, and other relevant stakeholders.

For example, there are shared responsibilities between the acquirer and supplier for the technical solution. The acquirer maintains configuration control of the contractual requirements and the supplier performs configuration management for the technical solution (e.g., establish and maintain the product baseline).

In this example, the acquirer retains the authority and responsibility for approving design changes that impact the product's ability to meet contractual requirements. The supplier manages other design changes. The acquirer maintains the right to access configuration data at any level required to implement planned or potential design changes and support options. Configuration management of legacy systems should be addressed on a case-by-case basis as design changes are contemplated.

Examples of work products that may be placed under configuration management include the following:

- Plans
- Process descriptions
- Requirements
- Acquisition strategies
- Solicitation packages
- Supplier agreements
- Supplier deliverables

Configuration management of work products may be performed at several levels of granularity. Configuration items can be decomposed into configuration components and configuration units. Only the term *configuration item* is used in this process area. Therefore, in these practices, *configuration item* may be interpreted as *configuration component* or *configuration unit,* as appropriate. (See the definition of "configuration item" in the glossary.)

Baselines provide a stable basis for the continuing evolution of configuration items.

> An example of an acquirer's baseline is a collection of acquirer work products such as contractual requirements and acceptance criteria that are related to the product baseline managed by the supplier.

Baselines are added to the configuration management system as they are developed. Changes to baselines and the release of work products built from the configuration management system are systematically controlled and monitored via the configuration control, change management, and configuration auditing functions of configuration management.

This process area applies not only to configuration management on projects, but also to configuration management on organizational work products such as standards, procedures, and reuse libraries.

Configuration management is focused on the rigorous control of the managerial and technical aspects of work products, including the delivered system.

This process area covers the practices for performing the configuration management function and is applicable to all work products that are placed under configuration management.

TIP

Many acquirer-developed work products, such as plans, requirements, and interfaces, are critical to guiding stakeholders through the life of the project. These work products must be maintained to reflect the current project scope and objectives.

HINT

Make explicit decisions about who has the authority in the project to approve baseline changes; document these decisions in project plans.

TIP

Any work product whose integrity should be ensured over a period of time might benefit from CM. For example, multiple acquisition programs may be ongoing and have schedule dependencies with one another. Establishing a cross-program CM approach may assist coordination efforts.

Related Process Areas

Refer to the Agreement Management process area for more information about formal acceptance of supplier deliverables.

Refer to the Project Planning process area for more information about developing plans and work breakdown structures, which may be useful for determining configuration items.

Refer to the Project Monitoring and Control process area for more information about performance analyses and corrective actions.

Specific Goal and Practice Summary

SG 1 Establish Baselines
- SP 1.1 Identify Configuration Items
- SP 1.2 Establish a Configuration Management System
- SP 1.3 Create or Release Baselines

SG 2 Track and Control Changes
- SP 2.1 Track Change Requests
- SP 2.2 Control Configuration Items

SG 3 Establish Integrity
- SP 3.1 Establish Configuration Management Records
- SP 3.2 Perform Configuration Audits

Specific Practices by Goal

SG 1 ESTABLISH BASELINES

Baselines of identified work products are established.

Specific practices to establish baselines are covered by this specific goal. The specific practices under the Track and Control Changes specific goal serve to maintain the baselines. The specific practices of the Establish Integrity specific goal document and audit the integrity of the baselines.

SP 1.1 IDENTIFY CONFIGURATION ITEMS

Identify configuration items, components, and related work products to be placed under configuration management.

Configuration identification is the selection, creation, and specification of the following:

- Products delivered to the customer
- Designated internal work products
- Acquired products
- Tools and other capital assets of the project's work environment
- Other items used in creating and describing these work products

Items under configuration management include specifications and interface documents that define requirements for the product. Other documents, such as test results, may also be included, depending on their importance to defining the product.

A *configuration item* is an entity designated for configuration management, which may consist of multiple related work products that form a baseline. This logical grouping provides ease of identification and controlled access. The selection of work products for configuration management should be based on criteria established during planning.

Configuration items may vary widely in complexity, size, and type, from an aircraft to commercial-of-the-shelf software to a test meter or a project plan. Any item required for product support and designated for separate procurement is a configuration item. Acquirer work products provided to suppliers such as solicitation packages and technical standards are typically designated as configuration items.

HINT

When developing your project plan, consider configuration items and work products you receive from customers, those you develop internally, and those delivered by suppliers.

Typical Work Products

1. Identified configuration items

Subpractices

1. Select configuration items and work products that compose them based on documented criteria.

HINT

Use criteria when selecting configuration items to ensure that the selection process is consistent and thorough.

Example criteria for selecting configuration items at the appropriate work-product level include the following:

- Work products that may be used by two or more groups
- Work products that are expected to change over time either because of errors or changes in requirements
- Work products that are dependent on each other (i.e., a change in one mandates a change in the others)
- Work products critical to project success

Examples of acquirer work products and supplier deliverables that may be part of a configuration item include the following:

- Process descriptions
- Requirements
- Acceptance criteria
- Supplier project progress and performance reports
- Supplier test results

2. Assign unique identifiers to configuration items.
3. Specify the important characteristics of each configuration item.
4. Specify when each configuration item is placed under configuration management.

HINT

Consider selecting tools that are compatible with the tools used by your suppliers and other stakeholders to ensure that unique identifiers are consistent.

TIP

Specifying when a configuration item must be placed under CM sets expectations among team members about the control of the project's work products.

Example criteria for determining when to place work products under configuration management include the following:

- Stage of the project lifecycle
- When the acquirer work product is ready for review and approval
- Degree of control desired on the work product
- Cost and schedule limitations
- Customer requirements

5. Identify the owner responsible for each configuration item.

SP 1.2 Establish a Configuration Management System

Establish and maintain a configuration management and change management system for controlling work products.

TIP

If the acquisition project maintains only the configuration of project documents, a simple spreadsheet or data management system may suffice. To maintain the configuration of products delivered to end users, more complex tools are necessary.

HINT

The number of baselines you need to maintain and the complexities of working with geographically dispersed teams are two typical considerations when selecting commercial software packages to help with CM.

HINT

When dealing with sensitive information during the acquisition process, you must consider taking additional steps to ensure the integrity of the acquisition process and its products.

TIP

Not all configuration items require the same level of control. Some may require more control as they move through the project lifecycle.

A configuration management system includes the storage media, procedures, and tools for accessing the system.

A change management system includes the storage media, procedures, and tools for recording and accessing change requests.

The acquirer considers how configuration items are shared between the acquirer and supplier as well as among relevant stakeholders. If the use of an acquirer's configuration management system is extended to a supplier, the acquirer must exercise security and access control procedures. In many cases, leaving acquired configuration items in the physical possession of the supplier and having access to supplier deliverables is an alternative solution. The supplier agreement specifies appropriate acquirer rights to supplier deliverables, in addition to requirements for delivery or access. Supplier work products, whenever they are delivered to the acquirer, are presented in accordance with accepted standards to ensure usability by the acquirer.

Typical Work Products

1. Configuration management system with controlled work products
2. Configuration management system access control procedures
3. Change request database

Subpractices

1. Establish a mechanism to manage multiple levels of control.

   The level of control is typically selected based on project objectives, risk, and resources. Levels of control can range from informal control that simply tracks changes made when configuration items are being developed by the acquirer or when supplier work products are delivered or made accessible to the acquirer, to formal configuration control using baselines that can only be changed as part of a formal configuration management process.

2. Store and retrieve configuration items in a configuration management system.
3. Share and transfer configuration items between control levels in the configuration management system.
4. Store and recover archived versions of configuration items.
5. Store, update, and retrieve configuration management records.
6. Create configuration management reports from the configuration management system.
7. Preserve the contents of the configuration management system.

> Examples of preservation functions of the configuration management system include the following:
> - Backup and restoration of configuration management files
> - Archive of configuration management files
> - Recovery from configuration management errors

8. Revise the configuration management structure as necessary.

TIP

A formal CM process is typically change-request-based and requires extensive tracking, review, and approval of all changes.

TIP

Version control is an important part of CM. There are different ways to identify versions. A standard way is to use sequential numbering.

HINT

Review the content of reports from the CM system regularly to ensure the integrity of configuration items and work products.

HINT

Review the CM system regularly to ensure that it is meeting the needs of the projects it serves.

SP 1.3 Create or Release Baselines

Create or release baselines for internal use and for delivery to the customer.

A baseline is a set of specifications or work products that has been formally reviewed and agreed on, that thereafter serves as the basis for further development or delivery, and that can be changed only through change control procedures. A baseline represents the assignment of an identifier to a configuration item or a collection of configuration items and associated entities. As a product evolves, several baselines may be used to control its development and testing.

The acquirer reviews and approves the release of product baselines created by the supplier. The acquirer creates baselines for acquirer work products that describe the project, requirements, funding, schedule, and performance measures and makes a commitment to manage the project to those baselines.

Typical Work Products

1. Baselines
2. Description of baselines

TIP

Since acquirer-developed work products drive the activities of the acquirer, supplier, and other key stakeholders, having a single source of "truth" is critical for project orchestration and success.

TIP

If the project or organization uses multiple baselines, it is critical to ensure that everyone is using the correct baseline.

Typical Supplier Deliverables

1. Product baselines
2. Description of product baselines

TIP

The acquisition project team may run or participate in several CCBs. These CCBs can be with customers, with members internal to the acquisition organization, with collaborating acquisition teams in a system of systems environment, or with suppliers. A clear and common understanding of how these CCBs interact is critical.

Subpractices

1. Obtain authorization from the configuration control board (CCB) before creating or releasing baselines of configuration items.
2. Create or release baselines only from configuration items in the configuration management system.
3. Document the set of configuration items that are contained in a baseline.
4. Make the current set of baselines readily available.

SG 2 TRACK AND CONTROL CHANGES

TIP

Depending on the types of work products and levels of control required, changes may be tracked and controlled by individuals through management forums or by using formal CCBs.

Changes to the work products under configuration management are tracked and controlled.

The specific practices under this specific goal serve to maintain baselines after they are established by specific practices under the Establish Baselines specific goal.

SP 2.1 TRACK CHANGE REQUESTS

Track change requests for configuration items.

TIP

Change requests must be sufficiently detailed to enable their analysis and disposition.

TIP

The acquirer may need to track change requests to supplier products that are not within the scope of the supplier's contract.

Change requests address not only new or changed requirements but also failures and defects in work products.

Change requests can be initiated either by the acquirer or supplier. Changes that impact acquirer work products and supplier deliverables as defined in the supplier agreement are handled through the acquirer's configuration management process.

Change requests are analyzed to determine the impact that the change will have on the work product, related work products, the budget, and the schedule.

Typical Work Products

1. Change requests

Typical Supplier Deliverables

1. Change requests

Subpractices

1. Initiate and record change requests in the change request database.
2. Analyze the impact of changes and fixes proposed in change requests.

   The acquirer analyzes the impact that submitted change requests may have on supplier agreements.

   Refer to the Solicitation and Supplier Agreement Development process area for more information about changing the supplier agreement.

3. Review change requests to be addressed in the next baseline with relevant stakeholders and get their agreement.

   Conduct the change request review with appropriate participants. Record the disposition of each change request and the rationale for the decision, including success criteria, a brief action plan if appropriate, and needs met or unmet by the change. Perform the actions required in the disposition, and report results to relevant stakeholders.

4. Track the status of change requests to closure.

SP 2.2 Control Configuration Items

Control changes to configuration items.

Control is maintained over the configuration of the work product baseline. This control includes tracking the configuration of each configuration item, approving a new configuration if necessary, and updating the baseline.

The acquirer decides which configuration items require version control, or more stringent levels of configuration control, and establishes mechanisms to ensure configuration items are controlled. Although the supplier may manage configuration items on the acquirer's behalf, the acquirer is responsible for approval and control of changes to these configuration items.

Typical Work Products

1. Revision history of configuration items
2. Archives of baselines

Subpractices

1. Control changes to configuration items throughout the life of the product.
2. Obtain appropriate authorization before changed configuration items are entered into the configuration management system.

TIP

A database provides a flexible environment for storing and tracking change requests.

TIP

The acquirer and end user may determine that certain change requests are outside the scope of current supplier agreements and may require the initiation of a new acquisition project for a follow-on system, major system modification, or rescoping of the current agreement; or the change may be deferred indefinitely.

HINT

Track change requests to closure to ensure that if a change request is not addressed, it was not lost or missed.

HINT

When deciding whether the acquirer or supplier maintains configuration control, consider the risk to the integrity of critical work products if the supplier fails to meet contractual requirements and it results in legal action.

TIP

A revision history usually contains not only what was changed but also who made the changes and when and why they were made.

TIP

The life of the product is typically longer than the life of the acquisition project. The responsibility for configuration items may change over time.

HINT

Define authorization procedures so that it is clear how to receive authorization to enter an updated configuration item into the CM system.

TIP

An important part of check-in and check-out is ensuring that only one copy of a configuration item is authorized for update at one time.

For example, authorization may come from the CCB, the project manager, or the customer.

3. Check in and check out configuration items in the configuration management system for incorporation of changes in a manner that maintains the correctness and integrity of configuration items.
4. Perform reviews to ensure that changes have not caused unintended effects on the baselines (e.g., ensure that changes have not compromised the safety and/or security of the system).
5. Record changes to configuration items and reasons for changes, as appropriate.

SG 3 Establish Integrity

Integrity of baselines is established and maintained.

TIP

Since baselines are often the "footprints" of a particular product, it is important that they are accurate.

The integrity of baselines, established by processes associated with the Establish Baselines specific goal, and maintained by processes associated with the Track and Control Changes specific goal, is addressed by the specific practices under this specific goal.

SP 3.1 Establish Configuration Management Records

Establish and maintain records describing configuration items.

TIP

When the acquisition project team is small and CM is informal, records describing the status of configuration items are as critical as they are with a large team. These records ensure a smooth handoff when team members leave the project.

Typical Work Products

1. Revision history of configuration items
2. Change log
3. Change request records
4. Status of configuration items
5. Differences between baselines

Typical Supplier Deliverables

1. Revision history of product and supplier deliverables defined in the supplier agreement

Subpractices

1. Record configuration management actions in sufficient detail so the content and status of each configuration item are known and previous versions can be recovered.
2. Ensure that relevant stakeholders have access to and knowledge of the configuration status of configuration items.

3. Specify the latest version of baselines.
4. Identify the version of configuration items that constitute a particular baseline.
5. Describe differences between successive baselines.
6. Revise the status and history (i.e., changes and other actions) of each configuration item as necessary.

HINT

When describing the differences between baselines, be detailed enough so that users of the baselines can differentiate them easily.

SP 3.2 Perform Configuration Audits

Perform configuration audits to maintain the integrity of configuration baselines.

Configuration audits confirm that the resulting baselines and documentation conform to a specified standard or requirement. Audit results should be recorded, as appropriate. (See the glossary for a definition of "configuration audit.")

HINT

Consider conducting audits prior to the handoff of work products among customer, acquirer, supplier, and other stakeholders.

Typical Work Products

1. Configuration audit results
2. Action items

Typical Supplier Deliverables

1. Supplier configuration audit results

Subpractices

1. Assess the integrity of baselines.
2. Confirm that configuration management records correctly identify configuration items.
3. Review the structure and integrity of items in the configuration management system.
4. Confirm the completeness and correctness of items in the configuration management system.

   Completeness and correctness of the configuration management system's content is based on requirements as stated in the plan and the disposition of approved change requests.
5. Confirm compliance with applicable configuration management standards and procedures.
6. Track action items from the audit to closure.

TIP

Integrity includes both accuracy and completeness.

TIP

An audit is effective only when all action items from the audit are addressed.

DECISION ANALYSIS AND RESOLUTION

A Support Process Area at Maturity Level 3

Purpose

The purpose of Decision Analysis and Resolution (DAR) is to analyze possible decisions using a formal evaluation process that evaluates identified alternatives against established criteria.

TIP

DAR provides organizations with a criteria-based approach to making important decisions objectively.

Introductory Notes

The Decision Analysis and Resolution process area involves establishing guidelines to determine which issues should be subject to a formal evaluation process and applying formal evaluation processes to these issues.

A formal evaluation process is a structured approach to evaluating alternative solutions against established criteria to determine a recommended solution.

A formal evaluation process involves the following actions:

- Establishing the criteria for evaluating alternatives
- Identifying alternative solutions
- Selecting methods for evaluating alternatives
- Evaluating alternative solutions using established criteria and methods
- Selecting recommended solutions from alternatives based on evaluation criteria

HINT

Many key acquisition decisions are made early in a project's lifecycle and have a major impact on project outcomes. Start by using formal evaluation methods on these key decisions before using them for selected day-to-day decisions. An effective source selection process or well-thought-out lifecycle milestone decisions are results of classic DAR activities.

Rather than using the phrase *alternative solutions to address issues* each time, in this process area, one of two shorter phrases are used: *alternative solutions* or *alternatives*.

A repeatable criteria-based decision-making process is especially important, both for making critical decisions that define and guide the acquisition process and later for critical decisions made with the selected supplier. The establishment of a formal process for decision

TIP

DAR takes the blame out of decision making. A bad decision is made when all the necessary information that might impact the decision was not considered and relevant stakeholders were not consulted.

HINT

Maintain the rationale for key decisions that drive the acquisition strategy to make early project thinking available to team members and stakeholders who join the project later.

X-REF

To see how to create an acquisition strategy, see "Techniques for Developing an Acquisition Strategy by Profiling Software Risks" at www.sei.cmu.edu/publications/documents/06.reports/06tr002.html.

TIP

Examples of nontechnical issues include staffing profiles for the acquisition project team over time and the mix of skills required to ensure project success.

TIP

Tools such as the Analytic Hierarchy Process (AHP), Quality Function Deployment (QFD), the Pugh Method, the Delphi Method, prioritization matrices, cause-and-effect diagrams, decision trees, weighted criteria spreadsheets, and simulations can incorporate weights in decision making.

making provides the acquirer with documentation of decision rationale. Such documentation allows criteria for critical decisions to be revisited when changes or technology insertion decisions that impact requirements or other critical project parameters are considered. A formal process also supports the communication of decisions between the acquirer and supplier.

A formal evaluation process reduces the subjective nature of a decision and provides a higher probability of selecting a solution that meets multiple demands of relevant stakeholders.

While the primary application of this process area is to technical concerns, formal evaluation processes can also be applied to many nontechnical issues, particularly when a project is being planned. Issues that have multiple alternative solutions and evaluation criteria lend themselves to a formal evaluation process.

Guidelines are created for deciding when to use formal evaluation processes to address unplanned issues. Guidelines often suggest using formal evaluation processes when issues are associated with medium to high risks or when issues affect the ability to achieve project objectives.

Formal evaluation processes can vary in formality, type of criteria, and methods employed. Less formal decisions can be analyzed in a few hours, use few criteria (e.g., effectiveness and cost to implement), and result in a one- or two-page report. More formal decisions may require separate plans, months of effort, meetings to develop and approve criteria, simulations, prototypes, piloting, and extensive documentation.

Both numeric and non-numeric criteria can be used in a formal evaluation process. Numeric criteria use weights to reflect the relative importance of criteria. Non-numeric criteria use a more subjective ranking scale (e.g., high, medium, or low). More formal decisions may require a full trade study.

A formal evaluation process identifies and evaluates alternative solutions. The eventual selection of a solution may involve iterative activities of identification and evaluation. Portions of identified alternatives may be combined, emerging technologies may change alternatives, and the business situation of suppliers may change during the evaluation period.

A recommended alternative is accompanied by documentation of selected methods, criteria, alternatives, and rationale for the recommendation. The documentation is distributed to relevant stakeholders; it provides a record of the formal evaluation process and rationale, which are useful to other projects that encounter a similar issue.

While some of the decisions made throughout the life of the project involve the use of a formal evaluation process, others do not. As mentioned earlier, guidelines should be established to determine which issues should be subject to a formal evaluation process.

Related Process Areas

Refer to the Project Planning process area for more information about general planning for projects.

Refer to the Integrated Project Management process area for more information about establishing the project's defined process. The project's defined process includes a formal evaluation process for each selected issue and incorporates the use of guidelines for applying a formal evaluation process to unforeseen issues.

Refer to the Risk Management process area for more information about identifying and mitigating risks. A formal evaluation process is often used to address issues with identified medium or high risks. Selected solutions typically affect risk mitigation plans.

X-REF

Refer to SSAD for more information about selecting one or more suppliers to deliver the product or service. The selection activities incorporate formal evaluation techniques and decision-making processes when selecting suppliers.

TIP

Many of the issues that may benefit from a formal evaluation process are addressed in PP, SSAD, RSKM, ARD, ATM, AVER, and AVAL.

DAR

Specific Goal and Practice Summary

SG 1 Evaluate Alternatives
- SP 1.1 Establish Guidelines for Decision Analysis
- SP 1.2 Establish Evaluation Criteria
- SP 1.3 Identify Alternative Solutions
- SP 1.4 Select Evaluation Methods
- SP 1.5 Evaluate Alternatives
- SP 1.6 Select Solutions

Specific Practices by Goal

SG 1 EVALUATE ALTERNATIVES

Decisions are based on an evaluation of alternatives using established criteria.

Issues requiring a formal evaluation process may be identified at any time. The objective should be to identify issues as early as possible to maximize the time available to resolve them.

SP 1.1 ESTABLISH GUIDELINES FOR DECISION ANALYSIS

Establish and maintain guidelines to determine which issues are subject to a formal evaluation process.

TIP

The terms *issues* and *decisions* are used interchangeably here.

Not every decision is significant enough to require a formal evaluation process. The choice between the trivial and the truly important are unclear without explicit guidance. Whether a decision is significant or not is dependent on the project and circumstances and is determined by established guidelines.

Typical guidelines for determining when to require a formal evaluation process include the following.

- A decision is directly related to topics that are medium or high risk.
- A decision is related to changing work products under configuration management.
- A decision would cause schedule delays over a certain percentage or amount of time.
- A decision affects the ability of the project to achieve its objectives.
- The costs of the formal evaluation process are reasonable when compared to the decision's impact.
- A legal obligation exists during a solicitation.
- There is a risk that the decision will have a significant adverse effect on cost, quality, resources, or schedule.
- Legal or supplier agreement issues must be resolved.

Refer to the Risk Management process area for more information about determining which issues are medium or high risk.

Examples of when to use a formal evaluation process include the following:

- On decisions to trade off performance, cost, and schedule requirements during an acquisition
- On selecting, terminating, or renewing suppliers
- On selecting training for project personnel
- On selecting a testing environment to be used for product validation
- On determining the items to be selected for reuse in related projects
- On selecting an approach for ongoing support (e.g., disaster recovery, service levels)

Typical Work Products

1. Guidelines for when to apply a formal evaluation process

HINT

Evaluate these guidelines periodically to ensure that they reflect the current needs of the project or organization.

Subpractices

1. Establish guidelines for when to use a formal evaluation process.
2. Incorporate the use of guidelines into the defined process as appropriate.

Refer to the Integrated Project Management process area for more information about establishing the project's defined process.

SP 1.2 Establish Evaluation Criteria

Establish and maintain criteria for evaluating alternatives, and the relative ranking of these criteria.

Evaluation criteria provide the basis for evaluating alternative solutions. Criteria are ranked so that the highest ranked criteria exert the most influence on the evaluation.

This process area is referenced by many other process areas in the model, and there are many contexts in which a formal evaluation process can be used. Therefore, in some situations you may find that criteria have already been defined as part of another process. This specific practice does not suggest that a second development of criteria be conducted.

Document the evaluation criteria to minimize the possibility that decisions will be second-guessed or that the reason for making the decision will be forgotten. Decisions based on criteria that are explicitly defined and established remove barriers to stakeholder buy-in.

TIP

In less formal cases, all criteria may be roughly equal and ranking may not be necessary.

HINT

Make sure you include participation of relevant customer and supplier stakeholders when selecting evaluation criteria.

Typical Work Products

1. Documented evaluation criteria
2. Rankings of criteria importance

Subpractices

1. Define the criteria for evaluating alternative solutions.

   Criteria should be traceable to requirements, scenarios, business case assumptions, business objectives, or other documented sources.

Types of criteria to consider include the following:

- Technology limitations
- Environmental impact
- Risks
- Total ownership and lifecycle costs

2. Define the range and scale for ranking the evaluation criteria.

   Scales of relative importance for evaluation criteria can be established with non-numeric values or with formulas that relate the evaluation parameter to a numeric weight.
3. Rank the criteria.
4. Assess the criteria and their relative importance.

TIP

An example of a non-numeric scale is one that ranks criteria based on low, medium, or high importance.

5. Evolve the evaluation criteria to improve their validity.
6. Document the rationale for the selection and rejection of evaluation criteria.

SP 1.3 Identify Alternative Solutions

Identify alternative solutions to address issues.

A wider range of alternatives can surface by soliciting as many stakeholders as practical for input. Input from stakeholders with diverse skills and backgrounds can help teams identify and address assumptions, constraints, and biases. Brainstorming sessions may stimulate innovative alternatives through rapid interaction and feedback.

Sufficient candidate solutions may not be furnished for analysis. As the analysis proceeds, other alternatives should be added to the list of potential candidate solutions. The generation and consideration of multiple alternatives early in a decision analysis and resolution process increases the likelihood that an acceptable decision will be made and that consequences of the decision will be understood.

HINT

When you are evaluating competing designs that are identified by your suppliers, make sure you solicit alternatives that may be more innovative and less obvious. Consider commissioning a special study by a team with a lower stake in the selection outcome to help ensure that a range of alternatives are identified.

Typical Work Products

1. Identified alternatives

Typical Supplier Deliverables

1. Supplier identified alternatives, if any

Subpractices

1. Perform a literature search.

   A literature search can uncover what others have done both inside and outside the organization. Such a search may provide a deeper understanding of the problem, alternatives to consider, barriers to implementation, existing trade studies, and lessons learned from similar decisions.
2. Identify alternatives for consideration in addition to those that may be provided with the issue.

   Evaluation criteria are an effective starting point for identifying alternatives. Evaluation criteria identify priorities of relevant stakeholders and the importance of technical, logistical, or other challenges.

   Combining key attributes of existing alternatives can generate additional and sometimes stronger alternatives.

   Solicit alternatives from relevant stakeholders. Brainstorming sessions, interviews, and working groups can be used effectively to uncover alternatives.
3. Document proposed alternatives.

SP 1.4 Select Evaluation Methods

Select evaluation methods.

Methods for evaluating alternative solutions against established criteria can range from simulations to the use of probabilistic models and decision theory. These methods must be carefully selected. The level of detail of a method should be commensurate with cost, schedule, performance, and risk impacts.

HINT

Make sure the method chosen is appropriate for the decision. A complex and time-consuming approach may be overkill for a simple binary decision.

While many problems may require only one evaluation method, some problems may require multiple methods. For instance, simulations may augment a trade study to determine which design alternative best meets a given criterion.

Suppliers competing to develop a technical solution for the acquirer may be directly evaluated in a final competition that involves a performance or functional demonstration of proposed solutions.

Typical Work Products

1. Selected evaluation methods

Subpractices

1. Select methods based on the purpose for analyzing a decision and on the availability of the information used to support the method.

> Typical evaluation methods include the following:
> - Benchmarking studies
> - Cost studies
> - Business opportunity studies
> - Surveys
> - Extrapolations based on field experience and prototypes
> - User review and comment
> - Judgment provided by an expert or group of experts (e.g., Delphi Method)

2. Select evaluation methods based on their ability to focus on the issues at hand without being overly influenced by side issues.
3. Determine the measures needed to support the evaluation method.

   Refer to the Measurement and Analysis process area for more information about specifying measures.

SP 1.5 Evaluate Alternatives

Evaluate alternative solutions using established criteria and methods.

Evaluating alternative solutions involves analysis, discussion, and review. Iterative cycles of analysis are sometimes necessary. Supporting analyses, experimentation, prototyping, piloting, or simulations may be needed to substantiate scoring and conclusions.

Often, the relative importance of criteria is imprecise and the total effect on a solution is not apparent until after the analysis is performed. In cases where the resulting scores differ by relatively small amounts, the best selection among alternative solutions may not be clear. Challenges to criteria and assumptions should be encouraged.

TIP

Evaluation criteria for a competitive source selection should be part of the solicitation package so that all stakeholders understand the relative importance of solicitation requirements.

X-REF

Refer to SP 1.2 of SSAD for more information on establishing evaluation criteria for use in selecting suppliers.

Typical Work Products

1. Evaluation results

Subpractices

1. Evaluate proposed alternative solutions using the established evaluation criteria and selected methods.
2. Evaluate assumptions related to the evaluation criteria and the evidence that supports the assumptions.
3. Evaluate whether uncertainty in the values for alternative solutions affects the evaluation and address these uncertainties, as appropriate.
4. Perform simulations, modeling, prototypes, and pilots as necessary to exercise the evaluation criteria, methods, and alternative solutions.

   Untested criteria, their relative importance, and supporting data or functions may cause the validity of solutions to be questioned. Criteria and their relative priorities and scales can be tested with trial runs against a set of alternatives. These trial runs of a select set of criteria allow for the evaluation of the cumulative impact of criteria on a solution. If trials reveal problems, different criteria or alternatives might be considered to avoid biases.
5. Consider new alternative solutions, criteria, or methods if proposed alternatives do not test well; repeat evaluations until alternatives do test well.

   Document the rationale for the addition of new alternatives or methods and changes to criteria, as well as the results of interim evaluations. Determine the scores for each alternative based on criteria evaluations and scoring methods previously determined.
6. Document the results of the evaluation.

SP 1.6 Select Solutions

Select solutions from alternatives based on evaluation criteria.

Selecting solutions involves weighing results from the evaluation of alternatives. Risks associated with the implementation of solutions must be assessed.

> **TIP**
>
> Selecting a solution still requires humans to make decisions. These decisions are informed by the results of evaluations. Other considerations (such as risk or external constraints) may cause a project to select solutions that score lower based on the chosen criteria. If this is the case, the rationale for the selection becomes even more critical to maintain.

Typical Work Products

1. Recommended solutions to address significant issues

Subpractices

1. Assess the risks associated with implementing the recommended solution.

   Refer to the Risk Management process area for more information about identifying and managing risks.

2. Document the results and rationale for the recommended solution.

INTEGRATED PROJECT MANAGEMENT

A Project Management Process Area at Maturity Level 3

Purpose

The purpose of Integrated Project Management (IPM) is to establish and manage the project and the involvement of the relevant stakeholders according to an integrated and defined process that is tailored from the organization's set of standard processes.

X-REF

IPM matures the project management activities described in PP and PMC so that they address the organizational requirements for projects described in OPF and OPD.

Introductory Notes

Integrated Project Management involves the following activities:

- Establishing the project's defined process at project startup by tailoring the organization's set of standard processes
- Managing the project using the project's defined process
- Establishing the work environment for the project based on the organization's work environment standards
- Establishing integrated teams that are tasked to accomplish project objectives
- Using and contributing to organizational process assets
- Enabling relevant stakeholders' concerns to be identified, considered, and, when appropriate, addressed during the development of the product
- Ensuring that relevant stakeholders perform their tasks in a coordinated and timely manner (1) to address product and product component requirements, plans, objectives, problems, and risks; (2) to fulfill their commitments; and (3) to identify, track, and resolve coordination issues

The integrated and defined process that is tailored from the organization's set of standard processes is called the project's defined process.

Managing the project's effort, cost, schedule, staffing, risks, and other factors is tied to the tasks of the project's defined process. The implementation and management of the project's defined process are typically described in the project plan. Certain activities may be covered in other plans that affect the project, such as the quality assurance plan, risk management strategy, and the configuration management plan.

Since the defined process for each project is tailored from the organization's set of standard processes, variability among projects is typically reduced and projects can more easily share process assets, data, and lessons learned.

TIP

Using IPM to guide project management activities enables project plans to be consistent with project activities because they are both derived from standard processes created by the organization. Further, plans tend to be more reliable and are developed more quickly, and new projects learn more quickly.

TIP

It is also easier to share resources (e.g., training and software tools) and to "load-balance" staff members across projects.

This process area also addresses the coordination of all activities associated with the project, such as the following:

- Development activities (e.g., requirements development, design, and verification)
- Service activities (e.g., delivery, help desk, operations, and customer contact)
- Acquisition activities (e.g., solicitation, agreement monitoring, and transition to operations)
- Support activities (e.g., configuration management, documentation, marketing, and training)

The working interfaces and interactions among relevant stakeholders internal and external to the project are planned and managed to ensure the quality and integrity of the entire product. Relevant stakeholders participate, as appropriate, in defining the project's defined process and the project plan. Reviews and exchanges are regularly conducted with relevant stakeholders to ensure that coordination issues receive appropriate attention and everyone involved with the project is appropriately aware of status, plans, and activities. (See the definition of "relevant stakeholder" in the glossary.) In defining the project's defined process, formal interfaces are created as necessary to ensure that appropriate coordination and collaboration occur.

TIP

A proactive approach to integrating plans and coordinating with relevant stakeholders outside the project is a key activity. This is particularly important when multiple projects must work together to provide needed capabilities.

The acquirer must involve and integrate all relevant acquisition, technical, support, and operational stakeholders. Depending on the scope and risk of the project, coordination efforts with the supplier can be significant.

Formal interfaces among relevant stakeholders take the form of memorandums of understanding, memorandums of agreement, contractual commitments, associated supplier agreements, and similar documents, depending on the nature of the interfaces and involved stakeholders.

This process area applies in any organizational structure, including projects that are structured as line organizations, matrix organizations, or integrated teams. The terminology should be appropriately interpreted for the organizational structure in place.

Related Process Areas

Refer to the Project Planning process area for more information about planning the project, which includes identifying relevant stakeholders and their appropriate involvement in the project.

Refer to the Project Monitoring and Control process area for more information about monitoring and controlling the project.

Refer to the Organizational Process Definition process area for more information about organizational process assets and work environment standards.

Refer to the Measurement and Analysis process area for more information about defining a process for measuring and analyzing processes.

Refer to the Agreement Management process area for more information about managing supplier agreements.

Specific Goal and Practice Summary

SG 1 Use the Project's Defined Process
- SP 1.1 Establish the Project's Defined Process
- SP 1.2 Use Organizational Process Assets for Planning Project Activities
- SP 1.3 Establish the Project's Work Environment
- SP 1.4 Integrate Plans
- SP 1.5 Manage the Project Using Integrated Plans
- SP 1.6 Establish Integrated Teams
- SP 1.7 Contribute to Organizational Process Assets

SG 2 Coordinate and Collaborate with Relevant Stakeholders
- SP 2.1 Manage Stakeholder Involvement
- SP 2.2 Manage Dependencies
- SP 2.3 Resolve Coordination Issues

TIP

In developing the acquisition model, what was the IPM IPPD addition in the CMMI-DEV model was consolidated into IPM SP 1.6 in the CMMI-ACQ model. Establishing integrated teams is an expected activity for conducting successful acquisitions. These teams often require participation beyond the project and may include customers and suppliers.

Specific Practices by Goal

SG 1 USE THE PROJECT'S DEFINED PROCESS

The project is conducted using a defined process tailored from the organization's set of standard processes.

The project's defined process must include those processes from the organization's set of standard processes that address all processes

TIP

All projects that use IPM use the organization's set of standard processes as a basis to begin planning all project activities.

necessary to acquire or develop and maintain the product. The product-related lifecycle processes, such as manufacturing and support processes, are developed concurrently with the product.

SP 1.1 Establish the Project's Defined Process

Establish and maintain the project's defined process from project startup through the life of the project.

Refer to the Organizational Process Definition process area for more information about organizational process assets.

Refer to the Organizational Process Focus process area for more information about organizational process needs and objectives and deploying the organization's set of standard processes on projects.

The project's defined process consists of defined processes that form an integrated, coherent lifecycle for the project.

The project's defined process logically sequences acquirer activities and supplier deliverables (as identified in the supplier agreement) to deliver a product that meets the requirements. The acquirer may require the supplier to align selected processes with the acquirer's defined process.

The project's defined process should satisfy the project's contractual requirements, operational needs, opportunities, and constraints. It is designed to provide a best fit for project needs.

A project's defined process is based on the following factors:

- Customer requirements
- Product and product component requirements
- Commitments
- Organizational process needs and objectives
- The organization's set of standard processes and tailoring guidelines
- The operational environment
- The business environment

Establishing the project's defined process at project startup helps to ensure that project staff and stakeholders implement a set of activities needed to efficiently establish an initial set of requirements and plans for the project. As the project progresses, the description of the project's defined process is elaborated and revised to better meet project requirements and the organization's process needs and objectives. Also, as the organization's set of standard processes changes, the project's defined process may need to be revised.

The project's defined process is driven by the acquisition strategy. The acquirer's defined process is affected, for example, by whether the acquisition strategy is to introduce new technology to the organization or to consolidate acquired products or services in use by the acquirer.

Typical Work Products

1. The project's defined process

Typical Supplier Deliverables

1. Tailored supplier processes that interface with the acquirer's defined process

Subpractices

1. Select a lifecycle model from those available in organizational process assets.

> Examples of project characteristics that could affect the selection of lifecycle models include the following:
> - Size of the project
> - Experience and familiarity of staff with implementing the process
> - Constraints such as cycle time and acceptable defect levels

2. Select standard processes from the organization's set of standard processes that best fit the needs of the project.
3. Tailor the organization's set of standard processes and other organizational process assets according to tailoring guidelines to produce the project's defined process.

   Sometimes the available lifecycle models and standard processes are inadequate to meet project needs. Sometimes the project is unable to produce required work products or measures. In such circumstances, the project must seek approval to deviate from what is required by the organization. Waivers are provided for this purpose.
4. Use other artifacts from the organization's process asset library, as appropriate.

> Other artifacts may include the following:
> - Lessons-learned documents
> - Templates
> - Example documents
> - Estimating models

X-REF

IPM depends strongly on OPD. It is impossible to fully implement the specific practices in IPM without having in place the organizational infrastructure described in OPD.

HINT

Tailor the organization's set of standard processes to address the project's specific needs and situation. Some questions to ask to determine specific needs include the following: Are stringent quality, safety, or security requirements in place? Are the customer's needs still evolving? Is the team working with a new customer, a new acquisition strategy, or a new supplier? Are there stringent schedule constraints?

5. Document the project's defined process.
6. Conduct peer reviews of the project's defined process.
7. Revise the project's defined process as necessary.

HINT

Maintain the process asset library to keep it current. Otherwise, it could become the dumping ground for all project information and quickly become unusable.

SP 1.2 *Use Organizational Process Assets for Planning Project Activities*

Use organizational process assets and the measurement repository for estimating and planning project activities.

TIP

These activities may be similar to what you were doing to address PP, but because data and experiences from other projects are now available and applicable, the accuracy of project planning improves.

Refer to the Organizational Process Definition process area for more information about organizational process assets and the organization's measurement repository.

When available, use results of previous planning and execution activities as predictors of the relative scope and risk of the effort being estimated for the current acquisition.

Typical Work Products

1. Project estimates
2. Project plans

Subpractices

1. Use the tasks and work products of the project's defined process as a basis for estimating and planning project activities.

   An understanding of the relationships among tasks and work products of the project's defined process and of the roles to be performed by relevant stakeholders is a basis for developing a realistic plan.
2. Use the organization's measurement repository in estimating the project's planning parameters.

TIP

Independent validation of data confirms that the historical data used is applicable to the project.

This estimate typically includes the following:
- Using appropriate historical data from this project or similar projects
- Accounting for and recording similarities and differences between the current project and those projects whose historical data will be used
- Ensuring historical data are valid
- Recording the reasoning, assumptions, and rationale used to select historical data

SP 1.3 *Establish the Project's Work Environment*

Establish and maintain the project's work environment based on the organization's work environment standards.

An appropriate work environment for a project comprises an infrastructure of facilities, tools, and equipment that people need to perform their jobs effectively in support of business and project objectives. The work environment and its components are maintained at a level of performance and reliability indicated by organizational work environment standards. As required, the project's work environment or some of its components can be developed internally or acquired from external sources.

The supplier's work environment should be compatible with the acquirer's work environment to enable efficient and effective transfer of work products.

The work environment might encompass environments for both verification and validation or these might be separate environments.

TIP

Often, the project's work environment contains components that are common to the organization's overall work environment. Many of these components may be provided by information technology (IT) or a facilities group.

Refer to the Establish Work Environment Standards specific practice in the Organizational Process Definition process area for more information about work environment standards.

Typical Work Products

1. Equipment and tools for the project
2. Installation, operation, and maintenance manuals for the project work environment
3. User surveys and results
4. Usage, performance, and maintenance records
5. Support services for the project's work environment

Subpractices

1. Plan, design, and install a work environment for the project.

   The critical aspects of the project work environment are, like any other product, requirements-driven. Work environment functionality and operations are explored with the same rigor as is done for any other product development.

TIP

A facilities group can use input from the project to create the work environment.

It may be necessary to make tradeoffs among performance, costs, and risks. The following are examples of each.

- Performance considerations may include timely interoperable communication, safety, security, and maintainability.
- Costs may include capital outlays, training, a support structure, disassembly and disposal of existing environments, and the operation and maintenance of the environment.
- Risks may include workflow and project disruptions.

Examples of equipment and tools include the following:

- Office software
- Decision support software
- Project management tools
- Requirements management tools and design tools
- Configuration management tools
- Evaluation tools
- Test and evaluation equipment

2. Provide ongoing maintenance and operational support for the project's work environment.

   Maintenance and support of the work environment can be accomplished either with capabilities found inside the organization or hired from outside the organization.

Examples of maintenance and support approaches include the following:

- Hiring people to perform maintenance and support
- Training people to perform maintenance and support
- Contracting maintenance and support
- Developing expert users for selected tools

3. Maintain the qualification of components of the project's work environment.

   Components include software, databases, hardware, tools, test equipment, and appropriate documentation. Qualification of software includes appropriate certifications. Hardware and test equipment qualification includes calibration and adjustment records and traceability to calibration standards.
4. Periodically review how well the work environment is meeting project needs and supporting collaboration, and take action, as appropriate.

TIP

One of the main differences between IPM and PP is that IPM is more proactive in coordinating with relevant stakeholders, both internal (different teams) and external (organizational functions, support groups, customers, and suppliers) to the project, and is concerned with the integration of plans.

SP 1.4 Integrate Plans

Integrate the project plan and other plans that affect the project to describe the project's defined process.

Refer to the Project Planning process area for more information about establishing and maintaining a project plan.

Refer to the Organizational Process Definition process area for more information about organizational process assets and, in particular, the organization's measurement repository.

Refer to the Organizational Process Focus process area for more information about organizational process needs and objectives.

This specific practice extends the specific practices for establishing and maintaining a project plan to address additional planning activities such as incorporating the project's defined process, coordinating with relevant stakeholders, using organizational process assets, incorporating plans for peer reviews, and establishing objective entry and exit criteria for tasks.

The development of the project plan should account for current and projected needs, objectives, and requirements of the organization, customer, suppliers, and end users, as appropriate.

TIP

To formulate estimates, data should be available from the organization's measurement repository. Additionally, templates, examples, and lessons-learned documents should be available from the organization's process asset library.

Typical Work Products

1. Integrated plans

Typical Supplier Deliverables

1. Supplier plans

Subpractices

1. Integrate other plans that affect the project with the project plan.

> Other plans that affect the project plan may include the following:
> - Quality assurance plans
> - Configuration management plans
> - Risk management strategy
> - Documentation plans

2. Incorporate into the project plan the definitions of measures and measurement activities for managing the project.

   Refer to the Measurement and Analysis process area for more information about defining measures and measurement activities and analyzing measurement data.

3. Identify and analyze product and project interface risks.

   Refer to the Risk Management process area for more information about identifying and analyzing risks.

4. Schedule tasks in a sequence that accounts for critical development factors and project risks.

Examples of factors considered in scheduling include the following:

- Size and complexity of tasks
- Needs of the customer and end users
- Availability of critical resources
- Availability of key personnel

5. Incorporate plans for performing peer reviews on work products of the project's defined process.
6. Incorporate the training needed to perform the project's defined process in the project's training plans.
7. Establish objective entry and exit criteria to authorize the initiation and completion of tasks described in the work breakdown structure (WBS).

   Refer to the Project Planning process area for more information about the WBS.

8. Ensure that the project plan is appropriately compatible with the plans of relevant stakeholders.
9. Identify how conflicts will be resolved that arise among relevant stakeholders.

   Refer to the Agreement Management process area for more information about resolving supplier agreement issues.

TIP

Because of the organizational inputs from the organization's set of standard processes, many of the activities in PP are performed in IPM in more detail; and because of the historical data and experiences captured in other organizational process assets, the detail is more reliable.
Because of the historical data and experience captured in organizational process assets, IPM allows a more detailed and more reliable approach to planning.

SP 1.5 MANAGE THE PROJECT USING INTEGRATED PLANS

Manage the project using the project plan, other plans that affect the project, and the project's defined process.

TIP

The prior specific practices established the plan—this specific practice implements and manages the project against that plan.

Refer to the Organizational Process Definition process area for more information about organizational process assets.

Refer to the Organizational Process Focus process area for more information about organizational process needs and objectives and coordinating process improvement activities with the rest of the organization.

Refer to the Risk Management process area for more information about managing risks.

Refer to the Project Monitoring and Control process area for more information about monitoring and controlling the project.

Typical Work Products

1. Work products created by performing the project's defined process
2. Collected measures (i.e., actuals) and progress records or reports

3. Revised requirements, plans, and commitments
4. Integrated plans

Typical Supplier Deliverables

1. Supplier project progress and performance reports

Subpractices

1. Implement the project's defined process using the organization's process asset library.

> This task typically includes the following activities:
> - Incorporating artifacts from the organization's process asset library into the project, as appropriate
> - Using lessons learned from the organization's process asset library to manage the project

2. Monitor and control the project's activities and work products using the project's defined process, project plan, and other plans that affect the project.

TIP

The organization's process improvement plan is another plan that might affect the project.

> This task typically includes the following activities:
> - Using the defined entry and exit criteria to authorize the initiation and determine the completion of tasks
> - Monitoring activities that could significantly affect actual values of the project's planning parameters
> - Tracking project planning parameters using measurable thresholds that will trigger investigation and appropriate actions
> - Monitoring product and project interface risks
> - Managing external and internal commitments based on plans for tasks and work products of the project's defined process

An understanding of the relationships among tasks and work products of the project's defined process and of the roles to be performed by relevant stakeholders, along with well-defined control mechanisms (e.g., peer reviews), achieves better visibility into project performance and better control of the project.

3. Obtain and analyze selected measures to manage the project and support organization needs.

Refer to the Measurement and Analysis process area for more information about obtaining and analyzing measures.

TIP

This specific practice should prove useful to any project that needs to bring individuals of differing views, cultures, and expertise together as a team. This practice is performed concurrently with the first five specific practices.

This specific practice is included to ensure that integrated teams are used for the purposes of addressing integration issues. Often, these occur across boundaries with customers, suppliers, and other critical acquisition efforts.

This specific practice addresses the tendency of team members to become insular in outlook and not feel responsible for larger project issues. This specific practice complements the specific practices of SG 2.

HINT

When a supplier is integrated into the project team, pick the best process for the situation and be sure it is covered in the supplier agreement.

TIP

Establishing the right team structure aids in planning, coordinating, and managing risk. Acquisition projects sometimes choose a single, top-level, integrated team that is in place for the duration of the acquisition project, but the rest of the project work is performed within traditional organizational boundaries. Such an approach can improve efficiency and be pursued if the product architecture aligns well with existing organizational boundaries.

4. Periodically review and align the project's performance with current and anticipated needs, objectives, and requirements of the organization, customer, and end users, as appropriate.

   This review includes alignment with organizational process needs and objectives.

Examples of actions that achieve alignment include the following:

- Accelerating the schedule, with appropriate adjustments to other planning parameters and project risks
- Changing requirements in response to a change in market opportunities or customer and end-user needs
- Terminating the project

SP 1.6 Establish Integrated Teams

Establish and maintain integrated teams.

The project is managed using integrated teams that reflect the organizational rules and guidelines for team structuring and forming. The project's shared vision is established prior to establishing the team structure, which may be based on the WBS. For small acquirer organizations, the whole organization and relevant external stakeholders can be treated as an integrated team.

Refer to the Establish Rules and Guidelines for Integrated Teams specific practice in the Organizational Process Definition process area for more information about establishing organizational rules and guidelines for structuring and forming integrated teams.

One of the best ways to ensure coordination and collaboration with relevant stakeholders, specific goal 2 of this process area, is to include them on an integrated team. For projects within a system of systems framework, the most important integrated team may be with stakeholders representing other systems.

Typical Work Products

1. Documented shared vision
2. List of team members assigned to each integrated team
3. Integrated team charters
4. Periodic integrated team status reports

Subpractices

1. Establish and maintain the project's shared vision.

   When creating a shared vision, it is critical to understand the interfaces between the project and stakeholders external to the project. The vision should be shared among relevant stakeholders through their agreement and commitment.

   The development of the CMMI Product Suite is an example of a project that uses integrated teams. The CMMI project communicated its shared vision broadly so that the management team guiding CMMI activities, the home organizations that sponsored project team members, and the broad community had a clear understanding of the project's objectives, values, and intended outcomes.

2. Establish and maintain the integrated team structure.

   Cost, schedule, project risks, resources, interfaces, the project's defined process, and organizational guidelines are evaluated to establish the basis for defining integrated teams and their responsibilities, authorities, and interrelationships.

3. Establish and maintain each integrated team.

   Establishing and maintaining integrated teams encompasses choosing team leaders and team members and establishing team charters for each team. It also involves providing resources required to accomplish tasks assigned to the team.

4. Periodically evaluate the integrated team structure and composition.

   Integrated teams should be monitored to detect malfunctions, mismanaged interfaces, and mismatches of tasks to team members. Take corrective action when performance does not meet expectations.

HINT

Achieve the right allocation of requirements to each integrated team in the team structure before teams are formed because deciding which requirements to allocate to which team determines how the teams are staffed.

TIP

It may be useful to "sunset" a team once the specific needs of the team are satisfied. It may also be useful to create new teams at various points in the acquisition lifecycle to meet new acquisition challenges.

TIP

Each member of the integrated team should have dual aspirations and expectations: those specific to the project and those related to their home organization.

Although the integrated team sponsor helps to form the team, he or she is usually not involved in daily activities. The sponsor may be part of the management team.

The leader of an integrated team is often a member of the integrated team one layer up in the team structure.

The charter is reviewed by all members of the team to ensure buy-in.

HINT

Often, each team member represents a specific and essential perspective. When team composition changes, you must review the roles of departing team members to see whether their perspectives are still represented on the team.

TIP

This specific practice provides feedback to the organization so that the organizational assets can be improved, and data and experiences can be shared with other projects.

SP 1.7 CONTRIBUTE TO ORGANIZATIONAL PROCESS ASSETS

Contribute work products, measures, and documented experiences to organizational process assets.

Refer to the Organizational Process Focus process area for more information about process improvement proposals.

Refer to the Organizational Process Definition process area for more information about organizational process assets, the organization's measurement repository, and the organization's process asset library.

This specific practice addresses collecting information from processes in the project's defined process.

Typical Work Products

1. Proposed improvements to organizational process assets
2. Actual process and product measures collected from the project
3. Documentation (e.g., exemplary process descriptions, plans, training modules, checklists, and lessons learned)
4. Process artifacts associated with tailoring and implementing the organization's set of standard processes on the project

Subpractices

X-REF

Improvements are proposed using "process improvement proposals." For more information, see OPF SP 2.4.

1. Propose improvements to organizational process assets.
2. Store process and product measures in the organization's measurement repository.

   Refer to the Project Planning process area for more information about recording planning and replanning data.

   Refer to the Measurement and Analysis process area for more information about recording measurement data.

3. Submit documentation for possible inclusion in the organization's process asset library.

> Examples of documentation include the following:
> - Exemplary process descriptions
> - Training modules
> - Exemplary plans
> - Checklists

4. Document lessons learned from the project for inclusion in the organization's process asset library.

5. Provide process artifacts associated with tailoring and implementing the organization's set of standard processes in support of the organization's process monitoring activities.

   Refer to the Monitor the Implementation specific practice of the Organizational Process Focus process area for more information about monitoring the implementation of the organization's set of standard processes and use of process assets on all projects.

SG 2 COORDINATE AND COLLABORATE WITH RELEVANT STAKEHOLDERS

Coordination and collaboration between the project and relevant stakeholders are conducted.

X-REF

Relevant stakeholders are identified in GP 2.7 and PP SP 2.6.

SP 2.1 MANAGE STAKEHOLDER INVOLVEMENT

Manage the involvement of relevant stakeholders in the project.

Stakeholder involvement is managed according to the project's integrated and defined process.

The supplier agreement provides the basis for managing supplier involvement in the project. Supplier agreements (e.g., interagency and intercompany agreements, memorandums of understanding, memorandums of agreement) that the acquirer makes with stakeholder organizations, which may be product or service providers or recipients, provide the basis for their involvement. These agreements are particularly important when the acquirer's project produces a system that must be integrated into a larger system of systems.

Refer to the Project Planning process area for more information about identifying stakeholders and their appropriate involvement and about establishing and maintaining commitments.

IPM

Typical Work Products

1. Agendas and schedules for collaborative activities
2. Documented issues
3. Recommendations for resolving relevant stakeholder issues

Subpractices

1. Coordinate with relevant stakeholders who should participate in project activities.
2. Ensure work products that are produced to satisfy commitments meet the requirements of the recipients.
3. Develop recommendations and coordinate actions to resolve misunderstandings and problems with requirements.

TIP

These commitments may be external commitments that the project staff is addressing.

TIP

Too often, project members assume that critical dependencies identified at the beginning of a project will not change or are someone else's responsibility.
Ironically, when time and money are limited, integration, coordination, and collaboration activities become more critical. Coordination helps to ensure that all involved parties contribute to the product in a timely way to minimize rework and delays.

SP 2.2 Manage Dependencies

Participate with relevant stakeholders to identify, negotiate, and track critical dependencies.

Refer to the Project Planning process area for more information about identifying stakeholders and their appropriate involvement and about establishing and maintaining commitments.

Typical Work Products

1. Defects, issues, and action items resulting from reviews with relevant stakeholders
2. Critical dependencies
3. Commitments to address critical dependencies
4. Status of critical dependencies

Typical Supplier Deliverables

1. Status of critical dependencies

Subpractices

1. Conduct reviews with relevant stakeholders.

   It is particularly important that acquirers or owners of systems that interact with the project in a system of systems be involved in these reviews to manage critical dependencies these types of systems create.
2. Identify each critical dependency.
3. Establish need dates and plan dates for each critical dependency based on the project schedule.
4. Review and get agreement on commitments to address each critical dependency with those responsible for providing the work product and those receiving the work product.
5. Document critical dependencies and commitments.

   The acquirer documents supplier commitments to meet critical dependencies in the supplier agreement. Supplier dependencies and acquirer dependencies are documented in an integrated plan.
6. Track critical dependencies and commitments and take corrective action, as appropriate.

   Refer to the Project Monitoring and Control process area for more information about tracking commitments.

X-REF

You can facilitate coordination on critical dependencies by determining need and plan dates for each critical dependency and then establishing and managing commitments as described in these subpractices and in PP and PMC.

Tracking critical dependencies typically includes the following:

- Evaluating the effects of late and early completion for impacts on future activities and milestones
- Resolving actual and potential problems with responsible parties whenever possible
- Escalating to the appropriate party the actual and potential problems not resolvable by the responsible individual or group

SP 2.3 Resolve Coordination Issues

Resolve issues with relevant stakeholders.

Examples of coordination issues include the following:

- Late critical dependencies and commitments
- Product-level problems
- Unavailability of critical resources or personnel
- Incomplete customer requirements
- Unresolved defects

TIP

These issues are typically resolved at the project level. However, since stakeholders may be from outside the project, issues may need to be escalated to the appropriate level of management to be resolved.

Typical Work Products

1. Relevant stakeholder coordination issues
2. Status of relevant stakeholder coordination issues

TIP

This specific practice is critical if integrated teams are to perform in a manner that is consistent with the project's shared vision.

Subpractices

1. Identify and document issues.
2. Communicate issues to relevant stakeholders.
3. Resolve issues with relevant stakeholders.
4. Escalate to appropriate managers those issues not resolvable with relevant stakeholders.
5. Track issues to closure.
6. Communicate with relevant stakeholders on the status and resolution of issues.

MEASUREMENT AND ANALYSIS

A Support Process Area at Maturity Level 2

Purpose

The purpose of Measurement and Analysis (MA) is to develop and sustain a measurement capability used to support management information needs.

HINT

Use this process area when you need to measure project progress, product size or quality, or process performance in support of making decisions and taking corrective action. In addition, use this process area when providing acquisition office perspectives on measurement data provided by suppliers.

Introductory Notes

The Measurement and Analysis process area involves the following activities:

- Specifying objectives of measurement and analysis so they are aligned with identified information needs and objectives
- Specifying measures, analysis techniques, and mechanisms for data collection, data storage, reporting, and feedback
- Implementing the collection, storage, analysis, and reporting of data
- Providing objective results that can be used in making informed decisions, and taking appropriate corrective action

TIP

This process area uses the term *objective* both as a noun meaning "a goal to be attained" (e.g., first bullet) and as an adjective meaning "unbiased" (e.g., fourth bullet).

The integration of measurement and analysis activities into the processes of the project supports the following:

- Objective planning and estimating
- Tracking actual performance against established plans and objectives
- Identifying and resolving process-related issues
- Providing a basis for incorporating measurement into additional processes in the future

TIP

Measurement involves everyone. A centralized group, such as a process group or a measurement group, may provide help in defining the measures, the analyses to perform, and the reporting content and charts used.

The staff required to implement a measurement capability may or may not be employed in a separate organization-wide program. Measurement capability may be integrated into individual projects or other organizational functions (e.g., quality assurance).

The initial focus for measurement activities is at the project level. However, a measurement capability may prove useful for addressing organization- and enterprise-wide information needs. To support this capability, measurement activities should support information needs at multiple levels, including the business, organizational unit, and project to minimize rework as the organization matures.

X-REF

Refer to SP 1.4 in OPD for more information about the organization's measurement repository.

Projects may choose to store project-specific data and results in a project-specific repository. When data are shared widely across projects, data may reside in the organization's measurement repository.

Measurement and analysis of product components provided by suppliers is essential for effective management of the quality and costs of the project. It is possible, with careful management of supplier agreements, to provide insight into data that support supplier-performance analysis.

TIP

It is important to include in the supplier agreement any measurement and analysis activities that you want the supplier to perform. Refer to SSAD, AM, and ATM for more information about supplier activities.

The acquirer specifies measures that enable it to gauge its own progress and output, supplier progress and output per contractual requirements, and the status of the evolving products acquired. An acquirer establishes measurement objectives for its activities and work products and supplier activities and deliverables. Measurement objectives are derived from information needs that come from project objectives, organizational objectives, and business needs.

Measurement objectives are used to define measures as well as collection, analysis, storage, and usage procedures for measures. These measures are specified in the project plan. Measures for the supplier, data collection processes and timing, expected analysis, and required storage should be specified in the supplier agreement.

In projects where multiple products are acquired to deliver a capability to the end user or where there are relationships with other projects to acquire joint capabilities, additional measures may be identified to track and achieve interoperability for programmatic, technical, and operational interfaces.

Related Process Areas

Refer to the Project Planning process area for more information about estimating project attributes and other planning information needs.

Refer to the Project Monitoring and Control process area for more information about monitoring project performance information needs.

Refer to the Configuration Management process area for more information about managing measurement work products.

Refer to the Requirements Management process area for more information about maintaining requirements traceability and related information needs.

Refer to the Solicitation and Supplier Agreement Development process area for more information about including supplier measures in the solicitation package and in the supplier agreement.

Refer to the Organizational Process Definition process area for more information about establishing the organization's measurement repository.

Refer to the Quantitative Project Management process area for more information about understanding variation and the appropriate use of statistical analysis techniques.

Specific Goal and Practice Summary

SG 1 Align Measurement and Analysis Activities
- SP 1.1 Establish Measurement Objectives
- SP 1.2 Specify Measures
- SP 1.3 Specify Data Collection and Storage Procedures
- SP 1.4 Specify Analysis Procedures

SG 2 Provide Measurement Results
- SP 2.1 Obtain Measurement Data
- SP 2.2 Analyze Measurement Data
- SP 2.3 Store Data and Results
- SP 2.4 Communicate Results

Specific Practices by Goal

SG 1 Align Measurement and Analysis Activities

Measurement objectives and activities are aligned with identified information needs and objectives.

The specific practices under this specific goal may be addressed concurrently or in any order:

- When establishing measurement objectives, experts often think ahead about necessary criteria for specifying measures and analysis procedures. They also think concurrently about the constraints imposed by data collection and storage procedures.
- Often, it is important to specify the essential analyses to be conducted before attending to details of measurement specification, data collection, or storage.

TIP

When starting a measurement program, an iterative process is usually helpful since you often do not know all of your objectives. On long acquisition projects, needed measurement activities may change significantly over the life of the project.

HINT

When establishing measurement objectives, ask yourself what question you are answering with the data, why you are measuring something, and how these measurements will affect project behavior.

HINT

Measurement can be an expensive activity. Think about why you are collecting the measures and try to ensure that the measures are used.

TIP

Avoid the temptation to measure only the suppliers' activities.

SP 1.1 *ESTABLISH MEASUREMENT OBJECTIVES*

Establish and maintain measurement objectives derived from identified information needs and objectives.

Measurement objectives document the purposes for which measurement and analysis are done and specify the kinds of actions that may be taken based on results of data analyses.

Measurement objectives focus on acquirer performance, supplier performance, and understanding the effects of their performance on customer operational and financial performance. Measurement objectives for the supplier enable defining and tracking service level expectations documented in the supplier agreement.

Measurement objectives identify what information is needed to do the following.

- Maintain alignment to project objectives and provide results that keep a project on track to its successful conclusion.
- Support the organization's ability to establish an infrastructure that reinforces and grows acquirer capabilities, including processes, people, and technologies, as appropriate.
- Support the enterprise's ability to monitor and manage its financial results and customer expectations, as appropriate.

Sources of measurement objectives include management, technical, project, product, and process implementation needs.

Measurement objectives may be constrained by existing processes, available resources, or other measurement considerations. Judgments may need to be made about whether the value of the result is commensurate with resources devoted to doing the work.

Modifications to identified information needs and objectives may, in turn, be indicated as a consequence of the process and results of measurement and analysis.

Example measurement objectives include the following.

- Reduce time to delivery.
- Reduce total lifecycle costs.
- Deliver the specified functionality completely.
- Improve prior levels of quality.
- Improve prior customer satisfaction ratings.
- Maintain and improve the relationships between the acquirer and supplier.

Sources of information needs and objectives may include the following:

- Project plans
- Project performance monitoring
- Interviews with managers and others who have information needs
- Established management objectives
- Strategic plans
- Business plans
- Formal requirements or contractual obligations
- Recurring or other troublesome management or technical problems
- Experiences of other projects or organizational entities
- External industry benchmarks
- Process improvement plans
- Supplier agreements and contractual requirements (e.g., service levels)
- Customer expectations

Refer to the Project Planning process area for more information about estimating project attributes and other planning information needs.

Refer to the Project Monitoring and Control process area for more information about project performance information needs.

Refer to the Requirements Management process area for more information about maintaining requirements traceability and related information needs.

Typical Work Products

1. Measurement objectives

Subpractices

1. Document information needs and objectives.
2. Prioritize information needs and objectives.
3. Document, review, and update measurement objectives.

   Carefully consider the purposes and intended uses of measurement and analysis.

   Measurement objectives are documented, reviewed by management and other relevant stakeholders, and updated as necessary. Completing these activities enables traceability to subsequent measurement and analysis activities and helps ensure that analyses will properly address identified information needs and objectives.
4. Provide feedback for refining and clarifying information needs and objectives as necessary.

   Identified information needs and objectives may be refined and clarified as a result of setting measurement objectives. Initial descriptions of information needs may be unclear or ambiguous. Conflicts may arise between existing needs and objectives. Precise targets on an already existing measure may be unrealistic.

5. Review appropriate measurement objectives with potential suppliers throughout the solicitation, obtaining their feedback and commitment.

   Refer to the Solicitation and Supplier Agreement Development process area for more information about solicitations and interacting with potential suppliers.

6. Maintain traceability of measurement objectives to identified information needs and objectives.

   Of course, measurement objectives may also change to reflect evolving information needs and objectives.

SP 1.2 SPECIFY MEASURES

Specify measures to address measurement objectives.

Measurement objectives are refined into precise, quantifiable measures.

Measurement of project and organizational work can typically be traced to one or more measurement information categories. These categories include the following: schedule and progress, effort and cost, size and stability, and quality.

Measures may be either *base* or *derived.* Data for base measures are obtained by direct measurement. Data for derived measures come from other data, typically by combining two or more base measures.

Derived measures typically are expressed as ratios, composite indices, or other aggregate summary measures. They are often more quantitatively reliable and meaningfully interpretable than the base measures used to generate them.

Base measures enable the creation of many derived measures or indicators from the same standard data sources. In addition, there is a direct relationship between measurement objectives, measurement categories, base measures, and derived measures. This direct relationship is depicted using some common examples in Table 9.1:

As a part of their measurement and analysis activities, projects may also consider the use of Earned Value Management (EVM) for measures related to cost and schedule [GEIA 748 2002]. EVM is a method for objectively measuring cost and schedule progress and for predicting estimated total costs and target completion dates based on past and current performance trends.

Typical EVM data include the planned cost of accomplishing specific and measurable tasks, the actual cost of completing tasks, and

TABLE 9.1 Example Measurement Relationships

Example Measurement Objectives	*Measurement Information Categories*	*Example Base Measures*	*Example Derived Measures*
Shorter Time to Delivery	Schedule and Progress	Estimated and Actual Start and End Dates by Task	Milestone Performance
			Percentage of Project on Time
		Estimated and Actual Start and End Dates of Acquisition Tasks	Schedule Estimation Accuracy
Reduced Total Lifecycle Cost	Effort and Cost	Estimated and Actual Effort Hours	Return on Investment
		Estimated and Actual Cost	Cost Variance
Deliver Specified Functionality Completely	Size and Stability	Requirements Count	Requirements Volatility
			Size Estimation Accuracy
		Function Point Count	Estimated and Actual Function Points Completed
		Lines of Code Count	Amount of New, Modified, and Reused Code
Improve Levels of Quality	Quality	Product Defects Count	Defect Removal Efficiency
			Number of Defects Per Phase
			Total Unresolved Defects
		Customer Satisfaction Survey Scores	Customer Satisfaction Trends
		Supplier Performance and Relationship Scores	Supplier Performance and Relationship Trends
		Web Site Response Time	Variance from Throughput Target

earned value, which is the planned cost of the work actually completed for each task. Using these or similar base measures, the project can calculate derived measures such as schedule and cost variance and more complex measures. These include schedule and cost performance indices. EVM derived measures can assist with estimating the cost for completion and additional resources that may be required.

TIP

Table 9.1 and the discussions of EVM are not currently captured in CMMI-DEV. Acquirers may wish to share these ideas with their suppliers to facilitate integrated approaches to this measurement challenge.

TIP

The project must determine when an integrated answer is needed with the supplier, and when it must deliver an independent analysis as part of its acquisition responsibilities.

To manage projects, an acquirer uses supplier data (i.e., base measures) and supplier-reported derived measures in addition to measures of acquirer progress and output. Supplier measures required by the acquirer allow the acquirer to comprehensively address measurement objectives and to comprehensively determine the progress of the project. In some cases, these supplier measures will augment acquirer measures (e.g., supplier's schedule performance index and size estimation accuracy).

In most cases, supplier measures are the primary source of data, especially with regard to the development of the acquired product or service. For instance, measurement and analysis of the product or product components provided by a supplier through technical performance measures is essential for effective management. Technical performance measures are precisely defined measures based on a product requirement, product capability, or some combination of requirements and capabilities.

TIP

An example of a derived measure that is typically expressed as a ratio is a productivity measure (e.g., proposal pages read per hour). An example of a derived measure that is typically expressed as a composite index is a process capability index (e.g., C_{pk}, which indicates how well centered and tightly distributed a stable process is relative to selected specification limits).

It is important to use measures to track high-risk items to closure and to help determine risk mitigation and corrective actions. These supplier measures must be defined in the supplier agreement, including a supplier's measurement collection requirements and measurement reports to be provided to the acquirer.

Typical Work Products

1. Specifications of base and derived measures
2. Acceptance criteria for supplier measures

Subpractices

1. Identify candidate measures based on documented measurement objectives.

   Measurement objectives are refined into measures. Identified candidate measures are categorized and specified by name and unit of measure.

2. Identify existing measures that already address measurement objectives.

   Specifications for measures may already exist, perhaps established for other purposes earlier or elsewhere in the organization.

X-REF

Operational definitions are a key to the effective specification of measures. Activities in ARD may be of assistance in determining many of these.

3. Specify operational definitions for measures.

   Operational definitions are stated in precise and unambiguous terms. They address two important criteria:

   - Communication: What has been measured, how was it measured, what are the units of measure, and what has been included or excluded?

- Repeatability: Can the measurement be repeated, given the same definition, to get the same results?

4. Specify acceptance criteria based on operational definitions for measures that come from suppliers to the acquirer in a way that enables their intended use.

   Measures may be provided by the supplier as detailed measurement data or measurement reports. Measures that come from suppliers must be associated with the acquirer's acceptance criteria for supplier measures. Acceptance criteria may be captured in measurement specifications or by checklists.

   Acceptance criteria should be defined in a way that enables the intended use of supplier measures, such as potential aggregation and analysis. These criteria must include criteria associated with the collection and transfer mechanisms and procedures that must be performed by the supplier. Consider all characteristics about supplier measures that may impact their use, such as differences in financial calendars used by different suppliers.

5. Prioritize, review, and update measures.

   Proposed specifications of measures are reviewed for their appropriateness with potential end users and other relevant stakeholders. Priorities are set or changed, and specifications of measures are updated as necessary.

X-REF

For additional information on specifying measures, see the SEI's Software Engineering Measurement and Analysis Web site (www.sei.cmu.edu/sema), the Practical Software & Systems Measurement Web site (www.psmsc.com), and the iSixSigma Web site (www.isixsigma.com).

SP 1.3 SPECIFY DATA COLLECTION AND STORAGE PROCEDURES

Specify how measurement data is obtained and stored.

Explicit specification of collection methods helps ensure that the right data are collected properly. This specification may also help further clarify information needs and measurement objectives.

Proper attention to storage and retrieval procedures helps ensure that data are available and accessible for future use.

The supplier agreement specifies the measurement data the supplier must provide to the acquirer, in what format they have to be provided to the acquirer, how the measurement data will be collected and stored by the supplier (e.g., retention period of data), how and how often they will be transferred to the acquirer, and who has access to data. Some supplier data may be considered proprietary by the supplier and may need to be protected as such by the acquirer. Also consider that some acquirer measurement data (e.g., total project cost data) may be proprietary and should not be shared with suppliers. An acquirer must plan for the collection, storage, and access control of sensitive data.

TIP

Ensuring appropriate accessibility of data and maintenance of data integrity are two key concerns related to data storage and retrieval. Both concerns are magnified when there are multiple suppliers or complex interactions among customers, acquirers, and suppliers.

The acquirer must ensure that appropriate mechanisms are in place to obtain measurement data from the supplier in a consistent way. It is critical for the acquirer to insist in the supplier agreement on accurate data collection by the supplier for the acquirer's measurement and analysis.

Typical Work Products

1. Data collection and storage procedures
2. Data collection tools

Typical Supplier Deliverables

1. Recommendations for data collection and storage procedures

Subpractices

1. Identify existing sources of data that are generated from current work products, processes, or transactions.
2. Identify measures for which data are needed but are not currently available.
3. Specify how to collect and store the data for each required measure.

   Explicit specifications are made of how, where, and when data will be collected. Procedures for collecting valid data are specified. Data are stored in an accessible manner for analysis. This analysis helps determine whether data will be saved for possible reanalysis or documentation purposes.

Questions to be considered typically include the following.

- Have the frequency of collection and points in the process where measurements will be made been determined?
- Has the timeline that is required to move measurement results from points of collection to repositories, other databases, or end users been established?
- Who is responsible for obtaining data?
- Who is responsible for data storage, retrieval, and security?
- Have necessary supporting tools been developed or acquired?
- Have required data collection requirements and applicable procedures been specified in supplier agreement standards and related documents?

4. Create data collection mechanisms and process guidance.

   Data collection and storage mechanisms are well integrated with other normal work processes. Data collection mechanisms may include manual or automated forms and templates. Clear, concise guidance on correct procedures is available to those responsible for doing the work. Training is provided as needed to clarify processes required for the collection of complete and accurate data and to minimize the burden on those who must provide and record data.

Create mechanisms to transfer data and process guidance from the supplier to the acquirer, as appropriate. Data collection from a supplier may be integrated with periodic monitoring and review of supplier activities. Applicable standard report formats and tools to be used for reporting by the supplier must be specified in the supplier agreement.

5. Support automatic collection of data as appropriate and feasible.
6. Prioritize, review, and update data collection and storage procedures.

   Proposed procedures are reviewed for their appropriateness and feasibility with those who are responsible for providing, collecting, and storing data. They also may have useful insights about how to improve existing processes or may be able to suggest other useful measures or analyses.

   Review data collection and storage procedures with potential suppliers throughout the solicitation. Update data collection and storage procedures, as appropriate, and obtain supplier commitment to collect and store measurement data and reference procedures in the supplier agreement.
7. Update measures and measurement objectives as necessary.

TIP

In today's environment, automation is often used. Further, some organizations use multiple tools and databases to address their measurement needs. If this is the case, you must carefully manage the compatibility among these tools and databases.

SP 1.4 Specify Analysis Procedures

Specify how measurement data are analyzed and communicated.

Specifying analysis procedures in advance ensures that appropriate analyses will be conducted and reported to address documented measurement objectives (and thereby the information needs and objectives on which they are based). This approach also provides a check that necessary data will, in fact, be collected.

The supplier agreement defines the required data analysis and the definition and examples of measures the supplier must provide to the acquirer.

TIP

Often, someone can manipulate data to provide the picture he or she wants to convey. By specifying the analysis procedures in advance, you can minimize this type of abuse.

Typical Work Products

1. Analysis specifications and procedures
2. Data analysis tools

Typical Supplier Deliverables

1. Recommendations for analysis specification and procedures

Subpractices

1. Specify and prioritize the analyses to be conducted and the reports to be prepared.

   Early on, pay attention to the analyses to be conducted and to the manner in which results will be reported. These should meet the following criteria.

   - The analyses explicitly address the documented measurement objectives.
   - Presentation of results is clearly understandable by the audiences to whom the results are addressed.

   Priorities may have to be set within available resources.

   Establish and maintain a description of the analysis approach for data elements, a description of reports that must be provided by the supplier, and a reference to analysis specifications and procedures in the supplier agreement.

2. Select appropriate data analysis methods and tools.

   Refer to the Select Measures and Analytic Techniques specific practice and the Apply Statistical Methods to Understand Variation specific practice of the Quantitative Project Management process area for more information about the appropriate use of statistical analysis techniques and understanding variation.

Descriptive statistics are typically used in data analysis to do the following.

- Examine distributions on specified measures (e.g., central tendency, extent of variation, or data points exhibiting unusual variation).
- Examine interrelationships among specified measures (e.g., comparisons of defects by phase of the product's lifecycle or by product component).
- Display changes over time.

TIP

Those responsible for analyzing the data and presenting the results should include those whose activities generated the measurement data or their management whenever possible. There should also be support provided by a process group, QA group, or measurement experts for these data-related activities.

3. Specify administrative procedures for analyzing data and communicating results.

   Data collected from a supplier are subject to validity checks that can be achieved by periodic audits of the supplier's execution of data collection and analysis procedures for acquirer-required measures. The acquirer's option to perform validity checks of measurement data collected by the supplier and the supplier's execution of required analysis procedures must be defined in the supplier agreement.

4. Review and update the proposed content and format of specified analyses and reports.

   All of the proposed content and format are subject to review and revision, including analytic methods and tools, administrative procedures, and priorities. Relevant stakeholders consulted should include end users, sponsors, data analysts, and data providers.

Review specified analyses and reports with suppliers and identify their commitment to support the analysis, and review recommendations they may provide related to the analysis of measurement data.

5. Update measures and measurement objectives as necessary.

   Just as measurement needs drive data analysis, clarification of analysis criteria can affect measurement. Specifications for some measures may be refined further based on specifications established for data analysis procedures. Other measures may prove unnecessary, or a need for additional measures may be recognized.

   Specifying how measures will be analyzed and reported may also suggest the need for refining measurement objectives themselves.

X-REF

Refer to specific practice 1.1 when refining your measurement objectives.

6. Specify criteria for evaluating the utility of analysis results and for evaluating the conduct of measurement and analysis activities.

Criteria for evaluating the utility of the analysis might address the extent to which the following apply.

- The results are (1) provided in a timely manner, (2) understandable, and (3) used for decision making.
- The work does not cost more to perform than is justified by the benefits it provides.

TIP

The criteria are divided into two lists. The first comprises criteria that any organization can use. The second is a bit more sophisticated and might be used by organizations once they establish their measurement program.

Criteria for evaluating the conduct of the measurement and analysis might include the extent to which the following apply.

- The amount of missing data or the number of flagged inconsistencies is beyond specified thresholds.
- There is selection bias in sampling (e.g., only satisfied end users are surveyed to evaluate end-user satisfaction, or only unsuccessful projects are evaluated to determine overall productivity).
- Measurement data are repeatable (e.g., statistically reliable).
- Statistical assumptions have been satisfied (e.g., about the distribution of data or about appropriate measurement scales).

SG 2 Provide Measurement Results

Measurement results, which address identified information needs and objectives, are provided.

The primary reason for conducting measurement and analysis is to address identified information needs and objectives. Measurement results based on objective evidence can help to monitor performance, fulfill obligations documented in a supplier agreement, make informed management and technical decisions, and enable corrective actions to be taken.

TIP

MA provides the foundation for the behavior required in high-maturity organizations. By the time organizations reach maturity level 4, management and staff members will use measurement results as part of their daily work.

SP 2.1 Obtain Measurement Data

Obtain specified measurement data.

Data necessary for analysis are obtained and checked for completeness and integrity.

Supplier measurement data are collected according to data collection and storage procedures as defined in the supplier agreement. Data necessary for analysis are obtained and checked for completeness and integrity.

Typical Work Products

1. Base and derived measurement data sets
2. Results of data integrity tests

Typical Supplier Deliverables

1. Base and derived supplier measurement data sets
2. Results of data integrity tests of supplier measurement data

Subpractices

1. Obtain data for base measures.

   Data are collected as necessary for previously used and newly specified base measures. Existing data are gathered from project records or elsewhere in the organization.

   Data are obtained from the supplier for base measures as defined in the supplier agreement.

2. Generate data for derived measures.

   Values are newly calculated for all derived measures.

   Derived measures are obtained from the supplier as defined in the supplier agreement.

3. Perform data integrity checks as close to the source of data as possible.

   All measurements are subject to error in specifying or recording data. It is always better to identify these errors and sources of missing data early in the measurement and analysis cycle.

   Checks can include scans for missing data, out-of-bounds data values, and unusual patterns and correlation across measures. It is particularly important to do the following.

   - Test and correct for inconsistency of classifications made by human judgment (i.e., to determine how frequently people make differing

TIP

If too much time has passed, it may be inefficient or even impossible to verify the integrity of a measure or to identify the source of missing data.

classification decisions based on the same information, otherwise known as *intercoder reliability*).

- Empirically examine the relationships among measures that are used to calculate additional derived measures. Doing so can ensure that important distinctions are not overlooked and that derived measures convey their intended meanings (otherwise known as *criterion validity*).

Use acceptance criteria to verify the results of data integrity tests conducted by the supplier and to verify the integrity of supplier data. Follow up with suppliers if data are not available or data integrity checks indicate potential errors in data.

Refer to the Agreement Management process area for more information about resolving supplier agreement issues.

SP 2.2 Analyze Measurement Data

Analyze and interpret measurement data.

Measurement data are analyzed as planned, additional analyses are conducted as necessary, results are reviewed with relevant stakeholders, and necessary revisions for future analyses are noted.

Typical Work Products

1. Analysis results and draft reports

Typical Supplier Deliverables

1. Responses to analysis results and draft reports

Subpractices

1. Conduct initial analyses, interpret results, and draw preliminary conclusions.

   The results of data analyses are rarely self-evident. Criteria for interpreting results and drawing conclusions should be stated explicitly. Discuss results and preliminary conclusions with suppliers, as appropriate.

2. Conduct additional measurement and analysis as necessary, and prepare results for presentation.

   Results of planned analyses may suggest (or require) additional, unanticipated analyses. In addition, these analyses may identify needs to refine existing measures, to calculate additional derived measures, or even to collect data for additional base measures to properly complete the planned analysis. Similarly, preparing initial results for presentation may identify the need for additional, unanticipated analyses. Coordinate additional analyses with suppliers, as appropriate.

TIP

Often, someone can misinterpret analyses and draw incorrect conclusions. By specifying criteria for interpreting results in advance, you can reduce the risk of drawing incorrect conclusions.

3. Review initial results with relevant stakeholders.

   It may be appropriate to review initial interpretations of results and the way in which these results are presented before disseminating and communicating them widely.

   Relevant stakeholders with whom reviews may be conducted include intended end users and sponsors, as well as data analysts and data providers.

   Review initial results related to supplier progress or output with suppliers and determine if revisions are appropriate based on their response.

4. Refine criteria for future analyses.

   Lessons that can improve future efforts are often learned from conducting data analyses and preparing results. Similarly, ways to improve measurement specifications and data collection procedures may become apparent, as may ideas for refining identified information needs and objectives.

   Update data acceptance criteria for supplier measures, as appropriate.

TIP

Measurement and analysis is a learning process. You will typically go through many cycles before the measures and analyses are fine-tuned. Recognize that this learning may also be occurring on the supplier side.

SP 2.3 Store Data and Results

Manage and store measurement data, measurement specifications, and analysis results.

Storing measurement-related information enables its timely and cost-effective use as historical data and results. The information also is needed to provide sufficient context for interpretation of data, measurement criteria, and analysis results.

Information stored typically includes the following:

- Measurement plans
- Specifications of measures
- Sets of data that were collected
- Analysis reports and presentations
- Retention period for data stored
- Data acceptance criteria for supplier data

Stored information contains or references other information needed to understand and interpret the measures and to assess them for reasonableness and applicability (e.g., measurement specifications used on different projects when comparing across projects).

Typically, data sets for derived measures can be recalculated and need not be stored. However, it may be appropriate to store summaries based on derived measures (e.g., charts, tables of results, or report prose).

HINT

Understand what to store, what can be recalculated or reconstructed, and what to discard.

Interim analysis results need not be stored separately if they can be efficiently reconstructed.

Projects may choose to store project-specific data and results in a project-specific repository. When data are shared across projects, they may reside in the organization's measurement repository.

Refer to the Establish the Organization's Measurement Repository specific practice of the Organizational Process Definition process area for more information about establishing the organization's measurement repository.

Refer to the Configuration Management process area for more information about managing measurement work products.

Typical Work Products

1. Stored data inventory

Subpractices

1. Review data to ensure their completeness, integrity, accuracy, and currency.
2. Store data according to data storage procedures.
3. Make stored contents available for use only to appropriate groups and personnel.

   The acquirer protects measurement data provided by the supplier according to the supplier agreement. The supplier agreement might specify that the acquirer must restrict access to a supplier's measurement data to acquirer employees only.
4. Prevent stored information from being used inappropriately.

Examples of inappropriate use include the following:

- Disclosure of information provided in confidence
- Faulty interpretations based on incomplete, out-of-context, or otherwise misleading information
- Measures used to improperly evaluate the performance of people or to rank projects
- Impugning the integrity of individuals

TIP

Inappropriate use of data will seriously undermine the credibility of your MA implementation. It may also threaten effective collaboration with customers and suppliers.

SP 2.4 COMMUNICATE RESULTS

Communicate results of measurement and analysis activities to all relevant stakeholders.

The results of the measurement and analysis process are communicated to relevant stakeholders in a timely and usable fashion to support decision making and assist in taking corrective action.

TIP

An indicator of a mature organization is the daily use of measurement data by both staff members and management to guide their activities. Such use of measurement data requires effective communication of measurement data and the results of analyses.

Relevant stakeholders include intended users, sponsors, data analysts, and data providers.

Relevant stakeholders also include suppliers.

Typical Work Products

1. Delivered reports and related analysis results
2. Contextual information or guidance to help interpret analysis results

Subpractices

1. Keep relevant stakeholders apprised of measurement results in a timely manner.

   To the extent possible and as part of the normal way they do business, users of measurement results are kept personally involved in setting objectives and deciding on plans of action for measurement and analysis. Users are regularly kept apprised of progress and interim results.

   Refer to the Project Monitoring and Control process area for more information about the use of measurement results.

2. Assist relevant stakeholders in understanding results.

   Results are communicated in a clear and concise manner appropriate to the methodological sophistication of relevant stakeholders. Results are understandable, easily interpretable, and clearly tied to identified information needs and objectives.

   The acquirer establishes and maintains a standard format for communicating measurement data to relevant stakeholders.

   Data are often not self-evident to practitioners who are not measurement experts. The following measurement choices should be explicitly clarified:

   - How and why base and derived measures were specified
   - How data were obtained
   - How to interpret results based on the data analysis methods used
   - How results address information needs

TIP

As organizations mature, management and staff members should become more comfortable with measurement, be more likely to interpret the analyses correctly, and be able to ask the right questions to help them draw the right conclusions.

Examples of actions to assist in understanding results include the following:

- Discussing the results with relevant stakeholders
- Providing a transmittal memo that provides background and explanation
- Briefing users on results
- Providing training on the appropriate use and understanding of measurement results

ORGANIZATIONAL INNOVATION AND DEPLOYMENT

A Process Management Process Area at Maturity Level 5

Purpose

The purpose of Organizational Innovation and Deployment (OID) is to select and deploy incremental and innovative improvements that measurably improve the organization's processes and technologies. These improvements support the organization's quality and process-performance objectives as derived from the organization's business objectives.

TIP

OID potentially improves the value of *all* processes and technology, through both innovative as well as incremental improvements.

Introductory Notes

The Organizational Innovation and Deployment process area enables the selection and deployment of improvements that can enhance the organization's ability to meet its quality and process-performance objectives. (See the definition of "quality and process-performance objectives" in the glossary.)

The term *improvement,* as used in this process area, refers to all ideas (proven and unproven) that would change the organization's processes and technologies to better meet the organization's quality and process-performance objectives.

TIP

Changes must be measurably better, not just different. In early improvement efforts, it is often difficult to measure the effects of changes, so sometimes things are just different and not better. This is one of the main reasons this process area is staged at the highest maturity level.

Quality and process-performance objectives that this process area might address include the following:

- Improved product quality (e.g., functionality, performance)
- Increased productivity
- Decreased cycle time
- Greater customer and end-user satisfaction
- Shorter development or production time to change functionality, add new features, or adapt to new technologies
- Reduce delivery time
- Reduce time to adapt to new technologies and business needs
- Improved performance of a supply chain involving multiple suppliers

- Improved intersupplier performance
- Improved utilization of resources across the organization

TIP

Those closest to a process are most familiar with its details and can identify incremental improvement opportunities. That is why everyone in the organization should be empowered and encouraged to suggest potential improvements. Change and the ability to manage change is one of the key characteristics of a mature organization; another is when the majority (70 percent to 90 percent) of the work force is involved in proposing and evaluating changes.

TIP

Participation in process improvement activities can also involve the acquirer's customers. Processes that improve the relationships across those boundaries can be improved as well.

Achievement of these objectives depends on the successful establishment of an infrastructure that enables and encourages all people in the organization to propose potential improvements to the organization's processes and technologies. Achievement of these objectives also depends on being able to effectively evaluate and deploy proposed improvements to the organization's processes and technologies. All members of the organization can participate in the organization's process- and technology-improvement activities. Their proposals are systematically gathered and addressed.

Improvements may be identified and executed by the acquirer or the supplier. The acquirer encourages all suppliers to participate in the acquirer's process- and technology-improvement activities. Some selected improvements may be deployed across acquirer and supplier organizations.

The acquirer and suppliers may share the costs and benefits of improvements. Acquirers may increase the incentive for suppliers to participate in improvement efforts across the supply chain by allowing suppliers to appropriate the entire value derived from a contributed improvement for an initial period (e.g., 6 to 18 months). Over time, the supplier may be expected to share a proportion of those savings with the acquirer (e.g., through cost reductions to the acquirer). Acquirer and supplier expectations related to participation in process- and technology-improvement activities, and the sharing of associated costs and benefits, should be documented in the supplier agreement.

Pilots are conducted to evaluate significant changes involving untried, high-risk, or innovative improvements before they are broadly deployed.

Process and technology improvements to be deployed across the organization are selected from process- and technology-improvement proposals based on the following criteria:

- A quantitative understanding of the organization's current quality and process performance
- The organization's quality and process-performance objectives
- Estimates of the improvement in quality and process performance resulting from deploying the process and technology improvements
- Estimated costs of deploying process and technology improvements, and resources and funding available for such deployment

Expected benefits added by the process and technology improvements are weighed against the cost and impact to the organization. Change and stability must be balanced carefully. Change that is too great or too rapid can overwhelm the organization, destroying its investment in organizational learning represented by organizational process assets. Rigid stability can result in stagnation, allowing the changing business environment to erode the organization's business position.

Improvements are deployed, as appropriate, to new and ongoing projects.

In this process area, the term *process and technology improvements* refers to incremental and innovative improvements to processes and also to process or product technologies (including project work environments).

The informative material in this process area is written assuming the specific practices are applied in an organization that has a quantitative understanding of its standard processes and their expected quality and performance in predictable situations. Specific practices of this process area may be applicable, but with reduced value, if this assumption is not met.

The specific practices in this process area complement and extend those found in the Organizational Process Focus process area. The focus of this process area is process improvement based on a quantitative understanding of the organization's set of standard processes and technologies and their expected quality and performance in predictable situations. In the Organizational Process Focus process area, no assumptions are made about the quantitative basis of improvement.

HINT

If a proposed improvement is unrelated to the organization's objectives, it probably is not worth pursuing. However, occasionally it may indicate an opportunity missed by those who created the objectives, so if appropriate, revisit the objectives to see whether they should be updated.

HINT

Although many changes may individually have merit, consider their cumulative impact on the organization.

HINT

For early, qualitative process improvement, OPF may give sufficient assistance for process improvement efforts. Select OID for use in your improvement program once the organization has the ability to statistically manage its critical subprocesses as a basis for estimating and determining the impact of a change.

Related Process Areas

Refer to the Organizational Process Focus process area for more information about soliciting, collecting, and handling process improvement proposals and coordinating the deployment of process improvements into projects' defined processes.

Refer to the Organizational Training process area for more information about providing updated training to support the deployment of process and technology improvements.

Refer to the Organizational Process Performance process area for more information about quality and process-performance objectives and process-performance models. Quality and process-performance objectives are used to analyze and select process- and technology-improvement proposals for deployment.

Process-performance models are used to quantify the impact and benefits of innovations.

Refer to the Measurement and Analysis process area for more information about establishing objectives for measurement and analysis, specifying measures and analyses to be performed, obtaining and analyzing measures, and reporting results.

Refer to the Integrated Project Management process area for more information about implementing process and technology improvements into the project's defined process and project work environment.

Refer to the Decision Analysis and Resolution process area for more information about formal evaluations when selecting improvement proposals and innovations.

Specific Goal and Practice Summary

SG 1 Select Improvements
- SP 1.1 Collect and Analyze Improvement Proposals
- SP 1.2 Identify and Analyze Innovations
- SP 1.3 Pilot Improvements
- SP 1.4 Select Improvements for Deployment

SG 2 Deploy Improvements
- SP 2.1 Plan the Deployment
- SP 2.2 Manage the Deployment
- SP 2.3 Measure Improvement Effects

Specific Practices by Goal

SG 1 SELECT IMPROVEMENTS

Process and technology improvements, which contribute to meeting quality and process-performance objectives, are selected.

SP 1.1 COLLECT AND ANALYZE IMPROVEMENT PROPOSALS

Collect and analyze process- and technology-improvement proposals.

Each process- and technology-improvement proposal must be analyzed.

The acquirer must continuously improve its processes and its alignment with its customer and suppliers. The acquirer may look for opportunities to maximize throughput based on the identification of the most limiting resource and, as a result, create a more agile supply chain (e.g., giving higher priority to improvement proposals that promote a supply chain that responds both quickly and cost effectively).

HINT

Everyone in the organization must be aware that he or she can submit an improvement proposal, and know how to submit one.

Simple process and technology improvements, with well-understood benefits and effects, will not usually undergo detailed evaluations.

> An example of a simple process and technology improvement is to establish guidelines for multiple-supplier interactions.

TIP

Ideas for incremental improvements often originate from within the organization; ideas for innovative improvements often originate from outside the organization.

Typical Work Products

1. Analyzed process- and technology-improvement proposals

Typical Supplier Deliverables

1. Process- and technology-improvement proposals

Subpractices

1. Collect process- and technology-improvement proposals.

   A process- and technology-improvement proposal documents proposed incremental and innovative improvements to processes and technologies. Managers and staff in the organization, as well as customers, end users, and suppliers can submit process- and technology-improvement proposals. Process and technology improvements may be implemented at the local level before being proposed for the organization.

HINT

You can collect proposals using open-ended mechanisms, surveys, or focus groups.

TIP

"Local level" refers to an individual project.

> Examples of sources for process- and technology-improvement proposals include the following:
>
> - Findings and recommendations from process appraisals
> - Templates for acquirer work products
> - The organization's quality and process-performance objectives
> - Analysis of data about customer and end-user problems as well as customer and end-user satisfaction
> - Analysis of data about project performance compared to quality and productivity objectives
> - Analysis of technical performance measures
> - Results of process and product benchmarking efforts
> - Analysis of data on defect causes
> - Measured effectiveness of process activities
> - Measured effectiveness of project work environments
> - Examples of process- and technology-improvement proposals that were successfully adopted elsewhere
> - Feedback on previously submitted process- and technology-improvement proposals
> - Spontaneous ideas from managers and staff
> - Findings and recommendations from joint acquirer and supplier study groups

Refer to the Organizational Process Focus process area for more information about process- and technology-improvement proposals.

TIP

Without a quantitative understanding of current performance, it is difficult to evaluate the effect of an improvement. Process-performance models help to predict the value of changing the processes.

2. Analyze the costs and benefits of process- and technology-improvement proposals, as appropriate.

   Criteria for evaluating costs and benefits include the following:

   - Contribution toward meeting the organization's quality and process-performance objectives
   - Effect on mitigating identified project and organizational risks
   - Ability to respond quickly to changes in project requirements, market situations, and the business environment
   - Effect on related processes and associated assets
   - Cost of defining and collecting data that support the measurement and analysis of the process- and technology-improvement proposal
   - Expected life span of the proposal

   Process-performance models provide insight into the effect of process changes on process capability and performance.

   Refer to the Organizational Process Performance process area for more information about process-performance models.

3. Identify the process- and technology-improvement proposals that are innovative.

   Innovative improvements are also identified and analyzed in the Identify and Analyze Innovations specific practice.

   Whereas this specific practice analyzes proposals that have been passively collected, the purpose of the Identify and Analyze Innovations specific practice is to actively search for and locate innovative improvements. The search primarily involves looking outside the organization.

   Innovative improvements are typically identified by reviewing process- and technology-improvement proposals or by actively investigating and monitoring innovations that are in use in other organizations or are documented in research literature. Innovation may be inspired by internal improvement objectives or by the external business environment.

   Innovative improvements are typically major changes to the process that represent a break from the old way of doing things (e.g., changing the lifecycle model). Innovative improvements may also include changes in products that support, enhance, or automate the process (e.g., using off-the-shelf products to support the process).

Examples of innovative improvements include addition of, or major updates to, the following:

- Support tools
- Processes or lifecycle models
- Interface standards
- Reusable components
- Management techniques and methodologies
- Quality-improvement techniques and methodologies

4. Identify potential barriers and risks to deploying each process- and technology-improvement proposal.

TIP

To identify barriers to deployment, it is helpful to understand the organization's attitude toward change and its ability to change. Such knowledge influences whether and how changes, especially large ones, are implemented.

Examples of barriers to deploying process and technology improvements include the following:

- Turf guarding and parochial perspectives
- Unclear or weak business rationale
- Lack of short-term benefits and visible successes
- Unclear picture of what is expected from everyone
- Too many changes at the same time
- Lack of involvement and support from relevant stakeholders

Examples of risk factors that affect the deployment of process and technology improvements include the following:

- Compatibility of the improvement with existing processes, values, and skills of potential end users
- Complexity of the improvement
- Difficulty implementing the improvement
- Ability to demonstrate the value of the improvement before widespread deployment
- Justification for large, up-front investments in areas such as tools and training
- Inability to overcome "technology drag" where the current implementation is used successfully by a large and mature installed base of end users
- Additional cost to the customer or supplier
- Misalignment of customer, acquirer, and supplier improvement priorities

5. Estimate the cost, effort, and schedule required for deploying each process- and technology-improvement proposal.

TIP

These subpractices represent the rigor that is expected of high-maturity organizations and is typically not possible at earlier stages of process improvement.

6. Select the process- and technology-improvement proposals to be piloted before broad-scale deployment.

   Since innovations, by definition, usually represent a major change, most innovative improvements will be piloted.
7. Document results of the evaluation of each process- and technology-improvement proposal.
8. Monitor the status of each process- and technology-improvement proposal.

SP 1.2 Identify and Analyze Innovations

Identify and analyze innovative improvements that could increase the organization's quality and process performance.

The specific practice, Collect and Analyze Improvement Proposals, analyzes proposals that are passively collected. The purpose of this specific practice is to actively search for, locate, and analyze innovative improvements. This search primarily involves looking outside the organization.

An acquirer's customers and suppliers are vital sources of innovative ideas. Interorganizational and organizational learning are therefore critical to actively identifying and analyzing innovations.

TIP

This practice is similar in approach to the Elicit Requirements specific practice in ARD. Potential innovative improvements are proactively sought after rather than passively collecting proposals.

Typical Work Products

1. Candidate innovative improvements
2. Analysis of proposed innovative improvements

Typical Supplier Deliverables

1. Candidate innovative improvements

Subpractices

1. Analyze the organization's set of standard processes to determine areas in which innovative improvements would be most helpful.

   These analyses are performed to determine which subprocesses are critical to achieving the organization's quality and process-performance objectives and which ones are good candidates to be improved.
2. Investigate innovative improvements that may improve the organization's set of standard processes.

   Investigating innovative improvements involves the following activities:
   - Systematically maintaining awareness of leading relevant technical work and technology trends
   - Periodically searching for commercially available innovative improvements

TIP

Investigating innovative improvements is an ongoing activity that involves monitoring the marketplace for innovations that could benefit the organization and help it reach its objectives.

- Collecting proposals for innovative improvements from projects and the organization
- Systematically reviewing processes and technologies used externally and comparing them to those used in the organization
- Identifying areas in which innovative improvements have been used successfully, and reviewing data and documentation of experience using these improvements
- Identifying improvements that integrate new technology into products and project work environments
- Determining where supplier products stand in relation to technology cycles and product lifecycles
- Monitoring economies all over the world to spot new supply bases and markets

3. Analyze potential innovative improvements to understand their effects on process elements and predict their influence on the process.

   The acquirer and its suppliers may establish an innovation review program. This program may create time-boxed innovation solicitation, which is a well-communicated formal process for analysis and guaranteed response to innovative ideas proposed by customers, employees, and suppliers.

   Process-performance models can provide a basis for analyzing possible effects of changes to process elements.

   Refer to the Organizational Process Performance process area for more information about process-performance models.

4. Analyze the costs and benefits of potential innovative improvements.
5. Create process- and technology-improvement proposals for those innovative improvements that would result in improving the organization's processes or technologies.
6. Select innovative improvements to be piloted before broad-scale deployment.

   Since innovations, by definition, usually represent a major change, most innovative improvements will be piloted.

7. Document results of evaluations of innovative improvements.

X-REF

When analyzing innovations, it is important to consider their role in business strategy and growth. For example, see *The Innovator's Solution: Creating and Sustaining Successful Growth* by Clayton M. Christensen and Michael E. Raynor (Harvard Business School Press).

SP 1.3 Pilot Improvements

Pilot process and technology improvements to select which ones to implement.

Pilots are performed to assess new and unproven major changes before they are broadly deployed, as appropriate.

TIP

Another purpose of a pilot is to gauge a change's applicability to other projects.

A pilot may involve a single project or a group of projects.

The implementation of this specific practice may overlap with the implementation of the Implement Action Proposals specific practice in the Causal Analysis and Resolution process area (e.g., when causal analysis and resolution is implemented organizationally or across multiple projects).

Typical Work Products

1. Pilot evaluation reports
2. Documented lessons learned from pilots

Typical Supplier Deliverables

1. Pilot evaluation reports for pilots executed in the supplier environment
2. Documented lessons learned from pilots executed in the supplier environment

Subpractices

TIP

Because of the need for careful coordination, pilots are often planned in the same manner as projects.

HINT

When planning a pilot, decide who will participate, how to conduct the pilot, how to collect results, and what information to collect to decide on broad-scale deployment.

1. Plan the pilots.

   When planning pilots, define quantitative criteria to be used for evaluating pilot results.
2. Review and get relevant stakeholder agreement on plans for pilots.
3. Consult with and assist those performing the pilots.
4. Perform each pilot in an environment that is characteristic of the environment present in a broad-scale deployment.
5. Track pilots against their plans.
6. Review and document results of pilots.

Pilot results are evaluated using the quantitative criteria defined during pilot planning. Reviewing and documenting results of pilots usually involves the following activities:

- Deciding whether to terminate the pilot, replan and continue the pilot, or proceed with deploying the process and technology improvement
- Updating the disposition of process- and technology-improvement proposals associated with the pilot
- Identifying and documenting new process- and technology-improvement proposals, as appropriate
- Identifying and documenting lessons learned and problems encountered during the pilot

SP 1.4 Select Improvements for Deployment

Select process and technology improvements for deployment across the organization.

Selection of process and technology improvements for deployment across the organization is based on quantifiable criteria derived from the organization's quality and process-performance objectives.

Typical Work Products

1. Process and technology improvements selected for deployment

Subpractices

1. Prioritize candidate process and technology improvements for deployment.

   Priority is based on an evaluation of the estimated cost-to-benefit ratio with regard to the quality and process-performance objectives.

   Refer to the Organizational Process Performance process area for more information about quality and process-performance objectives.

2. Select the process and technology improvements to be deployed.

   The selection of process improvements is based on their priorities and available resources.

3. Determine how each process and technology improvement will be deployed.

Examples of where the process and technology improvements may be deployed include the following:

- Organizational process assets
- Project-specific or common work environments
- Organization's product families
- Organization's capabilities
- Organization's projects
- Organizational groups

4. Document results of the selection process.

Results of the selection process usually include the following:

- The selection criteria for candidate improvements
- The disposition of each improvement proposal
- The rationale for the disposition of each improvement proposal
- The assets to be changed for each selected improvement

TIP

There is a need to balance stability with change. You can't afford to make every promising change; therefore, you must be selective about which changes you deploy across the organization.

TIP

The point of this subpractice is to determine the deployment approach in greater detail than was described in earlier steps (e.g., where the improvement will need to be incorporated).

TIP

Documenting the results of selection can help if the business environment changes enough for you to reconsider the decision and make a different selection.

TIP

The identification and analysis of improvement proposals and innovations (SG 1 specific practices) are typically ongoing activities. In contrast, the detailed planning for and deployment of improvements may be done periodically (e.g., quarterly or annually).

TIP

Depending on the magnitude of the change, it could take months or years before the change is fully deployed. Therefore, it is important to think about the retirement of those processes and products that the change will replace.

SG 2 Deploy Improvements

Measurable improvements to the organization's processes and technologies are continually and systematically deployed.

SP 2.1 Plan the Deployment

Establish and maintain plans for deploying selected process and technology improvements.

The plans for deploying selected process and technology improvements may be included in the organization's plan for organizational innovation and deployment or they may be documented separately.

An acquirer's plans for deploying improvements may include openly sharing most process knowledge and expertise with its suppliers. Any process-related knowledge that the acquirer or one of its suppliers possesses is viewed as accessible to virtually any other supplier in the acquirer's supply chain (perhaps with the exception of a direct competitor).

The implementation of this specific practice complements the Deploy Organizational Process Assets specific practice in the Organizational Process Focus process area and adds the use of quantitative data to guide the deployment and to determine the value of improvements with respect to quality and process-performance objectives.

Refer to the Organizational Process Focus process area for more information about deploying organizational process assets.

This specific practice plans the deployment of selected process and technology improvements. The Plan the Process generic practice addresses comprehensive planning that covers the specific practices in this process area.

Typical Work Products

1. Deployment plans for selected process and technology improvements

Subpractices

1. Determine how each process and technology improvement must be adjusted for organization-wide deployment.

   Process and technology improvements proposed in a limited context (e.g., for a single project) might need to be modified to work across the organization.

2. Determine the changes needed to deploy each process and technology improvement.

Examples of changes needed to deploy a process and technology improvement include the following:

- Process descriptions, standards, and procedures
- Work environments
- Education and training
- Skills
- Existing commitments
- Existing activities
- Continuing support to end users
- Organizational culture and characteristics
- Supplier agreements

3. Identify strategies that address potential barriers to deploying each process and technology improvement.
4. Establish measures and objectives for determining the value of each process and technology improvement with respect to the organization's quality and process-performance objectives.

Examples of measures for determining the value of a process and technology improvement include the following:

- Return on investment
- Time to recover the cost of the process or technology improvement
- Measured improvement in the project's or organization's product quality and process performance
- Number and types of project and organizational risks mitigated by the process or technology improvement
- Average time required to respond to changes in project requirements, market situations, and the business environment

Refer to the Measurement and Analysis process area for more information about establishing objectives for measurement and analysis, specifying measures and analyses to be performed, obtaining and analyzing measures, and reporting results.

5. Document the plans for deploying selected process and technology improvements.
6. Review and get agreement with relevant stakeholders on the plans for deploying selected process and technology improvements.
7. Revise the plans for deploying selected process and technology improvements as necessary.

SP 2.2 *Manage the Deployment*

Manage the deployment of selected process and technology improvements.

The implementation of this specific practice may overlap with the implementation of the Implement Action Proposals specific practice in the Causal Analysis and Resolution process area (e.g., when causal analysis and resolution is implemented organizationally or across multiple projects). The primary difference is that in the Causal Analysis and Resolution process area, planning is done to manage the removal of root causes of defects or problems from the project's defined process. In the Organizational Innovation and Deployment process area, planning is done to manage the deployment of improvements to the organization's processes and technologies that can be quantified against the organization's business objectives.

Typical Work Products

1. Updated training materials (to reflect deployed process and technology improvements)
2. Documented results of process- and technology-improvement deployment activities
3. Revised process- and technology-improvement measures, objectives, priorities, and deployment plans

Subpractices

1. Monitor the deployment of process and technology improvements using the deployment plans.
2. Coordinate the deployment of process and technology improvements across the organization.

   Coordinating deployment includes the following activities:

   - Coordinating activities of projects, support groups, and organizational groups for each process and technology improvement
   - Coordinating activities for deploying related process and technology improvements
3. Quickly deploy process and technology improvements in a controlled and disciplined manner, as appropriate.

TIP

One of the goals of most organizations is to be nimble and agile. Therefore, it is necessary to introduce small changes quickly, especially when they are limited and address an error.

Examples of methods for quickly deploying process and technology improvements include the following:

- Using red-lines, process change notices, or other controlled process documentation as interim process descriptions
- Deploying process and technology improvements incrementally, rather than as a single deployment
- Providing comprehensive consulting to early adopters of the process and technology improvement in lieu of revised formal training

4. Incorporate process and technology improvements into organizational process assets, as appropriate.

   Refer to the Organizational Process Definition process area for more information about organizational process assets.

5. Coordinate the deployment of process and technology improvements into the projects' defined processes, as appropriate.

   Refer to the Organizational Process Focus process area for more information about coordinating the deployment of process improvements into projects' defined processes.

6. Provide consulting, as appropriate, to support deployment of process and technology improvements.
7. Provide updated training materials to reflect improvements to organizational process assets.

   Refer to the Organizational Training process area for more information about training materials.

8. Confirm that the deployment of all process and technology improvements is completed.
9. Determine whether the ability of the defined process to meet quality and process-performance objectives is adversely affected by the process and technology improvement, and take corrective action as necessary.

   Refer to the Quantitative Project Management process area for more information about quantitatively managing the project's defined process to achieve the project's established quality and process-performance objectives.

10. Document and review results of process- and technology-improvement deployment.

    Documenting and reviewing results includes the following:

    - Identifying and documenting lessons learned

TIP

Extensive or complex improvements may require help, such as training, user support, or feedback on use of the new or updated process.

TIP

This should not be the first time the defined process with the improvement incorporated is analyzed to evaluate its impact on the organization's ability to meet its objectives. However, this further evaluation ensures that any unanticipated consequences have been addressed.

- Identifying and documenting new process- and technology-improvement proposals
- Revising process- and technology-improvement measures, objectives, priorities, and deployment plans

SP 2.3 Measure Improvement Effects

Measure effects of deployed process and technology improvements.

Refer to the Measurement and Analysis process area for more information about establishing objectives for measurement and analysis, specifying measures and analyses to be performed, obtaining and analyzing measures, and reporting results.

TIP

CAR addresses only the changes that were identified to prevent reoccurrence of a defect or problem. This specific practice looks at measuring the effects of all improvements that you are deploying across the organization.

The implementation of this specific practice may overlap with the implementation of the Evaluate the Effect of Changes specific practice in the Causal Analysis and Resolution process area (e.g., when causal analysis and resolution is implemented organizationally or across multiple projects).

Typical Work Products

1. Documented measures of the effects resulting from deployed process and technology improvements

Subpractices

1. Measure the actual cost, effort, and schedule for deploying each process and technology improvement.
2. Measure the value of each process and technology improvement.
3. Measure progress toward achieving the organization's quality and process-performance objectives.
4. Analyze progress toward achieving the organization's quality and process-performance objectives and take corrective action as needed.

   Refer to the Organizational Process Performance process area for more information about process-performance analyses.

5. Store measures in the organization's measurement repository.

TIP

Having measures available for reference may help evaluate newly proposed improvements that are similar to this one.

ORGANIZATIONAL PROCESS DEFINITION

A Process Management Process Area at Maturity Level 3

Purpose

The purpose of Organizational Process Definition (OPD) is to establish and maintain a usable set of organizational process assets and work environment standards.

Introductory Notes

Organizational process assets enable consistent process performance across the organization and provide a basis for cumulative, long-term benefits to the organization. (See the definition of "organizational process assets" in the glossary.)

The organization's process asset library is a collection of items maintained by the organization for use by the organization's people and projects. This collection of items includes descriptions of processes and process elements, descriptions of lifecycle models, process tailoring guidelines, process-related documentation, and data. The organization's process asset library supports organizational learning and process improvement by allowing the sharing of best practices and lessons learned across the organization.

The acquirer's organizational process assets also include acquisition guidance and practices established for use across acquisition projects and which refer to applicable statutes and regulations.

The organization's set of standard processes also describes standard interactions with suppliers. Supplier interactions are characterized by the following typical items: deliverables expected from suppliers, acceptance criteria applicable to those deliverables, standards (e.g., architecture and technology standards), and standard milestone and progress reviews.

The organization's set of standard processes is tailored by projects to create their defined processes. Other organizational process assets are used to support tailoring and implementing defined processes.

TIP

Acquisition organizations come in various configurations. For some larger acquisition programs, responsibility for the organizational elements of the model may rest within the program, giving guidance to the projects within. In others, there may be a collection of programs under a specific organizational executive. It is therefore difficult to provide specific guidance on the location of the various model elements associated with the Process Management category.

TIP

OPD contains specific practices that capture the organization's requirements, standards, and guidelines that are to be used by all projects across the organization.

HINT

As with any library, a key challenge is to enable staff members to locate information quickly. Therefore, it is necessary to catalog, maintain, and archive information.

Work environment standards are used to guide the creation of project work environments.

A standard process is composed of other processes (i.e., subprocesses) or process elements. A *process element* is the fundamental (i.e., atomic) unit of process definition that describes activities and tasks to consistently perform work. The process architecture provides rules for connecting the process elements of a standard process. The organization's set of standard processes may include multiple process architectures.

(See the definitions of "standard process," "process architecture," "subprocess," and "process element" in the glossary.)

TIP

CMMI models try to capture the "what" and not the "how." However, in notes and examples, guidance is provided to give you some tips on the interpretation and implementation of the concepts.

Organizational process assets may be organized in many ways, depending on the implementation of the Organizational Process Definition process area. Examples include the following.

- Descriptions of lifecycle models may be part of the organization's set of standard processes, or they may be documented separately.
- The organization's set of standard processes may be stored in the organization's process asset library, or it may be stored separately.
- A single repository may contain both measurements and process-related documentation, or they may be stored separately.

Related Process Areas

Refer to the Organizational Process Focus process area for more information about organizational process-related matters.

TIP

SP 1.7 is derived in part from CMMI-DEV but is not limited in application to IPPD and is not an optional addition as it is in that constellation.

Specific Goal and Practice Summary

SG 1 Establish Organizational Process Assets

SP 1.1 Establish Standard Processes
SP 1.2 Establish Lifecycle Model Descriptions
SP 1.3 Establish Tailoring Criteria and Guidelines
SP 1.4 Establish the Organization's Measurement Repository
SP 1.5 Establish the Organization's Process Asset Library
SP 1.6 Establish Work Environment Standards
SP 1.7 Establish Rules and Guidelines for Integrated Teams

Specific Practices by Goal

SG 1 Establish Organizational Process Assets

A set of organizational process assets is established and maintained.

SP 1.1 ESTABLISH STANDARD PROCESSES

Establish and maintain the organization's set of standard processes.

Standard processes may be defined at multiple levels in an enterprise and they may be related hierarchically. For example, an enterprise may have a set of standard processes that is tailored by individual organizations (e.g., a division or site) in the enterprise to establish their set of standard processes. The set of standard processes may also be tailored for each of the organization's business areas or product lines. Thus, the *organization's set of standard processes* can refer to the standard processes established at the organization level and standard processes that may be established at lower levels, although some organizations may have only one level of standard processes. (See the definitions of "standard process" and "organization's set of standard processes" in the glossary.)

Multiple standard processes may be needed to address the needs of different application domains, lifecycle models, methodologies, and tools. The organization's set of standard processes contains process elements (e.g., a work product size-estimating element) that may be interconnected according to one or more process architectures that describe relationships among process elements.

The organization's set of standard processes typically includes technical, management, administrative, support, and organizational processes.

Basing standard processes on industry standards and widely accepted models, with common terminology and lexicon, enables seamless interactions between the acquirer and supplier. In a multi-supplier environment, this seamless interaction is most important for acquirer standard processes that directly interface with supplier processes. Also, there may be cost and coordination benefits from having suppliers work together to develop or reconcile common support processes that are aligned with acquirer processes.

The level of detail required for standard processes depends on the flexibility needed by an enterprise, for instance, based on differences in business context, project types, and application domains.

The organization's set of standard processes should collectively cover all processes needed by the organization and projects, including those addressed by the process areas at maturity level 2.

Typical Work Products

1. Organization's set of standard processes

TIP

Organizational process assets support a fundamental change in behavior. Projects no longer create their processes from scratch but instead use the best practices of the organization, thus improving quality and saving time and money.

TIP

Standard processes define the key activities performed in an organization. Some examples of standard acquisition processes include source selection, contract negotiations, planning, and both technical and business reviews.

TIP

The organization's set of standard processes can include processes that are not directly addressed by CMMI, such as project acquisition strategy approval, financial management, and progress reporting to higher management or customers.

TIP

Often, organizations look at the exemplar processes from their successful acquisition projects or from other organizations as a starting point to populate the organization's set of standard processes.

TIP

The objective is to decompose and define the process so that it can be performed consistently across projects but will allow enough flexibility to meet the unique requirements of each project.

Subpractices

1. Decompose each standard process into constituent process elements to the detail needed to understand and describe the process.

   Each process element covers a bounded and closely related set of activities. The descriptions of process elements may be templates to be filled in, fragments to be completed, abstractions to be refined, or complete descriptions to be tailored or used unmodified. These elements are described in such detail that the process, when fully defined, can be consistently performed by appropriately trained and skilled people.

Examples of process elements include the following:

- Template for the conduct of management reviews
- Templates for supplier deliverables
- Common lexicon for directly interfacing acquirer and supplier processes
- Templates for standard supplier agreements
- Description of methods for verifying supplier estimates
- Description of standard acquisition approaches related to teaming with suppliers
- Description of standard acceptance criteria
- Description of standard decision making and issue resolution

2. Specify the critical attributes of each process element.

Examples of critical attributes include the following:

- Process roles
- Applicable standards
- Applicable procedures, methods, tools, and resources
- Process-performance objectives
- Entry criteria
- Inputs
- Product and process measures to be collected and used
- Verification points
- Outputs
- Interfaces
- Exit criteria

3. Specify relationships among process elements.

> Examples of relationships include the following:
> - Order of the process elements
> - Interfaces among process elements
> - Interfaces with external processes
> - Interdependencies among process elements

The rules for describing relationships among process elements are referred to as the *process architecture.* The process architecture covers essential requirements and guidelines. Detailed specifications of these relationships are covered in descriptions of defined processes that are tailored from the organization's set of standard processes.

4. Ensure that the organization's set of standard processes adheres to applicable policies, standards, and models.

   Adherence to applicable process standards and models is typically demonstrated by developing a mapping from the organization's set of standard processes to relevant process standards and models. This mapping is a useful input to future appraisals.

HINT

Your initial focus should be on standardizing what you already do well.

5. Ensure that the organization's set of standard processes satisfies the process needs and objectives of the organization.

   Refer to the Organizational Process Focus process area for more information about establishing and maintaining the organization's process needs and objectives.

6. Ensure that there is appropriate integration among processes that are included in the organization's set of standard processes.
7. Document the organization's set of standard processes.
8. Conduct peer reviews on the organization's set of standard processes.

   The acquirer's review of its standard processes can include the participation of suppliers for those processes and process elements that define standard interactions with suppliers.
9. Revise the organization's set of standard processes as necessary.

HINT

Break down stovepipes: When capabilities residing in different organizations are routinely needed to understand tradeoffs and resolve system-level problems, consider establishing a standard end-to-end process for performing joint work. To improve workflow, consider process integration between acquisition and supplier elements where appropriate.

SP 1.2 Establish Lifecycle Model Descriptions

Establish and maintain descriptions of lifecycle models approved for use in the organization.

Lifecycle models may be developed for a variety of customers or in a variety of situations, since one lifecycle model may not be appropriate for all situations. Lifecycle models are often used to define phases of the project. Also, the organization may define different lifecycle models for each type of product and service it delivers.

TIP

When managing a project, it is helpful to have a standard description for the phases the project moves through (i.e., project lifecycle model) to organize and assess the adequacy of project activities and to monitor progress.

Lifecycle models describe acquisition lifecycles, depending on the acquisition strategy chosen. The acquisition lifecycle typically begins with the pre-award phase of a supplier agreement, continues through the phases of awarding and managing the supplier agreement, and ends when the supplier agreement period of performance ends, usually with the acceptance and completion of the warranty for the acquired product and the transition of the product to the support organization.

Typical Work Products

1. Descriptions of lifecycle models

Subpractices

1. Select lifecycle models based on the needs of projects and the organization.
2. Document descriptions of lifecycle models.
   Lifecycle models may be documented as part of the organization's standard process descriptions or they may be documented separately.
3. Conduct peer reviews on lifecycle models.
   The acquirer's review of lifecycle models should include the participation of suppliers for those processes and process elements that define expectations and constraints for suppliers.
4. Revise the descriptions of lifecycle models as necessary.

TIP

It helps to provide guidance about which lifecycle models work best with which types of projects. This guidance may be found in organizations' process asset libraries based on their previous experiences.

SP 1.3 Establish Tailoring Criteria and Guidelines

Establish and maintain tailoring criteria and guidelines for the organization's set of standard processes.

Tailoring criteria and guidelines describe the following:

- How the organization's set of standard processes and organizational process assets are used to create defined processes
- Mandatory requirements that must be satisfied by defined processes (e.g., the subset of organizational process assets that are essential for any defined process)
- Options that can be exercised and criteria for selecting among options
- Procedures that must be followed in performing and documenting process tailoring

TIP

Tailoring allows projects to adapt the organization's set of standard processes and other assets to meet their needs. The challenge is to provide guidance that has sufficient flexibility to meet the unique needs of each project but at the same time ensure meaningful consistency.

Examples of reasons for tailoring include the following:

- Adapting the process for a new supplier
- Customizing the process for an application or class of similar applications
- Elaborating the process description so that the resulting defined process can be performed
- Accommodating supplier characteristics such as the number of projects executed for the acquirer and the supplier's process maturity
- Following the acquisition strategy

Flexibility in tailoring and defining processes is balanced with ensuring appropriate consistency of processes across the organization. Flexibility is needed to address contextual variables such as the domain; nature of the customer; cost, schedule, and quality tradeoffs; technical difficulty of the work; and experience of the people implementing the process. Consistency across the organization is needed so that organizational standards, objectives, and strategies are appropriately addressed, and process data and lessons learned can be shared.

Tailoring is a critical activity that allows controlled changes to processes due to the specific needs of a project or a part of the organization. Processes and process elements that are directly related to critical business goals and objectives should usually be defined as mandatory (allowing less variation), but processes and process elements that are less critical or only indirectly affect business objectives may allow for more tailoring (and therefore more variation). The amount of tailoring could also depend on the project's lifecycle model, the supplier, or the acquirer–supplier relationship.

TIP

Finding this balance usually takes time as the organization gains experience from using these assets.

Tailoring criteria and guidelines may allow for using a standard process "as is," with no tailoring.

Typical Work Products

1. Tailoring guidelines for the organization's set of standard processes

Subpractices

1. Specify selection criteria and procedures for tailoring the organization's set of standard processes.

   To fully leverage the supplier's process capability, the acquirer may choose to minimize the tailoring of the supplier's standard processes. Depending on the interfaces of the acquirer's processes with the supplier's processes, the acquirer's standard processes may be tailored to allow the supplier to execute its standard processes.

Examples of criteria and procedures include the following:

- Criteria for selecting lifecycle models from those approved by the organization
- Criteria for selecting process elements from the organization's set of standard processes
- Procedures for tailoring selected lifecycle models and process elements to accommodate process characteristics and needs
- Criteria for selecting an acquisition strategy and suppliers
- Criteria for selecting acquirer processes based on supplier process tailoring such as adding or combining testing cycles

Examples of tailoring include the following:

- Modifying a lifecycle model
- Combining elements of different lifecycle models
- Modifying process elements
- Replacing process elements
- Reordering process elements

HINT

Streamline the waiver process to enable new projects to establish their defined process quickly and to avoid stalling.

2. Specify the standards used for documenting defined processes.
3. Specify the procedures used for submitting and obtaining approval of waivers from requirements of the organization's set of standard processes.
4. Document tailoring guidelines for the organization's set of standard processes.
5. Conduct peer reviews on the tailoring guidelines.
6. Revise tailoring guidelines as necessary.

TIP

Both the tailoring process and guidelines may be documented as part of the organization's set of standard processes.

SP 1.4 Establish the Organization's Measurement Repository

Establish and maintain the organization's measurement repository.

Refer to the Use Organizational Process Assets for Planning Project Activities specific practice of the Integrated Project Management process area for more information about the use of the organization's measurement repository in planning project activities.

TIP

The organization's measurement repository is a critical resource that helps new projects plan by providing answers to questions about projects similar to their own (e.g., How long did it take? How much effort was expended? What was the resultant quality?).

The repository contains both product and process measures related to the organization's set of standard processes. It also contains or refers to information needed to understand and interpret measures and to assess them for reasonableness and applicability. For example, the definitions of measures are used to compare similar measures from different processes.

Standard measures that must be collected from the supplier are included as requirements in standard supplier agreements and may appear in the organization's measurement repository.

TIP

Although this practice concentrates on establishing and maintaining a repository, the real value occurs when the people in the organization begin to use the data in the repository when they establish defined processes and plans.

Typical Work Products

1. Definition of the common set of product and process measures for the organization's set of standard processes
2. Design of the organization's measurement repository
3. Organization's measurement repository (i.e., the repository structure and support environment)
4. Organization's measurement data

Subpractices

1. Determine the organization's needs for storing, retrieving, and analyzing measurements.
2. Define a common set of process and product measures for the organization's set of standard processes.

   Measures in the common set are selected based on the organization's set of standard processes. They are selected for their ability to provide visibility into process performance and to support expected business objectives. The common set of measures may vary for different standard processes.

   Standard measures are selected for their ability to provide visibility into processes critical to expected business objectives and to focus on elements significantly impacting performance within a project and across the organization.

   Measures defined include those related to agreement management, some of which may need to be collected from suppliers.

   Operational definitions for measures specify procedures for collecting valid data and the point in the process where data will be collected.

   Refer to the Measurement and Analysis process area for more information about defining measures.

TIP

These measures change over time and therefore should be reviewed periodically.

3. Design and implement the measurement repository.
4. Specify procedures for storing, updating, and retrieving measures.
5. Conduct peer reviews on definitions of the common set of measures and procedures for storing, updating, and retrieving measures.
6. Enter specified measures into the repository.

   Refer to the Measurement and Analysis process area for more information about collecting and analyzing data.
7. Make the contents of the measurement repository available for use by the organization and projects, as appropriate.

X-REF

Measurement and analysis practices (see MA) are a prerequisite to establishing the organization's measurement repository.

8. Revise the measurement repository, the common set of measures, and procedures as the organization's needs change.

> Examples of when the common set of measures may need to be revised include the following.
> - New processes are added.
> - Processes are revised and new measures are needed.
> - Finer granularity of data is required.
> - Greater visibility into the process is required.
> - Measures are retired.

SP 1.5 Establish the Organization's Process Asset Library

Establish and maintain the organization's process asset library.

HINT

Think of why you are storing this information and how often it will be retrieved.

> Examples of items to be stored in the organization's process asset library include the following:
> - Organizational policies
> - Defined process descriptions
> - Procedures (e.g., estimating procedure)
> - Development plans
> - Acquisition plans
> - Quality assurance plans
> - Training materials
> - Process aids (e.g., checklists)
> - Lessons-learned reports

Typical Work Products

1. Design of the organization's process asset library
2. The organization's process asset library
3. Selected items to be included in the organization's process asset library
4. The catalog of items in the organization's process asset library

Subpractices

TIP

A major objective of the process asset library is to ensure that information is easy to locate and use.

1. Design and implement the organization's process asset library, including the library structure and support environment.
2. Specify criteria for including items in the library.

   Items are selected based primarily on their relationship to the organization's set of standard processes.

3. Specify procedures for storing, updating, and retrieving items.
4. Enter selected items into the library and catalog them for easy reference and retrieval.
5. Make items available for use by projects.
6. Periodically review the use of each item and use results to maintain the library contents.
7. Revise the organization's process asset library as necessary.

> Examples of when the library may need to be revised include the following.
> - New items are added.
> - Items are retired.
> - Current versions of items are changed.

TIP

Library maintenance can quickly become an issue if all documents from every project are stored in the library. Some organizations regularly review their process asset library contents every 12 to 18 months to decide what to discard or archive.

SP 1.6 Establish Work Environment Standards

Establish and maintain work environment standards.

Work environment standards allow the organization and projects to benefit from common tools, training, and maintenance, as well as cost savings from volume purchases. Work environment standards address the needs of all stakeholders and consider productivity, cost, availability, security, and workplace health, safety, and ergonomic factors. Work environment standards can include guidelines for tailoring and the use of waivers that allow adaptation of the project's work environment to meet needs.

TIP

Work environment standards must make sense for your organization, its line of business, the degree of collaboration to be supported, and so on.

HINT

If your organization has a shared vision, your work environment must support it.

> Examples of work environment standards include the following:
> - Procedures for the operation, safety, and security of the work environment
> - Standard workstation hardware and software
> - Standard application software and tailoring guidelines for it
> - Standard production and calibration equipment
> - Process for requesting and approving tailoring or waivers

TIP

Typically, projects have additional requirements for their work environment. This specific practice establishes the standards to be addressed across the organization.

Typical Work Products

1. Work environment standards

Subpractices

1. Evaluate commercially available work environment standards appropriate for the organization.
2. Adopt existing work environment standards and develop new ones to fill gaps based on the organization's process needs and objectives.

TIP

Specific practice 1.7 is included in this process area to address the use of integrated teams, as these are more likely to be needed to meet the complex needs of the acquisition organization in its interactions with other acquisition organizations, supplier organizations, and customer organizations.

TIP

This specific practice establishes organizational rules and guidelines so that projects do not get "bogged down" when establishing their team structure, integrated teams in that structure, and adequate collaboration among interfacing teams.

SP 1.7 Establish Rules and Guidelines for Integrated Teams

Establish and maintain organizational rules and guidelines for the structure, formation, and operation of integrated teams.

In an acquisition organization, integrated teams are useful not just in the acquirer's organization but between the acquirer and supplier and among the acquirer, supplier, and other relevant stakeholders, as appropriate. Integrated teaming may be especially important in a system of systems environment.

Operating rules and guidelines for integrated teams define and control how teams are created and how they interact to accomplish objectives. Integrated team members must understand the standards for work and participate according to those standards.

Structuring integrated teams involves defining the number of teams, the type of each team, and how each team relates with the others in the structure. Forming integrated teams involves chartering each team, assigning team members and team leaders, and providing resources to each team to accomplish its work.

Typical Work Products

1. Rules and guidelines for structuring and forming integrated teams

Subpractices

TIP

Teams cannot operate at high performance if they must consult management for approval of every action or decision.

TIP

This specific practice also addresses issue resolution. The authority initially given to a newly formed team may be expanded later as project phases are completed and the team demonstrates mature use of the authority granted. The rules and guidelines for the degree of empowerment should support making such adjustments.

1. Establish and maintain empowerment mechanisms to enable timely decision making.

   In a successful teaming environment, clear channels of responsibility and authority must be established. Issues can arise at any level of the organization when integrated teams assume too much or too little authority and when it is unclear who is responsible for making decisions. Documenting and deploying organizational guidelines that clearly define the empowerment of integrated teams can prevent these issues.

2. Establish rules and guidelines for structuring and forming integrated teams.

Organizational process assets can help the project to structure and implement integrated teams. Such assets may include the following:

- Team structure guidelines
- Team formation guidelines
- Team authority and responsibility guidelines
- Guidelines for establishing lines of communication and authority
- Team leader selection criteria

3. Define the expectations, rules, and guidelines that guide how integrated teams work collectively.

These rules and guidelines establish organizational practices for consistency across integrated teams and can include the following:

- How interfaces among integrated teams are established and maintained
- How assignments are accepted
- How resources and inputs are accessed
- How work gets done
- Who checks, reviews, and approves work
- How work is approved
- How work is delivered and communicated
- Reporting chains
- Reporting requirements (e.g., cost, schedule, and performance status), measures, and methods
- Progress reporting measures and methods

4. Maintain the rules and guidelines for structuring and forming integrated teams.

X-REF

For more information on establishing integrated teams, see IPM SP 1.6.

5. Establish and maintain organizational guidelines to help team members balance their team and home organization responsibilities.

   A *home organization* is the part of the organization to which team members are assigned when they are not on an integrated team. A *home organization* may be called a *functional organization, home base, home office,* or *direct organization.*

ORGANIZATIONAL PROCESS FOCUS

A Process Management Process Area at Maturity Level 3

Purpose

The purpose of Organizational Process Focus (OPF) is to plan, implement, and deploy organizational process improvements based on a thorough understanding of current strengths and weaknesses of the organization's processes and process assets.

> **TIP**
>
> The many varied organizational approaches to structuring acquisition offices and positioning process improvement programs within them makes this process area vitally important for pursuing CMMI-ACQ beyond the basic acquisition best practices found in the CMMI-ACQ Primer at www.sei.cmu.edu/cmmi/models/.
>
> Our experience suggests that in some cases the organizational process improvement efforts are best managed at a site where multiple acquisition projects are operating. In other cases, process improvement efforts may be dispersed across regions or the globe with needed commitment to process discipline imposed from a central office, such as the office of the company CIO.

Introductory Notes

The organization's processes include all processes used by the organization and its projects. Candidate improvements to the organization's processes and process assets are obtained from various sources including the measurement of processes, lessons learned in implementing processes, results of process appraisals, results of product evaluation activities, results of benchmarking against other organizations' processes, and recommendations from other improvement initiatives in the organization.

Process improvement occurs in the context of the organization's needs and is used to address the organization's objectives. The organization encourages participation in process improvement activities by those who perform the process. The responsibility for facilitating and managing the organization's process improvement activities, including coordinating the participation of others, is typically assigned to a process group. The organization provides the long-term commitment and resources required to sponsor this group and to ensure the effective and timely deployment of improvements.

> **TIP**
>
> Although CMMI describes many of the processes that are critical to success, it does not contain everything. Therefore, you may improve processes such as portfolio management, which might not be discussed in CMMI.

The acquirer encourages supplier participation in process improvement activities.

Careful planning is required to ensure that process improvement efforts across the organization are adequately managed and implemented. The organization's process improvement planning results in a process improvement plan.

The organization's process improvement plan addresses appraisal planning, process action planning, pilot planning, and deployment planning. Appraisal plans describe the appraisal timeline and schedule, the scope of the appraisal, resources required to perform the appraisal, the reference model against which the appraisal will be performed, and logistics for the appraisal.

Process action plans usually result from appraisals and document how improvements targeting weaknesses uncovered by an appraisal will be implemented. Sometimes the improvement described in the process action plan should be tested on a small group before deploying it across the organization. In these cases, a pilot plan is generated.

Finally, when the improvement is to be deployed, a deployment plan is created. This plan describes when and how the improvement will be deployed across the organization.

Organizational process assets are used to describe, implement, and improve the organization's processes (see the definition of "organizational process assets" in the glossary).

TIP

Project participation is essential to any process improvement effort. Since acquisition success is dependent on both acquirers and suppliers, coordinated approaches offer a powerful synergy.

Especially in the early phases of process improvement, the process group must visibly demonstrate return on the organization's investment in process improvement.

TIP

When multiple organizations are involved in the success of the development of the product or service (e.g., acquirers and suppliers), coordinating and potentially sharing appraisal efforts deserves consideration.

HINT

Run your process improvement program like a project or series of projects. Use CMMI practices to help you plan, implement, and manage your process improvement activities.

TIP

With any type of change, an investment is required. These activities may require weeks, months, or even years. One challenge is to demonstrate improvements the organization can see quickly.

Related Process Areas

Refer to the Organizational Process Definition process area for more information about organizational process assets.

Refer to the Organizational Training process area for more information about the coordination of training.

Refer to the Measurement and Analysis process area for more information about analyzing measures.

Specific Goal and Practice Summary

SG 1 Determine Process Improvement Opportunities
- SP 1.1 Establish Organizational Process Needs
- SP 1.2 Appraise the Organization's Processes
- SP 1.3 Identify the Organization's Process Improvements

SG 2 Plan and Implement Process Actions
- SP 2.1 Establish Process Action Plans
- SP 2.2 Implement Process Action Plans

SG 3 Deploy Organizational Process Assets and Incorporate Experiences
- SP 3.1 Deploy Organizational Process Assets
- SP 3.2 Deploy Standard Processes
- SP 3.3 Monitor the Implementation
- SP 3.4 Incorporate Experiences into Organizational Process Assets

Specific Practices by Goal

SG 1 Determine Process Improvement Opportunities

Strengths, weaknesses, and improvement opportunities for the organization's processes are identified periodically and as needed.

Strengths, weaknesses, and improvement opportunities may be determined relative to a process standard or model such as a CMMI model or International Organization for Standardization (ISO) standard. Process improvements should be selected to address the organization's needs.

Changing business objectives, legal and regulatory requirements, and results of benchmarking studies may be sources of process improvement opportunities.

SP 1.1 Establish Organizational Process Needs

Establish and maintain the description of process needs and objectives for the organization.

The organization's processes operate in a business context that must be understood. The organization's business objectives, needs, and constraints determine the needs and objectives for the organization's processes. Typically, issues related to finance, technology, quality, human resources, and marketing are important process considerations.

TIP

Process improvement must relate directly to the organization's business objectives.

The organization's process needs and objectives cover aspects that include the following:

- Characteristics of processes
- Process-performance objectives, such as time-to-market and delivered quality
- Process effectiveness

Issues related to the organization's acquisition management needs are important process considerations.

Typical Work Products

1. The organization's process needs and objectives

Subpractices

1. Identify policies, standards, and business objectives that are applicable to the organization's processes.

2. Examine relevant process standards and models for best practices.
3. Determine the organization's process-performance objectives.

   Process-performance objectives may be expressed in quantitative or qualitative terms.

   Refer to the Measurement and Analysis process area for more information about establishing measurement objectives.

TIP

Examples of process-performance objectives include reducing defects identified by the end user in the field by 20 percent per year (quantitative) and increasing customer satisfaction (qualitative).

Examples of process-performance objectives include the following:
- Cycle time
- Defect removal rates
- Productivity

4. Define essential characteristics of the organization's processes.

   Essential characteristics of the organization's processes are determined based on the following:
   - Processes currently being used in the organization
   - Standards imposed by the organization
   - Standards commonly imposed by customers of the organization

HINT

Select the appraisal method that matches the purpose and information needed. Guide your selection by knowing the amount of information needed and the importance of its accuracy.

Examples of process characteristics include the following:
- Level of detail used to describe processes
- Process notation used
- Granularity of processes

TIP

Remember that these appraisals are of the acquisition organization seeking to improve its own process performance.

5. Document the organization's process needs and objectives.
6. Revise the organization's process needs and objectives as needed.

SP 1.2 Appraise the Organization's Processes

Appraise the organization's processes periodically and as needed to maintain an understanding of their strengths and weaknesses.

X-REF

Using appraisals as part of managing supplier activities is covered in SSAD and AM. Another useful resource for understanding how to best interpret appraisals is the guidebook, "Understanding and Leveraging a Supplier's CMMI Efforts: A Guidebook for Acquirers," at www.sei.cmu.edu/publications/documents/07.reports/07tr004.html.

Process appraisals may be performed for the following reasons:
- To identify processes to be improved
- To confirm progress and make the benefits of process improvement visible
- To satisfy the needs of a customer–supplier relationship
- To motivate and facilitate buy-in

The buy-in gained during a process appraisal can be eroded significantly if it is not followed by an appraisal-based action plan.

Typical Work Products

1. Plans for the organization's process appraisals
2. Appraisal findings that address strengths and weaknesses of the organization's processes
3. Improvement recommendations for the organization's processes

Subpractices

1. Obtain sponsorship of the process appraisal from senior management.

   Senior management sponsorship includes the commitment to have the organization's managers and staff participate in the process appraisal and to provide resources and funding to analyze and communicate findings of the appraisal.

TIP

The commitment of resources to the appraisal must be visible throughout the organization.

2. Define the scope of the process appraisal.

   Process appraisals may be performed on the entire organization or may be performed on a smaller part of an organization such as a single project or business area.

   The scope of the process appraisal addresses the following:

   - Definition of the organization (e.g., sites or business areas) to be covered by the appraisal
   - Identification of the project and support functions that will represent the organization in the appraisal
   - Processes to be appraised

3. Determine the method and criteria for the process appraisal.

   Process appraisals can occur in many forms. They should address the needs and objectives of the organization, which may change over time. For example, the appraisal may be based on a process model, such as a CMMI model, or on a national or international standard, such as ISO 9001 [ISO 2000]. Appraisals may also be based on a benchmark comparison with other organizations in which practices that may contribute to improved performance are identified. The appraisal method may assume a variety of characteristics, including time and effort, makeup of the appraisal team, and the method and depth of investigation.

TIP

Examples of appraisal methods include SCAMPI A, B, and C, as well as less formal gap analyses and surveys.

4. Plan, schedule, and prepare for the process appraisal.
5. Conduct the process appraisal.
6. Document and deliver the appraisal's activities and findings.

SP 1.3 Identify the Organization's Process Improvements

Identify improvements to the organization's processes and process assets.

Typical Work Products

1. Analysis of candidate process improvements
2. Identification of improvements for the organization's processes

Subpractices

HINT

In the early stages of process improvement, there are more candidate improvements than resources to address them. Prioritize these opportunities to be most effective.

1. Determine candidate process improvements.

Candidate process improvements are typically determined by doing the following:

- Measure processes and analyze measurement results
- Review processes for effectiveness and suitability
- Review lessons learned from tailoring the organization's set of standard processes
- Review lessons learned from implementing processes
- Review process improvement proposals submitted by the organization's managers, staff, and other relevant stakeholders
- Solicit inputs on process improvements from senior management and other leaders in the organization
- Examine results of process appraisals and other process-related reviews
- Review results of other organizational improvement initiatives

Candidate process improvements are also determined by doing the following:

- Reviewing process improvement proposals submitted by the organization's suppliers
- Obtaining feedback from suppliers on acquirer processes and supplier–acquirer interface points

HINT

Choose improvements that are visible to the organization, have a defined scope, and can be addressed successfully by available resources. If you try to do too much too quickly, it may result in failure and cause the improvement program to be questioned.

2. Prioritize candidate process improvements.

Examples of techniques to help determine and prioritize possible improvements to be implemented include the following:

- A cost-benefit analysis that compares the estimated cost and effort to implement the process improvements and their associated benefits
- A gap analysis that compares current conditions in the organization with optimal conditions
- A force-field analysis of potential improvements to identify potential barriers and strategies for overcoming those barriers
- Cause-and-effect analyses to provide information on the potential effects of different improvements that can then be compared

3. Identify and document the process improvements to be implemented.
4. Revise the list of planned process improvements to keep it current.

SG 2 Plan and Implement Process Actions

Process actions that address improvements to the organization's processes and process assets are planned and implemented.

The successful implementation of improvements requires participation in process action planning and implementation by process owners, those performing the process, and support organizations.

X-REF

Organizational process assets are those created by the activities in OPD.

TIP

Most of the acquisition organization should be involved in these activities.

SP 2.1 Establish Process Action Plans

Establish and maintain process action plans to address improvements to the organization's processes and process assets.

Establishing and maintaining process action plans typically involves the following roles:

- Management steering committees to set strategies and oversee process improvement activities
- Process groups to facilitate and manage process improvement activities
- Process action teams to define and implement process actions
- Process owners to manage deployment
- Practitioners to perform the process

This involvement helps to obtain buy-in on process improvements and increases the likelihood of effective deployment.

Process action plans are detailed implementation plans. These plans differ from the organization's process improvement plan by targeting improvements that were defined to address weaknesses, usually uncovered by appraisals.

Suppliers may be involved in developing process action plans if the processes that define interfaces between the acquirer and supplier are targeted for improvement.

TIP

Depending on the magnitude of the improvement, a process action plan can look similar to a project plan. If the improvement is small, the plan can look similar to a plan for a routine maintenance activity.

Typical Work Products

1. The organization's approved process action plans

Subpractices

1. Identify strategies, approaches, and actions to address identified process improvements.

X-REF

Piloting guidance can be found in OID and can be useful even if the thorough quantitative information expected by OID is not yet available.

New, unproven, and major changes are piloted before they are incorporated into normal use.

2. Establish process action teams to implement actions.

   Process action teams typically include process owners and those who perform the process. Process action teams may also include supplier representatives when suppliers interact with the acquirer process to be improved or provide supplemental resources to the acquirer to perform an acquirer process.

3. Document process action plans.

> Process action plans typically cover the following:
> - The process improvement infrastructure
> - Process improvement objectives
> - Process improvements to be addressed
> - Procedures for planning and tracking process actions
> - Strategies for piloting and implementing process actions
> - Responsibility and authority for implementing process actions
> - Resources, schedules, and assignments for implementing process actions
> - Methods for determining the effectiveness of process actions
> - Risks associated with process action plans

4. Review and negotiate process action plans with relevant stakeholders.
5. Review process action plans as necessary.

SP 2.2 Implement Process Action Plans

Implement process action plans.

TIP

Depending on the size of the organization and the extent of the change, the implementation activity can take days, weeks, months, or even years. Legacy acquisition programs may need to tailor changes to recognize existing agreements with customers and suppliers or with other acquisition offices in a system of systems environment.

Typical Work Products

1. Commitments among process action teams
2. Status and results of implementing process action plans
3. Plans for pilots

Subpractices

1. Make process action plans readily available to relevant stakeholders.
2. Negotiate and document commitments among process action teams and revise their process action plans as necessary.
3. Track progress and commitments against process action plans.
4. Conduct joint reviews with process action teams and relevant stakeholders to monitor the progress and results of process actions.

5. Plan pilots needed to test selected process improvements.
6. Review the activities and work products of process action teams.
7. Identify, document, and track to closure issues encountered when implementing process action plans.
8. Ensure that results of implementing process action plans satisfy the organization's process improvement objectives.

SG 3 DEPLOY ORGANIZATIONAL PROCESS ASSETS AND INCORPORATE EXPERIENCES

The organizational process assets are deployed across the organization and process-related experiences are incorporated into organizational process assets.

The specific practices under this specific goal describe ongoing activities. New opportunities to benefit from organizational process assets and changes to them may arise throughout the life of each project. Deployment of standard processes and other organizational process assets must be continually supported in the organization, particularly for new projects at startup.

OPF

SP 3.1 DEPLOY ORGANIZATIONAL PROCESS ASSETS

Deploy organizational process assets across the organization.

Deploying organizational process assets or changes to them should be performed in an orderly manner. Some organizational process assets or changes to them may not be appropriate for use in some parts of the organization (e.g., because of customer requirements or the current lifecycle phase being implemented). It is therefore important that those that are or will be executing the process, as well as other organization functions (e.g., training and quality assurance), be involved in the deployment as necessary.

HINT

Be sure to think about retiring the assets and work products that the change replaces. This activity is particularly important when acquisition organizations are dispersed regionally or globally.

Refer to the Organizational Process Definition process area for more information about how the deployment of organizational process assets is supported and enabled by the organization's process asset library.

Typical Work Products

1. Plans for deploying organizational process assets and changes to them across the organization
2. Training materials for deploying organizational process assets and changes to them
3. Documentation of changes to organizational process assets
4. Support materials for deploying organizational process assets and changes to them

Subpractices

1. Deploy organizational process assets across the organization.

> Typical activities performed as a part of this deployment include the following:
> - Identifying organizational process assets that should be adopted by those who perform the process
> - Determining how organizational process assets are made available (e.g., via a Web site)
> - Identifying how changes to organizational process assets are communicated
> - Identifying resources (e.g., methods and tools) needed to support the use of organizational process assets
> - Planning the deployment
> - Assisting those who use organizational process assets
> - Ensuring that training is available for those who use organizational process assets

   Refer to the Organizational Training process area for more information about the coordination of training.

2. Document changes to organizational process assets.

   Documenting changes to organizational process assets serves two main purposes:
   - To enable the communication of changes
   - To understand the relationship of changes in the organizational process assets to changes in process performance and results

3. Deploy changes that were made to organizational process assets across the organization.

> Typical activities performed as a part of deploying changes include the following:
> - Determining which changes are appropriate for those who perform the process
> - Planning the deployment
> - Arranging for the support needed to successfully transition changes

4. Provide guidance and consultation on the use of organizational process assets.

SP 3.2 Deploy Standard Processes

Deploy the organization's set of standard processes to projects at their startup and deploy changes to them, as appropriate, throughout the life of each project.

It is important that new projects use proven and effective processes to perform critical early activities (e.g., project planning, receiving requirements, and obtaining resources).

Projects should also periodically update their defined processes to incorporate the latest changes made to the organization's set of standard processes when it will benefit them. This periodic update helps to ensure that all project activities derive the full benefit of what other projects have learned.

Refer to the Organizational Process Definition process area for more information about the organization's set of standard processes and tailoring guidelines.

HINT

Project startup is the first and least expensive opportunity to get it right. Consider using experienced teams to help guide a project through high-risk areas selecting from and tailoring the organization's set of standard processes to mitigate project risk.

OPF

Typical Work Products

1. The organization's list of projects and the status of process deployment on each (i.e., existing and planned projects)
2. Guidelines for deploying the organization's set of standard processes on new projects
3. Records of tailoring and implementing the organization's set of standard processes

Subpractices

1. Identify projects in the organization that are starting up.
2. Identify active projects that would benefit from implementing the organization's current set of standard processes.
3. Establish plans to implement the organization's current set of standard processes on the identified projects.
4. Assist projects in tailoring the organization's set of standard processes to meet their needs.

   Refer to the Integrated Project Management process area for more information about tailoring the organization's set of standard processes to meet the unique needs and objectives of the project.

5. Maintain records of tailoring and implementing processes on the identified projects.
6. Ensure that the defined processes resulting from process tailoring are incorporated into plans for process-compliance evaluations.

   Process-compliance audits are objective evaluations of project activities against the project's defined process.

7. As the organization's set of standard processes are updated, identify which projects should implement the changes.

SP 3.3 Monitor the Implementation

Monitor the implementation of the organization's set of standard processes and use of process assets on all projects.

HINT

It is important not to limit improvement activities to just a few projects in your portfolio. Even legacy or small projects will benefit from the planned adoption of better process.

By monitoring implementation, the organization ensures that the organization's set of standard processes and other process assets are appropriately deployed to all projects. Monitoring implementation also helps the organization develop an understanding of the organizational process assets being used and where they are used in the organization. Monitoring also helps to establish a broader context for interpreting and using process and product measures, lessons learned, and improvement information obtained from projects.

Typical Work Products

1. Results of monitoring process implementation on projects
2. Status and results of process-compliance audits
3. Results of reviewing selected process artifacts created as part of process tailoring and implementation

Subpractices

1. Monitor projects for their use of the organization's process assets and changes to them.
2. Review selected process artifacts created during the life of each project.

   Reviewing selected process artifacts created during the life of a project ensures that all projects are making appropriate use of the organization's set of standard processes.
3. Review results of process-compliance audits to determine how well the organization's set of standard processes has been deployed.

   Refer to the Process and Product Quality Assurance process area for more information about objectively evaluating processes against applicable process descriptions, standards, and procedures.
4. Identify, document, and track to closure issues related to implementing the organization's set of standard processes.

SP 3.4 Incorporate Experiences into Organizational Process Assets

Incorporate process-related work products, measures, and improvement information derived from planning and performing the process into organizational process assets.

> **X-REF**
> Practices in IPM, OPF, and OPD are tightly related. OPD defines the organizational assets. OPF manages them, deploys them across the organization, and collects feedback. IPM uses the assets on the project and provides feedback to the organization.

Typical Work Products

1. Process improvement proposals
2. Process lessons learned
3. Measurements of organizational process assets
4. Improvement recommendations for organizational process assets
5. Records of the organization's process improvement activities
6. Information on organizational process assets and improvements to them

Subpractices

1. Conduct periodic reviews of the effectiveness and suitability of the organization's set of standard processes and related organizational process assets relative to the organization's business objectives.
2. Obtain feedback about the use of organizational process assets.
3. Derive lessons learned from defining, piloting, implementing, and deploying organizational process assets.
4. Make lessons learned available to people in the organization, as appropriate.

   Actions may be necessary to ensure that lessons learned are used appropriately.

> **TIP**
> Some feedback may be collected as part of quality assurance (QA) activities.

> **X-REF**
> Lessons learned are usually made available through the library established in OPD.

> Examples of inappropriate use of lessons learned include the following:
> - Evaluating the performance of people
> - Judging process performance or results

> Examples of ways to prevent inappropriate use of lessons learned include the following:
> - Controlling access to lessons learned
> - Educating people about the appropriate use of lessons learned

5. Analyze the organization's common set of measures.

   Refer to the Measurement and Analysis process area for more information about analyzing measures.

> **X-REF**
> Common sets of measures are usually kept in the organization's measurement repository, established in OPD.

Refer to the Organizational Process Definition process area for more information about establishing an organizational measurement repository, including common measures.

6. Appraise processes, methods, and tools in use in the organization and develop recommendations for improving organizational process assets.

> **TIP**
>
> We use the word *appraise* here more in line with Webster's definition of the word, rather than the appraisal term we use in CMMI.

This appraisal typically includes the following:

- Determining which processes, methods, and tools are of potential use to other parts of the organization
- Appraising the quality and effectiveness of organizational process assets
- Identifying candidate improvements to organizational process assets
- Determining compliance with the organization's set of standard processes and tailoring guidelines

7. Make the best of the organization's processes, methods, and tools available to people in the organization, as appropriate.
8. Manage process improvement proposals.

   Process improvement proposals can address both process and technology improvements.

The activities for managing process improvement proposals typically include the following:

- Soliciting process improvement proposals
- Collecting process improvement proposals
- Reviewing process improvement proposals
- Selecting the process improvement proposals to be implemented
- Tracking the implementation of process improvement proposals

   Process improvement proposals are documented as process change requests or problem reports, as appropriate.

   Some process improvement proposals may be incorporated into the organization's process action plans.

9. Establish and maintain records of the organization's process improvement activities.

ORGANIZATIONAL PROCESS PERFORMANCE

A Process Management Process Area at Maturity Level 4

Purpose

The purpose of Organizational Process Performance (OPP) is to establish and maintain a quantitative understanding of the performance of the organization's set of standard processes in support of achieving quality and process-performance objectives, and to provide process-performance data, baselines, and models to quantitatively manage the organization's projects.

X-REF

QPM and OPP are tightly coupled process areas. An organization seeking to implement one of these should implement both of them.

OPP

Introductory Notes

X-REF

The concept of "common measures" is further described in OPD SP 1.4.

Process performance is a measure of actual results achieved by following a process. Process performance is characterized by process measures (e.g., effort, cycle time, and defect removal effectiveness) and product measures (e.g., reliability, defect density, capacity, response time, and cost).

The common measures for the organization consist of process and product measures that can be used to characterize the actual performance of processes in the organization's individual projects. By analyzing the resulting measurements, a distribution or range of results can be established that characterize the expected performance of the process when used on any individual project.

TIP

A subprocess measure's "central tendency and spread," normalized appropriately (e.g., for work product size), can serve as its process performance baseline (PPB). Such a PPB can be displayed in different ways, such as by a control chart, box plot, or histogram. OPP practices assume, at a minimum, that PPBs are established for selected subprocess measures, but the organization and projects may benefit from establishing PPBs for other measures too.

In this process area, the phrase *quality and process-performance objectives* covers objectives and requirements for product quality, service quality, and process performance. As indicated earlier, the term *process performance* includes quality; however, to emphasize the importance of quality, the phrase *quality and process-performance objectives* is used rather than just *process-performance objectives*.

Measuring quality and process performance may involve combining existing measures into additional derived measures to provide more insight into the overall efficiencies and effectiveness at a project or organization level. The analysis at the organization level may be

TIP

This paragraph describes in a simplified way how the organization's process performance baselines (referred to here as "expected process performance") support QPM that, in turn, provides the data used to refine these baselines.

used to study productivity, improve efficiencies, and increase throughput across projects in the organization.

The expected process performance can be used in establishing the project's quality and process-performance objectives and can be used as a baseline against which actual project performance can be compared. This information is used to quantitatively manage the project. Each quantitatively managed project, in turn, provides actual performance results that become a part of baseline data for organizational process assets.

The acquirer may use quality and process-performance objectives to define performance and service level expectations for suppliers.

Process-performance models are used to represent past and current process performance and to predict future results of the process. For example, the latent defects in the delivered product can be predicted using measurements of defects identified during product verification activities.

X-REF

See the Brad Clark and Dave Zubrow presentation, "How Good Is the Software: A Review of Defect Prediction Techniques," from the SEPG 2001 conference (www.sei.cmu.edu/sema/pdf/defect-prediction-techniques.pdf). Some of these techniques can be the basis for process performance models.

The same measures of latent defects, analyzed using a supplier's past projects data, can be used to predict the quality of products delivered by that supplier. The acquirer can use supplier process-performance models to predict the overall capability of the acquirer to deliver the product.

When the organization has measures, data, and analytical techniques for critical process, product, and service characteristics, it is able to do the following.

- Determine whether processes are behaving consistently or have stable trends (i.e., are predictable).
- Identify processes in which performance is within natural bounds that are consistent across process implementation teams.
- Establish criteria for identifying whether a process or subprocess should be statistically managed, and determine pertinent measures and analytical techniques to be used in such management.
- Identify processes that show unusual (e.g., sporadic or unpredictable) behavior.
- Identify aspects of processes that can be improved in the organization's set of standard processes.
- Identify the implementation of a process that performs best.
- Identify aspects of processes that could be improved across acquirer–supplier interfaces.

Related Process Areas

Refer to the Quantitative Project Management process area for more information about the use of process-performance baselines and models.

Refer to the Measurement and Analysis process area for more information about specifying measures and collecting and analyzing data.

Refer to the Organizational Process Definition process area for more information about establishing organizational process assets.

TIP

Much of what is described in OPP (and in QPM) utilizes the practices described in MA. Mastering many of the practices in MA is a prerequisite to implementing OPP and QPM.

X-REF

A 2001 presentation made by Doug Smith and Craig Hollenbach at the CMMI Technology Conference and User Group (www.dtic.mil/ndia/2001cmmi/hollenbach.pdf) provides examples of process performance baselines and models.

Specific Goal and Practice Summary

SG 1 Establish Performance Baselines and Models

SP 1.1	Select Processes
SP 1.2	Establish Process-Performance Measures
SP 1.3	Establish Quality and Process-Performance Objectives
SP 1.4	Establish Process-Performance Baselines
SP 1.5	Establish Process-Performance Models

Specific Practices by Goal

SG 1 ESTABLISH PERFORMANCE BASELINES AND MODELS

Baselines and models, which characterize the expected process performance of the organization's set of standard processes, are established and maintained.

Prior to establishing process-performance baselines and models, it is necessary to determine which processes are suitable to be measured (the Select Processes specific practice), which measures are useful for determining process performance (the Establish Process-Performance Measures specific practice), and the quality and process-performance objectives for those processes (the Establish Quality and Process-Performance Objectives specific practice).

These specific practices are often interrelated and may need to be performed concurrently to select appropriate processes, measures, and quality and process-performance objectives. Often, the selection of one process, measure, or objective will constrain the selection of the others. For example, if a certain process is selected, the measures and objectives for that process may be constrained by the process itself.

HINT

Select process elements, not processes composed of multiple elements. Multiple sources of variation hidden in a process are not easily analyzed. What might appear to be a stable process may in fact be a collection of unstable process elements. This collection of process elements would leave you unable to correctly predict future behavior or accurately identify opportunities for improvement.

SP 1.1 SELECT PROCESSES

Select processes or subprocesses in the organization's set of standard processes to be included in the organization's process-performance analyses.

Refer to the Organizational Process Definition process area for more information about the structure of organizational process assets.

The organization's set of standard processes consists of a set of standard processes that, in turn, are composed of subprocesses.

Typically, it will not be possible, useful, or economically justifiable to apply statistical management techniques to all processes or subprocesses of the organization's set of standard processes. Selection of processes or subprocesses is based on the needs and objectives of both the organization and its projects.

The selection of subprocesses for analysis, the determination of process-performance objectives, and the selection of appropriate measures are often concurrent and iterative processes of both the organization and its projects.

When selecting processes or subprocesses for analyses, it is critical to understand the relationships between different processes and subprocesses and their impact on the acquirer and supplier delivering the product specified by the customer. Such an approach helps to ensure that quantitative and statistical management are applied where they have the most overall value to the organization.

TIP

These examples of criteria used to select subprocesses are fairly sophisticated and are typical of organizations almost at maturity level 4 or 5. At lower maturity levels, only a few of the criteria may be practical. The criteria used will grow in sophistication and the selection evolves as more experience and data are gained.

Examples of criteria that may be used for the selection of a process or subprocess for the organization's process-performance analysis include the following:

- The relationship of the subprocess to key business objectives
- Current availability of valid historical data relevant to the subprocess
- Current degree of data variability
- Subprocess stability (e.g., stable performance in comparable instances)
- The availability of corporate or commercial information that can be used to build predictive models

HINT

Because not all processes contribute equally to a business objective, and all such analyses consume time, effort, and money, you should start with a small selection. As you learn more, you can modify and expand the selection accordingly.

The existence of project data that indicates the process or subprocess has been or can be stabilized is a useful criterion that can be used for selecting a process or subprocess.

Typical Work Products

1. List of processes or subprocesses identified for process-performance analyses

SP 1.2 Establish Process-Performance Measures

Establish and maintain definitions of measures to be included in the organization's process-performance analyses.

Refer to the Measurement and Analysis process area for more information about specifying measures.

Typical Work Products

1. Definitions of selected measures of process performance

Subpractices

1. Determine which of the organization's business objectives for quality and process performance should be addressed by the measures.
2. Select measures that provide appropriate insight into the organization's quality and process performance.

   The measurement repository provides common measures for this purpose.

   For business objectives addressed through acquisition, select process, product, and service level measures that provide insight into the process performance of suppliers and into the quality of their deliverables.

Examples of criteria used to select measures include the following:
- Relationship of measures to the organization's business objectives
- Coverage that measures provide over the life of the product or service
- Visibility that measures provide into process performance
- Availability of measures
- Extent to which measures are objective
- Frequency at which observations of the measure can be collected
- Extent to which measures are controllable by changes to the process or subprocess
- Extent to which measures represent the users' view of effective process performance
- Extent to which measures provide insight that enables the acquirer to manage the project

3. Incorporate selected measures into the organization's set of common measures.

   Measures expected to be collected and reported by suppliers are incorporated into standard supplier agreement templates and standard service level agreements, as appropriate.

HINT

Analyze business objectives to identify process measures that provide insight into quality and process performance.

X-REF

The Goal Question Metric (GQM) is a well-known approach to deriving measures that provide insight into issues of interest. See www.cs.umd.edu/~mvz/handouts/gqm.pdf. The SEI's variant of GQM is called the Goal Question Indicator Metric (GQIM). See www.sei.cmu.edu/products/courses/implement.goal-driven.sw.meas.html.

X-REF

To begin systematic collection of these measures from new projects, incorporate them into the organization's set of common measures (OPD SP 1.4).

4. Revise the set of measures as necessary.

   Measures are periodically evaluated for their continued usefulness and ability to indicate process effectiveness.

SP 1.3 Establish Quality and Process-Performance Objectives

Establish and maintain the organization's quantitative objectives for quality and process performance.

The organization's quality and process-performance objectives should have the following attributes:

- Based on the organization's business objectives
- Based on the past performance of projects
- Gauges process performance in areas such as product quality, productivity, cycle time, or response time
- Accounts for the inherent variability or natural bounds of the selected process or subprocess
- Accounts for the inherent variability or natural bounds of supplier performance

TIP

Objectives based on the organization's business objectives may set the bar too high to motivate projects to identify process improvements. From a practical standpoint, what does the performance data show about how well a project can do relative to a particular process? In summary, there is need for balance between "desires" and "reality."

Typical Work Products

1. The organization's quality and process-performance objectives
2. Supplier service levels based on quality and process-performance objectives

Subpractices

1. Review the organization's business objectives related to quality and process performance.

TIP

OPP *aligns* the organization's process-performance analyses and management of projects with business objectives.

> Examples of business objectives include the following.
> - Achieve a development cycle of a specified duration for a specified release of a product.
> - Deliver the functionality of the product for a target percentage of estimated cost.
> - Decrease the cost of product maintenance by a specified percentage.

2. Define the organization's quantitative objectives for quality and process performance.

   Objectives may be established for process or subprocess measurements (e.g., effort, cycle time, and defect removal effectiveness) as well as for

TIP

The quantitative objectives for quality and process performance should be related to the organization's business objectives.

product measurements (e.g., reliability and defect density) and service measurements (e.g., capacity and response times) as appropriate.

> Examples of quality and process-performance objectives include the following.
> - Achieve a specified productivity.
> - Deliver work products with no more than a specified number of latent defects.
> - Shorten time to delivery within +/–5 percent of the process-performance baseline.
> - Reduce total lifecycle cost of new and existing products by 15 percent.
> - Deliver 100 percent of the specified functionality of the product.
> - Improve supplier performance and relationship scores to 4.8 (out of 5).

3. Define the priorities of the organization's objectives for quality and process performance.
4. Review, negotiate, and obtain commitment to the organization's quality and process-performance objectives and their priorities from relevant stakeholders.
5. Revise the organization's quantitative objectives for quality and process performance as necessary.

> Examples of when the organization's quantitative objectives for quality and process performance may need to be revised include the following:
> - When the organization's business objectives change
> - When the organization's processes change
> - When actual quality and process performance differ significantly from the objectives

TIP

Commitment to the organization's quality and process-performance objectives means senior management supports them by periodically reviewing how well projects are performing relative to them. Project management and senior technical staff members incorporate them into their projects and strive hard to achieve them.

OPP

SP 1.4 Establish Process-Performance Baselines

Establish and maintain the organization's process-performance baselines.

The organization's process-performance baselines are a measurement of performance for the organization's set of standard processes at various levels of detail, as appropriate. The processes include the following:

- Sequence of connected processes
- Processes that cover the entire life of the project
- Processes for developing individual work products

TIP

The term *process-performance baseline* is used instead of *process capability baseline* because *process capability* assumes the events are generated from the same process (and people). This may be a correct assumption in the case of a single project (*or team*), but not for the whole organization.

There may be several process-performance baselines to characterize performance for subgroups of the organization.

Examples of criteria used to categorize subgroups include the following:
- Product line
- Line of business
- Application domain
- Complexity
- Team size
- Work product size
- Process elements from the organization's set of standard processes
- Supplier-acquisition approach
- Agreement type (e.g., fixed price and time and effort)

Tailoring of the organization's set of standard processes may significantly affect the comparability of data for inclusion in process-performance baselines. Effects of tailoring should be considered in establishing baselines. Depending on the tailoring allowed, separate performance baselines may exist for each type of tailoring.

Refer to the Quantitative Project Management process area for more information about the use of process-performance baselines.

Typical Work Products

1. Baseline data on the organization's process performance

HINT

Record sufficient contextual information with a measurement to enable identification of the process-performance baseline it should be included in, when it was generated, and by whom.

Subpractices

1. Collect measurements from the organization's projects.

   The process or subprocess in use when the measurement was taken is recorded to enable appropriate use later.

   Refer to the Measurement and Analysis process area for more information about collecting and analyzing data.

TIP

Unless the process is stable, process-performance baselines will actually be a mixture of measurements taken from *different* processes. Such baselines are severely limited in their usefulness to projects (e.g., trial natural bounds are likely to be far apart).

2. Establish and maintain the organization's process-performance baselines from collected measurements and analyses.

   Refer to the Measurement and Analysis process area for more information about establishing objectives for measurement and analysis, specifying measures and analyses to be performed, obtaining and analyzing measures, and reporting results.

   Process-performance baselines are derived by analyzing collected measurements to establish a distribution or range of results that characterize the expected performance for selected processes or subprocesses when used on a project in the organization.

The measurements from stable subprocesses in projects should be used when possible; other data may not be reliable.

3. Review and get agreement with relevant stakeholders about the organization's process-performance baselines.
4. Make the organization's process-performance information available across the organization in the organization's measurement repository.
   The organization's process-performance baselines are used by projects to estimate the natural bounds for process performance.
5. Compare the organization's process-performance baselines to associated objectives.
6. Revise the organization's process-performance baselines as necessary.

Examples of when the organization's process-performance baselines may need to be revised include the following:

- When the processes change
- When the organization's results change
- When the organization's needs change
- When the suppliers' processes change
- When suppliers change

HINT

Investigate subgrouping when incorporating data from multiple projects (and teams) into the same process-performance baseline. Even if the process is stable in individual projects, it still might be executed sufficiently differently across projects to make establishment of a single baseline inappropriate.

TIP

OPP does not directly say what to do with the results of the comparison of the baseline to the objectives. Ideally, the objectives are attainable, but a stretch beyond the baseline. This comparison establishes feasible objectives. If the objectives are infeasible, revise them using CAR or OID to search for ways to improve performance.

SP 1.5 Establish Process-Performance Models

Establish and maintain process-performance models for the organization's set of standard processes.

Process-performance models are used to estimate or predict the value of a process-performance measure from the values of other process, product, and service measurements. These process-performance models typically use process and product measurements collected throughout the life of the project to estimate progress toward achieving objectives that cannot be measured until later in the project's life.

Process-performance models are used to estimate or predict when to fund, hold, cancel, migrate, reengineer, or retire a project. Process-performance models allow the acquirer to synchronize processes with customer needs. The organization's process-performance baselines provide quantitative data on those aspects of the projects and organization that can approximate the throughput potential of its processes. Focusing on these critical constraints, process-performance models allow the acquirer to predict how to best maximize the flow of work through projects and the organization.

HINT

Establish process-performance models that provide insight at different points in a project (e.g., at the end of each phase) to track progress.

Process-performance models are used as follows.

- The organization uses them for estimating, analyzing, and predicting the process performance associated with processes in and changes to the organization's set of standard processes.
- The organization uses them to assess the (potential) return on investment for process improvement activities.
- Projects use them for estimating, analyzing, and predicting the process performance of their defined processes.
- Projects use them for selecting processes or subprocesses for use.

Process-performance models are also used to set process-performance objectives for suppliers and to provide data that can help suppliers achieve these objectives.

These measures and models are defined to provide insight into and to provide the ability to predict critical process and product characteristics that are relevant to business value.

Results of the acquirer's process-performance models are shared with suppliers to help ensure the synchronized delivery of products and services.

Examples of areas of concern to projects in which models may be useful include the following:

- Schedule and cost
- Reliability
- Defect identification and removal rates
- Defect removal effectiveness
- Latent defect estimation
- Response time
- Project progress
- Combinations of these areas

X-REF

A paper by Tobias Häberlein, located at http://prosim.pdx.edu/prosim2003/paper/prosim03_haeberlein.pdf, concerns the application of system dynamics to acquisition. (System dynamics models were first used to model software.) The paper also has a good collection of references.

Examples of process-performance models include the following:

- System dynamics models
- Reliability growth models
- Complexity models
- Supply chain models

Refer to the Quantitative Project Management process area for more information about the use of process-performance models.

Typical Work Products

1. Process-performance models

Typical Supplier Deliverables

1. Supplier process-performance models

Subpractices

1. Establish process-performance models based on the organization's set of standard processes and the organization's process-performance baselines.
2. Calibrate process-performance models based on the organization's past results and current needs.
3. Review process-performance models and get agreement with relevant stakeholders.
4. Support the projects' use of the process-performance models.
5. Revise process-performance models as necessary.

Examples of when process-performance models may need to be revised include the following:
- When processes change
- When the organization's results change
- When the organization's needs change
- When supplier processes that directly interface with acquirer processes change
- When suppliers change

TIP

A review of the organization's set of standard processes helps to identify process and product characteristics that might assist in constructing a process-performance model. Process-performance baselines provide a primary source of the information needed to quantify and calibrate the model.

HINT

Meet with relevant stakeholders to discuss process-performance models (e.g., their usefulness and limitations) and the support required to make effective use of such models on projects.

X-REF

To use process-performance models effectively, project staff members and management may need significant support. The subpractices of OID SP 2.2 provide some example forms of support.

ORGANIZATIONAL TRAINING

A Process Management Process Area at Maturity Level 3

Purpose

The purpose of Organizational Training (OT) is to develop skills and knowledge of people so they can perform their roles effectively and efficiently.

Introductory Notes

Organizational Training includes training to support the organization's strategic business objectives and to meet the tactical training needs that are common across projects and support groups. Training needs identified by individual projects and support groups are handled at the project and support group level and are outside the scope of Organizational Training. Projects and support groups are responsible for identifying and addressing their training needs.

TIP

OT addresses the organization's training needs. The project's training needs are often more specific and are addressed in PP, PMC, and IPM.

OT

An organizational training program involves the following activities:

- Identifying the training needed by the organization
- Obtaining and providing training to address those needs
- Establishing and maintaining a training capability
- Establishing and maintaining training records
- Assessing training effectiveness

Effective training requires the assessment of needs, planning, instructional design, and appropriate training media (e.g., workbooks and computer software), as well as a repository of training process data. As an organizational process, the main components of training include a managed training development program, documented plans, personnel with appropriate mastery of disciplines and other areas of knowledge, and mechanisms for measuring the effectiveness of the training program.

TIP

Training data includes staff training records, dates of classes, and other training information.

Identifying process training needs is based primarily on the skills required to perform the organization's set of standard processes.

Identifying training needs may also address some training needs of suppliers, especially in those process elements that define interfaces with and expectations for suppliers.

TIP

Remember, CMMI sets expectations on *what* needs to be done, not *how* to do it. Therefore, each organization must decide what type of training is best for any situation.

Certain skills may be effectively and efficiently imparted through vehicles other than in-class training experiences (e.g., informal mentoring). Other skills require more formalized training vehicles, such as in a classroom, by Web-based training, through guided self-study, or via a formalized on-the-job training program. The formal or informal training vehicles employed for each situation should be based on an assessment of the need for training and the performance gap to be addressed. The term *training* used throughout this process area is used broadly to include all of these learning options.

TIP

To deploy these processes effectively across the organization, training is typically required.

Success in training can be measured by the availability of opportunities to acquire the skills and knowledge needed to perform new and ongoing enterprise activities.

Skills and knowledge may be technical, organizational, or contextual. Technical skills pertain to the ability to use equipment, tools, materials, data, and processes required by a project or process. Organizational skills pertain to behavior within and according to the employee's organization structure, role and responsibilities, and general operating principles and methods. Contextual skills are the self-management, communication, and interpersonal abilities needed to successfully perform in the organizational and social context of the project and support groups.

The phrase *project and support groups* is used frequently in the process area description to indicate an organization-level perspective.

TIP

Opportunities for joint training of acquirer and supplier team members should be explored, as they typically improve cross-functional activities.

This process area applies to developing acquirer skills and knowledge so that those in the organization can perform their roles effectively and efficiently. However, these practices can also apply to developing the supplier skills and knowledge. Topics can include acquirer business practices (e.g., acceptance and invoicing) as well as technical practices that the acquirer desires to be performed in a particular way (e.g., reflect lean thinking) or a collaborative way (e.g., using an agile approach).

Related Process Areas

Refer to the Organizational Process Definition process area for more information about the organization's process assets.

Refer to the Project Planning process area for more information about training needs identified by projects.

Refer to the Decision Analysis and Resolution process area for more information about applying evaluation criteria when selecting training approaches.

Specific Goal and Practice Summary

SG 1 Establish an Organizational Training Capability
- SP 1.1 Establish Strategic Training Needs
- SP 1.2 Determine Which Training Needs Are the Responsibility of the Organization
- SP 1.3 Establish an Organizational Training Tactical Plan
- SP 1.4 Establish a Training Capability

SG 2 Provide Necessary Training
- SP 2.1 Deliver Training
- SP 2.2 Establish Training Records
- SP 2.3 Assess Training Effectiveness

Specific Practices by Goal

SG 1 ESTABLISH AN ORGANIZATIONAL TRAINING CAPABILITY

A training capability, which supports the organization's management and technical roles, is established and maintained.

The organization identifies training required to develop the skills and knowledge necessary to perform enterprise activities. Once the needs are identified, a training program addressing those needs is developed.

SP 1.1 ESTABLISH STRATEGIC TRAINING NEEDS

Establish and maintain strategic training needs of the organization.

Strategic training needs address long-term objectives to build a capability by filling significant knowledge gaps, introducing new technologies, or implementing major changes in behavior. Strategic planning typically looks two to five years into the future.

HINT

Use strategic training to ensure that the organization continues as a learning organization, strengthens its core competencies, and remains competitive.

Examples of sources of strategic training needs include the following:
- The organization's standard processes
- The organization's strategic business plan
- The organization's process improvement plan
- Enterprise-level initiatives
- Skill assessments
- Risk analyses
- Acquisition and supplier management

Typical Work Products

1. Training needs
2. Assessment analysis

Subpractices

1. Analyze the organization's strategic business objectives and process improvement plan to identify potential training needs.
2. Document the strategic training needs of the organization.

> Examples of categories of training needs include (but are not limited to) the following:
> - Process analysis and documentation
> - Engineering (e.g., requirements analysis, design, testing, configuration management, and quality assurance)
> - Selection and management of suppliers
> - Management (e.g., estimating, tracking, and risk management)
> - Disaster recovery and continuity of operations
> - Acquisition management (e.g., solicitation, supplier selection, and supplier management)
> - Communication and negotiation skills

3. Determine the roles and skills needed to perform the organization's set of standard processes.

> Roles may include project manager, architects, business process analysts, and suppliers, especially in process elements that identify interfaces with and expectations from suppliers.

4. Document the training needed to perform roles in the organization's set of standard processes.
5. Document the training needed to maintain the safe, secure, and continued operation of the business.
6. Revise the organization's strategic needs and required training as necessary.

SP 1.2 Determine Which Training Needs Are the Responsibility of the Organization

Determine which training needs are the responsibility of the organization and which are left to the individual project or support group.

Refer to the Project Planning process area for more information about project- and support-group-specific plans for training.

In addition to strategic training needs, organizational training addresses training requirements that are common across projects and support groups. Projects and support groups have the primary responsibility for identifying and addressing their training needs. The organization's training staff is responsible only for addressing common cross-project and support group training needs (e.g., training in work environments common to multiple projects). In some cases, however, the organization's training staff may address additional training needs of projects and support groups, as negotiated with them, in the context of the training resources available and the organization's training priorities.

TIP

Small acquisition-specific organizations may choose to use the practices in this process area to address all of their training. If so, the scope and intent of the practices should be expanded appropriately.

Typical Work Products

1. Common project and support group training needs
2. Training commitments

Subpractices

1. Analyze the training needs identified by projects and support groups.

   Analysis of project and support group needs is intended to identify common training needs that can be most efficiently addressed organization-wide. These needs-analysis activities are used to anticipate future training needs that are first visible at the project and support group levels.

2. Negotiate with projects and support groups on how their training needs will be satisfied.

   The support provided by the organization's training staff depends on the training resources available and the organization's training priorities.

3. Document commitments for providing training support to projects and support groups.

> Examples of training appropriately performed by the project or support group include the following:
> - Training in the application or service domain of the project
> - Training in the unique tools and methods used by the project or support group
> - Training in safety, security, and human factors

SP 1.3 Establish an Organizational Training Tactical Plan

Establish and maintain an organizational training tactical plan.

The organizational training tactical plan is the plan to deliver the training that is the responsibility of the organization and is necessary

TIP

For many organizations, this planning is performed annually with a review each quarter.

for individuals to perform their roles effectively. This plan addresses the near-term execution of training and is adjusted periodically in response to changes (e.g., in needs or resources) and to evaluations of effectiveness.

Typical Work Products

1. Organizational training tactical plan

Subpractices

1. Establish the content of the plan.

> Organizational training tactical plans typically contain the following:
> - Training needs
> - Training topics
> - Schedules based on training activities and their dependencies
> - Methods used for training
> - Requirements and quality standards for training materials
> - Training tasks, roles, and responsibilities
> - Required resources including tools, facilities, environments, staffing, and skills and knowledge

2. Establish commitments to the plan.
   Documented commitments by those responsible for implementing and supporting the plan are essential for the plan to be effective.
3. Revise the plan and commitments as necessary.

SP 1.4 Establish a Training Capability

Establish and maintain a training capability to address organizational training needs.

Refer to the Decision Analysis and Resolution process area for more information about how to apply evaluation criteria when selecting training approaches and developing training materials.

Typical Work Products

1. Training materials and supporting artifacts

Subpractices

1. Select appropriate approaches to satisfy organizational training needs.
   Many factors may affect the selection of training approaches, including audience-specific knowledge, costs and schedule, and the work environment. Selecting an approach requires consideration of the

means to provide skills and knowledge in the most effective way possible given the constraints.

Examples of training approaches include the following:
- Classroom training
- Computer-aided instruction
- Guided self-study
- Formal apprenticeship and mentoring programs
- Facilitated videos
- Chalk talks
- Brown-bag lunch seminars
- Structured on-the-job training

2. Determine whether to develop training materials internally or to acquire them externally.

   Determine the costs and benefits of internal training development and of acquiring training externally.

Example criteria that can be used to determine the most effective mode of knowledge or skill acquisition include the following:
- Performance objectives
- Time available to prepare for project execution
- Business objectives
- Availability of in-house expertise
- Availability of training from external sources

Examples of external sources of training include the following:
- Customer-provided training
- Commercially available training courses
- Academic programs
- Professional conferences
- Seminars

3. Develop or obtain training materials.

   Training may be provided by the project, support groups, the organization, or an external organization. The organization's training staff coordinates the acquisition and delivery of training regardless of its source.

Examples of training materials include the following:
- Courses
- Computer-aided instruction
- Videos

4. Develop or obtain qualified instructors.

   To ensure that internal training instructors have the necessary knowledge and training skills, criteria can be defined to identify, develop, and qualify them. In the case of external training, the organization's training staff can investigate how the training provider determines which instructors will deliver the training. This can also be a factor in selecting or continuing to use a training provider.

5. Describe the training in the organization's training curriculum.

> Examples of the information provided in training descriptions for each course include the following:
> - Topics covered in the training
> - Intended audience
> - Prerequisites and preparation for participating
> - Training objectives
> - Length of the training
> - Lesson plans
> - Completion criteria for the course
> - Criteria for granting training waivers

6. Revise training materials and supporting artifacts as necessary.

> Examples of situations in which training materials and supporting artifacts may need to be revised include the following.
> - Training needs change (e.g., when new technology associated with the training topic is available).
> - An evaluation of the training identifies the need for change (e.g., evaluations of training effectiveness surveys, training program performance assessments, or instructor evaluation forms).

SG 2 PROVIDE NECESSARY TRAINING

Training necessary for individuals to perform their roles effectively is provided.

When selecting people to be trained, the following should be considered:

- Background of the target population of training participants
- Prerequisite background to receive training
- Skills and abilities needed by people to perform their roles
- Need for cross-discipline technical management training for all disciplines, including project management

- Need for managers to have training in appropriate organizational processes
- Need for training in basic principles of all appropriate disciplines or services to support personnel in quality management, configuration management, and other related support functions
- Need to provide competency development for critical functional areas
- Need to maintain competencies and qualifications of personnel to operate and maintain work environments common to multiple projects

SP 2.1 Deliver Training

Deliver training following the organizational training tactical plan.

Typical Work Products

1. Delivered training course

Subpractices

1. Select those who will receive the training necessary to perform their roles effectively.

   The acquirer includes supplier representatives, as appropriate, to ensure that selected suppliers can effectively interface with acquirer processes.

   Training is intended to impart knowledge and skills to people performing various roles in the organization. Some people already possess the knowledge and skills required to perform well in their designated roles. Training can be waived for these people, but care should be taken that training waivers are not abused.
2. Schedule the training, including any resources, as necessary (e.g., facilities and instructors).

   Training should be planned and scheduled. Training is provided that has a direct bearing on work performance expectations. Therefore, optimal training occurs in a timely manner with regard to imminent job-performance expectations.

> These performance expectations often include the following:
> - Training in the use of specialized tools
> - Training in procedures that are new to the person who will perform them

3. Conduct the training.

   Experienced instructors should conduct the training. When possible, training is conducted in settings that closely resemble actual performance conditions and includes activities to simulate actual work situations. This approach includes integration of tools, methods, and procedures for competency development. Training is tied to work responsibilities so that on-the-job activities or other outside experiences will reinforce the training within a reasonable time after the training was conducted.

4. Track the delivery of training against the plan.

SP 2.2 Establish Training Records

Establish and maintain records of organizational training.

TIP

To provide consistent and complete information on each employee, the training records may include all training, whether performed at the organization's level or by a project or support group.

This practice applies to the training performed at the organizational level. Establishment and maintenance of training records for project- or support-group-sponsored training is the responsibility of each individual project or support group.

Typical Work Products

1. Training records
2. Training updates to the organizational repository

Typical Supplier Deliverables

1. Training records, as appropriate

Subpractices

X-REF

To ensure that training records are accurate, you may want to use some CM practices.

1. Keep records of all students who successfully complete each training course or other approved training activity as well as those who are unsuccessful.
2. Keep records of all staff members who are waived from training.

   The rationale for granting a waiver should be documented, and both the manager responsible and the manager of the excepted individual should approve the waiver.
3. Keep records of all students who successfully complete their required training.
4. Make training records available to the appropriate people for consideration in assignments.

   Training records may be part of a skills matrix developed by the training organization to provide a summary of the experience and education of people, as well as training sponsored by the organization.

SP 2.3 Assess Training Effectiveness

Assess the effectiveness of the organization's training program.

A process should exist to determine the effectiveness of training (i.e., how well training is meeting the organization's needs).

> **TIP**
>
> Training effectiveness can change over time. Initially, training may be done using one medium or mode of delivery to train large numbers of people and another medium or mode of delivery to train the "stragglers."

Examples of methods used to assess training effectiveness include the following:

- Testing in the training context
- Post-training surveys of training participants
- Surveys of manager satisfaction with post-training effects
- Assessment mechanisms embedded in courseware

Measures may be taken to assess the benefits of training against both the project's and organization's objectives. Particular attention should be paid to the need for various training methods, such as training teams as integral work units. When used, performance objectives should be shared with course participants, unambiguous, observable, and verifiable. The results of the training-effectiveness assessment should be used to revise training materials as described in the Establish a Training Capability specific practice.

Typical Work Products

1. Training-effectiveness surveys
2. Training program performance assessments
3. Instructor evaluation forms
4. Training examinations

Subpractices

1. Assess in-progress or completed projects to determine whether staff knowledge is adequate for performing project tasks.
2. Provide a mechanism for assessing the effectiveness of each training course with respect to established organizational, project, or individual learning (or performance) objectives.
3. Obtain student evaluations of how well training activities met their needs.

PROJECT MONITORING AND CONTROL

A Project Management Process Area at Maturity Level 2

Purpose

The purpose of Project Monitoring and Control (PMC) is to provide an understanding of the project's progress so that appropriate corrective actions can be taken when the project's performance deviates significantly from the plan.

X-REF

PP provides the overall plan and PMC tracks activities against the plan.

Introductory Notes

A project's documented plan is the basis for monitoring activities, communicating status, and taking corrective action. Progress is primarily determined by comparing actual work product and task attributes, effort, cost, and schedule to the plan at prescribed milestones or control levels in the project schedule or WBS. Appropriate visibility of progress enables timely corrective action to be taken when performance deviates significantly from the plan. A deviation is significant if, when left unresolved, it precludes the project from meeting its objectives.

TIP

Initially, as processes based on PMC are introduced, project managers and staff members are reactive. However, as monitoring and control of activities become routine, project managers and staff members begin to anticipate problems and success in advance.

The term *project plan* is used throughout these practices to refer to the overall plan for controlling the project.

Monitoring and control functions are established early in the project as the project's planning is performed and the acquisition strategy is defined. As the acquisition of technology solutions unfolds, monitoring and control activities are essential to ensure that appropriate resources are being applied and that acquirer activities are progressing according to plan.

When actual status deviates significantly from expected values, corrective actions are taken, as appropriate. These actions may require replanning, which may include revising the original plan, establishing new agreements, or including additional mitigation activities in the current plan.

HINT

Normally, variation will occur. Perform corrective action only when a significant deviation occurs.

X-REF

Some corrective actions may require changes to agreements. These maintenance activities are covered in SSAD SP 3.2.

If corrective action is required to resolve variances from project plans, these actions should be defined and tracked to closure.

After one or more suppliers are selected and agreements are established, the role of monitoring and control becomes twofold: (1) The acquirer continues to monitor and control its activities and work products while also (2) monitoring and controlling the progress and performance of supplier activities that affect the overall project plan.

The supplier project progress and performance reporting requirements are established in the supplier agreement consistent with the needs of the project.

Related Process Areas

Refer to the Project Planning process area for more information about the project plan, including how it specifies the appropriate level of project monitoring, measures used to monitor progress, and known risks.

Refer to the Measurement and Analysis process area for more information about the process of measuring, analyzing, and recording information.

Refer to the Agreement Management process area for more information about resolving supplier agreement issues.

Refer to the Solicitation and Supplier Agreement Development process area for more information about making changes to the supplier agreement.

Specific Goal and Practice Summary

SG 1 Monitor the Project Against the Plan
- SP 1.1 Monitor Project Planning Parameters
- SP 1.2 Monitor Commitments
- SP 1.3 Monitor Project Risks
- SP 1.4 Monitor Data Management
- SP 1.5 Monitor Stakeholder Involvement
- SP 1.6 Conduct Progress Reviews
- SP 1.7 Conduct Milestone Reviews
- SP 1.8 Monitor Transition to Operations and Support

SG 2 Manage Corrective Action to Closure
- SP 2.1 Analyze Issues
- SP 2.2 Take Corrective Action
- SP 2.3 Manage Corrective Actions

Specific Practices by Goal

SG 1 Monitor the Project Against the Plan

Actual performance and progress of the project are monitored against the project plan.

Monitoring acquirer progress and performance begins as soon as a plan is established. The acquirer is responsible for monitoring the progress and output of the project. After a supplier is selected and a supplier agreement is put in place, the acquirer's monitoring and control activities extend to the supplier and its activities. The acquirer monitors supplier progress, including achievement of requirements established in the supplier agreement and using specified process, product, and service level measures.

SP 1.1 Monitor Project Planning Parameters

Monitor actual values of project planning parameters against the project plan.

Project planning parameters constitute typical indicators of project progress and performance and include attributes of work products and tasks, costs, effort, and schedule. Attributes of the work products and tasks include size, complexity, weight, form, fit, and function.

Monitoring typically involves measuring actual values of project planning parameters, comparing actual values to estimates in the plan, and identifying significant deviations. Recording actual values of project planning parameters includes recording associated contextual information to help understand measures. An analysis of the impact that significant deviations have on determining the corrective actions to take is handled in specific goal 2 and its specific practices in this process area.

TIP

Actual values gathered during the project are used as "historical data" to provide a basis for estimates in planning for similar projects in the future.

Typical Work Products

1. Records of project performance
2. Records of significant deviations
3. Cost performance reports

Typical Supplier Deliverables

1. Supplier project progress and performance reports
2. Records of significant deviations
3. Cost performance reports

X-REF

These subpractices mirror the specific practices in PP.

Subpractices

1. Monitor progress against the schedule.

Progress monitoring typically includes the following:
- Periodically measuring the actual completion of activities and milestones
- Comparing the actual completion of activities and milestones against the project plan schedule
- Identifying significant deviations from the project plan budget and schedule estimates

2. Monitor the project's costs and expended effort.

An example of a system for monitoring and updating the project's costs and expended effort is an Earned Value Management System (EVMS) [GEIA 748 2002].

Effort and cost monitoring typically includes the following:
- Periodically measuring the actual effort and costs expended and staff assigned
- Comparing actual effort, costs, staffing, and training to the project plan budget and estimates
- Identifying significant deviations from the project plan budget and schedule

3. Monitor the attributes of work products and tasks.

   Refer to the Project Planning process area for more information about the attributes of work products and tasks.

   Refer to the Measurement and Analysis process area for more information about measures defined to support management information needs.

Monitoring the attributes of work products and tasks typically includes the following:
- Periodically measuring the actual attributes of work products and tasks, such as size or complexity (and changes to these attributes)
- Comparing the actual attributes of work products and tasks (and changes to these attributes) to project plan estimates
- Identifying significant deviations from project plan estimates

Monitoring attributes applies to both acquirer and supplier work products and tasks.

4. Monitor resources provided and used.

   Refer to the Project Planning process area for more information about planned resources.

   This resource monitoring includes monitoring the availability of resources provided by the supplier for the project.

5. Monitor the knowledge and skills of project personnel.

   Refer to the Project Planning process area for more information about planning for the knowledge and skills needed to perform the project.

> Monitoring the knowledge and skills of project personnel typically includes the following:
> - Periodically measuring the acquisition of knowledge and skills by project personnel
> - Comparing actual training obtained to that documented in the project plan
> - Identifying significant deviations from estimates in the project plan

   Personnel monitoring includes monitoring the skills and knowledge of supplier personnel provided for the project.

6. Document significant deviations in project planning parameters.

   Document significant deviations that apply either to acquirer project execution or to supplier deviations from the project plan.

   Refer to the Solicitation and Supplier Agreement Development process area for more information about modifying supplier agreements to reflect change requests.

SP 1.2 Monitor Commitments

Monitor commitments against those identified in the project plan.

Resource commitments that result in expenditures (e.g., issued purchase orders and completed supplier deliverables that are accepted) are tracked when the expense is incurred, even prior to formal payment, to ensure that future financial and legal obligations are accounted for as soon as they are incurred. Commitments that do not result in expenditures (e.g., allocation of resources or skill sets) should also be monitored.

Supplier commitments for the project are also monitored by the acquirer through these practices.

> **TIP**
>
> Things happen that prevent appropriate follow-through with commitments, especially in an immature organization. Therefore, it is necessary to monitor commitments and take corrective action when commitments change.

Typical Work Products

1. Records of commitment reviews

Subpractices

1. Regularly review commitments (both external and internal).
2. Identify commitments that have not been satisfied or are at significant risk of not being satisfied.
3. Document the results of commitment reviews.

SP 1.3 Monitor Project Risks

Monitor risks against those identified in the project plan.

> **X-REF**
>
> Specific practice 1.3 is the handshake with the risks that were identified in PP. This practice is reactive and involves minimal risk management activities. For more complete and proactive handling of project risks, refer to RSKM.

Refer to the Project Planning process area for more information about identifying project risks.

Refer to the Risk Management process area for more information about risk management activities.

The acquirer monitors the overall project risk. Many risks are the sole responsibility of the acquirer and may include information that should not be shared with the supplier (e.g., source selection sensitive, recompetition, or internal staffing).

There can also be risks that require careful coordination with suppliers and the establishment of appropriate mechanisms for the escalation of risks and risk status (e.g., feasibility of the technology to meet end-user performance requirements). Shared risks may require jointly planned mitigations.

Typical Work Products

1. Records of project risk monitoring

Typical Supplier Deliverables

1. Records of supplier risk monitoring

Subpractices

1. Periodically review the documentation of risks in the context of the project's current status and circumstances.

   This review includes the risks defined in the solicitation package, those identified by the supplier in their proposal, and those raised as part of regular supplier status reporting.
2. Revise the documentation of risks as additional information becomes available.
3. Communicate the risk status to relevant stakeholders.

Examples of risk status include the following:

- A change in the probability that the risk occurs
- A change in risk priority

SP 1.4 Monitor Data Management

Monitor the management of project data against the project plan.

Refer to the Plan Data Management specific practice in the Project Planning process area for more information about identifying types of data to be managed and how to plan for their management.

Once plans for the management of project data are made, the management of that data must be monitored to ensure that those plans are accomplished.

Typical Work Products

1. Records of data management

Typical Supplier Deliverables

1. Records of supplier data management

Subpractices

1. Periodically review data management activities against their description in the project plan.
2. Identify and document significant issues and their impacts.
3. Document results of data management activity reviews.

SP 1.5 Monitor Stakeholder Involvement

Monitor stakeholder involvement against the project plan.

Refer to the Plan Stakeholder Involvement specific practice in the Project Planning process area for more information about identifying relevant stakeholders and planning appropriate involvement with them.

Once stakeholders are identified and the extent of their involvement in the project is specified in project planning, that involvement must be monitored to ensure that appropriate interactions are occurring.

This monitoring is particularly true in a system of systems environment in which the involvement of owners, acquirers, and customers of other systems in the system of systems is crucial to the success of that system of systems.

Typical Work Products

1. Records of stakeholder involvement

Typical Supplier Deliverables

1. Records of supplier involvement

Subpractices

1. Periodically review the status of stakeholder involvement.
2. Identify and document significant issues and their impacts.
3. Document the results of stakeholder involvement status reviews.

SP 1.6 Conduct Progress Reviews

Periodically review the project's progress, performance, and issues.

TIP

Progress reviews are held regularly (e.g., weekly, monthly, or quarterly).

Progress reviews are project reviews to keep stakeholders informed. These project reviews can be informal and may not be specified explicitly in project plans.

Refer to the Agreement Management process area for more information about conducting reviews with the supplier per the supplier agreement.

Refer to the Solicitation and Supplier Agreement Development process area for more information about establishing review requirements in the supplier agreement.

Typical Work Products

1. Documented project review results

Typical Supplier Deliverables

1. Supplier project progress and performance reports
2. Supplier review materials and reports
3. Documentation of product and document deliveries

Subpractices

1. Regularly communicate status on assigned activities and work products to relevant stakeholders.

   Managers, staff members, customers, end users, suppliers, and other relevant stakeholders in the organization are included in reviews, as appropriate.

2. Review the results of collecting and analyzing measures for controlling the project.

   Refer to the Measurement and Analysis process area for more information about measuring and analyzing project performance data.

Examples of classes of commonly used acquirer measures include the following:

- Requirements volatility
- Return on investment
- Cost performance index
- Number of defects per phase and by severity of defects
- Schedule performance index
- Customer satisfaction trends
- Supplier performance and relationship trends

3. Identify and document significant issues and deviations from the plan.

   This activity includes identifying and documenting both acquirer and supplier issues and deviations.

4. Document change requests and problems identified in work products and processes.

   Refer to the Configuration Management process area for more information about managing changes.

5. Document the results of reviews.
6. Track change requests and problem reports to closure.

SP 1.7 Conduct Milestone Reviews

Review the project's accomplishments and results at selected project milestones.

Refer to the Project Planning process area for more information about milestone planning.

Refer to the Measurement and Analysis process area for more information about the process of measuring, analyzing, and recording project performance data.

Milestone reviews are planned during project planning and are typically formal reviews.

TIP

Milestones are major events in a project. If you are using a project lifecycle model, milestones may be predetermined. Many professional organizations recommend iterative planning and managing at the "inchstone" level for near-term tasks to avoid surprises at the official milestone event.

Typical Work Products

1. Documented milestone review results

Typical Supplier Deliverables

1. Documented measurement results
2. Measurement analysis reports

Subpractices

1. Conduct milestone reviews with relevant stakeholders at meaningful points in the project's schedule, such as the completion of selected stages.

   Managers, staff members, customers, end users, suppliers, and other relevant stakeholders in the organization are included in milestone reviews, as appropriate.

   Conduct milestone reviews with the supplier as specified in the supplier agreement.

   Refer to the Acquisition Technical Management process area for more information about conducting technical reviews with the supplier per the supplier agreement.

   Refer to the Solicitation and Supplier Agreement Development process area for more information about establishing review requirements in the supplier agreement.

2. Review commitments, the plan, the status, and risks of the project.
3. Identify and document significant issues and their impacts.
4. Document results of the review, action items, and decisions.
5. Track action items to closure.

SP 1.8 MONITOR TRANSITION TO OPERATIONS AND SUPPORT

Monitor transition to operations and support.

TIP

A successful transition involves executing an effective plan for the appropriate facilities, training, use, maintenance, and support of the acquired capability.

The acquirer monitors and controls the transition of the accepted product or service against the plan for transition to operations and support.

Refer to the Plan Transition to Operations and Support specific practice in the Project Planning process area for more information about planning for the transition of the product or service to operations and support.

TIP

Sometimes the acquisition organization may be expected to perform specific transition activities itself. In still other cases, it may need to acquire a service supplier to support the capability provided to the customer.

Typically, the supplier has a role in integrating and packaging products and prepares for the transition to operations and support, including support for business user acceptance; the acquirer monitors these supplier activities. These expectations of the supplier and the acceptance criteria for transition to operations and support are included in the solicitation package and then the supplier agreement.

Typical Work Products

1. Transition readiness report
2. Records of transition to support reviews
3. Transition analysis report

Typical Supplier Deliverables

1. Training materials and supporting artifacts
2. Site readiness report
3. Verification reports
4. Training records
5. Operational readiness reports
6. Test results
7. Pilot results

Subpractices

1. Monitor the operations and support organization's capability and facilities designated to receive, store, use, and maintain acquired products.

   The acquirer makes adequate provisions through the supplier agreement or in-house operations and support organizations to operate the acquired product. Typically, the acquirer uses verification practices to confirm that the organization, physical environment, and operations and support resources are equipped to execute operations and support activities.

   The acquirer also reviews operations and support organizations designated to take responsibility for the operation of the product and to ensure that resources identified and budgeted are available when needed. The designated operations and support organizations demonstrate their readiness (i.e., capability and capacity) to accept responsibility for the product and to ensure uninterrupted support. Typically, a demonstration involves execution of all the activities of operations (e.g., a pilot).

2. Monitor the delivery of training for those involved in receiving, storing, using, and maintaining acquired products.

   Typically, the supplier develops training resources for the product. Training materials and resources are specified in the supplier agreement to meet the needs of various audiences (e.g., operations staff, support staff, end users). The acquirer verifies that training is provided at the appropriate time to the appropriate audience and determines whether the training capability provided is adequate.

3. Review pilot results, if any, and operational readiness reports for the acquired product.

   Determine readiness of the product and involved stakeholders, such as the operations and support organizations, for the transition of responsibility. The acquirer typically uses transition readiness criteria and verification and validation practices to determine if the supplier-delivered products meet specified requirements. The criteria also address the readiness of the product for maintenance over the intended product lifecycle.

4. Review and analyze the results of transition activities.

   The acquirer reviews and analyzes the results of transition activities and determines whether corrective actions must be completed before responsibility is transferred to the operational and support organizations.

> Example reports and logs used by the acquirer include the following:
> - Transition activity reports, including quality measures collected during the pilot and the warranty period
> - Problem tracking reports, detailing resolution time, escalation, and root cause analysis
> - Change management reports
> - Configuration management records
> - Operation logs to determine that sufficient information is stored to support reconstruction
> - Security reports
> - Actual operations and support costs compared to estimates

SG 2 MANAGE CORRECTIVE ACTION TO CLOSURE

Corrective actions are managed to closure when the project's performance or results deviate significantly from the plan.

When the acquirer determines (e.g., through its monitoring of measurement data) that supplier progress does not appear to be sufficient to meet a service level defined in the supplier agreement, then the acquirer initiates and manages corrective action with the supplier.

If the supplier does not comply appropriately with the acquirer's initiation of corrective action, the acquirer escalates and resolves this issue as a supplier agreement issue.

SP 2.1 ANALYZE ISSUES

Collect and analyze issues and determine corrective actions necessary to address them.

Corrective action is taken for both acquirer deviations and when supplier execution does not align with project planning (e.g., milestone and work product date slippages).

Many issues and corrective actions are the sole responsibility of the acquirer and may include information that should not be shared with the supplier (e.g., source selection sensitive, recompetition, and internal staffing).

Typical Work Products

1. List of issues needing corrective actions

Typical Supplier Deliverables

1. List of supplier issues needing corrective action by the acquirer

Subpractices

1. Gather issues for analysis.

   Issues are collected from reviews and the execution of other processes.

> Examples of issues to be gathered include the following:
> - Issues discovered when performing technical reviews, verification, and validation activities
> - Significant deviations in project planning parameters from estimates in the project plan
> - Commitments (either internal or external) that have not been satisfied
> - Significant changes in risk status
> - Data access, collection, privacy, or security issues
> - Stakeholder representation or involvement issues

2. Analyze issues to determine the need for corrective action.

   Refer to the Project Planning process area for more information about corrective action criteria.

   Corrective action is required when the issue, if left unresolved, may prevent the project from meeting its objectives.

SP 2.2 Take Corrective Action

Take corrective action on identified issues.

Some corrective actions may be assigned to a supplier. The acquirer oversees corrective actions assigned to the supplier, as appropriate.

> **TIP**
>
> In some cases, the corrective action can be to monitor the situation. A corrective action does not always result in a complete solution to the problem.

Typical Work Products

1. Corrective action plans

Typical Supplier Deliverables

1. Corrective action plans for supplier issues

TIP

When managing multiple suppliers, the acquirer may need to adjudicate the assignment of actions between the suppliers and itself. Consider including contractual language to set the expectation of suppliers when participating in issue allocation and resolution of issues. Such preparation becomes particularly important near the end of the project when funding is low and suppliers are eager to close out the contract.

Subpractices

1. Determine and document the appropriate actions needed to address identified issues.

   Refer to the Project Planning process area for more information about the project plan when replanning is needed.

> Examples of potential actions include the following:
> - Modifying the statement of work
> - Modifying requirements
> - Revising estimates and plans
> - Renegotiating commitments
> - Adding resources
> - Changing processes
> - Revising project risks

2. Review and get agreement with relevant stakeholders on the actions to be taken.
3. Negotiate changes to internal and external commitments.

SP 2.3 MANAGE CORRECTIVE ACTIONS

Manage corrective actions to closure.

Typical Work Products

1. Corrective action results

Typical Supplier Deliverables

1. Corrective action results for supplier issues

Subpractices

1. Monitor corrective actions for their completion.
2. Analyze results of corrective actions to determine the effectiveness of the corrective actions.
3. Determine and document appropriate actions to correct deviations from planned results for corrective actions.

   Lessons learned as a result of taking corrective action can be inputs to planning and risk management processes.

PROJECT PLANNING

A Project Management Process Area at Maturity Level 2

Purpose

The purpose of Project Planning (PP) is to establish and maintain plans that define project activities.

TIP

In planning, you determine the requirements to be fulfilled, the tasks to perform, and the resources and coordination required, and then you document all of this to obtain the needed resources and commitments.

Introductory Notes

The Project Planning process area involves the following activities:

- Developing the project plan
- Interacting with stakeholders appropriately
- Getting commitment to the plan
- Maintaining the plan

TIP

The plan is a declaration that the work has been rationally thought through and requests for resources are credible. If you ask management to commit resources, they want to know it is worth the investment. A project plan helps you to convince them.

Before committing resources to an acquisition project, management needs a clear plan.

Planning begins with requirements that define the product and project.

Project planning is based on the acquisition strategy, which is a guide for directing and controlling the project and a framework for integrating activities essential to acquiring an operational product or service. The acquisition strategy outlines acquisition objectives and constraints, availability of assets and technologies, consideration of acquisition methods, potential supplier agreement types and terms, accommodation of end-user considerations, considerations of risk, and support for the project throughout the project lifecycle.

X-REF

PMC addresses tracking of project activities in the plan.

Planning includes estimating the attributes of work products and tasks, determining the resources needed, negotiating commitments, producing a schedule, and identifying and analyzing project risks. Iterating through these activities may be necessary to establish the project plan. The project plan provides the basis for performing and controlling project activities that address commitments with the project's customer.

TIP

Project planning is not just for large projects. Research with the Personal Software Process has demonstrated that individuals working on tasks lasting only a few hours increase overall quality and productivity by making time to plan.

Project planning involves the development and maintenance of plans for all acquirer processes, including those required for effective acquirer–supplier interaction. Once the supplier agreement is signed and schedule, costs, and resources from the supplier are established, the acquirer takes the supplier estimations for the project into account at an appropriate level of detail in its project plan.

Project planning includes establishing and maintaining a plan for the orderly, smooth transition of the acquired product from a supplier to its use by the acquirer or its customers. In addition, if an existing product is to be replaced as part of the acquisition, the acquirer may be required to consider the disposal of the existing product as part of the planning for acquiring the new product. All transition activities are included in the project plan and provisions for accommodating such specialized requirements are also included.

All relevant stakeholders should be involved in the planning process from all lifecycle phases to ensure all technical and support activities are adequately addressed in project plans.

HINT

To limit change in the plan, determine early in the project when and what kind of changes will be accepted.

The project plan is usually revised as the project progresses to address changes in requirements and commitments, inaccurate estimates, corrective actions, and process changes. Specific practices describing both planning and replanning are contained in this process area.

Changes to the supplier agreement can also affect the project's planning estimates, budget, schedules, risks, project work tasks, commitments, and resources.

HINT

Both the organization and the project should define triggers for replanning.

The term *project plan* is used throughout the generic and specific practices in this process area to refer to the overall plan for controlling the project.

Related Process Areas

Refer to the Acquisition Requirements Development process area for more information about developing requirements.

Refer to the Requirements Management process area for more information about managing requirements needed for planning and replanning.

Refer to the Risk Management process area for more information about identifying and managing risks.

Refer to the Acquisition Technical Management process area for more information about evaluations and reviews that must be included in technical planning.

Refer to the Solicitation and Supplier Agreement Development process area for more information about establishing and maintaining supplier agreements.

Refer to the Measurement and Analysis process area for more information about specifying measures.

Specific Goal and Practice Summary

SG 1 Establish Estimates
- SP 1.1 Establish the Acquisition Strategy
- SP 1.2 Estimate the Scope of the Project
- SP 1.3 Establish Estimates of Work Product and Task Attributes
- SP 1.4 Define Project Lifecycle Phases
- SP 1.5 Estimate Effort and Cost

SG 2 Develop a Project Plan
- SP 2.1 Establish the Budget and Schedule
- SP 2.2 Identify Project Risks
- SP 2.3 Plan Data Management
- SP 2.4 Plan the Project's Resources
- SP 2.5 Plan Needed Knowledge and Skills
- SP 2.6 Plan Stakeholder Involvement
- SP 2.7 Plan Transition to Operations and Support
- SP 2.8 Establish the Project Plan

SG 3 Obtain Commitment to the Plan
- SP 3.1 Review Plans That Affect the Project
- SP 3.2 Reconcile Work and Resource Levels
- SP 3.3 Obtain Plan Commitment

Specific Practices by Goal

SG 1 ESTABLISH ESTIMATES

Estimates of project planning parameters are established and maintained.

Project planning parameters include all information needed by the project to perform necessary planning, organizing, staffing, directing, coordinating, reporting, and budgeting.

The acquirer develops estimates for project work based on the acquisition strategy, including high-level estimates for the work to be done by suppliers. Initial estimates may be revised based on supplier estimates in response to the solicitation package.

Estimates of planning parameters should have a sound basis to instill confidence that plans based on these estimates are capable of supporting project objectives.

X-REF

Specific goal 1 focuses on providing estimates of project planning parameters; actual values are monitored in PMC SP 1.1.

TIP

Project planning parameters are a key to managing a project. Planning parameters primarily include size, effort, and cost.

TIP

The basis for estimates can include historical data, the judgment of experienced estimators, and other factors.

Factors that are typically considered when estimating these parameters include the following:

- The acquisition strategy
- Project requirements, including product requirements, requirements imposed by the organization, requirements imposed by the customer, and other requirements that impact the project
- The scope of the project
- Identified tasks and work products
- The technical approach
- The selected project lifecycle model (e.g., waterfall, incremental, or spiral)
- Attributes of work products and tasks (e.g., size or complexity)
- The schedule
- Models or historical data used for converting attributes of work products and tasks into labor hours and costs
- The methodology (e.g., models, data, algorithms) used to determine needed material, skills, labor hours, and cost

HINT

Use this rationale to help justify to management why you need resources and why the effort and schedule estimates are appropriate.

The acquisition strategy is a key factor when estimating the project.

Documentation of the estimating rationale and supporting data is needed for stakeholder review and commitment to the plan and for maintenance of the plan as the project progresses.

SP 1.1 ESTABLISH THE ACQUISITION STRATEGY

Establish and maintain the acquisition strategy.

HINT

When you acquire a product or service, the *earlier* you prepare, the more likely you are to provide the right product of the right quality at the right time for project success.

TIP

The acquisition strategy should be developed to mitigate the unique technical and programmatic risks associated with the project.

The acquisition strategy is the business and technical management framework for planning, executing, and managing agreements for a project. The acquisition strategy relates to the objectives for the acquisition, the constraints, availability of resources and technologies, consideration of acquisition methods, potential supplier agreement types, terms and conditions, accommodation of business considerations, considerations of risk, and support for the acquired product over its lifecycle. The acquisition strategy reflects the entire scope of the project. It encompasses the work to be performed by the acquirer and the supplier, or in some cases multiple suppliers, for the full lifecycle of the product.

The acquisition strategy results from a thorough understanding of both the acquisition project and the general acquisition environment. The acquirer accounts for the potential value or benefit of the acquisition in the light of potential risks, considers constraints, and takes into account experiences with different types of suppliers, agreements, and terms. A well-developed strategy minimizes the time and cost required to satisfy approved capability needs, and maximizes affordability throughout the project lifecycle.

The acquisition strategy is the basis for formulating solicitation packages, supplier agreements, and project plans. The strategy evolves over time and should continuously reflect the current status and desired end point of the project.

X-REF

See "Techniques for Developing an Acquisition Strategy by Profiling Software Risks," CMU/SEI-2006-TR-002, for guidance on how to use a risk-based approach to develop an acquisition strategy for a software-intensive system.

Typical Work Products

1. Acquisition strategy

Subpractices

1. Identify the capabilities and objectives the acquisition is intended to satisfy or provide.

   The capabilities describe what the organization intends to acquire. Typically, the capabilities included in the acquisition strategy summary highlight product characteristics driven by interoperability or families of products. The acquisition strategy also identifies dependencies on planned or existing capabilities of other projects or products.

   Refer to the Acquisition Requirements Development process area for more information about determining capabilities and customer requirements.

   The acquirer defines objectives in terms of cost, schedule, and key process, product, and service level measures and technical performance measures as defined in requirements. These measures reflect customer expectations and threshold values representing acceptable limits that, in the customer's judgment, provide the needed capability. While the number and specificity of measures may change over the duration of an acquisition, the acquirer typically focuses on the minimum number of measures that, if thresholds are not met, will require a reevaluation of the project.

   The acquisition strategy establishes the milestone decision points and acquisition phases planned for the project. It prescribes the accomplishments for each phase and identifies the critical events affecting project management. Schedule parameters include, at a minimum, the projected dates for project initiation, other major decision points, and initial operational capability.

Examples of cost parameters include the following:

- Research, development, test, and evaluation costs
- Acquisition costs
- Acquisition-related operations, support, and disposal costs
- Total product quantity (to include both fully configured development and production units)

TIP

The type of acquisition varies according to the nature of products and services that are available to satisfy the project's needs and requirements (including commercial-off-the-shelf [COTS] products).

TIP

The acquisition approach and the supplier's development approach are complementary but not always the same. For example, the acquisition approach can be single-step whereas the supplier may use an incremental approach in developing the solution.

2. Identify the acquisition approach.

   The acquirer defines the approach the project will use to achieve full capability—either evolutionary or single step—and includes a brief rationale to justify the choice. When a project uses an evolutionary acquisition approach, the acquisition strategy describes the initial capability and how it will be funded, developed, tested, produced, and supported. The acquisition strategy previews similar planning for subsequent increments and identifies the approach to integrate or retrofit earlier increments with later increments.

Examples of additional considerations for the acquisition approach include the following:

- Actions a project team can take on its own if the acquiring organization has an acquisition, contracting, or purchasing department
- Who will prepare independent estimates and if these estimates are needed as evaluation criteria
- Managing multiple suppliers
- Anticipated lead times from potential suppliers to acquire items

3. Document business considerations.

   Business considerations include the type of competition planned for all phases of the acquisition or an explanation of why competition is not practicable or not in the best interests of the acquirer. Also included are considerations for establishing or maintaining access to competitive suppliers for critical products or product components. Availability and suitability of commercial items and the extent to which interfaces for these items have broad market acceptance, standards, organization support, and stability are other business considerations. Also included are considerations for both international and domestic sources that can meet the required need as primary sources of supply consistent with organizational policies and regulations.

Other examples of business considerations for an acquisition strategy include the following:

- Product and technology areas critical to satisfying or providing the desired capabilities
- Data rights
- Socio-economic constraints
- Safety and health issues
- Security issues (physical and information technology)

4. Identify major risks and which risks will be addressed jointly with the supplier.

   Major acquisition risks, whether primarily managed by the acquirer or supplier, should be identified and assessed by the acquirer. The acquisition strategy identifies major risks, which risks are to be shared with the supplier, and which are retained by the acquirer.

   Refer to the Risk Management process area for more information about establishing and maintaining a risk management strategy.

5. Identify the preferred supplier agreement type.

   The acquirer identifies standardized acquisition documents (e.g., standard supplier agreements), if any. The acquirer also determines the preferred type of supplier agreement (e.g., firm fixed-price; fixed-price incentive, firm target; cost plus incentive fee; or cost plus award fee) and the reasons it is suitable, including considerations of risk and reasonable risk-sharing by the acquirer and supplier.

   The acquisition strategy explains the planned incentive structure for the acquisition and how it encourages the supplier to provide the product or service at or below the established cost objectives and satisfy the schedule and key measurement objectives. Considerations should be given to using incentives to reduce primary project risks. If more than one incentive is planned for a supplier agreement, the acquisition strategy explains how the incentives complement one other and do not interfere with one another. The acquisition strategy identifies unusual terms and conditions of the planned supplier agreement and all existing or contemplated deviations to an organization's terms and conditions, if any.

6. Identify the product support strategy.

   The acquirer develops a product support strategy for lifecycle sustainment and continuous improvement of product affordability, reliability, and supportability, while sustaining readiness. The support strategy addresses how the acquirer will maintain oversight of the fielded product.

   If support is going to be performed by an organization different from the supplier, a sufficient overlap period should be defined to ensure smooth transition.

   The acquirer's sustainment organization or supplier typically participates in the development of the product support strategy.

7. Review and obtain agreement with senior management on the acquisition strategy.

   The development of the acquisition strategy for a project typically requires senior management sponsorship. Appropriate senior management must approve the acquisition strategy before initiating a project.

HINT

For some acquisition programs, the acquisition strategy is created by a project team that precedes the creation of the final acquisition project team.

SP 1.2 Estimate the Scope of the Project

Establish a top-level work breakdown structure (WBS) to estimate the scope of the project.

The acquirer establishes the objectives of the project in the acquisition strategy. An initial set of requirements and project objectives form the basis for establishing the WBS or for selecting a standard WBS from the organization's process assets. To ensure the full scope of the project is estimated, the WBS includes activities performed by the acquirer as well as milestones and deliverables for suppliers.

The acquisition strategy drives a key decision in this practice: specifically, how much work, and what work, to give to a supplier. The acquirer develops a WBS that clearly identifies the project work performed by the acquirer and the project work performed by the supplier. The supplier work identified in the WBS becomes the foundation for the statement of work defined in the Solicitation and Supplier Agreement Development process area. The WBS identifies deliverables from the supplier and work products developed by the acquirer.

HINT

To develop estimates, decompose the project into smaller work items (the WBS), estimate the resources needed by each item, and then roll these up. This activity will result in more accurate estimates.

TIP

Interaction and iteration among planning, requirements definition, and design are often necessary. A project can learn a lot from each iteration and can use this knowledge to update the plan, requirements, and design for the next iteration.

The WBS evolves with the project. Initially, a top-level WBS can serve to structure initial estimating. The development of a WBS divides the overall project into an interconnected set of manageable components. Typically, the WBS is a product-oriented structure that provides a scheme for identifying and organizing the logical units of work to be managed, which are called *work packages*. The WBS provides a reference and organizational mechanism for assigning effort, schedule, and responsibility and is used as the underlying framework to plan, organize, and control the work done on the project. Some projects use the term *contract WBS* to refer to the portion of the WBS placed under contract (possibly the entire WBS). Not all projects have a contract WBS (e.g., internally funded development).

Typical Work Products

1. Task descriptions
2. Work package descriptions
3. WBS

Subpractices

1. Develop a WBS based on the product architecture.

    The WBS should permit the identification of the following items:

- Risks and their mitigation tasks
- Tasks for deliverables and supporting activities
- Tasks for skill and knowledge acquisition
- Tasks for the development of needed support plans, such as configuration management, quality assurance, and verification plans
- Tasks for the integration and management of nondevelopmental items

2. Identify the work packages in sufficient detail to specify estimates of project tasks, responsibilities, and schedule.

   The top-level WBS is intended to help gauge the project work effort for tasks and organizational roles and responsibilities. The amount of detail in the WBS at this level helps in developing realistic schedules, thereby minimizing the need for management reserve.
3. Identify products and product components to be externally acquired.
4. Identify work products to be reused.

HINT

Use the WBS to help you define the product architecture.

You may select different suppliers to deliver different architectural components. Make sure you account for the integration activities if this is the case.

TIP

The level of detail often depends on the level and completeness of the requirements. Often, the work packages and estimates evolve as the requirements evolve.

HINT

Consider establishing a management reserve commensurate to the overall uncertainty that allows for the efficient allocation of resources to address the uncertainty of estimates.

SP 1.3 Establish Estimates of Work Product and Task Attributes

Establish and maintain estimates of work product and task attributes.

Size is the primary input to many models used to estimate effort, cost, and schedule. The models can also be based on inputs such as connectivity, complexity, and structure.

Examples of types of work products for which size estimates are made include the following:
- Deliverable and nondeliverable work products
- Documents and files
- Operational and support hardware, firmware, and software

Estimation methods include using historical acquirer and supplier data and standard estimating models to compare projects of similar complexity. Where historical size data are not available, develop an estimate based on the understanding of the design of similar products.

Estimation models can be built based on historical data as part of organizational process performance, and estimates for any project can be validated using these models.

Refer to the Organizational Process Performance process area for more information about process-performance models.

HINT

Learn to quantify the resources needed for particular tasks by associating size measures with each type of work product and building historical data. By collecting historical data from projects, you can learn how measured size relates to the resources consumed by tasks. This knowledge can then be used when planning the next project.

X-REF

For more information on tools and methods used for cost estimating, see www.cssc.usc.edu.

Examples of size measures include the following:

- Number of functions
- Function points
- Source lines of code
- Number of classes and objects
- Number of requirements
- Number and complexity of interfaces
- Number of pages
- Number of inputs and outputs
- Number of technical risk items
- Volume of data
- Number of logic gates for integrated circuits
- Number of parts (e.g., printed circuit boards, components, and mechanical parts)
- Physical constraints (e.g., weight and volume)

HINT

Consider providing guidelines on how to estimate the difficulty or complexity of a task to improve estimation accuracy, especially when size measures are not available.

The estimates should be consistent with project requirements to determine the project's effort, cost, and schedule. A relative level of difficulty or complexity should be assigned for each size attribute.

Typical Work Products

1. Technical approach
2. Size and complexity of tasks and work products
3. Estimating models
4. Attribute estimates

Subpractices

1. Determine the technical approach for the project.

   The technical approach defines a top-level strategy for development of the product. It includes decisions on architectural features, such as distributed or client/server; state-of-the-art or established technologies to be applied, such as robotics, composite materials, or artificial intelligence; and breadth of the functionality expected in the final products, such as safety, security, and ergonomics.

   The technical approach provides a basis for interoperability and supportability of the technical solution developed by the supplier.

X-REF

Mature organizations maintain historical data to help projects establish reasonable estimates (see MA SP 1.5 and IPM SP 1.2).

2. Use appropriate methods to determine the attributes of the work products and tasks to be used to estimate resource requirements.

   Methods for determining size and complexity should be based on validated models or historical data.

Examples of attributes include the following:
- Maturity of the technology specified in the technical solution
- Amount and complexity of the work potentially assigned to suppliers
- Number of locations where the product is to be installed

The methods for determining attributes evolve as the understanding of the relationship of product characteristics to attributes increases.

Examples of current methods include the following:
- Number of logic gates for integrated circuit design
- Lines of code or function points for software
- Number and complexity of requirements for systems engineering
- Number of square feet for standard-specified residential homes

3. Estimate the attributes of work products and tasks.

SP 1.4 Define Project Lifecycle Phases

Define project lifecycle phases on which to scope the planning effort.

The determination of a project's lifecycle phases provides for planned periods of evaluation and decision making. These periods are normally defined to support logical decision points at which significant commitments are made concerning resources and technical approach. Such points provide planned events at which project course corrections and determinations of future scope and cost can be made.

Project lifecycle phases must be defined depending on the scope of requirements, estimates for project resources, and the nature of the project.

The acquirer includes the entire project lifecycle (i.e., from user needs through initial and subsequent upgrades) when planning lifecycle phases and refines the acquisition strategy as appropriate. The acquirer considers all supplier agreements in the context of the acquisition so that an integrated approach results. A complex project can involve managing multiple supplier agreements simultaneously or in sequence. In such cases, any acquisition lifecycle can end during any phase of the project lifecycle. Depending on the acquisition strategy, there may be intermediate phases for the creation of prototypes, increments of capability, or spiral model cycles.

TIP

For example, in a single-step acquisition, at the end of the requirements analysis phase, the requirements are evaluated to assess consistency, completeness, and feasibility, and to decide whether the project is ready (from a technical and risk perspective) to commit resources for suppliers to begin the design phase.

Refer to the Establish Lifecycle Model Descriptions specific practice in the Organizational Process Definition process area for more information about acquisition lifecycles.

During establishment of the supplier agreement, the acquirer works with the supplier to understand supplier lifecycle models and processes, especially those that interact directly with acquirer processes. Agreement on the lifecycle models and processes to be used during the project enables seamless interactions between supplier and acquirer, resulting in a successful acquirer-supplier relationship.

Understanding the project lifecycle is crucial in determining the scope of the planning effort and the timing of initial planning, as well as the timing and criteria (critical milestones) for replanning.

Typical Work Products

1. Project lifecycle phases

SP 1.5 *Estimate Effort and Cost*

Estimate the project's effort and cost for work products and tasks.

HINT

Calibrate estimation techniques and methods to take into consideration the project's specific characteristics.

Estimates of effort and cost are generally based on results of analysis using models or historical data applied to size, activities, and other planning parameters. Confidence in these estimates is based on rationale for the selected model and the nature of the data. There may be occasions when available historical data does not apply, such as when efforts are unprecedented or when the type of task does not fit available models. An effort is unprecedented (to some degree) if a similar product or component has never been built. An effort may also be unprecedented if the development group has never built such a product or component.

TIP

Unprecedented efforts often require an evolutionary acquisition approach as part of the acquisition strategy. These methods provide frequent opportunities for feedback, which helps to resolve issues or risks and allows planning of the next iteration.

Unprecedented efforts are more risky, require more research to develop reasonable bases of estimate, and require more management reserve. The uniqueness of the project must be documented when using these models to ensure a common understanding of assumptions made in the initial planning stages.

Estimates address all processes and activities performed by the project for the project lifecycle, including an estimate of effort and cost for supplier work. The project estimate includes detailed estimates for activities performed by the acquirer and its stakeholders. The acquirer should include members of their technical community (e.g., systems, hardware, and software engineers) to ensure all technical considerations have been accounted for in the estimates. As the project evolves, these estimates may be revised based on changed conditions (e.g., new circumstances encountered during execution of the supplier agreement).

In addition to creating an estimate for the project work products, the acquirer is encouraged to have its estimate and WBS independently reviewed by individuals external to the project to ensure that the project estimation and WBS can be validated.

TIP

Differences between the acquirer's estimate and the supplier's estimate should be analyzed to uncover risks that may demand management attention.

Typical Work Products

1. Estimation rationale
2. Project effort estimates
3. Project cost estimates

Subpractices

1. Collect models or historical data to be used to transform the attributes of work products and tasks into estimates of labor hours and costs.

   Effort estimation at the work product and task level needs to be established for acquirer work. Effort estimation for supplier deliverables and processes must be established as well.

   Many parametric models have been developed to help estimate cost and schedule. The use of these models as the sole source of estimation is not recommended because these models are based on historical project data that may or may not be pertinent to your project. Multiple models and methods can be used to ensure a high level of confidence in the estimate.

   Historical data include the cost, effort, and schedule data from previously executed projects and appropriate scaling data to account for differing sizes and complexity.
2. Include supporting infrastructure needs when estimating effort and cost.

HINT

If you are using only one parametric model, make sure it is calibrated to your project's characteristics.

TIP

Scaling can be reliable when applied from experiences similar to the one at hand. However, increased complexity usually adds more interactions with other acquisition projects or legacy capabilities requiring additional coordination effort.

Examples of supporting infrastructure typically provided by the supplier include the following:

- Critical computing resources in the host and testing environment (e.g., memory, disk, and network capability)
- Test equipment

3. Estimate effort and cost using models and historical data.

Effort and cost inputs used for estimating typically include the following:

- Judgmental estimates provided by an expert or group of experts (e.g., Delphi Method)
- Estimates for the development of requirements
- Risks, including the extent to which the effort is unprecedented
- Critical competencies and roles needed to perform the work
- The WBS
- Costs of acquired work products
- Selected project lifecycle model and processes
- Lifecycle cost estimates
- Skill levels of managers and staff needed to perform the work
- Knowledge, skill, and training needs
- Facilities needed (e.g., office and meeting space and workstations)
- Travel required
- Level of security required for tasks, work products, hardware, software, personnel, and the work environment
- Service level agreements for call centers and warranty work
- Direct labor and overhead

The amount of supplier work for a project largely determines the amount of acquirer work required to manage the project and the supplier. Effort for the acquirer includes (1) effort associated with defining the scope of the project; (2) effort associated with the development of the solicitation and supplier agreement; agreement and technical management; project planning, monitoring, and control; acquisition requirements development, verification, and validation; configuration management; measurement and analysis; process and product quality assurance; requirements management; and risk management; (3) operating and maintenance effort associated with the sustainment of the solution; and (4) disposal effort.

TIP

In some cases, each project phase may have a more detailed and focused plan of its own, in addition to the overall project plan. Also, a detailed plan typically is provided for each increment or iteration when using an evolutionary acquisition approach and will focus on particular requirements issues, design issues, or other risks.

SG 2 *Develop a Project Plan*

A project plan is established and maintained as the basis for managing the project.

A project plan is a formal, approved document used to manage and control the execution of the project. It is based on project requirements and established estimates.

The project plan should consider all phases of the project lifecycle. Project planning should ensure that all plans affecting the project are consistent with the overall project plan.

SP 2.1 Establish the Budget and Schedule

Establish and maintain the project's budget and schedule.

The project's budget and schedule are based on developed estimates and ensure that budget allocation, task complexity, and task dependencies are appropriately addressed.

The project's budget and schedule (including the lifecycle-related activities of the acquirer), the supplier's efforts, and those of supporting organizations and other stakeholders (including any supplier that supports the acquirer) are established, tracked, and maintained for the duration of the project. In addition to creating a schedule for project work products, the acquirer should have the schedule independently reviewed by individuals external to the project to ensure that the project schedule can be validated.

Event-driven, resource-limited schedules have proven to be effective in dealing with project risk. Identifying accomplishments to be demonstrated before initiation of an event provides some flexibility in the timing of the event, a common understanding of what is expected, a better vision of the state of the project, and a more accurate status of the project's tasks.

TIP

Plans that may affect the project plan include configuration management plans, plans for interfacing acquisition projects, the system's support plan, the organization's process improvement plan, and the organization's training plan.

HINT

If the budget is dictated by others and it doesn't cover your estimated resource needs, replan to ensure that the project will be within budget. Likewise, if the schedule is dictated by others and it isn't consistent with your plan, replan to ensure that the project will be able to deliver the product on time (perhaps with fewer features).

TIP

In an event-driven schedule, tasks can be initiated only after certain criteria are met.

Typical Work Products

1. Project schedules
2. Schedule dependencies
3. Project budget

Subpractices

1. Identify major milestones.

   Milestones are often imposed to ensure completion of certain deliverables by the milestone. Milestones can be event-based or calendar-based. If calendar-based, once milestone dates have been agreed on, it is often difficult to change them.

2. Identify schedule assumptions.

   When schedules are initially developed, it is common to make assumptions about the duration of certain activities. These assumptions are frequently made on items for which little if any estimation data is available. Identifying these assumptions provides insight into the level of confidence (i.e., uncertainties) in the overall schedule.

3. Identify constraints.

   Factors that limit the flexibility of management options must be identified as early as possible. The examination of the attributes of work

X-REF

Defining event-based milestones and monitoring their completion (PMC SP 1.1 subpractice 1) provides visibility into the project's progress.

products and tasks often brings these issues to the surface. Such attributes can include task duration, resources, inputs, and outputs. Since key characteristics of prequalified or other potential suppliers are elements of project success, the acquirer considers these characteristics (e.g., technical and financial capability, management and delivery processes, production capacity, and business type and size) in identifying constraints for the project.

4. Identify task dependencies.

   Typically, the tasks for a project can be accomplished in some ordered sequence that minimizes the duration of the project. This sequencing involves the identification of predecessor and successor tasks to determine optimal ordering.

Examples of tools that can help determine optimal ordering of task activities include the following:

- Critical Path Method (CPM)
- Program Evaluation and Review Technique (PERT)
- Resource-limited scheduling
- Critical chain method

5. Define the budget and schedule.

An example of a system used for documenting the costs and schedule of a project is an EVMS [GEIA 748 2002].

Establishing and maintaining the project's budget and schedule typically includes the following:

- Defining the committed or expected availability of resources and facilities
- Determining the time phasing of activities
- Determining a breakout of subordinate schedules
- Defining dependencies among activities (predecessor or successor relationships)
- Defining schedule activities and milestones to support accuracy in progress measurement
- Identifying milestones for the delivery of products to the customer
- Defining activities of appropriate duration
- Defining milestones of appropriate time separation
- Defining a management reserve based on the confidence level in meeting the schedule and budget
- Using appropriate historical data to verify the schedule
- Defining incremental funding requirements
- Documenting project assumptions and rationale
- Determining the approach to incorporating supplier schedules at an appropriate level of detail

6. Establish corrective action criteria.

   Criteria are established for determining what constitutes a significant deviation from the project plan. A basis for gauging issues and problems is necessary to determine when corrective action should be taken. Corrective actions may require replanning, which may include revising the original plan, establishing new agreements, or including mitigation activities in the current plan.

   Criteria for corrective action are based on key objectives defined in the acquisition strategy using process, product, and service level measures. The measures represent key stakeholder needs and threshold values of acceptable limits that, in the stakeholder's judgment, will provide the needed capability. All measures that represent key stakeholder needs and other measures for monitoring the supplier are defined in the Statement of Work (SOW), along with their associated minimum allowed performance levels. These measures are used to identify issues and problems and gauge whether corrective actions should be taken. The plan should define how these measures will be assessed and evaluated.

HINT

Establish corrective action criteria early in the project to ensure that issues are addressed appropriately and consistently.

SP 2.2 Identify Project Risks

Identify and analyze project risks.

Refer to the Risk Management process area for more information about risk management activities.

Refer to the Monitor Project Risks specific practice in the Project Monitoring and Control process area for more information about risk monitoring activities.

Risks are identified or discovered and analyzed to support project planning. This specific practice should be extended to all plans that affect the project to ensure that appropriate interfacing is taking place among all relevant stakeholders on identified risks.

Project planning risk identification and analysis typically include the following:

- Identifying risks
- Analyzing risks to determine the impact, probability of occurrence, and time frame in which problems are likely to occur
- Prioritizing risks

TIP

Risk management is a key to project success.

HINT

Once suppliers are selected, the acquisition project should define how risks are continuously identified, managed, and escalated by all stakeholders. Don't rely on the supplier to do all the work; many risks are under the purview of the acquirer and must be identified, analyzed, and mitigated by the acquisition project team.

Risks are identified from multiple perspectives (e.g., acquisition, technical, management, operational, supplier agreement, industry, support, and end user) to ensure all project risks are considered comprehensively in planning activities. Applicable regulatory and statutory requirements with respect to safety and security must be considered while identifying risks.

The acquisition strategy and the risks identified in other project planning activities form the basis for some of the criteria used in evaluation practices in the Solicitation and Supplier Agreement Development process area. As the project evolves, risks may be revised based on changed conditions.

Typical Work Products

1. Identified risks
2. Risk impacts and probability of occurrence
3. Risk priorities

Subpractices

1. Identify risks.

   The identification of risks involves the identification of potential issues, hazards, threats, vulnerabilities, and so on that could negatively affect work efforts and plans. Risks must be identified and described in an understandable way before they can be analyzed. When identifying risks, it is a good idea to use a standard method for defining risks. Risk identification and analysis tools can be used to help identify possible problems.

Examples of risk identification and analysis tools include the following:
- Risk taxonomies
- Risk assessments
- Checklists
- Structured interviews
- Brainstorming
- Performance models
- Cost models
- Network analysis
- Quality factor analysis

TIP

Risk identification and analysis tools help to identify risks more completely and rapidly, analyzing them more consistently, and allowing what has been learned on previous projects to be applied to new projects.

Numerous risks are associated with acquiring products through suppliers (e.g., the stability of the supplier, the ability to maintain sufficient insight into the progress of their work, the supplier's capability to meet product requirements, and the skills and availability of supplier resources to meet commitments).

The process, product, and service level measures and associated thresholds should be analyzed to identify instances where thresholds are at risk of not being met. These project measures are key indicators of project risk.

2. Document risks.
3. Review and obtain agreement with relevant stakeholders on the completeness and correctness of documented risks.
4. Revise risks, as appropriate.

> **TIP**
> Managing risk can be considered a "team sport." It may be prudent to manage some risks with suppliers, gain insight on suppliers' handling of their unique risks, and manage specific acquisition risks independently.

Examples of when identified risks may need to be revised include the following:

- When new risks are identified
- When risks become problems
- When risks are retired
- When project circumstances change significantly

SP 2.3 PLAN DATA MANAGEMENT

Plan for the management of project data.

> **TIP**
> This specific practice helps to answer questions such as what data the project should collect, distribute, deliver, and archive; how and when it should do this; who should be able to access it; and how data will be stored to address the need for privacy and security, yet give access to those who need it.

Data are forms of documentation required to support a project in all of its areas (e.g., administration, engineering, configuration management, finance, logistics, quality, safety, manufacturing, and procurement). The data can take any form (e.g., reports, manuals, notebooks, charts, drawings, specifications, files, or correspondence). The data may exist in any medium (e.g., printed or drawn on various materials, photographs, electronic, or multimedia).

Data may be deliverable (e.g., items identified by a project's contract data requirements) or data may be nondeliverable (e.g., informal data, trade studies and analyses, internal meeting minutes, internal design review documentation, lessons learned, and action items). Distribution can take many forms, including electronic transmission.

> **HINT**
> Interpret data broadly to benefit from data management more fully.

Data requirements for the project should be established for both data items to be created and their content and form, based on a common or standard set of data requirements. Uniform content and format requirements for data items facilitate understanding of data content and help with consistent management of data resources.

> **TIP**
> Selecting a standard form can facilitate communication and understanding.

The reason for collecting each document should be clear. This task includes the analysis and verification of project deliverables and nondeliverables, data requirements, and customer-supplied data. Often, data are collected with no clear understanding of how they will be used. Data are costly and should be collected only when needed.

TIP

Providing a reason for the data being collected encourages cooperation from those providing the data.

Project data include both acquirer- and supplier-created data. The acquirer identifies the minimal data required to cost-effectively operate, maintain, and improve the acquired product and to foster source-of-support competition throughout the product's lifecycle in the acquirer's intended environment. Data should be available in a format that is compatible with the intended user's environment and a quality assurance program should be implemented to guarantee the accuracy and completeness of data.

HINT

In addition to making sure that all the relevant stakeholders (suppliers, end users, etc.) have access to project data, consider who you want *not* to have access. Doing so ensures that the acquisition process keeps competitors and adversaries in the dark.

The acquirer considers how data will be shared between acquirer and supplier as well as across relevant stakeholders. In many cases, leaving acquirer data in the physical possession of the supplier and having access to supplier data is the preferred solution. In addition to data access, the requirement for acquirer use, reproduction, manipulation, alteration, or transfer of possession of data should be part of the data management plan. The supplier agreement specifies appropriate acquirer rights to the data acquired, in addition to requirements for delivery or access.

Data, when delivered to the acquirer, are formatted according to accepted data standards to ensure their usability by the acquirer. Planning for managing data, including during transition to operations and support, is addressed as part of project planning to avoid unexpected costs to procure, reformat, and deliver data. Plans for managing data within project teams and the infrastructure required to manage data between the supplier, operational users, and other relevant stakeholders are included.

Project data and plans requiring version control or more stringent levels of configuration control are determined and mechanisms established to ensure project data are controlled. The implications of controlling access to classified and sensitive data (e.g., proprietary, export controlled, source selection sensitive) and other access-controlled data also must be considered.

Typical Work Products

TIP

The data management plan defines the data necessary for the project, who owns it, where it is stored, and how it is used. It may even specify what happens to the data after the project terminates.

1. Data management plan
2. Master list of managed data
3. Data content and format description
4. Lists of data requirements for acquirers and suppliers
5. Privacy requirements
6. Security requirements
7. Security procedures
8. Mechanisms for data retrieval, reproduction, and distribution

9. Schedule for the collection of project data
10. List of project data to be collected

Subpractices

1. Establish requirements and procedures to ensure privacy and the security of data.

   Not everyone will have the need or clearance necessary to access project data. Procedures must be established to identify who has access to which data as well as when they have access to which data. Security and access control are critical when the acquirer provides data access to the supplier. Security and access control includes access lists of authorized supplier personnel and nondisclosure agreements between the acquirer and supplier.

TIP

Data privacy and security should be considered, but may not be an applicable consideration for certain types of projects.

For example, when the supplier performs work for the acquirer off-site (e.g., off-shore development center), the acquirer must consider additional security measures such as a firewall between acquirer and supplier networks and restricted access to the acquirer's workplace.

2. Establish a mechanism to archive data and to access archived data.

   Accessed information should be in an understandable form (e.g., electronic or computer output from a database) or represented as originally generated.

   The data management plan is ideally supported by an integrated data system that meets the needs of both initial acquisition and support communities. Integrating acquisition and sustainment data systems into a total lifecycle integrated data environment provides the capability needed to plan effectively for sustainment and to facilitate technology insertion for affordability improvements during reprocurement and post-production support, while ensuring that acquisition planners have accurate information about total lifecycle costs.
3. Determine the project data to be identified, collected, and distributed.
4. Decide which project data and plans require version control or more stringent levels of configuration control and establish mechanisms to ensure project data are controlled.

X-REF

Measurement data is a subset of project data. See MA SPs 1.3 and 2.3 for more information on collecting, storing, and controlling access to measurement data.

SP 2.4 Plan the Project's Resources

Plan for necessary resources to perform the project.

TIP

This practice addresses *all* resources, not just personnel.

Defining project resources (e.g., labor, machinery/equipment, materials, and methods) and quantities needed to perform project activities, builds on the initial estimates and provides additional information that can be applied to expand the WBS used to manage the project.

The top-level WBS developed earlier as an estimation mechanism is typically expanded by decomposing these top levels into work packages that represent single work units that can be separately assigned, performed, and tracked. This subdivision is done to distribute management responsibility and provide better management control.

Each work package or work product in the WBS should be assigned a unique identifier (e.g., number) to permit tracking. A WBS can be based on requirements, activities, work products, or a combination of these items. A dictionary that describes the work for each work package in the WBS should accompany the work breakdown structure.

TIP

The WBS established in SP 1.2 is expanded to help identify roles as well as staffing, process, facility, and tool requirements; to assign work; to obtain commitment to perform the work; and to track it to completion. Automated tools can help you with these activities.

The resource plan must include planning for staff with appropriate training and experience to evaluate supplier proposals and participate in negotiations with suppliers. The resource plan identifies the project resources expected from the supplier, including critical facilities or equipment needed to support the work. The resource plan may be revised based on the supplier agreement or changes in conditions during project execution.

Typical Work Products

1. WBS work packages
2. WBS task dictionary
3. Staffing requirements based on project size and scope
4. Critical facilities and equipment list
5. Process and workflow definitions and diagrams
6. Project administration requirements list

Subpractices

1. Determine process requirements.

   The processes used to manage a project must be identified, defined, and coordinated with all relevant stakeholders to ensure efficient operations during project execution.

   The acquirer must determine how its processes interact with supplier processes to enable seamless execution of the project and successful acquirer–supplier relationships. Considerations include the use of a common process across multiple suppliers and the acquirer or the use of unique but compatible processes. At the very least, processes should be compatible across interfaces.

X-REF

At maturity level 3, the organization is typically the main source of process requirements, standard processes, and process assets that aid in their use (see OPF SP 2.3 and OPD).

2. Determine staffing requirements.

The staffing of a project depends on the decomposition of project requirements into tasks, roles, and responsibilities for accomplishing project requirements as laid out in the work packages of the WBS. Staffing requirements must consider the knowledge and skills required for each identified position, as defined in the Plan Needed Knowledge and Skills specific practice.

The acquirer determines its staffing requirements, including staffing for solicitation and supplier agreement management activities and staffing expected by the supplier to complete its portion of the work as defined in the WBS.

3. Determine facility, equipment, and component requirements.

   Most projects are unique in some sense and require a set of unique assets to accomplish project objectives. The determination and acquisition of these assets in a timely manner are crucial to project success. Lead-time items must be identified early to determine how they will be addressed. Even when required assets are not unique, compiling a list of all of facilities, equipment, and parts (e.g., number of computers for the personnel working on the project, software applications, and office space) provides insight into aspects of the scope of an effort that are often overlooked.

   The acquirer considers what it may need to provide for acceptance of supplier deliverables and for transition and support of the acquired product.

   The acquirer must also identify and ensure that facilities or equipment to be provided to the supplier for project work are accounted for in the project plan.

SP 2.5 Plan Needed Knowledge and Skills

Plan for knowledge and skills needed to perform the project.

Refer to the Organizational Training process area for more information about knowledge and skills information to be incorporated into the project plan.

Knowledge delivery to projects involves both training project personnel and acquiring knowledge from outside sources.

Staffing requirements are dependent on the knowledge and skills available to support the execution of the project.

The acquirer plans for knowledge and skills required by the project team to perform their tasks. Knowledge and skill requirements can be derived from project risk.

For example, if the acquirer is purchasing a software-intensive product, it ensures that acquisition personnel assigned to the project have expertise in systems and software engineering or provides training for the project team in these areas.

TIP

This practice addresses the training that is specific to the project.

TIP

At maturity level 2, the organization may not be capable of providing much training for its projects. Each project might address all of its knowledge and skill needs. At maturity level 3, the organization takes responsibility for addressing common training needs (e.g., training in the organization's set of standard processes).

Orientation and training in acquirer processes and the domain knowledge required to execute the project are also required. The acquirer also plans for knowledge and skills needed from the supplier.

> For example, the acquirer can provide role descriptions and skill profiles to the supplier as part of the solicitation package.

Planning for needed knowledge and skills includes ensuring that appropriate training is planned for personnel involved in receiving, storing, using, and supporting the transitioned product. Also included is ensuring that costs and funding sources to pay for training are available and lead times to obtain the funding are identified.

TIP

Either the project or the organization can maintain these typical work products.

Typical Work Products

1. Inventory of skill needs
2. Staffing and new hire plans
3. Databases (e.g., skills and training)
4. Training plans

HINT

Consider all knowledge and skills required for the project, not just the technical aspects.

Subpractices

1. Identify the knowledge and skills needed to perform the project.
2. Assess the knowledge and skills available.
3. Select mechanisms for providing needed knowledge and skills.

TIP

If a skill is needed for the current project, but is not expected to be needed for future projects, external skills acquisition may be the best choice. However, if the skill needed for the project is expected to continue, training existing employees or hiring a new employee should be explored.

> Example mechanisms include the following:
> - In-house training (both organizational and project)
> - External training
> - Staffing and new hires
> - External skill acquisition

The choice of in-house training or outsourced training for needed knowledge and skills is determined by the availability of training expertise, the project's schedule, and business objectives.

4. Incorporate selected mechanisms into the project plan.

X-REF

Identifying and involving relevant stakeholders is also addressed in PMC SP 1.5, IPM, and GP 2.7.

SP 2.6 Plan Stakeholder Involvement

Plan the involvement of identified stakeholders.

Stakeholders are identified from all phases of the project lifecycle by identifying the people and functions that need to be represented in the project and describing their relevance and the degree of interaction for project activities. A two-dimensional matrix with stakeholders along one axis and project activities along the other axis is a convenient format for accomplishing this identification. Relevance of the stakeholder to the activity in a particular project phase and the amount of interaction expected would be shown at the intersection of the project phase activity axis and the stakeholder axis.

Stakeholders can include operational users and project participants as well as potential suppliers. When acquiring products that must interoperate with other products, the acquirer plans the involvement of stakeholders from other projects or communities to ensure the delivered product can perform as required in its intended environment. Such planning often includes steps for establishing and maintaining supplier agreements with these stakeholders (e.g., interagency and intercompany agreements, memorandums of understanding, and memorandums of agreement).

For inputs of stakeholders to be useful, careful selection of relevant stakeholders is necessary. For each major activity, identify stakeholders who are affected by the activity and those who have expertise that is needed to conduct the activity. This list of relevant stakeholders will probably change as the project moves through phases of the project lifecycle. It is important, however, to ensure that relevant stakeholders in the latter phases of the lifecycle have early input to requirements and design decisions that affect them.

HINT

For each project phase, identify stakeholders important to the success of that phase and their role (e.g., implementer, reviewer, or consultant). Arrange this information into a matrix to aid in communication, obtain their commitment (SP 3.3), and monitor status (PMC SP 1.5).

TIP

Not all stakeholders identified will be relevant stakeholders. Only a limited number of stakeholders are selected for interaction with the project as work progresses.

Examples of the type of material that should be included in a plan for stakeholder interaction include the following:

- List of all relevant stakeholders
- Rationale for stakeholder involvement
- Roles and responsibilities of relevant stakeholders with respect to the project, by project lifecycle phase
- Relationships among stakeholders
- Relative importance of the stakeholder to the success of the project, by project lifecycle phase
- Resources (e.g., training, materials, time, and funding) needed to ensure stakeholder interaction
- Schedule for the phasing of stakeholder interaction

Implementing this specific practice relies on shared or exchanged information with the previous Plan Needed Knowledge and Skills specific practice.

Typical Work Products

1. Stakeholder involvement plan

SP 2.7 PLAN TRANSITION TO OPERATIONS AND SUPPORT

Plan transition to operations and support.

TIP

A successful transition involves planning for the appropriate facilities, training, use, maintenance, and support.

TIP

Acquirers should not overlook a supplier's responsibilities for ongoing maintenance and support. Long-term support needs should be considered when establishing the supplier agreement.

Planning for transition must be considered part of initial planning for the project.

Transition and support plans include the approach for introducing and maintaining readiness, sustainment, and the operational capability of the products delivered by the supplier. Plans for transitioning to operations and support include assignment of responsibility for transition to operations and support of the product, as well as all activities needed to manage the transition and to support the product in its intended environment (e.g., definition of transition readiness criteria agreed to by relevant stakeholders). These plans may include reasonable accommodations for potential risks and for the evolution of acquired products and their eventual removal from operational use.

Transition to operations and support plans typically include the following:

- Processes and procedures for the transition to operations and support
- Evaluation methods and acceptance criteria for transitioning the product to operations and support
- Readiness criteria for the product
- Readiness criteria for the operations organization
- Readiness criteria for the product support organization
- Expectations for supplier execution of the transition
- Warranty expectations for the acquired product
- Transition of intellectual property or other acquirer assets to the acquirer's designated repository
- Resolution steps if any problems are encountered

If support is to be provided by an organization different from the supplier, a sufficient overlap period should be included in the plan.

Typically, the acquirer develops initial transition and support plans and then reviews and approves more detailed transition and support plans.

Refer to the Agreement Management process area for more information about acceptance criteria and accepting the product.

Refer to the Acquisition Technical Management process area for more information about evaluation methods for the product.

Typical Work Products

1. Transition to operations and support plans

Subpractices

1. Determine the transition scope and objectives.
2. Determine transition requirements and criteria.
3. Determine transition responsibilities and resources to include post-transition support enhancements and lifecycle considerations.
4. Determine configuration management needs of the transition.
5. Determine training needs for operations and support.

SP 2.8 ESTABLISH THE PROJECT PLAN

Establish and maintain the overall project plan.

A documented plan that addresses all relevant planning items is necessary to achieve the mutual understanding, commitment, and performance of individuals, groups, and organizations that must execute or support the plans. The plan generated for the project defines all aspects of the effort, tying together the following in a logical manner: project lifecycle considerations; technical and management tasks; budgets and schedules; milestones; data management; risk identification; resource and skill requirements; and stakeholder identification and interaction. Infrastructure descriptions include responsibility and authority relationships for project staff, management, and support organizations.

The project plan may include multiple plans such as staffing plans, stakeholder involvement plans, measurement and analysis plans, monitoring and control plans, solicitation plans, agreement management plans, risk mitigation plans, transition plans, quality assurance plans, and configuration management plans. Regardless of form, the plan or plans should address the acquisition strategy as well as the cradle-to-grave considerations for the project and product to be acquired.

TIP

The plan document should reflect the project's status as requirements and the project environment change.
A documented plan communicates resources needed, expectations, and commitments; contains a game plan for relevant stakeholders, including the project team (SP 3.3); documents the commitment to management and other providers of resources; and is the basis for managing the project.

HINT

Most project plans change over time as requirements are better understood, so plan how and when you will update the plan.

Examples of plans that have been used in the U.S. Department of Defense community include the following:

- Integrated Master Plan: an event-driven plan that documents significant accomplishments with pass/fail criteria for both business and technical elements of the project and that ties each accomplishment to a key project event
- Integrated Master Schedule: an integrated and networked multilayered schedule of project tasks required to complete the work effort documented in a related Integrated Master Plan
- Systems Engineering Management Plan: a plan that details the integrated technical effort across the project
- Systems Engineering Master Schedule: an event-based schedule that contains a compilation of key technical accomplishments, each with measurable criteria, requiring successful completion to pass identified events
- Systems Engineering Detailed Schedule: a detailed, time-dependent, task-oriented schedule that associates dates and milestones with the Systems Engineering Master Schedule

TIP

Before making a commitment, a project member analyzes what it will take to meet the commitment. Project members who make commitments should continually evaluate their ability to meet their commitments, communicate immediately to those affected when they cannot meet their commitments, and mitigate the impacts of being unable to meet their commitments.

X-REF

Commitments are a recurring theme in CMMI. Requirements are committed to in REQM. Commitments are documented and reconciled in PP, monitored in PMC, and addressed more thoroughly in IPM.

HINT

Beware of commitments that are not given freely. A favorite quote that applies is "How bad do you want it? That is how bad you will get it!" If you do not allow commitments to be made freely, staff members most likely will try to provide the commitment you want to hear instead of a well-thought-out answer that is accurate.

Typical Work Products

1. Overall project plan

SG 3 OBTAIN COMMITMENT TO THE PLAN

Commitments to the project plan are established and maintained.

To be effective, plans require commitment by those responsible for implementing and supporting the plan.

Refer to the Solicitation and Supplier Agreement Development process area for more information about supplier agreements and finalizing supplier plans.

SP 3.1 REVIEW PLANS THAT AFFECT THE PROJECT

Review all plans that affect the project to understand project commitments.

Plans developed in other process areas typically contain information similar to that called for in the overall project plan. These plans may provide additional detailed guidance and should be compatible with and support the overall project plan to indicate who has the authority, responsibility, accountability, and control. All plans that affect the project should be reviewed to ensure they contain a common understanding of the scope, objectives, roles, and relationships that are required for the project to be successful. Many of these plans are described by the Plan the Process generic practice.

The project may have a hierarchy of plans (e.g., risk mitigation plans, transition plans, quality assurance plans, and configuration management plans). In addition, stakeholder plans (e.g., operational, test, support, and supplier plans) must be reviewed to ensure consistency among all project participants. Acquirer review of plans must include reviewing cross-supplier dependencies.

HINT

How related plans are documented is up to the project. Sometimes it makes sense to have all plans in one document. Other times it doesn't. However, all the plans must be consistent and be consistently updated.

Typical Work Products

1. Record of the reviews of plans that affect the project

SP 3.2 Reconcile Work and Resource Levels

Adjust the project plan to reconcile available and estimated resources.

To establish a project that is feasible, obtain commitment from relevant stakeholders and reconcile differences between estimates and available resources. Reconciliation is typically accomplished by lowering or deferring technical performance requirements, negotiating more resources, finding ways to increase productivity, outsourcing, adjusting the staff skill mix, or revising all plans that affect the project or its schedules.

TIP

A well-written plan includes estimates of the resources needed to complete the project successfully. When the estimates are higher than the resources available, the situation must be reconciled so that all relevant stakeholders can commit to a feasible plan (SP 3.3).

During supplier selection and negotiation of the supplier agreement, the acquirer reconciles overall project work and resource levels based on proposals from the supplier. Following completion of the supplier agreement, the acquirer incorporates supplier plans at an appropriate level of detail into the project plan to support the alignment of plans. For example, an acquirer may incorporate major supplier milestones, deliverables, and reviews.

TIP

Since resource availability can change, such reconciliation will likely need to be done multiple times during the life of the project.

Typical Work Products

1. Revised methods and corresponding estimating parameters (e.g., better tools and the use of off-the-shelf components)
2. Renegotiated budgets
3. Revised schedules
4. Revised requirements list
5. Renegotiated stakeholder agreements

SP 3.3 Obtain Plan Commitment

Obtain commitment from relevant stakeholders responsible for performing and supporting plan execution.

TIP

Commitments are a two-way form of communication.

TIP

In maturity level 1 organizations, management often communicates a different picture of the project than the staff does. This inconsistency indicates that commitments were not obtained.

TIP

Documenting commitments makes clear the responsibilities of those involved with the project.

HINT

Use the WBS to ensure that all tasks are considered when obtaining commitments. Use the stakeholder involvement plan (or matrix) to ensure that all relevant stakeholders are considered.

TIP

A commitment not documented is a commitment not made (memories are imperfect and thus unreliable).

TIP

Senior management must be informed of external commitments (especially those with customers, end users, and suppliers), as they can expose the organization to unnecessary risk.

X-REF

For more information on managing commitments, dependencies, and coordination issues among relevant stakeholders, see IPM SG 2. For more information on identifying and managing interfaces, see ATM SG 2.

Obtaining commitment involves interaction among all relevant stakeholders, both internal and external to the project. The individual or group making a commitment should have confidence that the work can be performed within cost, schedule, and performance constraints. Often, a provisional commitment is adequate to allow the effort to begin and to permit research to be performed to increase confidence to the appropriate level needed to obtain a full commitment.

Typical Work Products

1. Documented requests for commitments
2. Documented commitments

Subpractices

1. Identify needed support and negotiate commitments with relevant stakeholders.

    The WBS can be used as a checklist for ensuring that commitments are obtained for all tasks.

    The plan for stakeholder interaction should identify all parties from whom commitment should be obtained.

2. Document all organizational commitments, both full and provisional, ensuring the appropriate level of signatories.

    Commitments must be documented to ensure a consistent mutual understanding and for tracking and maintenance. Provisional commitments should be accompanied by a description of risks associated with the relationship.

3. Review internal commitments with senior management, as appropriate.
4. Review external commitments with senior management, as appropriate.

    Management may have the necessary insight and authority to reduce risks associated with external commitments.

5. Identify commitments regarding interfaces between project elements and other projects and organizational units so that these commitments can be monitored.

    Well-defined interface specifications form the basis for commitments.

PROCESS AND PRODUCT QUALITY ASSURANCE

A Support Process Area at Maturity Level 2

Purpose

The purpose of Process and Product Quality Assurance (PPQA) is to provide staff and management with objective insight into processes and associated work products.

TIP

PPQA is often referred to as the "eyes and ears" of the organization. It provides the insights needed so that the organization can determine whether its policies, practices, and processes are followed, are effective, and that the work products produced are meeting the needs of the organization or project.

Introductory Notes

The Process and Product Quality Assurance process area involves the following activities:

- Objectively evaluating performed processes, work products, and services against applicable process descriptions, standards, and procedures
- Identifying and documenting noncompliance issues
- Providing feedback to project staff and managers on the results of quality assurance activities
- Ensuring that noncompliance issues are addressed

TIP

The phrase *process descriptions, standards, and procedures* is used in PPQA (and in GP 2.9) to represent management's expectations as to how project work will be performed. Applicable process descriptions, standards, and procedures are typically identified during project planning.

The Process and Product Quality Assurance process area supports the delivery of high-quality products and services by providing project staff and managers at all levels with appropriate visibility into, and feedback on, processes and associated work products throughout the life of the project.

The acquirer evaluates critical acquirer work products, acquirer processes, results of supplier process quality assurance, and supplier deliverables. For example, process and product quality assurance ensures that the solicitation package was developed using standard processes agreed to by the organization and that it conforms to all applicable policies. The acquirer may review results of supplier quality assurance activities for selected supplier processes to ensure that the supplier is following its own processes.

HINT

During a SCAMPI, the appraisal team may not be able to judge the effectiveness of your processes or work products, but they do determine whether *you* have the ability to judge the effectiveness of your processes or work products and that you are taking appropriate action based on your determination.

Typically, selected supplier processes are critical processes, such as engineering or verification processes, where the supplier is required through the supplier agreement to follow project-specified standards. In exceptional cases, the acquirer may directly perform process and product quality assurance for selected supplier processes. The acquirer and supplier periodically share quality assurance issues and findings that are of mutual interest.

The practices in the Process and Product Quality Assurance process area ensure that planned processes are implemented, while the practices in the Acquisition Verification process area ensure that specified requirements are satisfied. These two process areas may on occasion address the same work product but from different perspectives. Projects should take advantage of the overlap in order to minimize duplication of effort while taking care to maintain separate perspectives.

TIP

Most acquirers don't use an independent quality assurance function to objectively evaluate process and product quality. Therefore, using objective criteria to evaluate quality and allowing for escalation of issues without retribution becomes even more critical.

Objectivity in process and product quality assurance evaluations is critical to the success of the project. (See the definition of "objectively evaluate" in the glossary.) Objectivity is achieved by both independence and the use of criteria. A combination of methods providing evaluations against criteria by those not producing the work product is often used. Less formal methods can be used to provide broad day-to-day coverage. More formal methods can be used periodically to assure objectivity.

TIP

For less mature acquisition organizations, it may be best to use personnel outside the project team, perhaps from another acquisition project, to help perform more formal audits of critical processes or work products.

Examples of ways to perform objective evaluations include the following:

- Formal audits by organizationally separate quality assurance organizations
- Peer reviews, which may be performed at various levels of formality
- In-depth review of work at the place it is performed (i.e., desk audits)
- Distributed review and comment of work products

Traditionally, a quality assurance group that is independent of the project provides objectivity. However, another approach may be appropriate in some organizations to implement the process and product quality assurance role without that kind of independence.

For example, in an organization with an open, quality-oriented culture, the process and product quality assurance role may be performed, partially or completely, by peers; and the quality assurance function may be embedded in the process. For small organizations, this might be the most feasible approach.

If quality assurance is embedded in the process, several issues must be addressed to ensure objectivity. Everyone performing quality assurance activities should be trained. Those performing quality assurance activities for a work product should be separate from those directly involved in developing or maintaining the work product. An independent reporting channel to the appropriate level of organizational management must be available so that noncompliance issues can be escalated as necessary.

TIP

Because most acquisition project teams are very small, team members tend to have multiple roles and quality assurance activities are embedded within the process; therefore, it is important to ensure that objectivity is achieved..

For example, when implementing peer reviews as an objective evaluation method, the following issues must be addressed.

- Members are trained and roles are assigned for people attending the peer reviews.
- A member of the peer review who did not produce this work product is assigned to perform the quality assurance role.
- Checklists are available to support the quality assurance activity.
- Defects are recorded as part of the peer review report and are tracked and escalated outside the project when necessary.

TIP

Acquisition project leadership must create an environment in which team members are encouraged to identify and fix process and product defects.

Quality assurance should begin in the early phases of a project to establish plans, processes, standards, and procedures that will add value to the project and satisfy the requirements of the project and organizational policies. Those performing quality assurance participate in establishing plans, processes, standards, and procedures to ensure that they fit project needs and that they will be usable for performing quality assurance evaluations. In addition, processes and associated work products to be evaluated during the project are designated. This designation may be based on sampling or on objective criteria that are consistent with organizational policies, project requirements, and needs.

HINT

Establish your quality assurance approach early in the project and continually focus on identifying constraints that may keep you from achieving project objectives.
Use a risk-based approach when designating which processes and work products to evaluate.

When noncompliance issues are identified, they are first addressed in the project and resolved there if possible. Noncompliance issues that cannot be resolved in the project are escalated to an appropriate level of management for resolution.

This process area applies primarily to evaluations of project activities and work products, but it also applies to other activities and work products, such as training organizational support groups. For these activities and work products, the term *project* should be appropriately interpreted.

TIP

Limit the appraisal scope to the supplier processes that are most critical to the current phase of the project and use Class B or Class C (nonbenchmarking) methods to help identify and mitigate project risk.

It also applies to the reviews of supplier process quality results as defined in the supplier agreement. For example, the supplier agreement can require the supplier to provide detailed appraisal results of mandatory, acquirer-scoped CMMI for Development appraisals of supplier processes.

X-REF

For more information about interpreting CMMI achievements made by your suppliers, see "Understanding and Leveraging a Supplier's CMMI Efforts: A Guidebook for Acquirers" at www.sei.cmu.edu/publications/documents/07.reports/07tr004.html.

Related Process Areas

Refer to the Solicitation and Supplier Agreement Development process area for more information about specifying evaluation of selected supplier processes and work products.

Refer to the Agreement Management process area for more information about managing conformance to supplier agreements.

Refer to the Acquisition Verification process area for more information about the verification of acquirer work products.

Refer to the Acquisition Technical Management process area for more information about evaluating the technical solution.

Specific Goal and Practice Summary

SG 1 Objectively Evaluate Processes and Work Products
- SP 1.1 Objectively Evaluate Processes
- SP 1.2 Objectively Evaluate Work Products and Services

SG 2 Provide Objective Insight
- SP 2.1 Communicate and Ensure the Resolution of Noncompliance Issues
- SP 2.2 Establish Records

Specific Practices by Goal

SG 1 OBJECTIVELY EVALUATE PROCESSES AND WORK PRODUCTS

Adherence of the performed process and associated work products and services to applicable process descriptions, standards, and procedures is objectively evaluated.

HINT

You will be able to determine the effectiveness of your processes and work products by evaluating adherence to objective criteria.
Regularly ask your customer and supplier how they perceive the effectiveness and efficiency of your processes and the quality of your work products contributing to their success.

SP 1.1 OBJECTIVELY EVALUATE PROCESSES

Objectively evaluate designated performed processes against applicable process descriptions, standards, and procedures.

Objectivity in quality assurance evaluations is critical to the success of the project. A description of the quality assurance reporting chain and how it ensures objectivity should be defined.

The description of the quality assurance reporting chain is extended to include the relationship between the acquirer and suppliers. It is important to ensure that acquirer and supplier processes comply with applicable statutory and regulatory requirements.

The acquirer evaluates the project's execution of acquirer processes, including interactions with suppliers, and reviews evaluation reports provided by suppliers to determine if they follow their processes. There should be sufficient process quality assurance to detect noncompliance issues as early as possible that may affect the acquirer's or supplier's ability to successfully deliver products to the customer.

Through the supplier agreement, the acquirer should retain the right to audit supplier processes if there is an indication that suppliers are not following acceptable processes.

TIP

Some of the most critical processes to evaluate are those that cross organizational boundaries. Acquirer-to-customer, acquirer-to-supplier, and acquirer-to-acquirer processes in a system of systems acquisition are good candidates to evaluate regularly.

Typical Work Products

1. Evaluation reports
2. Noncompliance reports
3. Corrective actions

Typical Supplier Deliverables

1. Reports resulting from evaluations carried out by the supplier
2. Noncompliance reports
3. Corrective actions

Subpractices

1. Promote an environment (created as part of project management) that encourages employee participation in identifying and reporting quality issues.
2. Establish and maintain clearly stated criteria for evaluations.
3. Use the stated criteria to evaluate performed processes for adherence to process descriptions, standards, and procedures.

   The supplier regularly provides process evaluation reports as defined in the supplier agreement.
4. Identify each noncompliance found during the evaluation.

   Analyze results of monitoring selected acquirer processes to detect issues as early as possible that may affect the supplier's ability to satisfy requirements of its agreement.
5. Identify lessons learned that could improve processes for future products and services.

TIP

Quality is everyone's job. It is important that everyone in the organization be comfortable identifying and openly discussing quality concerns.

HINT

The results of your quality assurance activities can identify best practices and processes that you should share with others in your organization. When working with multiple suppliers on the same project, best practices discovered through audit activities at one supplier location can become project-wide candidates for adoption to reduce project risk.

SP 1.2 Objectively Evaluate Work Products and Services

Objectively evaluate designated work products and services against applicable process descriptions, standards, and procedures.

In addition to objectively evaluating critical acquirer work products, the acquirer uses objective acceptance criteria to evaluate supplier deliverables throughout the project lifecycle. The acquirer's acceptance criteria for supplier deliverables are consistent with project objectives and sufficient to allow the supplier to satisfactorily demonstrate that the product conforms to contractual requirements.

Refer to the Acquisition Verification process area for more information about verifying selected work products.

HINT

Resist the temptation to put total attention on the suppliers' work products and not give "due diligence" to evaluating your own (acquirer) work products. Both must be of high quality to ensure program success. You can embed objective evaluations of work products within some of the verification activities—particularly, peer reviews—though doing so requires care. (See the introductory notes for more information.)

Typical Work Products

1. Evaluation reports
2. Noncompliance reports
3. Corrective actions

Subpractices

1. Select work products to be evaluated based on documented sampling criteria if sampling is used.
2. Establish and maintain clearly stated criteria for the evaluation of work products.
3. Use the stated criteria during evaluations of work products.
4. Evaluate work products before they are delivered to the customer.
5. Evaluate work products at selected milestones in their development.
6. Perform in-progress or incremental evaluations of work products and services against process descriptions, standards, and procedures.
7. Identify each case of noncompliance found during evaluations.
8. Identify lessons learned that could improve processes for future products and services.

HINT

Subpractices 4 through 6 recommend evaluation of work products at different times and from different perspectives. The important point is that you think broadly about what will give you the best objective insight you need during your project.

HINT

Your quality assurance activities can benefit other projects in your organization; share your results outside your project team.

SG 2 Provide Objective Insight

Noncompliance issues are objectively tracked and communicated, and resolution is ensured.

SP 2.1 Communicate and Ensure the Resolution of Noncompliance Issues

Communicate quality issues and ensure the resolution of noncompliance issues with the staff and managers.

Noncompliance issues are problems identified in evaluations that reflect a lack of adherence to applicable standards, process descriptions, or procedures. The status of noncompliance issues provides an indication of quality trends. Quality issues include noncompliance issues and trend analysis results.

When noncompliance issues cannot be resolved in the project, use established escalation mechanisms to ensure that the appropriate level of management can resolve the issue. Track noncompliance issues to resolution.

Noncompliance issues of both the acquirer and supplier are tracked and resolved.

HINT

Noncompliance issues may be common in low-maturity organizations and should be addressed at the lowest possible level. Don't "criminalize" those responsible for noncompliance.

HINT

Focus on fixing the process, not the people. Create an environment where everyone feels empowered to identify and correct errors without fear of retaliation.

Typical Work Products

1. Corrective action reports
2. Evaluation reports
3. Quality trends
4. Acquirer feedback to suppliers

Typical Supplier Deliverables

1. Corrective actions

Subpractices

1. Resolve each noncompliance with the appropriate members of the staff where possible.

   The acquirer involves suppliers when resolving noncompliance issues, as appropriate.

2. Document noncompliance issues when they cannot be resolved in the project.

> Examples of ways to resolve a noncompliance in the project include the following:
> - Fixing the noncompliance
> - Changing the process descriptions, standards, or procedures that were violated
> - Obtaining a waiver to cover the noncompliance

3. Escalate noncompliance issues that cannot be resolved in the project to the appropriate level of management designated to receive and act on noncompliance issues.
4. Analyze noncompliance issues to see if there are quality trends that can be identified and addressed.

TIP

In some cases, organizational requirements and project requirements are contradictory. These contradictions may be valid variation points that the organization could incorporate into requirements for future projects.

HINT

Quality assurance activities are often seen as nonvalue-added. The status and results of quality assurance activities should be reported regularly. Also, consider reporting a "compliance percentage" rather than the number of noncompliance issues. This may encourage friendly competition across projects and increase appreciation for the quality assurance role.

TIP

Records provide a way to identify trends in quality assurance activities (including noncompliance issues) that allow the organization to identify where additional guidance or process changes are needed.

5. Ensure that relevant stakeholders are aware of results of evaluations and quality trends in a timely manner.
6. Periodically review open noncompliance issues and trends with the manager designated to receive and act on noncompliance issues.
7. Track noncompliance issues to resolution.

SP 2.2 Establish Records

Establish and maintain records of quality assurance activities.

Typical Work Products

1. Evaluation logs
2. Quality assurance reports
3. Status reports of corrective actions
4. Reports of quality trends

Subpractices

1. Record process and product quality assurance activities in sufficient detail so that status and results are known.
2. Revise the status and history of quality assurance activities as necessary.

QUANTITATIVE PROJECT MANAGEMENT

A Project Management Process Area at Maturity Level 4

QPM

Purpose

The purpose of Quantitative Project Management (QPM) is to quantitatively manage the project's defined process to achieve the project's established quality and process-performance objectives.

TIP

QPM contains the set of tools to enable an acquirer to migrate from using the rear view mirror to manage the project to using predictive, forward-looking approaches to quantitatively understand the project's current state and to help steer the project to success.

Introductory Notes

The Quantitative Project Management process area involves the following activities:

- Establishing and maintaining the project's quality and process-performance objectives
- Identifying suitable subprocesses that compose the project's defined process based on historical stability and capability data found in process-performance baselines or models
- Selecting subprocesses within the project's defined process to be statistically managed
- Monitoring the project to determine whether the project's objectives for quality and process performance are being satisfied, and identifying appropriate corrective action
- Selecting measures and analytic techniques to be used in statistically managing selected subprocesses
- Establishing and maintaining an understanding of the variation of selected subprocesses using selected measures and analytic techniques
- Monitoring the performance of selected subprocesses to determine whether they are capable of satisfying their quality and process-performance objectives, and identifying corrective action
- Recording statistical and quality management data in the organization's measurement repository

TIP

The specific practices of QPM are best implemented by those who actually execute the project's defined process—not by management or consulting statisticians alone.

When effectively implemented, QPM empowers individuals and teams by enabling them to accurately estimate (make predictions) and make commitments to these estimates (predictions) with confidence. This implementation of QPM is a key indicator of a truly capable process and a mature organization.

X-REF

QPM and OPP are tightly coupled process areas. Each produces work products used by the other. An organization seeking to implement one of these should seek to implement both. Likewise, the capability level 4 generic practices (CL4 GPs) should not be addressed for any process area except in the context of implementing OPP and QPM.

X-REF

QPM selects the organizational process assets established in OPD based on a quantitative understanding of their ability to meet project-specific objectives.

The quality and process-performance objectives, measures, and baselines identified here are developed as described in the Organizational Process Performance process area. Subsequently, the results of performing the processes associated with the Quantitative Project Management process area (e.g., measurement definitions and measurement data) become part of the organizational process assets referred to in the Organizational Process Performance process area.

To effectively address the specific practices in this process area, the organization must have already established a set of standard processes and related organizational process assets, such as the organization's measurement repository and the organization's process asset library for use by each project in establishing its defined process.

The project's defined process is a set of subprocesses that form an integrated and coherent lifecycle for the project. It is established, in part, through selecting and tailoring processes from the organization's set of standard processes. (See the definition of "defined process" in the glossary.)

The project should ensure that supplier effort and progress measurements are made available. Establishing effective relationships with suppliers is also necessary for the successful implementation of this process area's specific practices.

The acquirer uses quantitative methods to manage its work and to gain insight into supplier work and products. In addition to its own quantitative data, the acquirer uses quantitative data provided by the supplier as specified in the supplier agreement to address the specific practices in this process area.

Process performance is a measure of actual process results achieved. Process performance is characterized by both process measures (e.g., effort, cycle time, and defect removal efficiency) and product measures (e.g., reliability, defect density, and response time).

Subprocesses are defined components of a larger defined process. The subprocesses themselves may be further decomposed into other subprocesses and process elements.

An essential element of quantitative management is having confidence in estimates (i.e., being able to predict the extent to which the project can fulfill its quality and process-performance objectives). Subprocesses to be statistically managed are chosen based on identified needs for predictable performance. (See the definitions of "statistically managed process," "quality and process-performance objective," and "quantitatively managed process" in the glossary.)

Another essential element of quantitative management is understanding the nature and extent of the variation experienced in process performance, and recognizing when the project's actual performance may not be adequate to achieve the project's quality and process-performance objectives.

Statistical management involves statistical thinking and the correct use of a variety of statistical techniques such as run charts, control charts, confidence intervals, prediction intervals, and tests of hypotheses. Quantitative management uses data from statistical management to help the project predict whether it will be able to achieve its quality and process-performance objectives and identify what corrective action should be taken.

TIP

By "statistical thinking," we mean using statistical analysis techniques as tools in appropriate ways to estimate the variation in the performance of a process, to investigate its causes, and to recognize from the data when the process is not performing as it should.

This process area applies to managing a project, but the concepts found here also apply to managing other groups and functions. Applying these concepts to managing other groups and functions may not necessarily contribute to achieving the organization's business objectives but may help these groups and functions control their processes.

Examples of other groups and functions that could benefit from using this process area include the following:

- Quality assurance
- Process definition and improvement
- Effort reporting
- Customer complaint handling
- Problem tracking and reporting

Related Process Areas

Refer to the Project Monitoring and Control process area for more information about monitoring and controlling the project and taking corrective action.

Refer to the Measurement and Analysis process area for more information about establishing measurable objectives, specifying measures and analyses to be performed, obtaining and analyzing measures, and reporting results.

Refer to the Organizational Process Performance process area for more information about the organization's quality and process-performance objectives, process-performance analyses, process-performance baselines, and process-performance models.

Refer to the Organizational Process Definition process area for more information about organizational process assets, including the organization's measurement repository.

X-REF

See *Measuring the Software Process, Statistical Process Control for Software Process Improvement* by William A. Florac and Anita D. Carleton (Addison-Wesley).
See *Understanding Statistical Process Control* (Second Edition) by Donald J. Wheeler and David S. Chambers (SPC Press, Inc.).
See *Understanding Variation: The Key to Managing Chaos* (Second Edition) by Donald J. Wheeler (SPC Press, Inc.).

Refer to the Integrated Project Management process area for more information about establishing and maintaining the project's defined process.

Refer to the Causal Analysis and Resolution process area for more information about identifying causes of defects and other problems and taking action to prevent them from occurring in the future.

Refer to the Organizational Innovation and Deployment process area for more information about selecting and deploying improvements that support the organization's quality and process-performance objectives.

Refer to the Solicitation and Supplier Agreement Development process area for more information about establishing reporting requirements for supplier measurement results and quantitative data in the supplier agreement.

Specific Goal and Practice Summary

SG 1 Quantitatively Manage the Project
- SP 1.1 Establish the Project's Objectives
- SP 1.2 Compose the Defined Process
- SP 1.3 Select Subprocesses to Be Statistically Managed
- SP 1.4 Manage Project Performance

SG 2 Statistically Manage Subprocess Performance
- SP 2.1 Select Measures and Analytic Techniques
- SP 2.2 Apply Statistical Methods to Understand Variation
- SP 2.3 Monitor the Performance of Selected Subprocesses
- SP 2.4 Record Statistical Management Data

Specific Practices by Goal

SG 1 QUANTITATIVELY MANAGE THE PROJECT

The project is quantitatively managed using quality and process-performance objectives.

TIP

Generally, these objectives are established early during project planning as customer requirements relating to product quality, service quality, and process performance are being established and analyzed. Once a supplier or set of suppliers are selected, revisit these objectives. Teaming with suppliers who have quantitatively managed processes may present opportunities to optimize across organizational boundaries.

SP 1.1 ESTABLISH THE PROJECT'S OBJECTIVES

Establish and maintain the project's quality and process-performance objectives.

When establishing the project's quality and process-performance objectives, it is often useful to think ahead about which processes from the organization's set of standard processes will be included in the project's defined process and what the historical data indicate regarding their process performance. These considerations will help in establishing realistic objectives for the project. Later, as the project's actual performance becomes known and more predictable, objectives may need to be revised.

The acquirer establishes the project's quality and process-performance objectives based on objectives of the organization, the customer, and other relevant stakeholders. The acquirer may also establish quality and process-performance objectives for supplier deliverables. These quantitative quality and process-performance objectives for the supplier are documented in the supplier agreement. The acquirer typically expects the supplier to execute its processes and apply its process-performance models toward achieving these objectives.

HINT

The project's quality and process-performance objectives can be challenging but must be achievable. In other words, balance senior management's desire for improvement with what projects are realistically capable of achieving. Supplier quality and process-performance objectives that are "specified" by the acquirer prior to contract award will need to be revised once the selected supplier's performance baselines are established.

Typical Work Products

1. The project's quality and process-performance objectives

Subpractices

1. Review the organization's objectives for quality and process performance.

   The intent of this review is to ensure that the project understands the broader business context in which the project must operate. The project's objectives for quality and process performance are developed in the context of these overarching organizational objectives.

   Refer to the Organizational Process Performance process area for more information about the organization's quality and process-performance objectives.

2. Identify the quality and process-performance needs and priorities of the customer, suppliers, end users, and other relevant stakeholders.

TIP

The project's objectives for quality and process performance are based, in part, on those of the organization (OPP SP 1.3). This approach helps to ensure that the project's objectives for quality and process performance are aligned with those of the organization.

Examples of quality and process-performance attributes for which needs and priorities might be identified include the following:

- Functionality
- Reliability
- Maintainability
- Usability
- Duration
- Predictability
- Timeliness
- Accuracy

3. Identify how process performance is to be measured.

   Consider whether measures established by the organization are adequate for assessing progress in fulfilling customer, end user, and other stakeholder needs and priorities. It may be necessary to supplement these measures with additional ones.

Refer to the Measurement and Analysis process area for more information about defining measures.

4. Define and document measurable quality and process-performance objectives for the project.

   Defining and documenting objectives for the project involve the following:

   - Incorporating the organization's quality and process-performance objectives
   - Writing objectives that reflect the quality and process-performance needs and priorities of the customer, end users, and other stakeholders, and the way these objectives should be measured

> Examples of quality attributes for which objectives might be written include the following:
> - Mean time between failures
> - Critical resource utilization
> - Number and severity of defects in the released product
> - Number and severity of customer complaints concerning the provided service

> Examples of process-performance attributes for which objectives might be written include the following:
> - Percentage of defects removed by product verification activities (perhaps by type of verification, such as peer reviews and testing)
> - Defect escape rates
> - Number and density of defects (by severity) found during the first year following product delivery (or start of service)
> - Cycle time
> - Percentage of rework time

HINT

Apply the organization's process-performance models to determine which interim objectives lead to the desired project outcomes. Review interim objectives later as part of monitoring the project's progress toward achieving its (overarching) objectives for quality and process performance. (See SP 1.4, subpractice 2.)

5. Derive interim objectives for each lifecycle phase, as appropriate, to monitor progress toward achieving the project's objectives.

> An example of a method to predict future results of a process is the use of process-performance models to predict latent defects in the delivered product using interim measures of defects identified during product verification activities (e.g., peer reviews and testing).

6. Resolve conflicts among the project's quality and process-performance objectives (e.g., if one objective cannot be achieved without compromising another).

Resolving conflicts involves the following activities:

- Setting relative priorities for objectives
- Considering alternative objectives in light of long-term business strategies as well as short-term needs
- Involving the customer, end users, senior management, project management, and other relevant stakeholders in tradeoff decisions
- Revising objectives as necessary to reflect results of conflict resolution

7. Establish traceability to the project's quality and process-performance objectives from their sources.

Examples of sources of objectives include the following:

- Requirements
- The organization's quality and process-performance objectives
- The customer's quality and process-performance objectives
- Business objectives
- Discussions with customers and potential customers
- Market surveys

An example of a method to identify and trace these needs and priorities is Quality Function Deployment (QFD).

8. Define and negotiate quality and process-performance objectives for suppliers.

   Refer to the Solicitation and Supplier Agreement Development process area for more information about incorporating project quality and process-performance objectives into solicitation packages and into supplier agreements.

9. Revise the project's quality and process-performance objectives as necessary.

SP 1.2 Compose the Defined Process

Select subprocesses that compose the project's defined process based on historical stability and capability data.

Refer to the Integrated Project Management process area for more information about establishing and maintaining the project's defined process.

Refer to the Organizational Process Definition process area for more information about the organization's process asset library, which might include a process element of known and needed capability.

TIP

Some organizations may have only one standard process (e.g., because the projects are sufficiently similar to one another). In such cases, there are still some choices to explore (e.g., which attributes of the acquisition strategy should be modified to achieve project objectives).

TIP

Sources of historical stability and capability data include the organization's process-performance baselines and models (OPP SPs 1.4 and 1.5). These organizational assets can help the project determine whether a defined process capable of achieving the project's objectives can be established from the organization's set of standard processes.

Refer to the Organizational Process Performance process area for more information about the organization's process-performance baselines and process-performance models.

Subprocesses are identified from process elements in the organization's set of standard processes and process artifacts in the organization's process asset library.

These subprocesses may include those used for interacting with a supplier (e.g., negotiating a supplier agreement and conducting supplier reviews).

Typical Work Products

1. Criteria used in identifying which subprocesses are valid candidates for inclusion in the project's defined process
2. Candidate subprocesses for inclusion in the project's defined process
3. Subprocesses to be included in the project's defined process
4. Identified risks when selected subprocesses lack a process-performance history

Subpractices

1. Establish the criteria to use in identifying which subprocesses are valid candidates for use.

> Identification may be based on the following:
> - Quality and process-performance objectives
> - Existence of process-performance data
> - Product line standards
> - Project lifecycle models
> - Customer requirements
> - Laws and regulations

2. Determine whether subprocesses that are to be statistically managed and were obtained from the organizational process assets are suitable for statistical management.

   A subprocess may be more suitable for statistical management if it has a history of the following:
   - Stable performance in previous comparable instances
   - Process-performance data that satisfy the project's quality and process-performance objectives

   Historical data are primarily obtained from the organization's process-performance baselines. However, these data may not be available for all subprocesses.

3. Analyze the interaction of subprocesses to understand relationships among subprocesses and measured attributes of the subprocesses.

Examples of analysis techniques include system dynamics models and simulations.

4. Identify the risk when no subprocess is available that is known to be capable of satisfying quality and process-performance objectives (i.e., no capable subprocess is available or the capability of the subprocess is not known).

   Even when a subprocess has not been selected to be statistically managed, historical data and process-performance models may indicate that the subprocess is not capable of satisfying quality and process-performance objectives.

   Refer to the Risk Management process area for more information about identifying and analyzing risks.

HINT

When acquirer subprocesses interact with supplier or end-user subprocesses, the dynamics may not be obvious. Use system dynamics models in concert with process-performance models to uncover hidden behavior and unintended consequences.

X-REF

To see how to use systems thinking to evaluate the underlying dynamics of common patterns of failure, see "Acquisition Archetypes: Changing Counterproductive Behaviors in Real Acquisitions" at www.sei.cmu.edu/programs/acquisition-support/pof-intro.html.

QPM

SP 1.3 Select Subprocesses to Be Statistically Managed

Select subprocesses of the project's defined process to be statistically managed.

Selecting subprocesses to be statistically managed is often a concurrent and iterative process of identifying applicable project and organization quality and process-performance objectives, selecting subprocesses, and identifying process and product attributes to measure and control. Often, the selection of a process, quality and process-performance objective, or measurable attribute will constrain the selection of the other two. For example, if a particular process is selected, measurable attributes and quality and process-performance objectives may be constrained by that process.

Typical Work Products

1. Quality and process-performance objectives to be addressed by statistical management
2. Criteria used in selecting which subprocesses will be statistically managed
3. Subprocesses to be statistically managed
4. Identified process and product attributes of selected subprocesses that should be measured and controlled

HINT

How many subprocesses must be statistically managed to be capability or maturity level 4? There is no universal answer, of course, but an initial approach might be to select subprocesses (1) that give visibility into what is happening within each major lifecycle phase (and for each team) and (2) whose behavior can be used to update or calibrate process-performance models to predict future project outcomes. This approach allows project members to regularly determine whether they are still on track toward meeting project objectives.

HINT

You can perform SPs 1.1 through 1.3 concurrently and iteratively.

TIP

This specific practice focuses on more than just selecting subprocesses. It also focuses on identifying the attributes of each subprocess by which it will be statistically managed.

HINT

Identify which objectives will be addressed through statistically managing attributes of one or more subprocesses. Avoid selecting objectives that are outside the acquisition team's ability to control. Objectives that are achieved by a supplier or end user are important to track, but difficult to quantitatively manage using statistical process control techniques because the processes are outside your control.

TIP

The project's selection of subprocesses to statistically manage is based, in part, on those selected by the organization (OPP SP 1.1).

TIP

The selection of subprocess attributes is not mentioned in OPP, or in any specific practice statement in QPM, and is thus easily overlooked.

Subpractices

1. Identify which of the project's quality and process-performance objectives will be statistically managed.
2. Identify criteria to be used in selecting subprocesses that are the main contributors to achieving identified quality and process-performance objectives and for which predictable performance is important.

Examples of sources for criteria used in selecting subprocesses include the following:

- Customer requirements related to quality and process performance
- Quality and process-performance objectives established by the customer
- Quality and process-performance objectives established by the organization
- The organization's performance baselines and models
- Stable performance of the subprocess on other projects
- Laws and regulations

3. Select subprocesses to be statistically managed using selection criteria.

   It may not be possible to statistically manage some subprocesses (e.g., where new subprocesses and technologies are being piloted). In other cases, it may not be economically justifiable to apply statistical techniques to certain subprocesses.
4. Identify product and process attributes of selected subprocesses to be measured and controlled.

Examples of product and process attributes include the following:

- Defect density
- Cycle time
- Test coverage

SP 1.4 Manage Project Performance

Monitor the project to determine whether the project's objectives for quality and process performance will be satisfied, and identify corrective action, as appropriate.

Refer to the Measurement and Analysis process area for more information about analyzing and using measures.

A prerequisite for such a determination is that the selected subprocesses of the project's defined process are statistically managed and their process capability is understood. Specific practices of specific goal 2 provide detail on statistically managing selected subprocesses.

The acquirer monitors the performance of selected subprocesses to assess whether the project is on track in achieving its quality and process-performance objectives. These subprocesses include those that involve interaction with a supplier. This selective monitoring provides the acquirer with insight into project and supplier performance to predict the likelihood of achieving project objectives for quality and process performance. The acquirer uses this information to manage the project and to initiate corrective actions in time to meet project objectives.

TIP

Expand your process improvement toolkit to include techniques such as Six Sigma or Theory of Constraints when deciding the corrective actions to take.

X-REF

To see how to use Six Sigma with CMMI see "CMMI and Six Sigma: Partners in Process Improvement," at www.sei.cmu.edu/publications/books/process/cmmi-six-sigma.html.
For more information on using Theory of Constraints and the Critical Thinking Tools, see *Thinking for a Change: Putting the TOC Thinking Processes to Use* by Lisa Scheinkopf (CRC).

Typical Work Products

1. Estimates (i.e., predictions) of the achievement of the project's quality and process-performance objectives
2. Documentation of risks in achieving the project's quality and process-performance objectives
3. Documentation of actions needed to address deficiencies in achieving project objectives

Typical Supplier Deliverables

1. Supplier process-performance data for quality and process-performance objectives and expected service levels

Subpractices

1. Periodically review the performance and capability of each subprocess selected to be statistically managed to appraise progress toward achieving the project's quality and process-performance objectives.

   The process capability of each selected subprocess is determined with respect to that subprocess's established quality and process-performance objectives. These objectives are derived from the project's quality and process-performance objectives, which are defined for the project as a whole.

2. Periodically review actual results achieved against established interim objectives for each phase of the project lifecycle to appraise progress toward achieving the project's quality and process-performance objectives.
3. Track supplier results for achieving their quality and process-performance objectives.
4. Use process-performance models calibrated with obtained measures of critical attributes to estimate progress toward achieving the project's quality and process-performance objectives.

HINT

In the case of statistically managed attributes, review the process capability (i.e., natural process bounds compared to derived objectives).

TIP

The organization's process-performance models (OPP SP 1.5) can help the project determine whether it will be able to achieve the project's objectives.

Process-performance models are used to estimate progress toward achieving objectives that cannot be measured until a future phase in the project lifecycle. An example is the use of process-performance models to predict latent defects in the delivered product using interim measures of defects identified during peer reviews.

Refer to the Organizational Process Performance process area for more information about process-performance models.

Calibration of the process-performance models is based on results obtained from performing the previous subpractices.

5. Identify and manage risks associated with achieving the project's quality and process-performance objectives.

   Refer to the Risk Management process area for more information about identifying and managing risks.

Example sources of risks include the following:

- Inadequate stability and capability data in the organization's measurement repository
- Subprocesses having inadequate performance or capability
- Suppliers not achieving their quality and process-performance objectives
- Lack of visibility into supplier capability
- Inaccuracies in the organization's process-performance models for predicting future performance
- Deficiencies in predicted process performance (estimated progress)
- Other identified risks associated with identified deficiencies

6. Determine and document actions needed to address deficiencies in achieving the project's quality and process-performance objectives.

   The intent of these actions is to plan and deploy the right set of activities, resources, and schedule to place the project back on a path toward achieving its objectives.

Examples of actions that can be taken to address deficiencies in achieving the project's objectives include the following:

- Changing quality and process-performance objectives so that they are within the expected range of the project's defined process
- Improving the implementation of the project's defined process to reduce its normal variability (reducing variability may bring the project's performance within the objectives without having to move the mean)
- Adopting new subprocesses and technologies that have the potential for satisfying objectives and managing associated risks
- Identifying the risk and risk mitigation strategies for deficiencies
- Terminating the project

Refer to the Project Monitoring and Control process area for more information about taking corrective action.

SG 2 Statistically Manage Subprocess Performance

The performance of selected subprocesses within the project's defined process is statistically managed.

Avoid the temptation of using cumulative data (e.g., Schedule Performance Index or Cost Performance Index) on control charts. Variation is masked because of the cumulative nature of the indicator and large variances associated with independent events can be missed. This specific goal describes an activity critical to achieving the Quantitatively Manage the Project specific goal of this process area. The specific practices under this specific goal describe how to statistically manage subprocesses whose selection was described in specific practices under specific goal 1. When selected subprocesses are statistically managed, their capability to achieve their objectives can be determined. By these means, it is possible to predict whether the project will be able to achieve its objectives, which is key to quantitatively managing the project.

TIP

A "statistically managed process" does not require or expect control charts per se, but rather techniques that help determine the natural bounds in process variation and detect anomalous events. To date, control charts are the most widely used statistical analysis technique. When the circumstances warrant (e.g., when dealing with time-ordered event data from statistically independent events), control charts are a practical technique for accomplishing these things.

SP 2.1 Select Measures and Analytic Techniques

Select measures and analytic techniques to be used in statistically managing selected subprocesses.

Refer to the Measurement and Analysis process area for more information about establishing measurable objectives; specifying the measures and analyses to be performed; obtaining, analyzing, and updating measures; and reporting results.

Typical Work Products

1. Definitions of measures and analytic techniques to be used in (or proposed for) statistically managing subprocesses
2. Operational definitions of measures, their collection points in subprocesses, and how the integrity of measures will be determined
3. Traceability of measures back to the project's quality and process-performance objectives
4. Instrumented organizational support environment that supports automatic data collection

Subpractices

1. Identify common measures from the organizational process assets that support statistical management.

TIP

The project's identification of common measures to support statistical management is based, in part, on measures established by the organization to be included in its process performance analyses (OPP SP 1.2).

Refer to the Organizational Process Definition process area for more information about common measures.

Product lines or other stratification criteria may categorize common measures.

TIP

Additional measures may be needed, for example, to address unique customer requirements or supplier approaches.

2. Identify additional measures that may be needed for this instance to cover critical product and process attributes of the selected subprocesses.

   In some cases, measures may be research-oriented. Such measures should be explicitly identified.

X-REF

Much of the material found in the remaining subpractices (3 through 8) is a direct application of MA SG 1, Align Measurement and Analysis Activities, to statistically managing the selected subprocesses.

3. Identify the measures that are appropriate for statistical management.

   Critical criteria for selecting statistical management measures include the following:
   - Controllable (e.g., can a measure's values be changed by changing how the subprocess is implemented?)
   - Adequate performance indicator (e.g., is the measure a good indicator of how well the subprocess is performing relative to the objectives of interest?)

Examples of subprocess measures include the following:
- Requirements volatility
- Ratios of estimated to measured values of planning parameters (e.g., size, cost, and schedule)
- Coverage and efficiency of peer reviews
- Test coverage and efficiency
- Effectiveness of training (e.g., percent of planned training completed and test scores)
- Reliability
- Percentage of total defects inserted or found in different phases of the project lifecycle
- Percentage of total effort expended in different phases of the project lifecycle

4. Specify the operational definitions of measures, their collection points in subprocesses, and how the integrity of measures will be determined.

   Operational definitions are stated in precise and unambiguous terms. They address two important criteria:
   - Communication: What has been measured, how it was measured, what are the units of measure, and what has been included or excluded?
   - Repeatability: Is the measurement repeatable, given the same definition, to get the same results?

5. Analyze the relationship of identified measures to the objectives of the organization and its projects, and derive objectives that state target measures or ranges to be met for each measured attribute of each selected subprocess.
6. Instrument the organizational or project support environment to support collection, derivation, and analysis of statistical measures.
   This instrumentation is based on the following:
   - Description of the organization's set of standard processes
   - Description of the project's defined process
   - Capabilities of the organizational or project support environment
7. Identify appropriate statistical analysis techniques that are expected to be useful in statistically managing the selected subprocesses.
   The concept of "one size does not fit all" applies to statistical analysis techniques. What makes a particular technique appropriate is not just the type of measures but, more important, how the measures will be used and whether the situation warrants applying that technique. The appropriateness of the selection may need to be reviewed from time to time.
   Examples of statistical analysis techniques are given in the next specific practice.
8. Revise measures and statistical analysis techniques as necessary.

TIP

Control charts and other statistical techniques (ANOVA and regression analyses, their nonparametric equivalents, and other Six Sigma analysis techniques) provide value in examining relationships among processes, their inputs, and sources that can assist in understanding process variation.

SP 2.2 Apply Statistical Methods to Understand Variation

Establish and maintain an understanding of the variation of selected subprocesses using selected measures and analytic techniques.

Refer to the Measurement and Analysis process area for more information about collecting, analyzing, and using measurement results.

Understanding variation is achieved, in part, by collecting and analyzing process and product measures so that special causes of variation can be identified and addressed to achieve predictable performance.

A special cause of process variation is characterized by an unexpected change in process performance. Special causes are also known as *assignable causes* because they can be identified, analyzed, and addressed to prevent recurrence.

The identification of special causes of variation is based on departures from the system of common causes of variation. These departures can be identified by the presence of extreme values or other identifiable patterns in data collected from the subprocess or associated work products. Typically, knowledge of variation and insight about potential sources of anomalous patterns are needed to detect special causes of variation.

TIP

Achieving a stable subprocess (in which special causes of variation are detected and removed) is not enough. A subprocess that otherwise appears to be stable may demonstrate unacceptably wide variation, which should arouse suspicion. In any case, such a subprocess is not very predictable.

HINT

To address unacceptably wide variation, investigate the sources of that variation. How does the subprocess behave on certain data? How is its performance affected by upstream and lower-level subprocesses? The answers are opportunities to reduce variation in subprocess performance and more accurately predict future performance.

Sources of anomalous patterns of variation may include the following:

- Lack of process compliance
- Undistinguished influences of multiple underlying subprocesses on the data
- Ordering or timing of activities within the subprocess
- Uncontrolled inputs to the subprocess
- Environmental changes during subprocess execution
- Schedule pressure
- Inappropriate sampling or grouping of data

Typical Work Products

1. Collected measurements
2. Natural bounds of process performance for each measured attribute of each selected subprocess
3. Process performance compared to the natural bounds of process performance for each measured attribute of each selected subprocess

Typical Supplier Deliverables

1. Collected supplier measurements
2. Natural bounds of supplier process performance for each measured attribute of each selected subprocess
3. Supplier process performance compared to the natural bounds of process performance for each measured attribute of each selected subprocess

Subpractices

1. Establish trial natural bounds for subprocesses having suitable historical performance data.

    Refer to the Organizational Process Performance process area for more information about organizational process-performance baselines.

    Natural bounds of an attribute are the range within which variation normally occurs. All processes show some variation in process and product measures each time they are executed. The issue is whether this variation is due to common causes of variation in the normal performance of the process or to some special cause that can and should be identified and removed.

    When a subprocess is initially executed, suitable data for establishing trial natural bounds are sometimes available from prior instances of the subprocess or comparable subprocesses, process-performance baselines, or process-performance models. Typically, these data are contained in the organization's measurement repository. As the subprocess is executed, data specific to that instance are collected and used to update and replace the trial natural bounds. However, if the subprocess has been materially tailored, or if conditions are materially different from those in previous instantiations, data in the repository may not be relevant and should not be used.

In some cases, there may be no comparable historical data (e.g., when introducing a new subprocess, when entering a new application domain, or when significant changes have been made to the subprocess). In such cases, trial natural bounds will have to be made from early process data of this subprocess. These trial natural bounds must then be refined and updated as subprocess execution continues.

Examples of criteria for determining whether data are comparable include the following:

- Product lines
- Application domain
- Work product and task attributes (e.g., size of product)
- Size of project

2. Collect data, as defined by selected measures, on subprocesses as they execute.
3. Calculate the natural bounds of process performance for each measured attribute.

Examples of statistical techniques for calculating natural bounds include the following:

- Control charts
- Confidence intervals (for parameters of distributions)
- Prediction intervals (for future outcomes)

4. Identify special causes of variation.

An example of a criterion for detecting a special cause of process variation in a control chart is a data point that falls outside 3-sigma control limits.

The criteria for detecting special causes of variation are based on statistical theory and experience and depend on economic justification. As criteria are added, special causes are more likely to be identified if they are present, but the likelihood of false alarms also increases.

5. Analyze special cause of process variation to determine the reasons the anomaly occurred.

TIP

If the circumstances of subprocess execution are similar to those on which a process-performance baseline is based, such a baseline may be used to help establish trial natural bounds.

HINT

If all other means of establishing trial natural bounds fail, use the first measurements obtained from performing the subprocess. Estimate natural bounds (a.k.a. trial control limits) when there are only three or four data points, but take care not to overinterpret "assignable cause signals" until natural bounds become substantiated with further data.

TIP

Control charts (in particular, XmR and XbarR charts) are a widely used statistical analysis technique for calculating natural bounds.

TIP

Special causes of variation need to be identified and addressed to maintain predictable performance of the subprocess.

X-REF

For more information, see the references in "Related PAs" and the entry for "Control Charts" in Wikipedia, www.wikipedia.org.

HINT

To better understand subprocess variation, investigate at a lower level of granularity. Restratify the data (grouped to match input types or teams that will execute the subprocess), and test data subsequences for stability to obtain tighter control. See Example 7.1 in *Measuring the Software Process—Statistical Process Control for Software Process Improvement* by William A. Florac and Anita D. Carleton (Addison-Wesley).

TIP

The focus of the corrective action is on correcting subprocess execution, not subprocess definition. However, special causes of process variation may bring to light new promising candidate practices to be considered for future incorporation into the subprocess definition.

TIP

When corrective action is taken to address a special cause of variation, the affected data point (or data points) must be removed.

Examples of techniques for analyzing the reasons for special causes of variation include the following:

- Cause-and-effect (fishbone) diagrams
- Designed experiments
- Control charts (applied to subprocess inputs or lower-level subprocesses)
- Subgrouping (analyzing the same data segregated into smaller groups based on an understanding of how the subprocess was implemented facilitates isolation of special causes)

Some anomalies may simply be extremes of the underlying distribution rather than problems. Those implementing a subprocess are usually the ones best able to analyze and understand special causes of variation.

6. Determine the corrective action to be taken when special causes of variation are identified.

   Removing a special cause of process variation does not change the underlying subprocess. It addresses an error in the way the subprocess is executed.

   Refer to the Project Monitoring and Control process area for more information about taking corrective action.

7. Recalculate natural bounds for each measured attribute of the selected subprocesses as necessary.

   Recalculating the (statistically estimated) natural bounds is based on measured values that signify that the subprocess has changed, not on expectations or arbitrary decisions.

Examples of when natural bounds may need to be recalculated include the following.

- There are incremental improvements to the subprocess.
- New tools are deployed for the subprocess.
- A new subprocess is deployed.
- The collected measures suggest that the subprocess mean has permanently shifted or the subprocess variation has permanently changed.

SP 2.3 MONITOR THE PERFORMANCE OF SELECTED SUBPROCESSES

Monitor the performance of selected subprocesses to determine their capability to satisfy their quality and process-performance objectives, and identify corrective action as necessary.

The intent of this specific practice is to do the following:

- Statistically determine process behavior expected from the subprocess
- Appraise the probability that the subprocess will meet its quality and process-performance objectives
- Identify the corrective action to be taken based on a statistical analysis of process-performance data

Corrective action may include renegotiating affected project objectives, identifying and implementing alternative subprocesses, or identifying and measuring lower-level subprocesses to achieve greater detail in performance data.

These actions are intended to help the project use a more capable process. (See the definition of "capable process" in the glossary.)

A prerequisite for comparing the capability of a selected subprocess against its quality and process-performance objectives is that the measured attributes of the subprocess indicate that its performance is stable and predictable.

Process capability is analyzed for those subprocesses and measured attributes for which (derived) objectives are established. Not all subprocesses or measured attributes that are statistically managed are analyzed regarding process capability.

Historical data may be inadequate for initially determining whether the subprocess is capable. It also is possible that the estimated natural bounds for subprocess performance may shift away from quality and process-performance objectives. In either case, statistical control implies monitoring capability as well as stability.

Typical Work Products

1. Natural bounds of process performance for each selected subprocess compared to its established (derived) objectives
2. The process capability of each subprocess
3. The actions needed to address deficiencies in the process capability of each subprocess

Typical Supplier Deliverables

1. Actions needed to address deficiencies in supplier process performance or the quality of deliverables

HINT

For each stable subprocess (i.e., stable relative to a particular attribute to be controlled), compare its natural bounds against its associated objectives for quality and process performance and take corrective action as necessary.

TIP

This comparison of the natural bounds against derived objectives is called "determining the process capability" and "comparing the 'voice of the process' tohe 'voice of the customer'."

TIP

To determine whether a subprocess is capable relative to a particular attribute you must first know whether it is stable relative to that attribute.

HINT

Display the comparison graphically instead of computing capability indices because the latter are more confusing when communicating to non-SPC experts.

Subpractices

1. Compare quality and process-performance objectives to the natural bounds of the measured attribute.

   This comparison provides an appraisal of the process capability for each measured attribute of a subprocess. These comparisons can be displayed graphically in ways that relate the estimated natural bounds to the objectives or as process capability indices, which summarize the relationship of objectives to natural bounds.
2. Monitor changes in quality and process-performance objectives and the process capability of the selected subprocess.
3. Identify and document deficiencies in subprocess capability.
4. Determine and document actions needed to address deficiencies in subprocess capability.

HINT

Sometimes you can change the objectives derived for a particular attribute so that the subprocess's capability meets them by investigating whether some other subprocesses can give up some needed slack.

> Examples of actions that can be taken when the performance of a selected subprocess does not satisfy its objectives include the following:
> - Rederiving quality and process-performance objectives for each selected subprocess so that they can be met given the performance of the selected subprocesses
> - Improving the implementation of the existing subprocess to reduce its normal variability (reducing variability may bring natural bounds within the objectives without having to move the mean)
> - Adopting new process elements, subprocesses, and technologies that have the potential to satisfy objectives and manage associated risks
> - Identifying risks and risk mitigation strategies for each deficiency in subprocess capability

Refer to the Project Monitoring and Control process area for more information about taking corrective action.

SP 2.4 RECORD STATISTICAL MANAGEMENT DATA

X-REF

Statistical and quality management data may contribute to a future revision of the organization's process-performance baselines and models (OPP SPs 1.4 and 1.5).

Record statistical and quality management data in the organization's measurement repository.

Refer to the Measurement and Analysis process area for more information about managing and storing data, measurement definitions, and results.

Refer to the Organizational Process Definition process area for more information about the organization's measurement repository.

Typical Work Products

1. Statistical and quality management data recorded in the organization's measurement repository

REQUIREMENTS MANAGEMENT

A Project Management Process Area at Maturity Level 2

Purpose

The purpose of Requirements Management (REQM) is to manage requirements of the project's products and product components and to identify inconsistencies between those requirements and the project's plans and work products.

X-REF

REQM does not address eliciting or developing requirements. For more information on these topics, refer to the ARD process area.

REQM

Introductory Notes

Requirements management processes manage all requirements received or generated by the project, including both technical and nontechnical requirements as well as requirements levied on the project by the organization.

In particular, if the Acquisition Requirements Development process area is implemented, the resulting processes will generate customer and contractual requirements to be managed by requirements management processes. When the Requirements Management and the Acquisition Requirements Development process areas are both implemented, their associated processes may be closely tied and performed concurrently.

The project takes appropriate steps to ensure that the agreed-on set of requirements is managed to support the planning and execution needs of the project. When a project receives requirements from an approved requirements provider, these requirements are reviewed with the requirements provider to resolve issues and prevent misunderstanding before requirements are incorporated into project plans. Once the requirements provider and the requirements receiver reach an agreement, commitment to the requirements is obtained from project participants. The project manages changes to requirements as they evolve and identifies inconsistencies that occur among plans, work products, and requirements.

TIP

REQM addresses *all* customer and contractual *requirements* handled by the project, thus providing a stable foundation for acquisition activities and for suppliers to perform project planning, development, testing, and delivery activities. Nontechnical requirements include requirements such as cost, schedule, packaging, delivery, and other requirements not associated directly with attributes of the product or service. ARD develops customer and contractual requirements, SSAD formally hands them off to the supplier, ATM ensures that selected supplier work products meet these requirements, AVAL ensures that the resultant products are usable in their intended environment, and REQM manages requirements throughout the project's life into transition and eventual disposal.

Part of managing requirements is documenting requirements changes and their rationale and maintaining bidirectional traceability between source requirements and all product and product component requirements. (See the definition of "bidirectional traceability" in the glossary.)

Throughout the process areas, where we use the terms *product* and *product component*, they are intended to include service and service component and should be interpreted in that way.

TIP

Requirements providers can include customers, end-users, suppliers, management, regulatory agencies, and standards bodies.

Sometimes the customer requirements baseline is different from the contractual baseline that the suppliers are working on. The acquisition project must maintain both baselines and plan to resolve or negotiate inconsistencies. The project will have similar, but often more complex, challenges when multiple systems are being acquired to provide a final capability.

TIP

Bidirectional traceability is important when evaluating the impact of supplier product and service changes with respect to customer needs and when evaluating the impact of customer need changes with respect to the supplier's contractual baselines, products, and services.

HINT

When acquiring services, customer and contractual requirements changes must continue to be managed.

Consider using the practices in REQM to manage the requirements associated with other processes such as training, human resources, and so on.

Related Process Areas

Refer to the Acquisition Requirements Development process area for more information about transforming stakeholder needs into customer requirements and allocating requirements to supplier deliverables.

Refer to the Project Planning process area for more information about how project plans reflect requirements and must be revised as requirements change.

Refer to the Configuration Management process area for more information about baselines and controlling changes to requirements documents.

Refer to the Project Monitoring and Control process area for more information about tracking and controlling activities and work products that are based on requirements and taking appropriate corrective action.

Refer to the Risk Management process area for more information about identifying and handling risks associated with requirements.

Specific Goal and Practice Summary

SG 1 Manage Requirements

- SP 1.1 Understand Requirements
- SP 1.2 Obtain Commitment to Requirements
- SP 1.3 Manage Requirements Changes
- SP 1.4 Maintain Bidirectional Traceability of Requirements
- SP 1.5 Identify Inconsistencies Between Project Work and Requirements

Specific Practices by Goal

SG 1 MANAGE REQUIREMENTS

Requirements are managed and inconsistencies with project plans and work products are identified.

The project maintains a current and approved set of requirements over the life of the project by doing the following:

- Managing all changes to requirements
- Maintaining relationships among requirements, project plans, and work products
- Identifying inconsistencies among requirements, project plans, and work products
- Taking corrective action

Refer to the Project Monitoring and Control process area for more information about taking corrective action.

Requirements management typically includes directly managing changes to customer and contractual requirements developed by the acquirer and overseeing the supplier's requirements management process. Requirements changes may result in changes to the supplier agreement.

SP 1.1 Understand Requirements

Develop an understanding with requirements providers on the meaning of requirements.

To avoid requirements creep, criteria are established to designate appropriate channels or official sources from which to receive requirements. Those receiving requirements conduct analyses of them with the provider to ensure that a compatible, shared understanding is reached on the meaning of requirements. The result of these analyses and dialog is an agreed-to set of requirements.

Typical Work Products

1. Lists of criteria for distinguishing appropriate requirements providers
2. Criteria for evaluation and acceptance of requirements
3. Results of analyses against criteria
4. An agreed-to set of requirements

Subpractices

1. Establish criteria for distinguishing appropriate requirements providers.
2. Establish objective criteria for the evaluation and acceptance of requirements.

   Lack of evaluation and acceptance criteria often results in inadequate verification, costly rework, or customer rejection.

TIP

Requirements are a vehicle used to communicate expectations with customers and suppliers. These expectations evolve as the project progresses.

TIP

"Requirements creep" is the tendency for requirements to continually flow into a project (often from multiple sources) and expand the project's scope beyond what was planned. "Unfunded requirements" or "mandates" are frequent sources of cost and schedule overruns.

Requirements come from many stakeholders. Sometimes the eventual end-user community is too diverse to work with directly and will identify a surrogate to act as its representative. This additional layer between the acquirer and the end user is a potential source of risk for requirements interpretation issues.

TIP

Examples of agreed-to sets of requirements include an operational requirements document capturing customer needs and a technical requirements document provided to suppliers as part of the solicitation package, both with appropriate sign-offs from relevant stakeholders.

TIP

Having clear lines of communication and authority when dealing with requirements helps to keep requirements creep under control.

TIP

Maintaining two-way communication through the life of the project is critical to ensuring that a shared understanding of requirements is maintained between the project and the requirements providers.

Examples of evaluation and acceptance criteria include the following:
- Clearly and properly stated
- Complete
- Consistent with one another
- Uniquely identified
- Appropriate to implement
- Verifiable (testable)
- Traceable

3. Analyze requirements to ensure that established criteria are met.
4. Reach an understanding of requirements with requirements providers so that project participants can commit to them.

HINT

If you expect changes in requirements to occur, make sure your acquisition strategy and supplier agreements include explicit mechanisms for dealing with these changes.

TIP

Project members who make commitments must continually evaluate whether they can meet their commitments, communicate immediately when they realize they cannot meet a commitment, and mitigate the impacts of not being able to meet a commitment. Commitments are a recurring theme in CMMI. They are also documented and reconciled in PP, monitored in PMC, and addressed more thoroughly in IPM.

HINT

When commitment changes cross organizational boundaries, use more formal processes and documentation to capture the changes, new commitments, and rationale for the change.

SP 1.2 Obtain Commitment to Requirements

Obtain commitment to requirements from project participants.

Refer to the Project Monitoring and Control process area for more information about monitoring the commitments made.

The previous specific practice dealt with reaching an understanding with requirements providers. This specific practice deals with agreements and commitments among those who must carry out activities necessary to implement requirements. Requirements evolve throughout the project. As requirements evolve, this specific practice ensures that project participants commit to the current and approved requirements and the resulting changes in project plans, activities, and work products.

Changes to requirements may lead to changes in supplier agreements. These changes must be agreed on by the acquirer and supplier after appropriate negotiations.

Typical Work Products

1. Requirements impact assessments
2. Documented commitments to requirements and requirements changes

Typical Supplier Deliverables

1. Supplier requirements impact assessments

Subpractices

1. Assess the impact of requirements on existing commitments.
2. Negotiate and record commitments.

Changes to existing commitments should be negotiated before project participants commit to a requirement or requirements change.

The acquirer negotiates commitments with the customer and supplier before committing to requirements changes.

> **TIP**
>
> Commitments comprise both the resources involved and the schedule for completion.

SP 1.3 Manage Requirements Changes

Manage changes to requirements as they evolve during the project.

> **TIP**
>
> Controlling changes ensures that customers, acquisition project members, and suppliers all have a clear and shared understanding of the requirements.

Refer to the Configuration Management process area for more information about maintaining and controlling the requirements baseline and making requirements and change data available to the project.

During the project, requirements change for a variety of reasons. As needs change and as work proceeds, changes may have to be made to existing requirements. It is essential to manage these additions and changes efficiently and effectively. To effectively analyze the impact of changes, it is necessary that the source of each requirement is known and the rationale for the change is documented. The project may, however, want to track appropriate measures of requirements volatility to judge whether new or revised controls are necessary.

If contractual requirements defined in the supplier agreement are affected by the changes, the supplier agreement also must be aligned with the changed requirements.

> **TIP**
>
> "Requirements volatility" is the rate at which requirements change once implementation begins. Customer requirements and contractual requirements should be assessed for volatility. Customer requirements volatility could impact the acquisition strategy and contractual requirements volatility will impact the suppliers' ability to progress as planned. It is important to identify when requirements volatility is increasing so that appropriate action can be taken.

REQM

Typical Work Products

1. Requirements change requests
2. Requirements change impact reports
3. Requirements status
4. Requirements database
5. Requirements decision database

> **HINT**
>
> Many tools are available to help acquirers manage requirements. Consider using a tool compatible with tools used by customers or suppliers to aid in requirements traceability.

Typical Supplier Deliverables

1. Requirements change requests
2. Requirements change impact reports

Subpractices

1. Document all requirements and requirements changes that are given to or generated by the project.
2. Maintain a requirements change history, including the rationale for changes.

   Maintaining the change history helps track requirements volatility.

TIP

Documentation of requirements can take many forms, including databases, electronic files, and prototypes. Sources of requirements changes can be customers, acquisition project needs and constraints, regulatory changes, or suppliers.

TIP

A change history should include rationale for the change to allow project members and other stakeholders to review why decisions were made when they are questioned later.

TIP

The acquirer maintains an important link between customer and supplier requirements. Understanding the relationship between end-user needs and how those needs are implemented in supplier products or services is critical when performing ATM and AVAL activities.

TIP

Maintaining traceability across horizontal relationships can greatly reduce problems encountered in transition to operations and support activities.

TIP

A traceability matrix can take many forms: a spreadsheet, a database, and so on.

3. Evaluate the impact of requirements changes from the standpoint of relevant stakeholders.
4. Make requirements and change data available to the project.

SP 1.4 Maintain Bidirectional Traceability of Requirements

Maintain bidirectional traceability among requirements and work products.

The intent of this specific practice is to maintain the bidirectional traceability of requirements. (See the definition of "bidirectional traceability" in the glossary.) When requirements are managed well, traceability can be established from a source requirement to its lower-level requirements and from those lower-level requirements back to their source requirements. Such bidirectional traceability helps to determine whether all source requirements have been completely addressed and whether all lower-level requirements can be traced to a valid source.

Requirements traceability can also cover relationships to other entities such as intermediate and final work products, changes in design documentation, and test plans. Traceability can cover horizontal relationships, such as across interfaces, as well as vertical relationships. Traceability is particularly needed in conducting the impact assessment of requirements changes on project activities and work products.

The supplier maintains comprehensive bidirectional traceability to requirements defined in the supplier agreement by the acquirer, and the acquirer verifies that traceability. The acquirer maintains bidirectional traceability between customer requirements and contractual requirements.

Typical Work Products

1. Requirements traceability matrix
2. Requirements tracking system

Typical Supplier Deliverables

1. Comprehensive requirements traceability matrix managed by the supplier as required by the supplier agreement

Subpractices

1. Maintain requirements traceability to ensure that the source of lower-level (derived) requirements is documented.

Traceability from customer to contractual requirements is maintained by the acquirer. Traceability from contractual requirements to derived or additional requirements is maintained by the supplier.

2. Maintain requirements traceability from a requirement to its derived requirements and allocation to functions, interfaces, objects, people, processes, and work products.
3. Generate a requirements traceability matrix.

   A comprehensive traceability matrix tracing from customer requirements to contractor requirements is maintained by the acquirer. A comprehensive traceability matrix tracing from contractual requirements to lower-level requirements is maintained by the supplier.

HINT

When a requirement changes, use the traceability matrix to evaluate the impact that change has on supplier deliverables and customer needs.

SP 1.5 Identify Inconsistencies Between Project Work and Requirements

Identify inconsistencies between project plans and work products and requirements.

Refer to the Project Monitoring and Control process area for more information about monitoring and controlling project plans and work products for consistency with requirements and taking corrective actions when necessary.

This specific practice finds inconsistencies between requirements and project plans and work products and initiates corrective actions to resolve them.

Corrective actions taken by the project to resolve inconsistencies may also result in changes to project plans and supplier agreements.

Typical Work Products

1. Documentation of inconsistencies between requirements and project plans and work products, including sources and conditions
2. Corrective actions

Subpractices

1. Review project plans, activities, and work products for consistency with requirements and changes made to them.
2. Identify the source of the inconsistency.
3. Identify changes that must be made to plans and work products resulting from changes to the requirements baseline.
4. Initiate corrective actions.

TIP

Especially for large projects, product components are developed in parallel, sometimes by multiple suppliers, and it is challenging to keep all work products fully consistent with changes to the requirements.

HINT

Make sure acquisition planning documents, such as systems engineering plans and operational test and evaluation plans, are consistent. When a supplier or suppliers are selected, review supplier plans to ensure that they are consistent with acquisition planning documents.

TIP

A traceability matrix can help with this review of project plans, activities, and work products.

RISK MANAGEMENT

A Project Management Process Area at Maturity Level 3

Purpose

The purpose of Risk Management (RSKM) is to identify potential problems before they occur so that risk-handling activities can be planned and invoked as needed across the life of the product or project to mitigate adverse impacts on achieving objectives.

TIP

RSKM also can apply to identifying, evaluating, and maximizing (or realizing) *opportunities*. In a dynamic environment, risk management must be a continuous process of identifying, analyzing, and monitoring risks.

Introductory Notes

Risk management is a continuous, forward-looking process that is an important part of project management. Risk management should address issues that could endanger achievement of critical objectives. A continuous risk management approach effectively anticipates and mitigates risks that may have a critical impact on a project.

Effective risk management includes early and aggressive risk identification through collaboration and the involvement of relevant stakeholders as described in the stakeholder involvement plan addressed in the Project Planning process area. Strong leadership across all relevant stakeholders is needed to establish an environment for free and open disclosure and discussion of risk.

Risk management must consider both internal and external sources of cost, schedule, performance, and other risks. Early and aggressive detection of risk is important because it is typically easier, less costly, and less disruptive to make changes and correct work efforts during the earlier, rather than the later, phases of the project.

When the project identifies and assesses project risks during project planning and manages risks throughout the life of the project, risk identification includes identifying risks associated with the acquisition process and the use of a supplier to perform project work. Initially, the acquisition strategy identifies risks associated with an acquisition. The approach to the acquisition is planned based on those risks. As the project progresses to the selection of a

TIP

Without a free and open environment, many risks remain undisclosed until they surface as problems, when it is often too late to address them. Free and open discussions should involve customers and other stakeholders when the acquisition strategy is being formulated; involve potential suppliers when negotiations are taking place; and involve suppliers when the supplier agreement is being established and throughout the project.

X-REF

PP and PMC contain risk-management-related practices: See PP SP 2.2, Identify Project Risks; and PMC SP 1.3, Monitor Project Risks.

HINT

Relevant stakeholders external to the project bring perspectives and insight into identifying and evaluating risks. This is particularly true when your project is contributing to a system of systems. It is important to maintain a dialog on related risks pertaining to other systems in the system of systems.

TIP

For an acquisition organization, sources of risk are not just technical, but are often programmatic and related to funding. Although it may be valuable to manage risks with the supplier, recognize that there are supplier risks, acquirer risks, and shared risks. Each needs to be managed by the appropriate stakeholders.

HINT

Make sure you include end users. Capabilities are acquired to mitigate operational risk; however, the deployment of new capabilities may increase operational risk if they are not managed properly.

X-REF

To help end users participate in the risk process, see the SEI report, "A Taxonomy of Operational Risks" (CMU/SEI-2005-TN-036).

supplier, risks specific to the supplier's technical and management approach become important to the success of the acquisition.

These risks refer to the capability of the supplier to meet contractual requirements, including schedules and cost targets. When the project selects a supplier and awards the supplier agreement, the acquirer continues to manage project risks, including risks related to the supplier meeting its contractual requirements. Typically, the acquirer does not manage risks being addressed or managed by the supplier.

Risk management can be divided into three parts: defining a risk management strategy; identifying and analyzing risks; and handling identified risks, including the implementation of risk mitigation plans as needed.

Both the acquirer and supplier must understand project risks and how to modify the risk management strategy and plans as a project progresses through its lifecycle. Managing project risks requires a close partnership between the acquirer and supplier. Both must share appropriate risk management documentation, understand the risks, and develop and execute risk management activities.

The complexity of an acquirer–supplier relationship increases the need for early and aggressive risk identification. For example, acquirer capabilities, supplier experience working with the acquirer, financial stability of the supplier, and availability of well-defined dispute resolution processes all influence the risk of a project.

As represented in the Project Planning and Project Monitoring and Control process areas, organizations initially may focus on risk identification for awareness, and react to the realization of these risks as they occur. The Risk Management process area describes an evolution of these specific practices to systematically plan, anticipate, and mitigate risks to proactively minimize their impact on the project.

Although the primary emphasis of the Risk Management process area is on the project, these concepts can also be applied to manage organizational risks.

Related Process Areas

Refer to the Project Planning process area for more information about identifying project risks and planning the involvement of relevant stakeholders.

Refer to the Project Monitoring and Control process area for more information about monitoring project risks.

Refer to the Decision Analysis and Resolution process area for more information about using a formal evaluation process to evaluate alternatives for the selection and mitigation of identified risks.

Refer to the Solicitation and Supplier Agreement Development process area for more information about establishing supplier agreements.

HINT

A precondition to efficient risk management is to have shared and consistent project objectives among customers, the acquisition organization, and suppliers. Project objectives provide focus to risk management and help guide its activities.

Specific Goal and Practice Summary

SG 1 Prepare for Risk Management
- SP 1.1 Determine Risk Sources and Categories
- SP 1.2 Define Risk Parameters
- SP 1.3 Establish a Risk Management Strategy

SG 2 Identify and Analyze Risks
- SP 2.1 Identify Risks
- SP 2.2 Evaluate, Categorize, and Prioritize Risks

SG 3 Mitigate Risks
- SP 3.1 Develop Risk Mitigation Plans
- SP 3.2 Implement Risk Mitigation Plans

X-REF

For more information, see "Software Risk Management: Principles and Practices" by Barry Boehm (IEEE Software, 1990); Project Management Institute, *A Guide to the Project Management Body of Knowledge* (PMBOK Guide) Third Edition, 2004 (Chapter 11 deals with risk management); and www.sei.cmu.edu/risk/.

Specific Practices by Goal

SG 1 Prepare for Risk Management

Preparation for risk management is conducted.

Prepare for risk management by establishing and maintaining a strategy for identifying, analyzing, and mitigating risks. Typically, this strategy is documented in a risk management plan. The risk management strategy addresses specific actions and the management approach used to apply and control the risk management program. The strategy typically includes identifying sources of risk, the scheme used to categorize risks, and parameters used to evaluate, bound, and control risks for effective handling.

TIP

If your project uses safety and security analysis methods, incorporate these methods as part of the risk management strategy.

SP 1.1 Determine Risk Sources and Categories

Determine risk sources and categories.

Identifying risk sources provides a basis for systematically examining changing situations over time to uncover circumstances that impact the ability of the project to meet its objectives. Risk sources are both internal and external to the project. As the project progresses, additional sources of risk may be identified. Establishing categories for risks provides a mechanism for collecting and organizing risks as well as ensuring appropriate scrutiny and management attention to risks that can have serious consequences on meeting project objectives.

Acquirers initially identify and categorize risk sources and categories for the project and refine those sources and categories over time (e.g., schedule, cost, sourcing, contract management, supplier execution, technology readiness, human safety, reliability-related risks, and other issues outside the control of the acquirer). The supplier is also a source of risk (e.g., financial stability of the supplier and the possibility of the supplier's acquisition by another organization).

TIP

Under stress, people lose perspective when it comes to risks. Some risks (e.g., those external to the project) may be given too much emphasis and others too little. Having a list of risk sources, both internal and external, helps bring objectivity to the identification of risks.

Typical Work Products

1. Risk source lists (external and internal)
2. Risk categories list

Subpractices

1. Determine risk sources.

   Risk sources are fundamental drivers that cause risks in a project or organization. There are many sources of risks, both internal and external to a project. Risk sources identify where risks may originate.

TIP

In a typical project, risks and their status change. A standard list of risk sources enables a project to be thorough in its identification of risks at each point in the project.

Typical internal and external risk sources include the following:
- Uncertain requirements
- Unprecedented efforts (i.e., estimates unavailable)
- Infeasible design
- Unavailable technology
- Unrealistic schedule estimates or allocation
- Inadequate staffing and skills
- Cost or funding issues
- Uncertain or inadequate subcontractor capability
- Uncertain or inadequate supplier capability
- Inadequate communication with customers
- Disruptions to the continuity of operations

TIP

Disruption to the continuity of operations is an external source. If neglected, it may have huge consequences. If mitigated, the mitigation is often cost-effective.

   Many of these sources of risk are often accepted without adequately planning for them. Early identification of both internal and external sources of risk can lead to early identification of risks. Risk mitigation plans can then be implemented early in the project to preclude occurrence of risks or reduce consequences of their occurrence.

2. Determine risk categories.

   Risk categories are the "bins" used for collecting and organizing risks. Identifying risk categories aids the future consolidation of activities in risk mitigation plans.

The following factors may be considered when determining risk categories:

- Phases of the project's lifecycle model (e.g., requirements, design, manufacturing, test and evaluation, delivery, and disposal)
- Types of processes used
- Types of products used
- Project management risks (e.g., contract risks, budget/cost risks, schedule risks, resource risks, performance risks, and supportability risks)
- Supplier risks (e.g., financial viability of the supplier and the geographic location of supplier resources)
- Product safety, security, and reliability

TIP

Categories are used to group related risks that can often be addressed by the same mitigation activities, thereby increasing risk management efficiency.

TIP

Risks are often grouped by lifecycle phase.

A risk taxonomy can be used to provide a framework for determining risk sources and categories.

SP 1.2 Define Risk Parameters

Define parameters used to analyze and categorize risks and to control the risk management effort.

Parameters for evaluating, categorizing, and prioritizing risks include the following:

- Risk likelihood (i.e., probability of risk occurrence)
- Risk consequence (i.e., impact and severity of risk occurrence)
- Thresholds to trigger management activities

Risk parameters are used to provide common and consistent criteria for comparing risks to be managed. Without these parameters, it is difficult to gauge the severity of an unwanted change caused by a risk and to prioritize the actions required for risk mitigation planning.

Acquirers should document the parameters used to analyze and categorize risks so they are available for reference throughout the life of the project since circumstances change over time. Using these parameters, risks can easily be recategorized and analyzed when changes occur.

The acquirer may use tools such as *failure mode and effects analysis* to examine risks such as potential failures in products or processes. A tool may also be used to evaluate risk management priorities for mitigating known threat vulnerabilities.

X-REF

The risk taxonomies developed at the SEI and mentioned in Barry Boehm's and Vic Basili's "Top 10" Software Risks (www.cebase.org/www/AboutCebase/News/top-10-defects.html) are useful even after a decade.

Typical Work Products

1. Risk evaluation, categorization, and prioritization criteria
2. Risk management requirements (e.g., control and approval levels and reassessment intervals)

Subpractices

1. Define consistent criteria for evaluating and quantifying risk likelihood and severity levels.

   Consistently used criteria (e.g., bounds on likelihood and severity levels) allow impacts of different risks to be commonly understood, to receive the appropriate level of scrutiny, and to obtain the management attention warranted. In managing dissimilar risks (e.g., personnel safety versus environmental pollution), it is important to ensure consistency in the end result (e.g., a high risk of environmental pollution is as important as a high risk to personnel safety).

2. Define thresholds for each risk category.

   For each risk category, thresholds can be established to determine acceptability or unacceptability of risks, prioritization of risks, or triggers for management action.

> Examples of thresholds include the following.
> - Project-wide thresholds could be established to involve senior management when product costs exceed 10 percent of the target cost or when cost performance indices (CPIs) fall below 0.95.
> - Schedule thresholds could be established to involve senior management when schedule performance indices (SPIs) fall below 0.95.
> - Performance thresholds could be established to involve senior management when specified key items (e.g., processor utilization or average response times) exceed 125 percent of the intended design.

   For each identified risk, establish points at which more aggressive risk monitoring is employed or to signal the implementation of risk mitigation plans. These points can be redefined later in the project as necessary.

3. Define bounds on the extent to which thresholds are applied against or within a category.

   There are few limits to which risks can be assessed in either a quantitative or qualitative fashion. Definition of bounds (or boundary conditions) can be used to help define the extent of the risk management effort and avoid excessive resource expenditures. Bounds may include the exclusion of a risk source from a category. These bounds can also exclude any condition that occurs less than a given frequency.

TIP

To be effective, risk management must be objective and quantitative. Therefore, you must treat risks consistently with respect to key parameters. Defining criteria for evaluating risks helps to ensure consistency

TIP

In the middle of a project, you often lose perspective. Defining thresholds in advance enables a more objective treatment of risks.

TIP

These thresholds may need to be refined later as part of risk mitigation planning.

TIP

Bounds are intended to scope the risk management effort in sensible ways that help to conserve project resources.

SP 1.3 Establish a Risk Management Strategy

Establish and maintain the strategy to be used for risk management.

A comprehensive risk management strategy addresses items such as the following:

TIP

The risk management strategy documents the results of the first two specific practices.

- The scope of the risk management effort
- Methods and tools to be used for risk identification, risk analysis, risk mitigation, risk monitoring, and communication
- Project-specific sources of risks
- How risks are to be organized, categorized, compared, and consolidated
- Parameters used for taking action on identified risks, including likelihood, consequence, and thresholds
- Risk mitigation techniques to be used, such as prototyping, piloting, simulation, alternative designs, or evolutionary development
- The definition of risk measures used to monitor the status of risks
- Time intervals for risk monitoring or reassessment

The risk management strategy should be guided by a common vision of success that describes desired future project outcomes in terms of the product delivered, its cost, and its fitness for the task. The risk management strategy is often documented in an organizational or project risk management plan. This strategy is reviewed with relevant stakeholders to promote commitment and understanding.

A risk management strategy must be developed early in the project so that relevant risks are identified and managed aggressively. The acquisition strategy evolves based on risk identification and analysis. Early identification and assessment of critical risks allows the acquirer to formulate risk-handling approaches and streamline the project definition and solicitation around critical product and process risks.

TIP

Some large acquisition organizations develop a standard risk management strategy template that is tailored to meet the needs of individual projects.

Typical Work Products

1. Project risk management strategy

TIP

The risk management strategy is often documented as part of a risk management plan, or as a section in the project plan. All relevant stakeholders must understand fully the risk management strategy.

SG 2 Identify and Analyze Risks

Risks are identified and analyzed to determine their relative importance.

The degree of risk affects the resources assigned to handle the risk and the timing of when appropriate management attention is required.

Risk analysis entails identifying risks from identified internal and external sources and evaluating each identified risk to determine its likelihood and consequences. Risk categorization, based on an evaluation against established risk categories and criteria developed for the risk management strategy, provides information needed for risk-handling. Related risks may be grouped to enable efficient handling and effective use of risk management resources.

TIP

Risk identification and analysis is an activity that continues for the duration of the project.

TIP

"Can a project have no risks?" "Can multiple projects have the same risk lists?" If these questions are asked, someone does not understand risks. Some risks may be product-specific, contract-specific, or supplier-specific.

TIP

The context, conditions, and consequences of a risk statement provide much of the information that is needed later to understand and evaluate the risk.

HINT

Establish a work environment in which risks can be disclosed and discussed openly, without fear of repercussions. (Don't shoot the messenger!)

TIP

Many of the methods used for identifying risks use organizational process assets such as a risk taxonomy, risk repository, and lessons learned from past projects. Subject-matter experts may also be utilized. Other methods involve reviewing project artifacts such as the project's shared vision, project interfaces, and contractual requirements.

SP 2.1 Identify Risks

Identify and document risks.

Identifying potential issues, hazards, threats, and vulnerabilities that could negatively affect work efforts or plans is the basis for sound and successful risk management. Risks must be identified and described understandably before they can be analyzed and managed properly. Risks are documented in a concise statement that includes the context, conditions, and consequences of risk occurrence.

Risk identification should be an organized, thorough approach to seek out probable or realistic risks that may affect achieving objectives. To be effective, risk identification should not attempt to address every possible event regardless of how improbable it may be. Using categories and parameters developed in the risk management strategy and identified sources of risk can provide the discipline and streamlining appropriate for risk identification. Identified risks form a baseline for initiating risk management activities. Risks should be reviewed periodically to reexamine possible sources of risk and changing conditions to uncover sources and risks previously overlooked or nonexistent when the risk management strategy was last updated.

Risk identification focuses on identifying risks, not placement of blame. The results of risk identification activities should never be used by management to evaluate the performance of individuals.

There are many methods used for identifying risks. Typical identification methods include the following.

- Examine each element of the project work breakdown structure.
- Conduct a risk assessment using a risk taxonomy.
- Interview subject-matter experts.
- Review risk management efforts from similar products.
- Examine lessons-learned documents or databases.
- Examine design specifications and agreement requirements.

Some risks are identified by examining the supplier's WBS, product, and processes using the categories and parameters developed in the risk management strategy. Risks can be identified in many areas (e.g., requirements, technology, design, testing, vulnerability to threats, and lifecycle costs). An examination of the project in these areas can help to develop or refine the acquisition strategy and the risk-sharing structure between the acquirer and supplier.

The acquirer considers risks associated with a supplier's capability (e.g., meeting schedule and cost requirements for the project), including potential risks to the acquirer's intellectual capital or security vulnerabilities introduced by using a supplier.

Typical Work Products

1. List of identified risks, including the context, conditions, and consequences of risk occurrence

Typical Supplier Deliverables

1. List of identified risks, including the context, conditions, and consequences of risk occurrence

Subpractices

1. Identify the risks associated with cost, schedule, and performance.

   Cost, schedule, and performance risks should be examined in the acquirer's intended environment to the extent that they impact project objectives. Potential risks may be discovered that are outside the scope of project objectives but are vital to customer interests. For example, risks in development costs, product acquisition costs, cost of spare (or replacement) products, and product disposition (or disposal) costs have design implications. The customer may not have considered the full cost of supporting a fielded product or using a delivered service. The customer should be informed of such risks, but actively managing those risks may not be necessary. Mechanisms for making such decisions should be examined at project and organization levels and put in place if deemed appropriate, especially for risks that impact the project's ability to verify and validate the product.

   In addition to the cost risks identified earlier, other cost risks may include those associated with funding levels, funding estimates, and distributed budgets.

   Schedule risks may include risks associated with planned activities, key events, and milestones.

Performance risks may include risks associated with the following:

- Requirements
- Analysis and design
- Application of new technology
- Physical size
- Shape
- Weight
- Manufacturing and fabrication
- Functional performance and operation
- Verification
- Validation
- Performance maintenance attributes

TIP

One approach to identifying risks is to consider the cost, schedule, and performance issues associated with each lifecycle phase. Since each phase typically has a clear set of objectives and a completion milestone, a phase is a suitable context for identifying the risks associated with that phase.

HINT

When necessary, explain to customers the implications of their requirements, as they may not be aware of the acquisition risks associated with certain requirements. However, once they are aware of the risk, they may decide to keep the requirements as desired.

TIP

Performance risks may be associated with lifecycle phases, new technology, or desired attributes of the product.

Performance maintenance attributes are those characteristics that enable an in-use product or service to provide required performance, such as maintaining safety and security performance.

There are other risks that do not fall into cost, schedule, or performance categories.

Examples of these other risks include those related to the following:
- Strikes
- Diminishing sources of supply
- Technology cycle time
- Competition

TIP

Environmental risks are often ignored, even though some cost-effective mitigation activities are possible.

2. Review environmental elements that may impact the project.

   Risks to a project that frequently are missed include those supposedly outside the scope of the project (i.e., the project does not control whether they occur but can mitigate their impact), such as weather, natural or manmade disasters that affect the continuity of operations, political changes, and telecommunications failures.
3. Review all elements of the work breakdown structure as part of identifying risks to help ensure that all aspects of the work effort have been considered.
4. Review all elements of the project plan as part of identifying risks to help ensure that all aspects of the project have been considered.

   Refer to the Project Planning process area for more information about identifying project risks.

TIP

A good risk statement is fact-based, actionable, and brief.

TIP

A standard format for documenting risks makes it easier to train personnel on what is needed in risk statements.

5. Document the context, conditions, and potential consequences of each risk.

   Risk statements are typically documented in a standard format that contains the risk context, conditions, and consequences of occurrence. The risk context provides additional information about the risk such as the relative time frame of the risk, the circumstances or conditions surrounding the risk that have brought about the concern, and any doubt or uncertainty.
6. Identify the relevant stakeholders associated with each risk.

SP 2.2 EVALUATE, CATEGORIZE, AND PRIORITIZE RISKS

Evaluate and categorize each identified risk using defined risk categories and parameters, and determine its relative priority.

The evaluation of risks is needed to assign a relative importance to each identified risk and is used in determining when appropriate management attention is required. Often, it is useful to aggregate risks based on their interrelationships and to develop options at an aggregate level. When an aggregate risk is formed by a roll-up of lower-level risks, care must be taken to ensure that important lower-level risks are not ignored.

Collectively, the activities of risk evaluation, categorization, and prioritization are sometimes called a *risk assessment* or *risk analysis*.

The acquirer should conduct a risk assessment before solicitation to evaluate if the project can achieve its technical, schedule, and budget constraints. Technical, schedule, and cost risks should be discussed with potential suppliers before the solicitation is released. Using this approach, critical risks inherent in the project can be identified and addressed in the solicitation.

HINT

You can simplify risk management when you can treat a number of risks as one group from evaluation and mitigation perspectives.

Typical Work Products

1. List of risks and their assigned priority

Typical Supplier Deliverables

1. List of risks and their assigned priority

Subpractices

1. Evaluate identified risks using defined risk parameters.

   Each risk is evaluated and assigned values according to defined risk parameters, which may include likelihood, consequence (severity or impact), and thresholds. The assigned risk parameter values can be integrated to produce additional measures, such as risk exposure, which can be used to prioritize risks for handling.

   Often, a scale with three to five values is used to evaluate both likelihood and consequence.

TIP

Risk exposure is the result of the combination of the likelihood and the consequence of a risk (expressed quantitatively).

Likelihood, for example, can be categorized as remote, unlikely, likely, highly likely, or near certainty.

Example categories for consequence include the following:

- Low
- Medium
- High
- Negligible
- Marginal
- Significant
- Critical
- Catastrophic

TIP

Determining values for risk likelihood and consequence is easier and more repeatable if objectives are stated clearly, criteria exist for assigning values, relevant stakeholders are appropriately represented, and personnel have been trained.

Probability values are frequently used to quantify likelihood. Consequences are generally related to cost, schedule, environmental impact, or human measures (e.g., labor hours lost and severity of injury).

Risk evaluation is often a difficult and time-consuming task. Specific expertise or group techniques may be needed to assess risks and gain confidence in the prioritization. In addition, priorities may require reevaluation as time progresses.

2. Categorize and group risks according to defined risk categories.

   Risks are categorized into defined risk categories, providing a means to review them according to their source, taxonomy, or project component. Related or equivalent risks may be grouped for efficient handling. The cause-and-effect relationships between related risks are documented.

An acquirer's risk categories may include sourcing, contract management, and supplier execution, in addition to project management, technology, and requirements.

3. Prioritize risks for mitigation.

   A relative priority is determined for each risk based on assigned risk parameters. Clear criteria should be used to determine risk priority.

   Risk prioritization helps to determine the most effective areas to which resources for risks mitigation can be applied with the greatest positive impact to the project.

TIP

Priority assignment can likewise be a repeatable process.

SG 3 *Mitigate Risks*

Risks are handled and mitigated, as appropriate, to reduce adverse impacts on achieving objectives.

X-REF

RSKM heavily influences technical management (i.e., to adjust requirements, design, implementation, verification, and validation in light of risks and risk mitigation), project management (i.e., to plan for these activities and monitor thresholds that trigger the deployment of mitigation plans), and agreement management (i.e., to understand how these activities are reflected in the supplier agreement).

The steps in handling risks include developing risk-handling options, monitoring risks, and performing risk-handling activities when defined thresholds are exceeded. Risk mitigation plans are developed and implemented for selected risks to proactively reduce the potential impact of risk occurrence. Risk mitigation planning can also include contingency plans to deal with the impact of selected risks that may occur despite attempts to mitigate them. Risk parameters used to trigger risk-handling activities are defined by the risk management strategy.

SP 3.1 *Develop Risk Mitigation Plans*

Develop a risk mitigation plan for the most important risks to the project as defined by the risk management strategy.

A critical component of a risk mitigation planning is developing alternative courses of action, workarounds, and fallback positions, and a recommended course of action for each critical risk. The risk mitigation plan for a given risk includes techniques and methods used to avoid, reduce, and control the probability of risk occurrence, the extent of damage incurred should the risk occur (sometimes called a *contingency plan*), or both. Risks are monitored, and when they exceed established thresholds risk mitigation plans are deployed to return the impacted effort to an acceptable risk level. If the risk cannot be mitigated, a contingency plan can be invoked. Both risk mitigation and contingency plans often are generated only for selected risks for which consequences of the risks are high or unacceptable; other risks may be accepted and simply monitored.

TIP

The risk management literature uses the term *contingency plans* in various ways. In CMMI, a risk contingency plan is the part of a risk mitigation plan that addresses what actions to take *after* a risk is realized.

HINT

Reward personnel who prevent crises, not those who allow a crisis to happen and then heroically resolve it.

Options for handling risks typically include alternatives such as the following:

- Risk avoidance: changing or lowering requirements while still meeting user needs
- Risk control: taking active steps to minimize risks
- Risk transfer: reallocating requirements to lower risks
- Risk monitoring: watching and periodically reevaluating the risk for changes in assigned risk parameters
- Risk acceptance: acknowledging risk but not taking action

HINT

One way to identify actions that will avoid, reduce, or control a risk is to perform a causal analysis on the sources of the risk. Actions that eliminate or reduce causes may be suitable candidates for inclusion in a risk mitigation plan.

Often, especially for high risks, more than one approach to handling a risk should be generated.

TIP

A risk mitigation plan should, when its associated threshold is exceeded, return the project to an acceptable risk level.

For example, in the case of an event that disrupts the continuity of operations, approaches to risk management can include establishing the following:

- Resource reserves to respond to disruptive events
- Lists of available back-up equipment
- Back-up personnel for key personnel
- Plans for and results of testing emergency response systems
- Posted procedures for emergencies
- Disseminated lists of key contacts and information resources for emergencies

In many cases, risks are accepted or watched. Risk acceptance is usually done when the risk is judged too low for formal mitigation or when there appears to be no viable way to reduce the risk. If a risk is accepted, the rationale for this decision should be documented. Risks are watched when there is an objectively defined,

HINT

You can establish thresholds for different attributes (e.g., cost, schedule, and performance) and trigger different activities (e.g., contingency plan deployment and risk mitigation planning).

verifiable, and documented threshold of performance, time, or risk exposure (i.e., the combination of likelihood and consequence) that will trigger risk mitigation planning or invoke a contingency plan.

Thresholds for supplier risks that affect the project (e.g., schedule, quality, or risk exposure due to supplier risks) are specified in the supplier agreement along with escalation procedures if thresholds are exceeded.

Adequate consideration should be given early to technology demonstrations, models, simulations, pilots, and prototypes as part of risk mitigation planning.

Typical Work Products

1. Documented handling options for each identified risk
2. Risk mitigation plans
3. Contingency plans
4. Disaster recovery or continuity plans
5. List of those responsible for tracking and addressing each risk

Typical Supplier Deliverables

1. Documented handling options for each identified risk
2. Risk mitigation plans
3. Contingency plans
4. Disaster recovery or continuity plans
5. List of those responsible for tracking and addressing each risk

Subpractices

TIP

Thresholds trigger actions that may impact the work of personnel and relevant stakeholders. Thus, it is important to ensure that the motivation for particular thresholds and the actions they invoke are well understood by all who will be affected.

TIP

Assigning responsibility for risk mitigation is easier to do if mitigation activities and responsibilities are documented in a plan, such as the project plan.

1. Determine the levels and thresholds that define when a risk becomes unacceptable and triggers the execution of a risk mitigation plan or contingency plan.

   Risk level (derived using a risk model) is a measure combining the uncertainty of reaching an objective with the consequences of failing to reach the objective.

   Risk levels and thresholds that bound planned or acceptable performance must be clearly understood and defined to provide a means with which risk can be understood. Proper categorization of risk is essential for ensuring an appropriate priority based on severity and the associated management response. There may be multiple thresholds employed to initiate varying levels of management response. Typically, thresholds for the execution of risk mitigation plans are set to engage before the execution of contingency plans.

2. Identify the person or group responsible for addressing each risk.

3. Determine the cost-to-benefit ratio of implementing the risk mitigation plan for each risk.

   Risk mitigation activities should be examined for benefits they provide versus resources they will expend. Just like any other design activity, alternative plans may need to be developed and costs and benefits of each alternative assessed. The most appropriate plan is selected for implementation.

4. Develop an overall risk mitigation plan for the project to orchestrate the implementation of individual risk mitigation and contingency plans.

   The complete set of risk mitigation plans may not be affordable. A tradeoff analysis should be performed to prioritize risk mitigation plans for implementation.

5. Develop contingency plans for selected critical risks in the event their impacts are realized.

   Risk mitigation plans are developed and implemented as needed to proactively reduce risks before they become problems. Despite best efforts, some risks may be unavoidable and will become problems that impact the project. Contingency plans can be developed for critical risks to describe actions a project may take to deal with the occurrence of this impact. The intent is to define a proactive plan for handling the risk, either to reduce the risk (mitigation) or to respond to the risk (contingency), but in either event to manage the risk.

   Some risk management literature may consider contingency plans a synonym or subset of risk mitigation plans. These plans also may be addressed together as risk-handling or risk action plans.

TIP

Alternative risk mitigation plans may be formally evaluated (using DAR) to choose the best one. Relevant stakeholders may play an important role in such an evaluation (particularly for risks that impact them).

HINT

If you integrate all risk mitigation plans and find that the result is not affordable, trim the list using the priorities assigned in SP 2.2 or reprioritize them using a group-consensus approach (e.g., multivoting within risk categories).

SP 3.2 Implement Risk Mitigation Plans

Monitor the status of each risk periodically and implement the risk mitigation plan, as appropriate.

To effectively control and manage risks during the work effort, follow a proactive program to regularly monitor risks and the status and results of risk-handling actions. The risk management strategy defines the intervals at which risk status should be revisited. This activity may result in the discovery of new risks or new risk-handling options that can require replanning and reassessment. In either event, acceptability thresholds associated with the risk should be compared to the risk status to determine the need for implementing a risk mitigation plan.

The acquirer shares selected risks with the supplier. Risks associated with the acquisition process are tracked and resolved or controlled until mitigated. This monitoring includes risks that may be escalated by the supplier.

HINT

Make sure you monitor both the mitigation activity as well as the risk itself. Don't assume the risk is mitigated simply because the mitigation plan is executed. Unintended consequences or additional complexity may cause the risk exposure to increase when you expect it to decrease.

TIP

Weekly or monthly updates to risk status are typical.

TIP

Incorporating risk mitigation plans into the project plan enables their status to be reviewed as part of the project's regular progress reviews.

Typical Work Products

1. Updated lists of risk status
2. Updated assessments of risk likelihood, consequence, and thresholds
3. Updated list of risk-handling options
4. Updated list of actions taken to handle risks
5. Risk mitigation plans

Typical Supplier Deliverables

1. Updated list of risk status
2. Updated assessments of risk likelihood, consequence, and thresholds
3. Updated list of risk-handling options
4. Updated list of actions taken to handle risks
5. Risk mitigation plans

Subpractices

1. Monitor risk status.

   After a risk mitigation plan is initiated, the risk is still monitored. Thresholds are assessed to check for the potential execution of a contingency plan.

   A mechanism for monitoring should be employed.

2. Provide a method for tracking open risk-handling action items to closure.

   Refer to the Project Monitoring and Control process area for more information about tracking action items.

3. Invoke selected risk-handling options when monitored risks exceed defined thresholds.

   Often, risk-handling is performed only for risks judged to be "high" and "medium." The risk-handling strategy for a given risk may include techniques and methods to avoid, reduce, and control the likelihood of the risk or the extent of damage incurred should the risk (anticipated event or situation) occur or both. In this context, risk-handling includes both risk mitigation plans and contingency plans.

   Risk-handling techniques are developed to avoid, reduce, and control adverse impact to project objectives and to bring about acceptable outcomes in light of probable impacts. Actions generated to handle a risk require proper resource loading and scheduling in plans and baseline schedules. This replanning must closely consider the effects on adjacent or dependent work initiatives or activities.

   Refer to the Project Monitoring and Control process area for more information about revising the project plan.

TIP

To ensure that risk mitigation activities are performed properly, they must be planned, scheduled, and resourced, just like any other project activity.

4. Establish a schedule or period of performance for each risk-handling activity that includes a start date and anticipated completion date.
5. Provide a continued commitment of resources for each plan to allow the successful execution of risk-handling activities.
6. Collect performance measures on risk-handling activities.

SOLICITATION AND SUPPLIER AGREEMENT DEVELOPMENT

An Acquisition Process Area at Maturity Level 2

Purpose

The purpose of Solicitation and Supplier Agreement Development (SSAD) is to prepare a solicitation package, select one or more suppliers to deliver the product or service, and establish and maintain the supplier agreement.

HINT

SSAD helps you prevent such problems as suppliers that can't meet requirements, supplier agreements that prevent a proactive approach to supplier management, and suppliers that provide poor visibility into their activities.

Introductory Notes

The Solicitation and Supplier Agreement Development process area provides a set of practices that enables the acquirer to initialize and formalize a relationship with the supplier for the successful execution of the project. A supplier agreement is an agreement between the acquirer and supplier. This agreement may be a contract, license, or memorandum of agreement. The acquired product or service is delivered to the acquirer from the supplier according to the supplier agreement.

A supplier agreement created using these practices enables the acquirer to monitor and control supplier activities using other process areas, such as Project Monitoring and Control and Agreement Management.

The practices of this process area apply equally to initial supplier agreements and to subsequent change orders, task orders, or amendments related to those agreements.

The acquirer is responsible for establishing and maintaining ground rules for communicating with the supplier, documenting decisions, and resolving conflict through the life of the agreement. The acquirer facilitates these activities with relevant stakeholders. Roles and responsibilities of relevant stakeholders during the interaction with suppliers are defined, coordinated, and adhered to.

The specific goals and specific practices of this process area build on each other. The Prepare for Solicitation and Supplier Agreement

X-REF

The entry point for SSAD is normally PP SP 1.1, once the acquisition strategy is established.

TIP

By maturing the approach to SSAD, an agreement can be developed more quickly. Uniform selection approaches and standardized agreements benefit both the acquisition organization and its suppliers. Effective emphasis on SSAD ensures that AM processes flow more easily.

HINT

Taking a broad view when applying SSAD can help reduce business-critical risks in obtaining products and services from suppliers.

TIP

In some cases, agreements may also be necessary with the customer, particularly when the customer organization is significantly different from the acquisition organization. If a customer agreement is useful, the practices in SSAD can be tailored to aid the creation of these agreements as well. The acquirer, in these cases, may be viewed as the supplier to the ultimate customer.

Development specific goal and its associated specific practices identify potential suppliers and develop and distribute the solicitation package, including evaluation criteria and the statement of work. The solicitation package is developed using work products from other process areas (e.g., requirements and design constraints from Acquisition Requirements Development, supplier project and technical measures and objectives from Project Planning and Measurement and Analysis).

The Select Suppliers specific goal and its associated specific practices use work products from the preparation of the solicitation to solicit responses from potential suppliers, evaluate these responses, negotiate with potential suppliers, and select a supplier who can best deliver. Subsequently, the Establish Supplier Agreements specific goal and its associated specific practices are used to establish and maintain the supplier agreement. In turn, data provided by the supplier and documented in the supplier agreement (e.g., cost, schedule, risks) are used by Project Planning practices to update the project plan.

This process area contains many lists of examples to include in work products. As in other process areas, these lists are not all-inclusive and the acquirer should rely on other related lists when building work products. Considerations for supplier agreement content are described throughout the process areas.

Although this process area describes acquisition practices for a project, an acquirer would use the same practices in establishing a supplier agreement for multiple projects. The requirements included in the solicitation package and the supplier agreement would reflect a broader scope, and the evaluation and selection process would require an appropriate level of review before a selection is made.

Related Process Areas

Refer to the Project Planning process area for more information about planning for solicitation, developing and documenting the project plan for the acquisition, estimating the supplier's work, and revising the project plan.

Refer to the Measurement and Analysis process area for more information about specifying project measurement data.

Refer to the Acquisition Requirements Development process area for more information about defining customer and contractual requirements.

Refer to the Requirements Management process area for more information about managing requirements, including changes to requirements and traceability of requirements for products acquired from suppliers.

Refer to the Agreement Management process area for more information about monitoring and analyzing selected supplier activities and processes based on the supplier agreement.

Refer to the Decision Analysis and Resolution process area for more information about formal evaluation methods that can be used to select suppliers.

Specific Goal and Practice Summary

SG 1 Prepare for Solicitation and Supplier Agreement Development
- SP 1.1 Identify Potential Suppliers
- SP 1.2 Establish a Solicitation Package
- SP 1.3 Review the Solicitation Package
- SP 1.4 Distribute and Maintain the Solicitation Package

SG 2 Select Suppliers
- SP 2.1 Evaluate Proposed Solutions
- SP 2.2 Establish Negotiation Plans
- SP 2.3 Select Suppliers

SG 3 Establish Supplier Agreements
- SP 3.1 Establish an Understanding of the Agreement
- SP 3.2 Establish the Supplier Agreement

Specific Practices by Goal

SG 1 Prepare for Solicitation and Supplier Agreement Development

Preparation for solicitation and supplier agreement development is performed.

SP 1.1 Identify Potential Suppliers

Identify and qualify potential suppliers.

Consistent with internal organizational policy, the acquisition strategy, and project scope and requirements, the acquirer identifies potential suppliers to receive the solicitation. The acquirer can identify suppliers from a variety of sources (e.g., employees, international seminars, market analysis reports, pre-established schedules).

In some organizations, acquirers may solicit proposals from a limited number of suppliers to reduce their cost and efforts for the solicitation. Acquirers must, however, ensure that they include suppliers who are capable of meeting the requirements and that a sufficient number of suppliers are included to provide a competitive environment. This competition enhances the leverage of the acquirer in achieving its objectives (e.g., providing different approaches to meeting requirements).

TIP

Often, preferred-supplier lists may exist within the organization that reduce the scope of the needed selection activities and the risks associated with unknown suppliers.

Depending on applicable regulations and project characteristics, the acquirer may determine to pursue a sole-source acquisition rather than a competitive bid. Acquirers should document the rationale for determining potential suppliers, particularly in the case of sole-source selection.

Typical Work Products

1. List of potential suppliers prepared to respond to the solicitation

Subpractices

1. Develop a list of potential suppliers.

   To develop a list of potential suppliers, the acquirer considers which suppliers have experience with similar systems or projects, the performance the acquirer has experienced with suppliers on previous projects, which suppliers are likely to provide the capabilities needed for the project, and the availability of critical resources to staff and support the project. In addition to assessing supplier capabilities, a risk assessment is prepared on the suppliers' financial capabilities (e.g., credit worthiness, financial stability and access to capital, and the impact to the supplier of a successful bid).

2. Communicate with potential suppliers concerning the forthcoming solicitation.

   The acquirer contacts suppliers to outline plans for the solicitation, including the projected schedule for releasing the solicitation package and expected dates for responses from suppliers. If a supplier expresses interest in responding to the solicitation, the appropriate confidentiality agreements are put in place.

Typical communication to candidate suppliers includes the following:

- Anticipated scope of the solicitation
- Schedule for release of the solicitation package
- Overall project schedule
- Approach and procedures to be used throughout the solicitation process
- High-level criteria for evaluating proposal responses
- Required supplier qualifications
- Schedule for the return of proposals
- Date when the supplier must indicate if it will or will not participate in the solicitation

3. Verify participants who will evaluate supplier proposals.
4. Verify participants in supplier negotiations.

SP 1.2 ESTABLISH A SOLICITATION PACKAGE

Establish and maintain a solicitation package that includes the requirements and proposal evaluation criteria.

Solicitation packages are used to seek proposals from potential suppliers. The acquirer structures the solicitation package to facilitate an accurate and complete response from each potential supplier and to enable an effective comparison and evaluation of proposals.

The solicitation package includes a description of the desired form of the response, the relevant statement of work for the supplier, and required provisions in the supplier agreement (e.g., a copy of the standard supplier agreement or nondisclosure provisions). In government acquisitions, some or all of the content and structure of the solicitation package may be defined by regulation.

The solicitation package typically contains the following:

- The statement of work for the supplier, including supplier process, product, and service level measures
- Guidance on how potential suppliers are to respond to the solicitation package
- A description and criteria to be used to evaluate proposals
- Documentation requirements to submit with the response (e.g., project plans)
- The schedule for completing the solicitation process
- Procedures for addressing questions and contacts

The solicitation package is rigorous enough to ensure consistent and comparable responses but flexible enough to allow consideration of supplier suggestions for better ways to satisfy requirements. The acquirer can invite suppliers to submit a proposal that is wholly responsive to the request for proposal and to provide a proposed alternative solution in a separate proposal.

The complexity and level of detail of the solicitation package should be consistent with the value of, and risk associated with, the planned acquisition. In some cases, the solicitation may not include detailed requirements (e.g., it may be a solicitation for development of detailed requirements or it may include a statement of objectives to provide the supplier greater flexibility in addressing the scope of the project).

Proposal and supplier evaluation criteria are identified and documented.

Typical Work Products

1. Solicitation package
2. Supplier and proposal evaluation criteria

Subpractices

1. Develop the statement of work for the supplier.

   The statement of work for the supplier defines, for those items being acquired, the portion of the project scope that is included in the related supplier agreement. The statement of work for a supplier is developed from the project scope, the work breakdown structure, and the task dictionary.

   The statement of work for the supplier is written to be clear, complete, and concise. It describes the acquired product or service in sufficient detail to allow prospective suppliers to determine if they are capable of providing the product or service.

Example content of the statement of work for the supplier includes the following:

- Project objectives
- Requirements (including period of performance; milestones; work location; legal, statutory, and regulatory requirements; delivery format; quantities; and content requirements)
- Design constraints
- Deliverables and rights (e.g., work breakdown structure of the supplier's work, detailed design, and test results)
- An overview of the project with sufficient information for the supplier to understand the project environment and risks
- Expectations of the supplier's transition of the product to operations and support
- Expectations for process, product, and service level measures and reports that provide the acquirer visibility into supplier progress and performance
- Collateral services required (e.g. study reports, development of training materials, delivery of training to end users)
- Acquirer-specified standard processes for the project (e.g., configuration management, issue escalation and resolution, corrective action for nonconformances, and change management)
- The type of reviews to be conducted with the supplier and other communication processes and procedures
- Product acceptance criteria and required supplier involvement in the acquirer's validation and acceptance activities
- Post-project support

The statement of work for the supplier can be revised and refined as it moves through the solicitation, negotiation, and supplier agreement development processes until it is incorporated into a signed supplier agreement. For example, a prospective supplier can suggest a more efficient approach or a less costly product than those originally specified.

2. Specify the process, product, and service level measures for acceptance.

   The measures specify customer expectations and threshold values and are used to monitor the supplier and gauge the supplier's adherence to requirements.

   Service levels are an indicator of performance relative to an agreed-on service level measure. Service levels are designed to support the acquisition strategy. (See the definitions of "service level" and "measure" in the glossary.)

3. Develop supplier evaluation and proposal evaluation criteria.

   Evaluation criteria are developed and used to rate or score proposals. Evaluation criteria are included in the solicitation package. Evaluation criteria can be limited to purchase price if the acquisition item is readily available from a number of acceptable suppliers. Purchase price in this context includes both the cost of the item and ancillary expenses such as delivery. Other selection criteria can be identified and documented to support an evaluation of a more complex product or service (e.g., the individuals identified in the Project Planning resource plan develop and document criteria for evaluating potential suppliers and their proposals).

Examples of areas used to evaluate a potential supplier's ability and proposal include the following:

- Compliance to stated requirements contained in the solicitation package
- Experience with similar products or services (e.g., data on most recent similar projects with the associated cost, schedule, and quality performance and the degree to which requirements were fulfilled)
- Familiarity with acquirer processes, the technical environment, and the core business
- Total ownership and lifecycle costs
- Technical capability (e.g., expected functional and performance compliance to requirements and criteria given the architecture and technical solution proposed)
- Management, development, and delivery processes and procedures
- Proposed technical methodologies, techniques, solutions, and services
- Financial capability
- Production capacity and interest (e.g., staff available to perform the effort, available facilities, and other available resources)
- Business size and type
- Intellectual property and proprietary rights

TIP

The criteria used to select a supplier depend on the project, its requirements, and other factors. If you enter "supplier selection criteria" into your favorite search engine, you will be amazed by both the commonality and the variety of supplier selection criteria used in different industries.

Risks are typically included as criteria in a formal evaluation.

4. Document the proposal content that suppliers must submit with their response.

Examples of proposal content required for suppliers to submit include the following:

- Compliance with requirements
- References, company overview, and case studies
- Evidence of the supplier's organizational processes on which supplier processes for the project will be based and the commitment to execute those processes from project inception
- Plan describing how the supplier will carry out the scope and content of the solicitation package, including any improvements of execution capability over the duration of the supplier agreement
- Understanding of the size and complexity of the requested work based on requirements
- The pricing and compensation methodology that enables calculation of charges for the services being provided to the acquirer pursuant to supplier agreement terms and conditions, including taxes, credits, foreign currency translation, licenses, pass-through costs, and travel reimbursements
- Pricing and compensation schedules that provide for charges for the products and services provided, including frequency, term, and pricing type (e.g., fixed price, lump sum, time and materials) as well as rate cards, and a skills matrix
- Compliance with acquirer travel reimbursement policies
- References and experience validating the capability of the supplier's proposed approach to meet proposed funding, schedule, and quality targets
- Risk management plan describing how the supplier will periodically manage risks throughout the life of the project and how risks documented in the solicitation package will be managed
- Methods for early defect identification and the prevention of defects in delivered products
- The supplier's approach to assuring the quality of the product
- Approach to the escalation and resolution of issues
- Description of the supplier's proposed use of COTS and rationale for the supplier's confidence that COTS can achieve the requirements
- Description of the supplier's proposed reuse of previously developed hardware and software, rationale for the supplier's confidence that reuse can be achieved, and associated information about data rights
- Approach to providing visibility of development progress and costs at a level appropriate for the type of agreement and commensurate with the degree of risk
- Retention of critical staff during the project
- Identification of work to be performed by subcontractors

5. Incorporate the acquirer's (standard) supplier agreement, terms and conditions, and additional information into the solicitation package.

Supplier agreement terms and conditions typically include the following:

- Recitals
- Deliverables and rights
- Compensation and payments
- Confidentiality
- Privacy statements
- Continuous improvement and best practices
- Exclusive services, key employees, supplier personnel at acquirer sites
- Information-gathering practices and ethical representation
- Force majeure
- Term
- Termination for insolvency, breach, or nonperformance
- Termination for convenience
- Termination assistance
- Indemnification
- Insurance
- Right to audit
- Notices

Typical considerations for additional instructions and general information to help the supplier when responding to the solicitation package include the following:

- Submission of intent to submit proposal
- Submission due date, time, and destination
- Number of proposal copies that must be submitted
- Proposal format
- Noncomplying proposals
- Proposal ownership
- Bidder inquiries
- Key dates and activities
- Discretionary selection and potential modifications of the solicitation process
- No implied offer
- Response constitutes an offer to do business
- Confidentiality of information
- Publicity
- Use of subcontractors
- Due diligence

Continues

Continued

- Incurred costs
- Language requirements
- Statutory units
- Warranty provisions
- Licensing provisions

SP 1.3 Review the Solicitation Package

Review the solicitation package with stakeholders to ensure that the approach is realistic and can reasonably lead to the acquisition of a usable product.

The solicitation package is reviewed with stakeholders to ensure requirements have been accurately and sufficiently stated so that the solicitation can lead to a manageable agreement. The acquirer establishes traceability between requirements and the solicitation package. Suppliers may be included as stakeholders in the review of the solicitation package. The acquirer wants the solicitation package to attract a variety of responses and encourage competition. The acquirer also wants the solicitation package to be legally inclusive of all qualified suppliers.

Refer to the Perform Peer Reviews specific goal of the Acquisition Verification process area for more information about conducting peer reviews.

The acquirer may use standard templates and checklists to verify that the necessary components (e.g., skills, standards, verification and validation methods, measures, and acceptance criteria) are covered in the solicitation package.

Refer to the Organizational Process Definition process area for more information about standard checklists and templates in the organizational process assets.

The independent cost and schedule estimates for the supplier's project work are reviewed.

Typical Work Products

1. Record of the reviews of the solicitation package

SP 1.4 Distribute and Maintain the Solicitation Package

Distribute the solicitation package to potential suppliers for their response and maintain the package throughout the solicitation.

The solicitation package is distributed to potential suppliers in accordance with approved acquirer solicitation policies and procedures.

Refer to the Project Planning process area for more information about planning solicitation activities as necessary.

Refer to the Project Monitoring and Control process area for more information about monitoring and controlling solicitation activities as necessary.

Typical Work Products

1. Responses to supplier questions
2. Amendments to the solicitation package

Typical Supplier Deliverables

1. Supplier proposals
2. Supplier questions and requests for clarification

Subpractices

1. Finalize a list of potential suppliers.
2. Distribute the solicitation package to potential suppliers.
3. Document and respond to supplier questions according to the instructions in the solicitation package.

   Verify that all potential suppliers have equal access and opportunity to provide feedback on the solicitation package. Provide the opportunity for selected potential suppliers and stakeholders to clarify points of ambiguity in requirements as well as disconnects or concerns with requirements.
4. Acknowledge the receipt of supplier proposals according to the schedule identified in the solicitation package.
5. Verify conformance to requirements and completeness of supplier responses.

   Contact suppliers if the response is nonconforming or incomplete for corrective action.
6. Issue amendments to the solicitation package when changes are made to the solicitation.

SG 2 Select Suppliers

Suppliers are selected using a formal evaluation.

TIP

If a supplier is using CMMI-DEV, supplier capability evaluations can be aided by the types of activities outlined in the technical report "Understanding and Leveraging a Supplier's CMMI Efforts: A Guidebook for Acquirers" (CMU/SEI-2007-TR-004).

X-REF

Capability evaluation methods associated with CMMI include the SCAMPI B and C appraisal methods. See www.sei.cmu.edu/appraisal-program for more information. Some organizations hire a cadre of supplier selection personnel to facilitate these processes. Selection personnel are most effective when teamed with acquisition personnel who manage the agreement.

Suppliers are selected according to approved acquirer selection policies and procedures.

Refer to the Decision Analysis and Resolution process area for more information about formal evaluation approaches that can be used to select suppliers.

SP 2.1 Evaluate Proposed Solutions

Evaluate proposed solutions according to documented proposal evaluation criteria.

Proposals submitted in response to solicitation packages are evaluated in accordance with an overall established timeline, preliminary project plans, and proposal evaluation criteria. Proposal evaluation criteria are used to evaluate potential supplier responses to the solicitation. Evaluation results and decision-making notes (e.g., advantages and disadvantages of potential suppliers and scoring against criteria) should be documented and maintained.

For task orders or changes in the terms of an existing supplier agreement, the acquirer uses documented evaluation criteria to evaluate task order responses or proposed changes to terms of the agreement. In a sole-source or change order environment, this practice is critical to enable relevant stakeholder understanding of the intent of the effort or changes before placing additional work against the supplier agreement.

Typical Work Products

1. Clarification correspondence between the acquirer and potential suppliers
2. Evaluation results and rationale
3. List of candidate suppliers

Typical Supplier Deliverables

1. Proposal revisions based on clarifications
2. Supplier documentation of their approach to the project work, their capabilities, and a preliminary technical solution

Subpractices

1. Distribute supplier proposals to individuals identified by the acquirer to perform the evaluation.
2. Schedule an acquirer evaluation review of supplier proposals to consolidate questions, concerns, and issues.
3. Schedule supplier presentations.

4. Confirm the mutual understanding of the statement of work.

   A good practice is to compare the supplier's estimates to those developed in project planning; this comparison provides a means to determine if there is a mutual understanding of requirements and the associated work to fulfill them.

5. Evaluate supplier proposals and document findings.

6. Execute due diligence.

   Due diligence provides an opportunity for the acquirer to further clarify requirements, particularly those related to the acquirer's existing environment and products in use. Potential suppliers ask questions and gain understanding, which enables them to make realistic proposals. It also enables the acquirer to gain insight into the capability of the potential suppliers' proposed solutions to meet requirements. Due diligence helps to eliminate assumptions and replace them with facts, to identify and document risks and their mitigation plans or effect on the agreement, and to list issues and dependencies between the acquirer and supplier to include in the agreement.

Examples of typical due diligence activities include the following:

- Reviews of requirements with the current supplier or acquirer resources maintaining the products or providing the services
- Reviews of interfaces of a system with other systems maintained by the acquirer
- Reviews and validations of supplier references
- Reviews of the operating environment's facilities and capabilities
- Reviews of regulatory and security requirements
- Reviews of supplier capabilities

7. Document candidate supplier recommendations based on the proposal evaluation.

SP 2.2 Establish Negotiation Plans

Establish and maintain negotiation plans to use in completing a supplier agreement.

The acquirer develops and refines a negotiation plan for each of the candidate suppliers based on the evaluation of the suppliers and their proposals.

The proposal evaluation and negotiations with suppliers provide the basis for selecting the supplier best able to meet the requirements of the solicitation.

The size of a negotiation team depends on the size and complexity of the project. Typically, the team is led by acquirer management and includes individuals who have detailed knowledge of the statement of work documented in the solicitation package. The negotiation team is typically supported by legal staff, a financial analyst, purchasing, and the project manager.

Negotiations between acquirers and suppliers may be restricted by regulation. Review all regulations affecting negotiations before entering into them with a supplier.

Examples of items included in a negotiation plan include the following:

- Roles and responsibilities of negotiation team members
- Key issues to be negotiated from supplier responses
- Negotiation "levers" and where and when they should be used
- The sequence of events to negotiate issues
- Fall-back or compromise positions as necessary on given issues (possible concessions and trades)
- List of items that are non-negotiable
- External factors that could influence negotiations; (e.g., other pending deals and strategic plans)
- Prior experiences with supplier agreements to discover previous positions and issues (and negotiating styles)
- Schedule and sequence of supplier negotiation meetings
- Objectives for each negotiating session
- Risks, consequences, and mitigation alternatives

Typical Work Products

1. Negotiation plan for each candidate supplier

SP 2.3 Select Suppliers

HINT

Select a capable supplier that can meet your requirements with a quality product on time and within costs.

Select suppliers based on an evaluation of their ability to meet specified requirements and established criteria.

Proposal evaluation results are used to finalize a supplier selection based on the outcome of negotiations or responses to acquirer questions provided by potential suppliers. Negotiations enable the acquirer to select the best supplier for the project. In some cases, the acquirer may take the top two proposals and use negotiations to make the final selection decision.

Evaluation results and negotiation results support the selection decision or cause the acquirer to take other action, as appropriate. If the return on investment is not sufficient, the acquirer may decide to defer or cancel the project.

Typical Work Products

1. Revisions due to negotiations
2. Supplier selection decision
3. Evaluation reports

Subpractices

1. Evaluate supplier proposals.
2. Negotiate with suppliers to determine the best fit for the project.

   Negotiate with the selected supplier or candidate suppliers to resolve issues identified during due diligence and to address remaining issues with requirements. Revise requirements to be fulfilled by the supplier as appropriate.
3. Select a supplier to be awarded the supplier agreement.

   Refer to the Decision Analysis and Resolution process area for more information about formal evaluation methods that can be used to select suppliers.
4. Document the selection.

HINT

Strongly consider using DAR when evaluating potential suppliers. These subpractices describe some of what is involved in such an evaluation.

TIP

A proactive approach provides benefits such as addressing the capability gap of the organization uniformly, reducing the time that projects take to select suppliers, establishing a more efficient umbrella agreement with a preferred supplier, and protecting core competencies.

SG 3 ESTABLISH SUPPLIER AGREEMENTS

Supplier agreements are established and maintained.

A supplier agreement is established and maintained based on the supplier selection decision.

SP 3.1 ESTABLISH AN UNDERSTANDING OF THE AGREEMENT

Establish and maintain a mutual understanding of the agreement with selected suppliers and end users based on acquisition needs and the suppliers' proposed approaches.

Points of clarification and ambiguities may arise after award of the supplier agreement; therefore, the acquirer should work with the supplier to ensure that a mutual understanding is maintained through the life of the project (e.g., supplier workshops and executive meetings).

Typical Work Products

1. Correspondence clarifying elements of the agreement
2. Frequently asked questions (for use with end users and other suppliers)

HINT

If it's not documented in the supplier agreement, don't count on it happening! Renegotiating an agreement can be expensive, so make sure it covers everything that is important to you for managing the supplier and receiving the product that you are expecting.

HINT

Create a supplier agreement in the form suitable to the nature of the business transaction.

SP 3.2 Establish the Supplier Agreement

Establish and maintain the supplier agreement.

The agreement may be either a stand-alone agreement or part of a master agreement. When part of a master agreement, the project agreement may be an addendum, work order, or service request to the master agreement.

Typical Work Products

1. Supplier agreement (including terms and conditions)

Subpractices

1. Establish the supplier agreement.

Supplier agreement provisions typically include the following:

- The statement of work, specification, terms and conditions, list of deliverables, schedule, budget, and acceptance process
- Product acceptance criteria to be satisfied by the supplier
- Mechanisms and deliverables that provide sufficient data to allow the acquirer to evaluate and analyze acquired products
- Which acquirer and supplier representatives are responsible and authorized to make changes to the supplier agreement
- How requirements changes and changes to the supplier agreement are determined, communicated, and addressed
- Standards and procedures to be followed (e.g., configuration management, escalation, nonconformances, conflicts, and issues)
- Requirements for the supplier to establish a corrective action system that includes a change control process for rework and reevaluation
- Critical dependencies between the acquirer and supplier
- Documentation of what the acquirer will provide to the supplier (e.g., facilities, tools, software, documentation, and services)
- Analysis methods and acceptance criteria for designated supplier deliverables
- The types of reviews to be conducted with the supplier
- The supplier's responsibilities to execute corrective actions when initiated by project monitoring and control processes
- Nonhire and noncompete clauses
- Confidentiality, nondisclosure, and intellectual capital clauses pertaining to process and product quality assurance, measurement data, and personnel who would perform audits or are authorized to validate measurement data

Continues

Continued

- The supplier's responsibilities for preparing the site and training the support and operations organizations according to acquirer-specified standards, tools, and methods
- The supplier's responsibilities for ongoing maintenance and support of acquired products and their role as a stakeholder
- Requirements for the supplier to maintain bidirectional traceability to requirements provided in the supplier agreement
- Requirements for the supplier to be involved in deployment as necessary
- Warranty, ownership, usage, and data rights for acquired products
- Schedule for supplier compensation
- Security and legal penalty recoveries
- Dispute resolution procedures

2. Verify that all parties to the agreement understand and agree to all requirements by signing the supplier agreement.

   The acquirer should ensure that the supplier makes a commitment in the agreement to execute its proposed processes.

3. Notify those suppliers not selected for the award.
4. Communicate the supplier agreement in the organization as required.
5. Maintain the supplier agreement as required.

   After establishment of the supplier agreement, the acquirer may find requirements that are no longer optimal or applicable based on the supplier's progress or environment changes. Examples include the availability of new technology, overly burdensome documentation, and reporting requirements. Changes to supplier agreements may also occur when the supplier's processes or products fail to meet agreed-to criteria.

   Revise the supplier agreement and internal project documents to reflect changes in conditions as appropriate. Update cost, schedule, and budget documents as needed.

   All changes are formally documented and approved by both the acquirer and supplier before being implemented by this specific practice. Approved change requests can include modifications to terms and conditions of the supplier agreement, including the statement of work, pricing, and the descriptions of products, services, or results to be acquired.

   Refer to the Configuration Management process area for more information about tracking and controlling changes.

6. Ensure that all records related to the supplier agreement are stored, managed, and controlled for future use.

TIP

The acquirer must engage the supplier in reviews, monitoring, and evaluations to a depth and breadth appropriate to the circumstances and risks. The supplier agreement must cover details of these reviews.

X-REF

The project's progress and milestone reviews are covered in PMC SPs 1.6 and 1.7. Management reviews of the supplier are covered in AM SP 1.1, and technical reviews of the supplier's technical solutions are covered in ATM SP 1.3.

X-REF

Establishing (and revising) an agreement often requires *negotiation skills*. See *Getting to Yes: Negotiating Agreement Without Giving In*, Revised Second Edition, by William Ury, Roger Fisher, and Bruce Patton (Penguin USA).

TIP

Especially with long-term agreements (more than one year), technical and nontechnical requirements may change. It is necessary to document these changes in the supplier agreement because this is often the legal document that will make these significant changes binding.

HINT

The supplier agreement is the basis for monitoring your supplier and accepting the product. Make sure it covers all critical information.

PART THREE

The Appendices and Glossary

APPENDIX A

REFERENCES

Ahern 2008 Ahern, Dennis M.; Armstrong, Jim; Clouse, Aaron; Ferguson, Jack R.; Hayes, Will; and Nidiffer, Kenneth E. *CMMI SCAMPI Distilled: Appraisals for Process Improvement*. Boston: Addison-Wesley, 2005.

Bernard 2005 Bernard, Tom, et al. *CMMI Acquisition Module, Version 1.1* (CMU/SEI-2005-TR-011, ADA441245). Pittsburgh: Software Engineering Institute, Carnegie Mellon University, May 2005. www.sei.cmu.edu/publications/documents/05.reports/05tr011.html.

Crosby 1979 Crosby, Philip B. *Quality Is Free: The Art of Making Quality Certain*. New York: McGraw-Hill, 1979.

Curtis 2001 Curtis, Bill; Hefley, William E.; and Miller, Sally A. *The People Capability Maturity Model: Guidelines for Improving the Workforce*. Boston: Addison-Wesley, 2001.

Deming 1986 Deming, W. Edwards. *Out of the Crisis*. Cambridge, MA: MIT Press, 1986.

DoD 2006 *DoD Directive, 5000.1, Defense Acquisition Guidebook*. https://akss.dau.mil/dag/, 2006.

DoD 2008 England, Gordon. *DoD Directive, 5010.42, DoD-Wide Continuous Process Improvement (CPI)/Lean Six Sigma (LSS) Program*. www.dtic.mil/whs/directives/corres/pdf/501042p.pdf, 2008.

Dodson 2006 Dodson, Kathryn M., et al. *Adapting CMMI for Acquisition Organizations: A Preliminary Report* (CMU/SEI-2006-SR-005, ADA453524). Pittsburgh: Software Engineering Institute, Carnegie Mellon University, June 2006. www.sei.cmu.edu/publications/documents/06.reports/06sr005.html.

EIA 2002 Electronic Industries Alliance. *Systems Engineering Capability Model (EIA/IS-731.1)*. Washington, DC, 2002.

EIA 2003 Electronic Industries Alliance. *EIA Interim Standard: Systems Engineering (EIA/IS-632)*. Washington, DC, 2003.

Finley 2008 Finley, James I., and McQueary, Charles E. *Memorandum for Component Acquisition Executives.* https://acc.dau.mil/CommunityBrowser.aspx?id=215765, 2008.

GEIA 748 2002 Government Electronics and Information Technology Alliance. *Earned Value Management Systems (ANSI/EIA-748).* New York, 2002. www.nssn.org/search/DetailResults.aspx?docid=338699.

Gibson 2006 Gibson, Diane L.; Goldenson, Dennis R.; and Kost, Keith. *Performance Results of CMMI-Based Process Improvement* (CMU/SEI-2006-TR-004, ADA454687). Pittsburgh: Software Engineering Institute, Carnegie Mellon University, August 2006. www.sei.cmu.edu/publications/documents/06.reports/06tr004.html.

Higuera 1994 Higuera, R.; Dorofee, A.; Walker, J.; and Williams, R. *Team Risk Management: A New Model for Customer-Supplier Relationships* (CMU/SEI-94-SR-005). Pittsburgh: Software Engineering Institute, Carnegie Mellon University, 1994.

Humphrey 1989 Humphrey, Watts S. *Managing the Software Process.* Reading, MA: Addison-Wesley, 1989.

IEEE 1991 Institute of Electrical and Electronics Engineers. *IEEE Standard Computer Dictionary: A Compilation of IEEE Standard Computer Glossaries.* New York: IEEE, 1991.

ISO 1995 International Organization for Standardization and International Electrotechnical Commission. *ISO/IEC TR 12207 Information Technology—Software Life Cycle Processes,* 1995. www.iso.org/iso/iso_catalogue/catalogue_tc/catalogue_detail.htm?csnumber=21208.

ISO 2000 International Organization for Standardization. *ISO 9001, Quality Management Systems—Requirements,* 2000. www.iso.org/iso/en/CatalogueDetailPage.CatalogueDetail?CSNUMBER=21823&ICS1=3&ICS2=120&ICS3=10.

ISO 2002a International Organization for Standardization and International Electrotechnical Commission. *ISO/IEC 15288 Systems Engineering—System Life Cycle Processes,* 2002. www.jtc1-sc7.org/.

ISO 2002b International Organization for Standardization and International Electrotechnical Commission. *ISO/IEC 15939 Software and Systems Engineering—Measurement Process,* 2002. www.jtc1-sc7.org/.

ISO 2005 International Organization for Standardization and International Electrotechnical Commission. *ISO/IEC 20000-1 Information Technology – Service Management, Part 1: Specification; ISO/IEC 20000-2 Information Technology – Service Management, Part 2: Code of Practice,* 2005. www.iso.org/iso/iso_catalogue/catalogue_tc/catalogue_detail.htm?csnumber=41333.

ISO 2006 International Organization for Standardization and International Electrotechnical Commission. *ISO/IEC TR 15504 Information*

Technology—Software Process Assessment Part 1: Concepts and Vocabulary; Part 2: Performing an Assessment; Part 3: Guidance on Performing an Assessment; Part 4: Guidance on Use for Process Improvement and Process Capability Determination; Part 5: An Exemplar Process Assessment Model, 2003–2006. www.iso.org/iso/search.htm?qt=15504&published=true&active_tab=standards.

IT Governance 2005 IT Governance Institute. *CobiT 4.0*. Rolling Meadows, IL: IT Governance Institute, 2005. www.isaca.org/Content/NavigationMenu/Members_and_Leaders/COBIT6/Obtain_COBIT/Obtain_COBIT.htm.

Juran 1988 Juran, Joseph M. *Juran on Planning for Quality*. New York: Macmillan, 1988.

Kadish 2006 Kadish, Lieutenant General Ronald. *Defense Acquisition Performance Assessment.* https://acc.dau.mil/CommunityBrowser.aspx?id=17721, 2006.

McFeeley 1996 McFeeley, Robert. *IDEAL: A User's Guide for Software Process Improvement* (CMU/SEI-96-HB-001, ADA305472). Pittsburgh: Software Engineering Institute, Carnegie Mellon University, February 1996. www.sei.cmu.edu/publications/documents/96.reports /96.hb.001.html.

Meyers 2006a Meyers, B. Craig; Smith, James D.; Capell, Peter; and Place, Patrick. *Requirements Management in a System of Systems Context: A Workshop* (CMU/SEI-2006-TN-015). Pittsburgh: Software Engineering Institute, Carnegie Mellon University, 2006.

Meyers 2006b Meyers, B. Craig. *Risk Management Considerations for Interoperable Acquisition* (CMU/SEI-2006-TN-032). Pittsburgh: Software Engineering Institute, Carnegie Mellon University, 2006.

Meyers 2006c Meyers, B. Craig, and Sledge, Carol A. *Schedule Considerations for Interoperable Acquisition* (CMU/SEI-2006-TN-035). Pittsburgh: Software Engineering Institute, Carnegie Mellon University, 2006.

Meyers 2008 Meyers, B. Craig, and Smith, James D. *Programmatic Interoperability* (CMU/SEI-2008-TN-012). Pittsburgh: Software Engineering Institute, Carnegie Mellon University, 2008.

Morris 2004 Morris, Ed; Levine, Linda; Meyers, B. Craig; Place, Patrick R. H.; and Plakosh, Daniel. *System of Systems Interoperability (SOSI); Final Report* (CMU/SEI-2004-TR-004). Pittsburgh: Software Engineering Institute, Carnegie Mellon University, 2004.

SEI 1995 Software Engineering Institute. *The Capability Maturity Model: Guidelines for Improving the Software Process*. Reading, MA: Addison-Wesley, 1995.

SEI 2002 Software Engineering Institute. *Software Acquisition Capability Maturity Model (SA-CMM) Version 1.03* (CMU/SEI-2002-TR-010,

ADA399794). Pittsburgh: Software Engineering Institute, Carnegie Mellon University, March 2002. www.sei.cmu.edu/publications/documents/02.reports/02tr010.html.

SEI 2006a CMMI Product Team. *CMMI for Development, Version 1.2* (CMU/SEI-2006-TR-008, ADA455858). Pittsburgh: Software Engineering Institute, Carnegie Mellon University, August 2006. www.sei.cmu.edu/publications/documents/06.reports/06tr008.html.

SEI 2006b SCAMPI Upgrade Team. *Standard CMMI Appraisal Method for Process Improvement (SCAMPI) A, Version 1.2: Method Definition Document* (CMU/SEI-2006-HB-002). Pittsburgh: Software Engineering Institute, Carnegie Mellon University, August 2006. www.sei.cmu.edu/publications/documents/06.reports/06hb002.html.

SEI 2006c SCAMPI Upgrade Team. *Appraisal Requirements for CMMI, Version 1.2 (ARC, V1.2)* (CMU/SEI-2006-TR-011, ADA454612). Pittsburgh: Software Engineering Institute, Carnegie Mellon University, August 2006. www.sei.cmu.edu/publications/documents/06.reports/06tr011.html.

SEI 2007 CMMI Guidebook for Acquirers Team. *Understanding and Leveraging a Supplier's CMMI Efforts: A Guidebook for Acquirers* (CMU/SEI-2007-TR-004). Pittsburgh: Software Engineering Institute, Carnegie Mellon University, March 2007. www.sei.cmu.edu/publications/documents/07.reports/07tr004.html.

Shewhart 1931 Shewhart, Walter A. *Economic Control of Quality of Manufactured Product.* New York: Van Nostrand, 1931.

Smith 2005 Smith, James D., and Meyers, B. Craig. *Exploring Programmatic Interoperability: Army Future Force Workshop* (CMU/SEI-2005-TN-042). Pittsburgh: Software Engineering Institute, Carnegie Mellon University, 2005.

Smith 2006 Smith, James D., and Phillips, D. Mike. *Interoperable Acquisition for Systems of System: The Challenges* (CMU/SEI-2006-TN-034). Pittsburgh: Software Engineering Institute, Carnegie Mellon University, 2006.

AUTHORS' NOTE

Between publication of the CMMI-ACQ model and this book, many of these references have been updated, and the reader is encouraged to look for the latest versions. For example, both ISO/IEC 15288 and 12207 now have 2008 versions.

AUTHORS' NOTE

A book that is not listed in the model but is a useful resource for those using CMMI for process improvement is *CMMI Distilled: A Practical Introduction to Integrated Process Improvement.* The third edition was released in May 2008.

APPENDIX B

ACRONYMS

ACQ Acquisition constellation
AM Agreement Management (process area)
ARC Appraisal Requirements for CMMI
ARD Acquisition Requirements Development (process area)
ATM Acquisition Technical Management (process area)
AVAL Acquisition Validation (process area)
AVER Acquisition Verification (process area)
CAR Causal Analysis and Resolution (process area)
CCB configuration control board
CL capability level
CM Configuration Management (process area)
CMM Capability Maturity Model
CMMI Capability Maturity Model Integration
CMMI-ACQ CMMI for Acquisition
CMMI-DEV CMMI for Development
COTS commercial off the shelf
CPI cost performance index
CPM critical path method
DAR Decision Analysis and Resolution (process area)
DEV Development constellation
DoD Department of Defense
EDS Electronic Data Systems
EIA Electronic Industries Alliance
EIA/IS Electronic Industries Alliance/Interim Standard
GG generic goal
GP generic practice

GM General Motors

IBM International Business Machines

IDEAL Initiating, Diagnosing, Establishing, Acting, Learning

IEEE Institute of Electrical and Electronics Engineers

IPD-CMM Integrated Product Development Capability Maturity Model

IPM Integrated Project Management (process area)

ISO International Organization for Standardization

ISO/IEC International Organization for Standardization and International Electrotechnical Commission

IT Information technology

MA Measurement and Analysis (process area)

MDD Method Definition Document

ML maturity level

NDIA National Defense Industrial Association

OID Organizational Innovation and Deployment (process area)

OPD Organizational Process Definition (process area)

OPF Organizational Process Focus (process area)

OPP Organizational Process Performance (process area)

OT Organizational Training (process area)

OUSD (AT&L) Office of the Under Secretary of Defense (Acquisition, Technology, and Logistics)

P-CMM People Capability Maturity Model

PA process area

PERT Program Evaluation and Review Technique

PMC Project Monitoring and Control (process area)

PP Project Planning (process area)

PPQA Process and Product Quality Assurance (process area)

QA quality assurance

QFD Quality Function Deployment

QPM Quantitative Project Management (process area)

REQM Requirements Management (process area)

RSKM Risk Management (process area)

SA-CMM Software Acquisition Capability Maturity Model

SCAMPI Standard CMMI Appraisal Method for Process Improvement

SECM Systems Engineering Capability Model

SEI Software Engineering Institute

SG specific goal

SP specific practice

SPI schedule performance index

SSAD Solicitation and Supplier Agreement Development (process area)

SW-CMM Capability Maturity Model for Software or Software Capability Maturity Model

WBS work breakdown structure

APPENDIX C

PROJECT PARTICIPANTS

Many talented people were part of the product team that developed CMMI-ACQ. The following lists comprise those who participated in one or more of the following teams during the development of CMMI-ACQ. The organizations listed by members' names are those they represented at the time of their team membership.

Seven primary groups were involved in the development of this model:

The initial draft development team
The CMMI Architecture Team
The CMMI-ACQ, V1.2 Model Team
The CMMI-ACQ, V1.2 Training Team
The CMMI-ACQ, V1.2 Quality Team
The CMMI Acquisition Advisory Board
The CMMI Steering Group

Initial Draft Development Team

The initial draft development team created the document used as the initial baseline for the development of CMMI-ACQ, Version 1.2. This document was piloted by a few select organizations and publicly reviewed.

Kathryn M. Dodson, EDS
Matt Fisher, Software Engineering Institute
Hubert F. Hofmann, General Motors
Keith Kost, Software Engineering Institute
Gowri S. Ramani, Hewlett-Packard
Deborah K. Yedlin, General Motors

CMMI Architecture Team

In 2005 and 2006, the CMMI Architecture Team updated the architecture used to build components of the CMMI Product Suite, such as models and training materials.

Roger Bate, Software Engineering Institute
Mary Beth Chrissis, Software Engineering Institute
Hubert F. Hofmann, General Motors
Craig Hollenbach, Northrop Grumman
Lisa Ming, BAE Systems
Mike Phillips, Software Engineering Institute
John Scibilia, U.S. Army
Hal Wilson, Northrop Grumman
Gary Wolf, Raytheon

CMMI-ACQ, V1.2 Model Team

The Version 1.2 CMMI-ACQ Model Team used the baseline developed by the initial draft development team and input from reviewers and users to revise the initial draft and create CMMI-ACQ, Version 1.2.

Lloyd Anderson, Department of Homeland Security
Larry Baker, Defense Acquisition University
Roger Bate, Software Engineering Institute
Rhonda Brown, Software Engineering Institute
Aaron Clouse, Software Engineering Institute
Brad Doohan, Defence Materiel Organisation
Tom Keuten, General Motors
Mike Konrad, Software Engineering Institute
Keith Kost, Software Engineering Institute
Madhav S. Panwar, U.S. Government Accountability Office
Mike Phillips, Software Engineering Institute
Margaret Porteus, Institute for Defense Analyses
George Prosnik, Defense Acquisition University
Karen Richter, Institute for Defense Analyses
John Scibilia, U.S. Army
Sandy Shrum, Software Engineering Institute
Deborah K. Yedlin, Borland Software Corporation

CMMI-ACQ, V1.2 Training Team

The Version 1.2 CMMI-ACQ Training Team included a core team of developers and many reviewers. The development team used baselines created by the CMMI-ACQ, V1.2 Model Team and the existing "Introduction to CMMI" course to develop training for CMMI-ACQ, V1.2.

Bruce Allgood, U.S. Air Force
Rhonda Brown, Software Engineering Institute
Peter Capell, Software Engineering Institute
Mary Beth Chrissis, Software Engineering Institute
Aaron Clouse, Software Engineering Institute
Erin Czerwinski, Software Engineering Institute
Jack Ferguson, Software Engineering Institute
Matt Fisher, Software Engineering Institute
Thierry Girou, Thales
Jon Gross, Software Engineering Institute
Tom Keuten, General Motors
Mike Konrad, Software Engineering Institute
Phil Miller, Software Engineering Institute
Mike Phillips, Software Engineering Institute
Christine Safa, Thales
Sandy Shrum, Software Engineering Institute
Barbara Tyson, Software Engineering Institute
Christian Zion, Thales

CMMI-ACQ, V1.2 Quality Team

The Version 1.2 CMMI-ACQ Quality Team used a process developed over the years for CMMI model quality assurance. The team tailored the quality assurance (QA) process to CMMI-ACQ, V1.2 to prepare it and the training material developed by the CMMI-ACQ, V1.2 Training Team for release.

Rhonda Brown, Software Engineering Institute
Pamela Curtis, Software Engineering Institute
Keith Kost, Software Engineering Institute
Sandy Shrum, Software Engineering Institute

CMMI Acquisition Advisory Board

The CMMI Acquisition Advisory Board was responsible for providing direction to and approving the development work of the CMMI-ACQ, Version 1.2 Model Team. The board had final authority regarding decisions that impacted CMMI-ACQ, Version 1.2.

Kristen Baldwin, OUSD (AT&L) SSE/SSA
Tony D'Agosto, U.S. Army
Richard Frost, General Motors
Hubert F. Hofmann, General Motors
Guy Mercurio, Defense Contract Management Agency
Lawrence Osiecki, U.S. Army
Madhav Panwar, U.S. Government Accountability Office
Bob Rassa, National Defense Industry Association
Linda Roush, U.S. Navy
Katie Smith, U.S. Navy
Michael W. Smith, Missile Defense Agency
Bob Swarz, U.S. Air Force (The MITRE Corporation)

CMMI Steering Group

The CMMI Steering Group has guided and approved the plans of the Version 1.2 CMMI Product Team, provided consultation on significant CMMI project issues, ensured involvement from a variety of interested communities, and approved the final release of this model.

Steering Group Members

Kristen Baldwin, OUSD (AT&L) SSE/SSA
Clyde Chittister, Software Engineering Institute
Jim Gill, Boeing Integrated Defense Systems
John Kelly, NASA HQ
Kathy Lundeen, Defense Contract Management Agency
Larry McCarthy, Motorola, Inc.
Mike Nicol, U.S. Air Force ASC/EN
Lawrence Osiecki, U.S. Army
Bill Peterson, Software Engineering Institute
Bob Rassa, Raytheon Space & Airborne Systems
Joan Weszka, Lockheed Martin
Hal Wilson, Northrop Grumman Mission Systems
Brenda Zettervall, U.S. Navy, ASN/RDA CHENG

Ex-Officio Steering Group Members

Lloyd Anderson, Department of Homeland Security
Roger Bate, chief architect, Software Engineering Institute
Mike Phillips, CMMI program manager, Software Engineering Institute
Beth Sumpter, National Security Agency

Steering Group Support: Acquisition

Brian Gallagher, Software Engineering Institute

Steering Group Support: CCB

Mike Konrad, Software Engineering Institute

During the development of CMMI-ACQ, others served temporarily on the CMMI Steering Group. Anthony D'Agosto (U.S. Army RDECOM ARDEC) was a full Steering Group member. Thomas Drake (SES) and Deborah K. Yedlin (General Motors) were ex-officio members.

APPENDIX D

GLOSSARY

The glossary defines the basic terms used in CMMI models. Glossary entries are typically multiple-word terms consisting of a noun and one or more restrictive modifiers. (Some exceptions to this rule account for one-word terms in the glossary.)

To formulate definitions appropriate for CMMI, we consulted multiple sources. We first consulted the *Merriam-Webster OnLine* dictionary (www.m-w.com) and the source models (i.e., CMMI v1.2, EIA 731, SW-CMM v2, draft C, and IPD-CMM v0.98). We also consulted other standards as needed, including the following:

- ISO 9000 [ISO 2000]
- ISO/IEC 12207 [ISO 1995]
- ISO/IEC 15504 [ISO 2006]
- ISO/IEC 15288 [ISO 2002a]
- ISO/IEC 15939 [ISO 2002b]
- ISO 20000-1 [ISO 2005]
- IEEE [IEEE 1991]
- CobiT v. 4.0 [IT Governance 2005]
- SW-CMM v1.1
- EIA 632 [EIA 2003]
- SA-CMM [SEI 2002]
- P-CMM [Curtis 2001]

We developed the glossary recognizing the importance of using terminology that all model users can understand. We also recognized that words and terms can have different meanings in different contexts and environments. The glossary in CMMI models is designed to document the meanings of words and terms that should have the widest use and understanding by users of CMMI products.

Because CMMI for Acquisition was designed to apply to acquisition environments for both products and services, many of the terms in the glossary include both products and services in their definitions.

acceptance criteria The criteria that a deliverable must satisfy to be accepted by a user, customer, or other authorized entity. (See also "deliverable.")

acceptance testing Formal testing conducted to enable a user, customer, or other authorized entity to determine whether to accept a deliverable. (See also "unit testing.")

achievement profile In the continuous representation, a list of process areas and their corresponding capability levels that represent the organization's progress for each process area while advancing through the capability levels. (See also "capability level profile," "target profile," and "target staging.")

acquirer The stakeholder that acquires or procures a product or service from a supplier. (See also "stakeholder.")

acquisition The process of obtaining products or services through supplier agreements. (See also "supplier agreement.")

acquisition strategy The specific approach to acquiring products and services that is based on considerations of supply sources, acquisition methods, requirements specification types, contract or agreement types, and related acquisition risks.

adequate Interpret goals and practices in light of the organization's business objectives. When using any CMMI model, practices should be interpreted in a way that works for the organization. This term is used in goals and practices in which certain activities may not be equally relevant in all situations. (See also "appropriate" and "as needed.")

allocated requirement Requirement that levies all or part of the performance and functionality of a higher-level requirement on a lower-level architectural element or design component.

alternative practice A practice that is a substitute for one or more generic or specific practices contained in CMMI models that achieves an equivalent effect toward satisfying the generic or specific goal associated with it. Alternative practices are not necessarily one-for-one replacements for generic or specific practices.

amplifications Amplifications are informative model components that contain information relevant to a particular discipline. For example, to find amplifications for software engineering, look in the model for items labeled "For Software Engineering." The same is true for amplifications for other disciplines.

appraisal In the CMMI Product Suite, an examination of one or more processes by a trained team of professionals using an appraisal reference model as the basis for determining, at a minimum, strengths and weaknesses. (See also "assessment.")

appraisal findings The results of an appraisal that identify the most important issues, problems, or opportunities for process improvement within the appraisal scope. Appraisal findings are inferences drawn from corroborated objective evidence.

appraisal participants Members of the organizational unit who participate in providing information during an appraisal.

appraisal rating As used in CMMI appraisal materials, the value assigned by an appraisal team to (a) a CMMI goal or process area, (b) the capability level of a process area, or (c) the maturity level of an organizational unit. A rating is determined by enacting the defined rating process for the appraisal method being employed.

appraisal reference model As used in CMMI appraisal materials, the CMMI model to which an appraisal team correlates implemented process activities.

appraisal scope The definition of the boundaries of an appraisal encompassing the organizational limits and CMMI model limits within which the processes to be investigated operate.

appraisal team leader A person who leads the activities of an appraisal and has satisfied qualification criteria for experience, knowledge, and skills defined by the appraisal method.

appropriate Interpret goals and practices in light of the organization's business objectives. When using any CMMI model, practices should be interpreted in a way that works for the organization. This term is used in goals and practices in which certain activities may not be equally relevant in all situations. (See also "adequate" and "as needed.")

as needed Interpret goals and practices in light of the organization's business objectives. When using any CMMI model, practices should be interpreted in a way that works for the organization. This term is used in goals and practices in which certain activities may not be equally relevant in all situations. (See also "adequate" and "appropriate.")

assessment In the CMMI Product Suite, an appraisal that an organization does internally for the purposes of process improvement. The word *assessment* is also used in the CMMI Product Suite in an everyday English sense (e.g., risk assessment). (See also "appraisal.")

assignable cause of process variation In CMMI, the term *special cause of process variation* is used in place of *assignable cause of* *process variation* to ensure consistency. The two terms are defined identically. (See "special cause of process variation.")

audit In CMMI process improvement work, an objective examination of a work product or set of work products against specific criteria (e.g., requirements).

base measure A distinct property or characteristic of an entity and the method for quantifying it. (See also "derived measures.")

baseline A set of specifications or work products that has been formally reviewed and agreed on, which thereafter serves as the basis for further development, and which can be changed only through change control procedures. (See also "configuration baseline" and "product baseline.")

bidirectional traceability An association among two or more logical entities that is discernable in either direction (i.e., to and from an entity). (See also "requirements traceability" and "traceability.")

business objectives (See "organization's business objectives.")

capability level Achievement of process improvement within an individual process area. A capability level is defined by appropriate specific and generic practices for a process area. (See also "generic goal," "generic practice," "maturity level," and "process area.")

capability level profile In the continuous representation, a list of process areas and their corresponding capability levels. (See also "achievement profile," "target profile," and "target staging.")

A capability level profile may be an achievement profile when it represents the organization's progress for each process area while advancing through the capability levels. Or, it may be a target profile when it represents an objective for process improvement.

capability maturity model A model that contains the essential elements of effective processes for one or more disciplines and describes an evolutionary improvement path from ad hoc, immature processes to disciplined, mature processes with improved quality and effectiveness.

capable process A process that can satisfy its specified product quality, service quality, and process-performance objectives. (See also "stable process," "standard process," and "statistically managed process.")

causal analysis The analysis of defects to determine their cause.

change management Judicious use of means to effect a change, or a proposed change, to a product or service. (See also "configuration management.")

CMMI Framework The basic structure that organizes CMMI components, including elements of current CMMI models as well as rules and methods for generating models, appraisal methods (including associated artifacts), and training materials. The framework enables new disciplines to be added to CMMI so that they will integrate with the existing ones. (See also "CMMI model" and "CMMI Product Suite.")

CMMI model A model generated from the CMMI Framework. (See also "CMMI Framework" and "CMMI Product Suite.")

CMMI model component Any of the main architectural elements that compose a CMMI model. Some of the main elements of a CMMI model include specific practices, generic practices, specific goals, generic goals, process areas, capability levels, and maturity levels.

CMMI Product Suite The complete set of products developed around the CMMI concept. These products include the framework itself, models, appraisal methods, appraisal materials, and training materials. (See also "CMMI Framework" and "CMMI model.")

common cause of process variation The variation of a process that exists because of normal and expected interactions among components of a process. (See also "special cause of process variation.")

concept of operations (See "operational concept.")

configuration audit An audit conducted to verify that a configuration item, or a collection of configuration items that make up a baseline, conforms to a specified standard or requirement. (See also "audit," "configuration item," "functional configuration audit," and "physical configuration audit.")

configuration baseline The configuration information formally designated at a specific time during a product's or product component's life. Configuration baselines, plus approved changes from those baselines, constitute the current configuration information. (See also "product lifecycle.")

configuration control An element of configuration management consisting of the evaluation, coordination, approval or disapproval, and implementation of changes to configuration items after formal establishment of their configuration identification. (See also "configuration identification," "configuration item," and "configuration management.")

configuration control board A group of people responsible for evaluating and approving or disapproving proposed changes to configuration items and for ensuring implementation of approved changes. (See also "configuration item.")

Configuration control boards are also known as change control boards.

configuration identification An element of configuration management consisting of selecting the configuration items for a product, assigning unique identifiers to them, and recording their functional and physical characteristics in technical documentation. (See also "configuration item," "configuration management," and "product.")

configuration item An aggregation of work products that is designated for configuration management and treated as a single entity in the configuration management process. (See also "configuration management.")

configuration management A discipline applying technical and administrative direction and surveillance to (1) identify and document the functional and physical characteristics of a configuration item, (2) control changes to those characteristics, (3) record and report change processing and implementation status, and (4) verify compliance with specified requirements. (See also "configuration audit," "configuration control," "configuration identification," and "configuration status accounting.")

configuration status accounting An element of configuration management consisting of the recording and reporting of information needed to manage a configuration effectively. This information includes a list of the approved configuration, the status of proposed changes to the configuration, and the implementation status of approved changes. (See also "configuration identification" and "configuration management.")

continuous representation A capability maturity model structure wherein capability levels provide a recommended order for approaching process improvement within each specified process area. (See also "capability level," "process area," and "staged representation.")

contractual requirements The result of the analysis and refinement of customer requirements into a set of requirements suitable to be included in one or more solicitation packages, formal contracts, or supplier agreements between the acquirer and other appropriate organizations. (See also "acquirer," "customer requirement," "supplier agreement," and "solicitation package.")

Contractual requirements include both technical and nontechnical requirements necessary for the acquisition of a product or service.

corrective action Acts or deeds used to remedy a situation, remove an error, or adjust a condition.

commercial-off-the-shelf Items that can be purchased from a commercial supplier.

customer The party (individual, project, or organization) responsible for accepting the product or for authorizing payment. The customer is external to the project (except possibly when integrated teams are used) but not necessarily external to the project's organization. The customer may be a higher-level project. Customers are a subset of stakeholders. (See also "stakeholder.")

In most cases where this term is used, the preceding definition is intended; however, in some contexts, the term *customer* is intended to include other relevant stakeholders. (See also "customer requirement.")

customer requirement The result of eliciting, consolidating, and resolving conflicts among the needs, expectations, constraints, and interfaces of the product's relevant stakeholders in a way that is acceptable to the customer. (See also "customer.")

data Recorded information, regardless of the form or method of recording, including technical data, computer software documents, financial information, management information, representation of facts, numbers, or datum of any nature that can be communicated, stored, and processed.

data management The disciplined processes and systems that plan for, acquire, and provide stewardship for business and technical data, consistent with data requirements, throughout the data lifecycle.

defect density Number of defects per unit of product size (e.g., problem reports per thousand lines of code).

defined process A managed process that is tailored from the organization's set of standard processes according to the organization's tailoring guidelines; has a maintained process description; and contributes work products, measures, and other process improvement information to organizational process assets. (See also "managed process" and "measure.")

deliverable An item to be provided to an acquirer or other designated recipient as specified in an agreement. This item can be a document, hardware item, software item, service, or any type of work product. (See also "acquirer.")

derived measure A measure that is defined as a function of two or more values of base measures. (See also "base measure.")

derived requirements Requirements that are not explicitly stated in customer requirements but are inferred (1) from contextual requirements (e.g., applicable standards, laws, policies, common practices, and management decisions) or (2) from requirements needed to specify a product or service component. Derived requirements can also arise during analysis and design of components of the product or service. (See also "product requirements.")

design review A formal, documented, comprehensive, and systematic examination of a design to determine if the design meets the applicable requirements, to identify problems, and to propose solutions.

development In the CMMI Product Suite, not only development activities but also maintenance activities. Development projects that benefit from CMMI best practices can focus on development, maintenance, or both.

development plan A plan for guiding, implementing, and controlling the design and development of one or more products or services. (See also "product lifecycle" and "project plan.")

discipline In the CMMI Product Suite, the bodies of knowledge available when selecting a CMMI model (e.g., systems engineering). The CMMI Product Team envisions that other bodies of knowledge will be integrated into the CMMI Framework in the future.

document A collection of data, regardless of the medium on which it is recorded, that generally has permanence and can be read by humans or machines. So, documents include both paper and electronic documents.

enterprise The full composition of a company. A company may consist of many organizations in many locations with different customers. (See also "organization.")

entry criteria States of being that must be present before an effort can begin successfully.

equivalent staging A target staging, created using the continuous representation, which is defined so that the results of using the target staging can be compared to maturity levels of the staged representation. (See also "capability level profile," "maturity level," "target profile," and "target staging.")

Such staging permits benchmarking of progress among organizations, enterprises, and projects, regardless of the CMMI representation used. The organization may implement components of CMMI models beyond those reported as part of equivalent staging. Equivalent staging is only a measure to relate how the organization is compared to other organizations in terms of maturity levels.

establish and maintain This phrase means more than a combination of its component terms; it includes documentation and usage. For example, "Establish and maintain an organizational policy for planning and performing the organizational process focus process" means that not only must a policy be formulated, but it also must be documented and it must be used throughout the organization.

evidence (See "objective evidence.")

executive (See "senior manager.")

exit criteria States of being that must be present before an effort can end successfully.

expected CMMI components CMMI components that explain what may be done to satisfy a required CMMI component. Model users can implement the expected components explicitly or implement equivalent alternative practices to these components. Specific and generic practices are expected model components.

findings (See "appraisal findings.")

formal evaluation process A structured approach to evaluating alternative solutions against established criteria to determine a recommended solution to address an issue.

framework (See "CMMI Framework.")

functional analysis Examination of a defined function to identify all the subfunctions necessary to accomplish that function; identification of functional relationships and interfaces (internal and external) and capturing these in a functional architecture; and flow down of upper-level performance requirements and assignment of these requirements to lower-level subfunctions. (See also "functional architecture.")

functional architecture The hierarchical arrangement of functions, their internal and external (external to the aggregation itself) functional interfaces and external physical interfaces, their respective functional and performance requirements, and their design constraints.

functional configuration audit An audit conducted to verify that the development of a configuration item has been completed satisfactorily, that the item has achieved the performance and functional characteristics specified in the functional or allocated configuration identification, and that its operational and support documents are complete and satisfactory. (See also "configuration audit," "configuration management," and "physical configuration audit.")

generic goal A required model component that describes characteristics that must be present to institutionalize processes that implement a process area. (See also "institutionalization.")

generic practice An expected model component that is considered important in achieving the associated generic goal. The generic practices associated with a generic goal describe the activities that are expected to result in achievement of the generic goal and contribute to the institutionalization of the processes associated with a process area.

generic practice elaboration An informative model component that appears after a generic practice to provide guidance on how the generic practice should be applied to the process area. (This model component is not present in all CMMI models.)

goal A required CMMI component that can be either a generic goal or a specific goal. The word *goal* in a CMMI model always refers to a model component (e.g., generic goal and specific goal). (See also "generic goal," "objective," and "specific goal.")

hardware engineering The application of a systematic, disciplined, and quantifiable approach to transforming a set of requirements that represent the collection of stakeholder needs, expectations, and constraints, using documented techniques and technology to design, implement, and maintain a tangible product. (See also "software engineering" and "systems engineering.")

In CMMI, hardware engineering represents all technical fields (e.g., electrical or mechanical) that transform requirements and ideas into tangible and producible products.

higher-level management The person or persons who provide the policy and overall guidance for the process but do not provide the direct day-to-day monitoring and controlling of the process. Such persons belong to a level of management in the organization above the immediate level responsible for the process and can be (but are not necessarily) senior managers. (See also "senior manager.")

incomplete process A process that is not performed or is performed only partially (also known as capability level 0). One or more of the specific goals of the process area are not satisfied.

informative CMMI components CMMI components that help model users understand the required and expected components of a model. These components can contain examples, detailed explanations, or other helpful information. Subpractices, notes, references, goal titles, practice titles, sources, typical work products, amplifications, and generic practice elaborations are informative model components.

institutionalization The ingrained way of doing business that an organization follows routinely as part of its corporate culture.

integrated team A group of people with complementary skills and expertise who are committed to delivering specified work products in timely collaboration. Integrated team members provide skills and advocacy appropriate to all phases of the work products' life and are collectively responsible for delivering work products as specified. An integrated team should include empowered representatives from organizations, disciplines, and functions that have a stake in the success of the work products.

interface control In configuration management, the process of (1) identifying all functional and physical characteristics relevant to the interfacing of two or more configuration items provided by one or more organizations and (2) ensuring that proposed changes to these characteristics are evaluated and approved prior to implementation. (See also "configuration item" and "configuration management.")

lifecycle model A partitioning of the life of a product, service, or project into phases.

managed process A performed process that is planned and executed in accordance with policy; employs skilled people having adequate resources to produce controlled outputs; involves relevant stakeholders; is monitored, controlled, and reviewed; and is evaluated for adherence to its process description. (See also "performed process.")

manager In the CMMI Product Suite, a person who provides technical and administrative direction and control to those performing tasks or activities within the manager's area of responsibility. The traditional functions of a manager include planning, organizing, directing, and controlling work within an area of responsibility.

maturity level Degree of process improvement across a predefined set of process areas in which all goals in the set are attained. (See also "capability level" and "process area.")

measure (noun) Variable to which a value is assigned as a result of measurement. (See also "base measure," "derived measure," and "measurement.")

measurement A set of operations to determine the value of a measure. (See also "measure.")

memorandum of agreement Binding document of understanding or agreement between two or more parties. Also known as a "memorandum of understanding."

natural bounds The inherent process reflected by measures of process performance; sometimes referred to as "voice of the process."

Techniques such as control charts, confidence intervals, and prediction intervals are used to determine whether the variation is due to common causes (i.e., the process is predictable or stable) or is due to some special cause that can and should be identified and removed. (See also "measure" and "process performance.")

nondevelopmental item An item that was developed prior to its current use in an acquisition or development process. Such an item may require minor modifications to meet the requirements of its current intended use.

nontechnical requirements Requirements affecting product and service acquisition or development that are not properties of the product or service.

Examples include numbers of products or services to be delivered, data rights for delivered COTS nondevelopmental items, delivery dates, and milestones with exit criteria. Other nontechnical requirements include work constraints associated with training, site provisions, and deployment schedules.

objective When used as a noun in the CMMI Product Suite, the term *objective* replaces the word *goal* as used in its common everyday sense, since the word *goal* is reserved for use when referring to CMMI model components called *specific goals* and *generic goals*. (See also "goal.")

objective evidence As used in CMMI appraisal materials, documents or interview results used as indicators of the implementation or institutionalization of model practices. Sources of objective evidence can include instruments, presentations, documents, and interviews. (See also "institutionalization.")

objectively evaluate To review activities and work products against criteria that minimize subjectivity and bias by the reviewer. An example of an objective evaluation is an audit against requirements, standards, or procedures by an independent quality assurance function. (See also "audit.")

observation As used in CMMI appraisal materials, a written record that represents the appraisal team members' understanding of information either seen or heard during appraisal data collection activities. The written record may take the form of a statement or may take alternative forms as long as the content is preserved.

operational concept A general description of the way in which an entity is used or operates. (Also known as "concept of operations.")

operational scenario A description of an imagined sequence of events that includes the interaction of the product or service with its environment and users, as well as interaction among its product or service components. Operational scenarios are used to evaluate the requirements and design of the system and to verify and validate the system.

optimizing process A quantitatively managed process that is improved based on an understanding of the common causes of variation inherent in the process. The focus of an optimizing process is on continually improving the range of process performance through both incremental and innovative improvements. (See also "common cause of process variation," "defined process," and "quantitatively managed process.")

organization An administrative structure in which people collectively manage one or more projects as a whole and whose projects share a senior manager and operate under the same policies. However, the word *organization* as used throughout CMMI models can also apply to one person who performs a function in a small organization that might be performed by a group of people in a large organization. (See also "enterprise" and "organizational unit.")

organizational maturity The extent to which an organization has explicitly and consistently deployed processes that are documented, managed, measured, controlled, and continually improved. Organizational maturity may be measured via appraisals.

organizational policy A guiding principle typically established by senior management that is adopted by an organization to influence and determine decisions.

organizational process assets Artifacts that relate to describing, implementing, and improving processes (e.g., policies, measurements, process descriptions, and process implementation support tools). The term *process assets* is used to indicate that these artifacts are developed or acquired to meet the business objectives of the organization and that they represent investments by the organization that are expected to provide current and future business value. (See also "process asset library.")

organizational unit The part of an organization that is the subject of an appraisal. An organizational unit deploys one or more processes that have a coherent process context and operates within a coherent set of business objectives. An organizational unit is typically part of a larger organization, although in a small organization the organizational unit may be the whole organization.

organization's business objectives Senior management developed strategies designed to ensure an organization's continued existence and enhance its profitability, market share, and other factors influencing the organization's success. (See also "quality and process-performance objectives" and "quantitative objective.")

Such objectives may include reducing the number of change requests during a system's integration phase, reducing development cycle time, increasing the number of errors found in a product's first or second phase of development, and reducing the number of customer-reported defects when applied to systems engineering activities.

organization's measurement repository A repository used to collect and make measurement data available on processes and work products, particularly as they relate to the organization's set of standard processes. This repository contains or references actual measurement data and related information needed to understand and analyze measurement data.

organization's process asset library A library of information used to store and make process assets available that are useful to those who are defining, implementing, and managing processes in the organization. This library contains process assets that include process-related documentation such as policies, defined processes, checklists, lessons-learned documents, templates, standards, procedures, plans, and training materials.

organization's set of standard processes A collection of definitions of the processes that guide activities in an organization. These process descriptions cover the fundamental process elements (and their relationships to each other, such as ordering and interfaces) that must be incorporated into the defined processes that are implemented in projects across the organization. A standard process enables consistent development and maintenance activities across the organization and is essential for long-term stability and improvement. (See also "defined process" and "process element.")

outsourcing (See "acquisition.")

peer review The review of work products performed by peers during development of the work products to identify defects for removal. The term *peer review* is used in the CMMI Product Suite instead of the term *work product inspection*. (See also "work product.")

performed process A process that accomplishes the needed work to produce work products. The specific goals of the process area are satisfied.

physical configuration audit An audit conducted to verify that a configuration item, as built, conforms to the technical documentation that defines and describes it. (See also "configuration audit," "configuration management," and "functional configuration audit.")

planned process A process that is documented by both a description and a plan. The description and plan should be coordinated, and the plan should include standards, requirements, objectives, resources, and assignments.

policy (See "organizational policy.")

process In the CMMI Product Suite, activities that can be recognized as implementations of practices in a CMMI model. These activities can be mapped to one or more practices in CMMI process areas to allow a model to be useful for process improvement and process appraisal. (See also "process area," "subprocess," and "process element.")

There is a special use of the phrase *the process* in the statements and descriptions of the generic goals and generic practices. *The process*, as used in Part Two, is the process or processes that implement the process area.

process action plan A plan, usually resulting from appraisals, that documents how specific improvements targeting the weaknesses uncovered by an appraisal will be implemented.

process action team A team that has the responsibility to develop and implement process improvement activities for an organization as documented in a process action plan.

process and technology improvements Incremental and innovative improvements to processes and to process, product, or service technologies.

process architecture The ordering, interfaces, interdependencies, and other relationships among the process elements in a standard process. Process architecture also describes the interfaces, interdependencies, and other relationships between process elements and external processes (e.g., contract management).

process area A cluster of related practices in an area that, when implemented collectively, satisfies a set of goals considered important for making improvement in that area. All CMMI process areas are common to both continuous and staged representations.

process asset Anything the organization considers useful in attaining the goals of a process area. (See also "organizational process assets.")

process asset library A collection of process asset holdings that can be used by an organization or project. (See also "organization's process asset library.")

process attribute A measurable characteristic of process capability applicable to any process.

process capability The range of expected results that can be achieved by following a process.

process context The set of factors, documented in the appraisal input, that influences the judgment and comparability of appraisal ratings.

These factors include but are not limited to (a) the size of the organizational unit to be appraised; (b) the demographics of the organizational unit; (c) the application domain of the products or services; (d) the size, criticality, and complexity of the products or services; and (e) the quality characteristics of the products or services.

process definition The act of defining and describing a process. The result of process definition is a process description. (See also "process description.")

process description A documented expression of a set of activities performed to achieve a given purpose.

A process description provides an operational definition of the major components of a process. The description specifies, in a complete, precise, and verifiable manner, the requirements, design, behavior, or other characteristics of a process. It also may include procedures for determining whether these provisions have been satisfied. Process descriptions can be found at the activity, project, or organizational level.

process element The fundamental unit of a process. A process can be defined in terms of subprocesses or process elements. A subprocess can be further decomposed into subprocesses or process elements; a process element cannot. (See also "process" and "subprocess.")

Each process element covers a closely related set of activities (e.g., estimating element and peer review element). Process elements can be portrayed using templates to be completed, abstractions to be refined, or descriptions to be modified or used. A process element can be an activity or task.

process group A collection of specialists who facilitate the definition, maintenance, and improvement of processes used by the organization.

process improvement A program of activities designed to improve the performance and maturity of the organization's processes, and the results of such a program.

process improvement objectives A set of target characteristics established to guide the effort to improve an existing process in a specific, measurable way either in terms of resultant product or service characteristics (e.g., quality, performance, and conformance to standards) or in the way in which the process is executed (e.g., elimination of redundant process steps, combination of process steps, and improvement of cycle time). (See also "organization's business objectives" and "quantitative objective.")

process improvement plan A plan for achieving organizational process improvement objectives based on a thorough understanding of current strengths and weaknesses of the organization's processes and process assets.

process measurement A set of operations used to determine values of measures of a process and its resulting products or services for the purpose of characterizing and understanding the process. (See also "measurement.")

process owner The person (or team) responsible for defining and maintaining a process. At the organizational level, the process owner is the person (or team) responsible for the description of a standard process; at the project level, the process owner is the person (or team) responsible for the description of the defined process. A process may therefore have multiple owners at different levels of responsibility. (See also "defined process" and "standard process.")

process performance A measure of actual results achieved by following a process. It is characterized by both process measures (e.g., effort, cycle time, and defect removal efficiency) and product or service measures (e.g., reliability, defect density, and response time). (See also "measure.")

process-performance baseline A documented characterization of actual results achieved by following a process, which is used as a benchmark for comparing actual process performance against expected process performance. (See also "process performance.")

process-performance model A description of relationships among attributes of a process and its work products that is developed from historical process-performance data and calibrated using collected process and product or service measures from the project and that are used to predict results to be achieved by following a process. (See also "measure.")

process tailoring Making, altering, or adapting a process description for a particular end. For example, a project tailors its defined process from the organization's set of standard processes to meet objectives, constraints, and the environment of the project. (See also "defined process," "organization's set of standard processes," and "process description.")

product In the CMMI Product Suite, a work product that is intended for delivery to a customer or end user. The form of a product can vary in different contexts. (See also "customer," "product component," "service" and "work product.")

product component In the CMMI Product Suite, a work product that is a lower-level component of the product. Product components are integrated to produce the product. There may be multiple levels of product components. (See also "product" and "work product.")

Throughout the process areas, where the terms *product* and *product component* are used, they are intended to include service and service component and should be interpreted in that way.

product component requirements A complete specification of a product or service component, including fit, form, function, performance, and any other requirement.

product lifecycle The period of time, consisting of phases, that begins when a product or service is conceived and ends when the product or service is no longer available for use. Since an organization may be producing multiple products or services for multiple customers, one description of a product lifecycle may not be adequate. Therefore, the organization may define a set of approved product lifecycle models. These models are typically found in published literature and are likely to be tailored for use in an organization.

A product lifecycle could consist of the following phases: (1) concept and vision, (2) feasibility, (3) design/development, (4) production, and (5) phase out.

product line A group of products or services sharing a common, managed set of features that satisfy specific needs of a selected market or mission.

product-related lifecycle processes Processes associated with a product or service throughout one or more phases of its life (e.g., from conception through disposal), such as manufacturing and support processes.

product requirements A refinement of customer requirements into the developers' language, making implicit requirements into explicit derived requirements. (See also "derived requirements" and "product component requirements.")

The developer uses product requirements to guide the design and building of the product or service.

product suite (See "CMMI Product Suite.")

profile (See "achievement profile" and "target profile.")

program (1) A project. (2) A collection of related projects and the infrastructure that supports them, including objectives, methods, activities, plans, and success measures. (See also "project.")

project In the CMMI Product Suite, a managed set of interrelated resources that delivers one or more products or services to a customer or end user. A project has a definite beginning (i.e., project startup) and typically operates according to a plan. Such a plan is frequently documented and specifies what is to be delivered or implemented, the resources and funds to be used, the work to be done, and a schedule for doing the work. A project can be composed of projects. (See also "project startup.")

project manager In the CMMI Product Suite, the person responsible for planning, directing, controlling, structuring, and motivating the project. The project manager is responsible for satisfying the customer.

project plan A plan that provides the basis for performing and controlling the project's activities, which addresses the commitments to the project's customer.

Project planning includes estimating the attributes of work products and tasks, determining the resources needed, negotiating commitments, producing a schedule, and identifying and analyzing project risks. Iterating through these activities may be necessary to establish the project plan.

project progress and performance What a project achieves with respect to implementing project plans, including effort, cost, schedule, and technical performance. (See also "technical performance.")

project startup When a set of interrelated resources are directed to develop or deliver one or more products or services for a customer or end user. (See also "project.")

project's defined process The integrated and defined process that is tailored from the organization's set of standard processes. (See also "defined process.")

prototype A preliminary type, form, or instance of a product, service, product component, or service component that serves as a model for later stages or for the final, complete version of the product or service.

This model (e.g., physical, electronic, digital, and analytical) can be used for the following (and other) purposes:

- Assessing the feasibility of a new or unfamiliar technology
- Assessing or mitigating technical risk
- Validating requirements
- Demonstrating critical features
- Qualifying a product or service
- Qualifying a process
- Characterizing performance or features of the product or service
- Elucidating physical principles

quality The ability of a set of inherent characteristics of a product, service, product component, service component, or process to fulfill requirements of customers.

quality and process-performance objectives Objectives and requirements for product quality, service quality, and process performance.

Process-performance objectives include quality; however, to emphasize the importance of quality in the CMMI Product Suite, the phrase *quality and process-performance objectives* is used rather than just *process-performance objectives.*

quality assurance A planned and systematic means for assuring management that the defined standards, practices, procedures, and methods of the process are applied.

quantitative objective Desired target value expressed as quantitative measures. (See also "measure," "process improvement objectives," and "quality and process-performance objectives.")

quantitatively managed process A defined process that is controlled using statistical and other quantitative techniques. The product quality, service quality, and process-performance attributes are measurable and controlled throughout the project. (See also "defined process," "optimizing process," and "statistically managed process.")

rating (See "appraisal rating.")

reference An informative model component that points to additional or more detailed information in related process areas.

reference model A model that is used as a benchmark for measuring an attribute.

relevant stakeholder A stakeholder that is identified for involvement in specified activities and is included in a plan. (See also "stakeholder.")

representation The organization, use, and presentation of a CMM's components. Overall, two types of approaches to presenting best practices are evident: the staged representation and the continuous representation.

required CMMI components CMMI components that are essential to achieving process improvement in a given process area. These components are used in appraisals to determine process capability. Specific goals and generic goals are required model components.

requirement (1) A condition or capability needed by a user to solve a problem or achieve an objective. (2) A condition or capability that must be met or possessed by a product, service, product component, or service component to satisfy a supplier agreement, standard, specification, or other formally imposed documents. (3) A documented representation of a condition or capability as in (1) or (2). (See also "supplier agreement.")

requirements analysis The determination of product- or service-specific performance and functional characteristics based on analyses of customer needs, expectations, and constraints; operational concept; projected utilization environments for people, products, services, and processes; and measures of effectiveness. (See also "operational concept.")

requirements elicitation Using systematic techniques, such as prototypes and structured surveys, to proactively identify and document customer and end-user needs.

requirements management The management of all requirements received by or generated by the project, including both technical and nontechnical requirements as well as those requirements levied on the project by the organization. (See also "nontechnical requirement.")

requirements traceability A discernable association between requirements and related requirements, implementations, and verifications. (See also "bidirectional traceability" and "traceability.")

return on investment The ratio of revenue from output (product or service) to production costs, which determines whether an organization benefits from performing an action to produce something.

risk analysis The evaluation, classification, and prioritization of risks.

risk identification An organized, thorough approach to seek out probable or realistic risks in achieving objectives.

risk management An organized, analytic process to identify what might cause harm or loss (identify risks); to assess and quantify the identified risks; and to develop and, if needed, implement an appropriate approach to prevent or handle causes of risk that could result in significant harm or loss.

risk management strategy An organized, technical approach to identify what might cause harm or loss (identify risks); to assess and quantify the identified risks; and to develop and, if needed, implement an appropriate approach to prevent or handle causes of risk that could result in significant harm or loss.

Typically, risk management is performed for a project, organization, or product or service developing organizational units.

root cause A source of a defect such that if it is removed, the defect is decreased or removed.

senior manager In the CMMI Product Suite, a management role at a high-enough level in an organization that the primary focus of the person filling the role is the long-term vitality of the organization rather than short-term project concerns and pressures. A senior manager has authority to direct the allocation or reallocation of resources in support of organizational process improvement effectiveness. (See also "higher-level management.")

A senior manager can be any manager who satisfies this description, including the head of the organization. Synonyms for senior manager include *executive* and *top-level manager.* However, to ensure consistency and usability, these synonyms are not used in CMMI models.

service In the CMMI Product Suite, a service is a product that is intangible and nonstorable. (See also "product," "customer," and "work product.")

service level Current performance related to an agreed-on service level measure. (See also "measure" and "service.")

service level agreement Written agreement that documents agreed-on performance targets for agreed-on service level measures. (See also "measure" and "service.")

service level measure Measure of service performance that can be used as a target for acceptable results or behavior. (See also "measure" and "service.")

shared vision A common understanding of guiding principles, including mission, objectives, expected behavior, values, and final outcomes, which are developed and used by a project.

software engineering (1) The application of a systematic, disciplined, quantifiable approach to the development, operation, and maintenance of software. (2) The study of approaches as in (1). (See also "hardware engineering," and "systems engineering.")

solicitation The process of preparing a package to be used in selecting a supplier. (See also "solicitation package.")

solicitation package A collection of formal documents that includes a description of the desired form of response from a potential supplier, the relevant statement of work for the supplier, and required provisions in the supplier agreement.

special cause of process variation A cause of a defect that is specific to some transient circumstance and is not an inherent part of a process. (See also "common cause of process variation.")

specific goal A required model component that describes the unique characteristics that must be present to satisfy the process area. (See also "capability level," "generic goal," "organization's business objectives," and "process area.")

specific practice An expected model component that is considered important in achieving the associated specific goal. The specific practices describe the activities expected to result in achievement of the specific goals of a process area. (See also "process area" and "specific goal.")

stable process The state in which all special causes of process variation have been removed and prevented from recurring so that only common causes of process variation of the process remain. (See also "capable process," "common cause of process variation," "special cause of process variation," "standard process," and "statistically managed process.")

staged representation A model structure wherein attaining the goals of a set of process areas establishes a maturity level; each level builds a foundation for subsequent levels. (See also "maturity level" and "process area.")

stakeholder In the CMMI Product Suite, a group or individual that is affected by or is in some way accountable for the outcome of an undertaking. Stakeholders may include project members, suppliers, customers, end users, and others. (See also "customer" and "relevant stakeholder.")

standard (noun) Formal requirements developed and used to prescribe consistent approaches to development (e.g., ISO/IEC standards, IEEE standards, and organizational standards).

Instead of using *standard* as an adjective in its common everyday sense, we use another term that means the same thing (e.g., typical, traditional, usual, or customary).

standard process An operational definition of the basic process that guides the establishment of a common process in an organization.

A standard process describes the fundamental process elements that are expected to be incorporated into any defined process. It also describes relationships (e.g., ordering and interfaces) among these process elements. (See also "defined process.")

statement of work A description of work to be performed.

statistical predictability The performance of a quantitative process that is controlled using statistical and other quantitative techniques.

statistical process control Statistically based analysis of a process and measures of process performance, which identify common and special causes of variation in process performance and maintain process performance within limits. (See also "common cause of process variation," "special cause of process variation," and "statistically managed process.")

statistical techniques An analytic technique that employs statistical methods (e.g., statistical process control, confidence intervals, and prediction intervals).

statistically managed process A process that is managed by a statistically based technique in which processes are analyzed, special causes of process variation are identified, and performance is contained within well-defined limits. (See also "capable process," "special cause of process variation," "stable process," "standard process," and "statistical process control.")

subpractice An informative model component that provides guidance for interpreting and implementing specific or generic practices. Subpractices may be worded as if prescriptive, but they are actually meant only to provide ideas that may be useful for process improvement.

subprocess A process that is part of a larger process. A subprocess can be decomposed into subprocesses and/or process elements. (See also "process," "process description," and "process element.")

supplier (1) An entity delivering products or performing services being acquired. (2) An individual, partnership, company, corporation, association, or other service having an agreement with an acquirer for the design, development, manufacture, maintenance, modification, or supply of items under the terms of an agreement. (See also "acquirer.")

supplier agreement A documented agreement between the acquirer and supplier (e.g., contract, license, or memorandum of agreement).

sustainment The processes used to ensure that a product or service remains operational.

systems engineering The interdisciplinary approach governing the total technical and managerial effort required to transform a set of customer needs, expectations, and constraints into a solution and to support that solution throughout its life. (See also "hardware engineering" and "software engineering.")

This approach includes the definition of technical performance measures, the integration of engineering specialties toward the establishment of an architecture, and the definition of supporting lifecycle processes that balance cost, performance, and schedule objectives.

system of systems A set or arrangement of systems that results when independent and useful systems are integrated into a large system that delivers unique capabilities.

tailoring Tailoring a process makes, alters, or adapts a process description for a particular end. For example, a project establishes its defined process by tailoring from the organization's set of standard processes to meet the objectives, constraints, and environment of the project.

tailoring guidelines Organizational guidelines that enable projects, groups, and organizational functions to appropriately adapt standard processes for their use. The organization's set of standard processes is described at a general level that may not be directly usable to perform a process.

Tailoring guidelines aid those who establish the defined processes for projects. Tailoring guidelines cover (1) selecting a standard process, (2) selecting an approved lifecycle model, and (3) tailoring the selected standard process and lifecycle model to fit project needs. Tailoring guidelines describe what can and cannot be modified and identify process components that are candidates for modification.

target profile In the continuous representation, a list of process areas and their corresponding capability levels that represent an objective for process improvement. (See also "achievement profile" and "capability level profile.")

target staging In the continuous representation, a sequence of target profiles that describes the path of process improvement to be followed by the organization. (See also "achievement profile," "capability level profile," and "target profile.")

technical performance Characteristic of a process, product, or service, generally defined by a functional or technical requirement (e.g., estimating accuracy, user functions, security functions, response time, component accuracy, maximum weight, minimum throughput, and allowable range).

technical performance measure Precisely defined technical measure of a requirement, capability, or some combination of requirements and capabilities. (See also "measure.")

technical requirements Properties (i.e., attributes) of products or services to be acquired or developed.

test procedure Detailed instructions for the setup, execution, and evaluation of results for a given test.

traceability A discernable association among two or more logical entities such as requirements, system elements, verifications, or tasks. (See also "bidirectional traceability" and "requirements traceability.")

trade study An evaluation of alternatives, based on criteria and systematic analysis, to select the best alternative for attaining determined objectives.

training Formal and informal learning options, which may include in-class training, informal mentoring, Web-based training, guided self-study, and formalized on-the-job training programs. The learning options selected for each situation are based on an assessment of the need for training and the performance gap to be addressed.

typical work product An informative model component that provides sample outputs from a specific practice. These examples are called typical work products because there are often other work products that are just as effective but are not listed.

unit testing Testing of individual hardware or software units or groups of related units. (See also "acceptance testing.")

validation Confirmation that the product or service, as provided (or as it will be provided), will fulfill its intended use. In other words, validation ensures that "you built the right thing." (See also "verification.")

verification Confirmation that work products properly reflect the requirements specified for them. In other words, verification ensures that "you built it right." (See also "validation.")

version control The establishment and maintenance of baselines and the identification of changes to baselines that make it possible to return to the previous baseline.

work breakdown structure (WBS) An arrangement of work elements, and their relationship to each other and to the end product or service.

work product In the CMMI Product Suite, a useful result of a process. This can include files, documents, products, parts of a product, services, process descriptions, specifications, and invoices. A key distinction between a work product and a product component is that a work product is not necessarily part of the end product. (See also "product" and "product component.")

In CMMI models, the definition of "work product" includes services, however, the phrase "work products and services" is used to emphasize the inclusion of services in the discussion.

work product and task attributes Characteristics of products, services, and project tasks used to help in estimating project work. These characteristics include items such as size, complexity, weight, form, fit, and function. They are typically used as one input to deriving other project and resource estimates (e.g., effort, cost, and schedule).

Book Contributors

BOOK AUTHORS

Brian P. Gallagher

Director, Systems Engineering
ISR Systems Division
Northrop Grumman Mission Systems

Brian P. Gallagher is the director of ISR Mission Systems Engineering within the ISR Systems Division, Mission Systems Sector, Northrop Grumman, where he is responsible for leading a team of senior engineers with expertise in the discipline of systems engineering and its practical application to large-scale, mission-critical ISR systems. Prior to this position, Brian was director of acquisition support at the Software Engineering Institute, where he was responsible for building teams from across the SEI's disciplines to support the Department of Defense and other government agency acquisition programs. Brian was previously employed with the Aerospace Corporation, where he worked as a software acquisition and engineering advisor for several Air Force and NRO projects. During his Air Force career, he was the deputy chief of Software Engineering with an Air Intelligence Agency remote intelligence site, chief software engineer on the Range Operations Control Center Project at Cape Canaveral AFS, FL, a software project manager for the Titan IV Program Office, and a software engineer with Strategic Air Command. He received his B.S. in management information systems from Peru State College and M.S. in computer science/software engineering from Florida Institute of Technology.

Mike Phillips

Program Manager
CMMI Initiative
Software Engineering Institute

Mike Phillips is the program manager for CMMI at the Software Engineering Institute, a position created to lead the CMMI Product Suite evolution for the SEI. He was previously responsible for Transition Enabling activities at the SEI. He has authored technical reports, technical notes, and various articles and has a regular column in news@SEI, the SEI's newsletter. Mike also presents at many conferences around the world about CMMI. Prior to his retirement as a colonel from the Air Force, he was the program manager of the $36 billion development program for the B-2 stealth bomber in the B-2 System Program Office at Wright-Patterson AFB, Ohio. In addition to more than five years of B-2 experience, he has four years of experience guiding acquisition programs in the Pentagon for both the Air Force and the Office of the Secretary of Defense. His bachelor's degree in astronautical engineering is from the Air Force Academy, and his master's degrees are in nuclear engineering from Georgia Tech, in systems management from the University of Southern California, and in international affairs from Salve Regina College and the Naval War College. He is a graduate of the Program Management Course at the Defense Systems Management College and of the Air Force Test Pilot School.

Dr. Karen J. Richter

Research Analyst and
Senior Project Leader
Institute for Defense Analyses

Dr. Karen J. Richter is a research analyst and senior project leader at the Institute for Defense Analyses (IDA), a research and development "think tank" for the Department of Defense. She has led numerous projects for the Office of the Under Secretary of Defense for Acquisition, Technology, and Logistics (OUSD(AT&L)) in acquisition management; systems and software engineering, integration, and interoperability; system lifecycle process management; integrated product and process development (IPPD) and concurrent engineering; advanced manufacturing practices and virtual enterprises; system quality, reliability, and maintainability; design and manufacturing technology including modeling and simulation; and lifecycle affordability. She also led or participated in projects for the Office of the Under Secretary of Defense for Policy (OUSD(P)) and the Assistant Secretary of Defense for Networks and Information Integration (ASD(NII)). She was a member of the development teams for the CMMI SE/SW/IPPD and CMMI-DEV models and cochair of the development team for CMMI-ACQ. She has served on the CMMI Configuration Control Board and the CMMI Steering Group. She helped develop international standards on lifecycle process management, systems engineering, software engineering, and quality management as a member of both ISO/JTC1/Subcommittee 7 (Software and Systems Engineering) Working Group 7 (Life Cycle Management) and ISO/TC176 (Quality). She taught in the Department of Engineering Mechanics at the University of Wisconsin–Madison and in the Departments of Mechanical Engineering at The Ohio State University and the University of Maryland at College Park. She is the coauthor of three college engineering textbooks. She earned a B.A. in mathematics from Knox College and an M.S. and Ph.D. in engineering mechanics from the University of Wisconsin–Madison.

Sandy Shrum

Senior Writer/Editor
Communications
Software Engineering Institute

Sandy Shrum is a senior writer/editor at the Software Engineering Institute. She has been with the SEI since 1995 and has been a member of the CMMI Development Team since the CMMI project's inception in 1998. Her roles on the project have included model author, reviewer, editor, model development process coordinator, and quality assurance process owner. Sandy also is the secretary for the CMMI Configuration Control Board, a member of the internal configuration control board, and the CMMI communications coordinator. Before joining the SEI, Sandy spent eight years as a document developer with Legent Corporation, a Virginia-based software company. Her experience as a technical communicator dates back to 1988, when she earned her M.S. in professional writing from Carnegie Mellon University. Her undergraduate degree, a B.S. in business administration, was earned at Gannon University.

CASE STUDY AUTHORS

Dr. Richard Frost

Dr. Richard Frost is the global director of Systems Delivery Process and Tools at General Motors (GM). He is responsible for driving software engineering and system delivery globally for GM. Within GM, he has spearheaded numerous initiatives to accelerate business innovation and streamline development, including incremental development, requirements visualization, and process optimization. He is a member of the CMMI-ACQ Advisory Board at the Software Engineering Institute and was a driving force in the global implementation of CMMI-ACQ at GM. Before joining GM, Richard was an IT executive at Volkswagen of America, where he was focused on streamlining development and aligning IT and business strategies. His tenure at Volkswagen included executive leadership of Systems Development, eBusiness, and CRM technologies. His background includes more than 25 years of executive and technical leadership in a variety of technologies. Richard received a Ph.D. in systems engineering from Oakland University and bachelor's and master's degrees in computer science from the University of Michigan.

Tom Keuten

Tom Keuten works with General Motors as a process improvement lead. He was a member of the CMMI-ACQ Model Team and has been trained as a SCAMPI Lead Appraiser. His focus lies in the areas of organizational project management, quality assurance, and measurement and analysis. Tom has been a principal in multiple start-up management consulting organizations that focus on helping information technology organizations deliver innovative solutions to help their business customers. Prior to these roles, Tom played almost every role in the system delivery lifecycle working with many large and small clients of Hitachi Consulting and BDO Seidman. Tom earned an M.B.A. from the University of Notre Dame and a B.S. in business administration from Central Michigan University.

OTHER CONTRIBUTORS

Andrew D. Boyd
Software Engineering Institute

Richard Freeman
Air Force Center for Systems Engineering
Air Force Institute of Technology

Craig Meyers
Software Engineering Institute

INDEX

A

D

E

F

G

H

I

N

O

P

Q

R

U

V

W

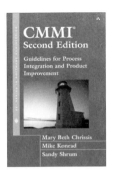

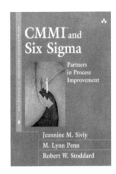

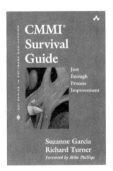

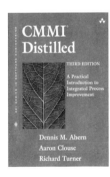

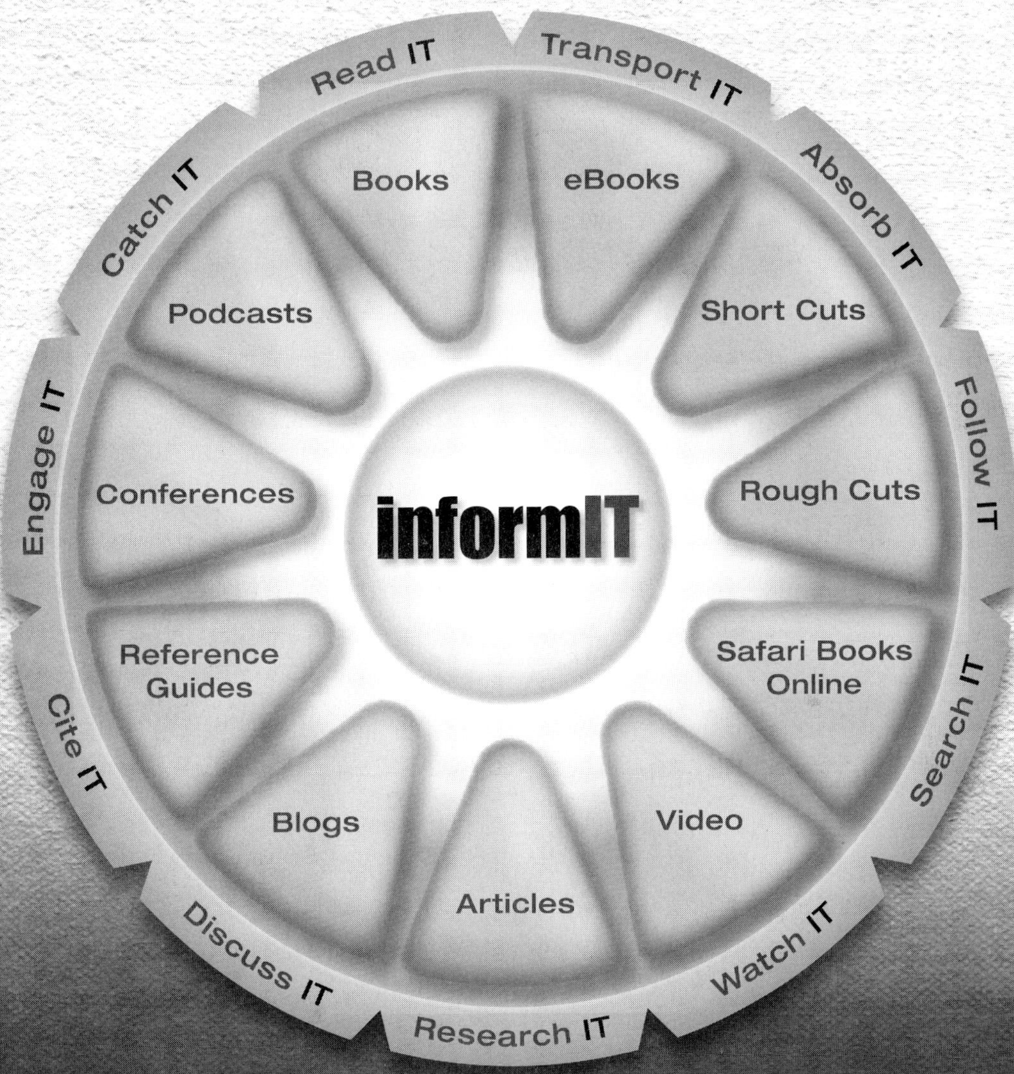

Process Areas by Maturity Level

Maturity Level 2

- Agreement Management (AM)
- Acquisition Requirements Development (ARD)
- Configuration Management (CM)
- Measurement and Analysis (MA)
- Project Monitoring and Control (PMC)
- Project Planning (PP)
- Process and Product Quality Assurance (PPQA)
- Requirements Management (REQM)
- Solicitation and Supplier Agreement Development (SSAD)

Maturity Level 3

- Acquisition Technical Management (ATM)
- Acquisition Validation (AVAL)
- Acquisition Verification (AVER)
- Decision Analysis and Resolution (DAR)
- Integrated Project Management (IPM)
- Organizational Process Definition (OPD)
- Organizational Process Focus (OPF)
- Organizational Training (OT)
- Risk Management (RSKM)

Maturity Level 4

- Organizational Process Performance (OPP)
- Quantitative Project Management (QPM)

Maturity Level 5

- Causal Analysis and Resolution (CAR)
- Organizational Innovation and Deployment (OID)